Health Care USA

Understanding Its Organization and Delivery

Seventh Edition

Harry A. Sultz, DDS, MPH
Professor Emeritus
Social and Preventive Medicine
School of Medicine and Biomedical Sciences

Dean Emeritus
School of Health Related Professions
State University of New York at Buffalo
Buffalo, New York

Kristina M. Young, MS
Instructor
School of Public Health and Health Professions
State University of New York at Buffalo
Buffalo, New York

Instructor
Canisius College
Buffalo, New York

President
Kristina M. Young & Associates, Inc.
Buffalo, New York

JONES & BARTLETT
LEARNING

World Headquarters
Jones & Bartlett Learning
40 Tall Pine Drive
Sudbury, MA 01776
978-443-5000
info@jblearning.com
www.jblearning.com

Jones & Bartlett Learning
Canada
6339 Ormindale Way
Mississauga, Ontario L5V 1J2
Canada

Jones & Bartlett Learning
International
Barb House, Barb Mews
London W6 7PA
United Kingdom

Jones & Bartlett Learning books and products are available through most bookstores and online booksellers. To contact Jones & Bartlett Learning directly, call 800-832-0034, fax 978-443-8000, or visit our website, www.jblearning.com.

Substantial discounts on bulk quantities of Jones & Bartlett Learning publications are available to corporations, professional associations, and other qualified organizations. For details and specific discount information, contact the special sales department at Jones & Bartlett Learning via the above contact information or send an email to specialsales@jblearning.com.

This publication is designed to provide accurate and authoritative information in regard to the Subject Matter covered. It is sold with the understanding that the publisher is not engaged in rendering legal, accounting, or other professional service. If legal advice or other expert assistance is required, the service of a competent professional person should be sought.

Production Credits
Publisher: Michael Brown
Editorial Assistant: Teresa Reilly
Editorial Assistant: Catie Haverling
Production Director: Amy Rose
Production Manager: Tracey Chapman
Associate Production Editor: Lisa Lamenzo
Senior Marketing Manager: Sophie Fleck
Manufacturing and Inventory Control
   Supervisor: Amy Bacus

Composition: Arlene Apone
Cover Design: Scott Moden
Cover Image: © Carsten Reisinger/
   ShutterStock, Inc.
Printing and Binding: Malloy, Inc.
Cover Printing: Malloy, Inc.

Library of Congress Cataloging-in-Publication Data
Sultz, Harry A.
  Health care USA : understanding its organization and delivery / Harry A. Sultz, Kristina M. Young. -- 7th ed.
      p. ; cm.
  Includes bibliographical references and index.
  ISBN-13: 978-0-7637-8458-4
  ISBN-10: 0-7637-8458-3
  1. Medical care--United States. 2. Medical policy--United States. I. Young, Kristina M. II. Title.
  [DNLM: 1. Delivery of Health Care--United States. 2. Health Policy--United States. W 84 AA1 S96h 2011]
  RA395.A3S897 2011
  362.10973--dc22
                        2010010691
6048

Printed in the United States of America
14 13 12 11 10   10 9 8 7 6 5 4 3 2 1

This book is dedicated to our parents, William and Marabelle Sultz and Jacob Jay and Marie Young. Guiding these warm, loving, and dignified people through the health care system during the last years of their lives taught us more about the feats, functions, and foibles of medical care than all the research conducted, literature read, and services administered.

Contents

Foreword

The Patient Protection and Affordable Care Act proposed by President Obama and passed by Congress early in 2010 has the potential to bring about major changes in the tradition-bound and health insurance company-dominated United States health care system. Unlike the opponents of health care reform, respected economists and system analysts from independent organizations and major universities predict that this legislation will provide tools to improve the quality and lower the costs of medical care. Whether the vested interests in the current U.S. health system's status quo will resist or accept the changes contained in the new legislation is a matter of conjecture.

In this period of speculation and turmoil in the health care delivery system, the seventh edition of *Health Care USA* has heightened significance. The text offers a clear overview of the health care industry and the issues that surround it. It describes the changing roles of the system's components as well as the technical, economic, political, and social forces responsible for those changes. Students of health care and related professions as well as neophyte practitioners need a broad understanding of the reformed U.S. health care system. Critical insights into diverse health care topics and issues are necessary to function effectively, and to relate intelligently, to the various segments of the health care sector.

In this edition, as in previous ones, the authors have meticulously screened vast amounts of new information and included the most critical points to update this work. This text continues to retain its balanced population perspective, allowing the reader to understand the forces driving rapid changes in the organization and financing of health care as well as the changes themselves.

The breadth of this book is ambitious, as is necessary for any text in a course that attempts to analyze the complex structures, processes, and relationships of health care in the United States. The authors have crafted an exceptionally readable text by integrating the diverse subject matter and presenting it in appropriate depth for an introductory course on this topic. Because a "population" rather than an "individual" health care perspective is the direction of the reformed delivery system, the authors' public health orientation makes this text particularly valuable. Their combined experience in the public health and medical care fields has allowed them to interpret health care developments with objectivity. It is an important feature in an introductory text that strives toward analysis of evidence, not advocacy, thereby allowing the formulation of one's own position.

Michel A. Ibrahim, MD, PhD
Professor of Epidemiology
Editor-in-Chief, "Epidemiological Reviews"
Johns Hopkins Bloomberg School of Public Health
and
Dean and Professor Emeritus
School of Public Health
University of North Carolina at Chapel Hill

Acknowledgments

Because one of us has an academic base as a professor emeritus of social and preventive medicine and a former academic dean, and the other has served in a variety of executive positions in voluntary agencies, hospitals, a managed care organization, and in her own consultant business and executive director of a regional public health organization, we bring different experiences to our interpretations of health care developments. When we taught together, as we often did, our students were at first amused and then intrigued by the differences between academic and applied perspectives. They learned, by our willingness to debate the merits of different interpretations of the same information, to appreciate that health care is fraught with variance in understandings, dissonance in values, and contradictions in underlying assumptions.

We are grateful therefore to the students in the Schools of Medicine, Public Health and Health Professions, Management, Law, and Millard Fillmore College of the University at Buffalo and Canisius College who contributed to our knowledge and experience by presenting challenging viewpoints, engaging us in spirited discussions, and providing thoughtful course evaluations. Over the years, their enthusiasm for the subject stimulated us to enrich our coursework constantly in an effort to meet and exceed their expectations.

We acknowledge with our sincerest gratitude Susan V. McLeer, MD, MS, Professor and Chair of the Department of Psychiatry, Drexel University College of Medicine, Philadelphia, Pennsylvania, who contributed the chapter on mental health services. A consummate clinician and academician, Dr. McLeer provided an exceptionally clear and insightful overview of the complex issues and service responses that characterize the field of mental health.

We are grateful to Michel Ibrahim, MD, PhD, Professor, Johns Hopkins Bloomberg School of Public Health and Dean and Professor Emeritus of the School of Public Health at the University of North Carolina at Chapel Hill who encouraged us to write this book and has contributed the "Foreword" to each edition.

We also thank Ebrahim Randeree, MBA, PhD(ABD), Assistant Dean, College of Communication & Information, The Florida State University, who gave us the benefit of his expertise and experience in the fast growing field of health information technology.

We also appreciate those who helped turn teachers into authors by providing the necessary editing, literature searches, word processing, and other support services. The early editions of this book benefited from the library and information science expertise of Karen Buchinger, and the literary competence and editing skill of Alice Stein. All manuscripts of the seven editions of this book were word processed for submission to our publisher by Sharon Palisano. Each edition was produced with unparalleled attention to every aspect of the publisher's requirements. We are extremely grateful for her meticulous attention to the details of these very large texts.

We also wish to recognize the important contributions of our publisher's staff who encourage our efforts, help shape the results, and motivate us to improve the book's utility to its users. To each of you we offer our profound thanks.

About the Authors

Harry A. Sultz, DDS, MPH, is Professor Emeritus of Social and Preventive Medicine at the University at Buffalo School of Medicine and Biomedical Sciences and Dean Emeritus of its School of Health Related Professions. He has also served as Adjunct Professor at the School of Law; Adjunct Professor, Health Systems Management, School of Management; and Clinical Assistant Professor, Department of Family Medicine.

Dr. Sultz has written six previous books, contributed chapters to several other books for professional audiences, and published numerous articles for medical and allied health journals. An epidemiologist, health care services planner, and researcher, he established and, for 26 years, directed the Health Services Research Program of Buffalo's School of Medicine. His extensive research experience serves as background for the various editions of this book and for the courses that he taught about health care and health policy. He also has long service as an expert consultant to several governmental and voluntary agencies and institutions.

Kristina M. Young, MS, is an instructor at the University at Buffalo, School of Public Health and Health Professions, State University of New York, where she teaches graduate courses in health care organization and health policy for students in the fields of public health, law, and management.

Ms. Young is the Executive Director of the Western New York Public Health Alliance, Inc., an organization that administers government and private funds to support public health activities in the western New York region. She also is President and Owner of Kristina M. Young & Associates, Inc., a management consulting and training firm specializing in health and human services organizations. Previously, she served as

President of a corporate training and development organization; as Executive Vice President of a not-for-profit organization dedicated to advancing the joint interests of a major teaching hospital and a health maintenance organization; and as the Vice President for Research and Development for a teaching hospital system and Executive Director of its health, education, and research foundation.

Introduction

In spite of its long history and common use, the U.S. health care system has been a complex puzzle to many Americans. Medical care in the United States is an enormous $2.5 trillion industry. It includes thousands of independent medical practices and partnerships and provider organizations; public and nonprofit institutions such as hospitals, nursing homes, and other specialized care facilities; and major private corporations. In dollar volume, the U.S. health care industry is second only to the manufacturing sector. For personal consumption, Americans spend more only on food and housing than they do on medical care. Furthermore, health care is by far the largest service industry in the country. In fact, the U.S. health care system is the world's eighth largest economy, second to that of France, and is larger than the total economy of Italy.[1]

More intimidating than its size, however, is its complexity. Not only is health care labor intensive at all levels, but also the types and functions of its numerous personnel change periodically to adjust to new technology, knowledge, and ways of delivering health care services.

As is frequently associated with progress, medical advances often create new problems while solving old ones. The explosion of medical knowledge that produced narrowly defined medical specialties has compounded a long-standing shortcoming of American medical care. The delivery of sophisticated high-tech health care requires the support of an incredibly complicated infrastructure that allows too many opportunities for patients to fall through the cracks between its narrowly defined services and specialists. In addition, our system has proven to be inept in securing even a modicum of universal coverage. Currently, over 47 million Americans are uninsured.

The size and complexity of health care in the United States contributes to its long-standing problems of limited consumer access, inconsistent quality, and uncontrolled costs. In addition, the U.S. health care system has done little to address the unnecessary and wasteful duplication of certain services in some areas and the absence of essential services in others.

These problems have worried this country's political and medical leaders for decades and have motivated legislative proposals that are aimed at reform by eight U.S. presidents. President Clinton's National Health Security Act of 1993 produced an unusually candid and sometimes acrimonious congressional debate. Vested interests advocating change and those defending the status quo both lobbied extensively to influence public and political opinion. In the end, the stakeholders in the traditional system convinced a public—apprehensive about more governmental control over personal health services—that the Clinton plan was too much, too liberal, and too costly, and it was therefore defeated.

President Obama's 2009 proposal for a major reform of the U.S. health care system produced an even more boisterous response by those with vested interests in the status quo. Led by the lobbyists of the insurance and pharmaceutical industries who envision constraints on their long history of unlimited profits, opponents of expanding the role of government, and supported by folks frightened of change or the scare tactics of reform opponents, the debate has been partisan and vigorous.

As 2009 ended, both houses of Congress had passed landmark, but somewhat different, health care reform bills by the slimmest of margins. In March 2010 the two versions of health care reform legislation were reconciled, signed by President Obama, and the long-awaited health care reform movement is underway. In subsequent chapters the proposed legislative changes are described.

Regardless of the forthcoming governmental intervention, health care is already undergoing a revolution. Health care reform has been occurring as a market-driven, not a policy-driven, phenomenon. In a world of accelerating consolidation to achieve ever higher standards of effectiveness and economy, there has been a surge of health care facility and service mergers and acquisitions, new programs, new names, and new roles that signal the onset of fundamental changes throughout the system. Hospitals are competing for patients, clinics have sprung up in shopping plazas, and physicians are creating larger and larger group practices.

The practice of medicine, long a cottage industry that valued individual entrepreneurship and control, has undergone dramatic change and physicians have been most affected. Physicians who cherished the individual autonomy and privileged position afforded them now face the vexing oversight of case and utilization management, practice guidelines, critical pathways, and clinical report cards. Unfortunately, the loss of professional control has also been accompanied by the loss of control over the allocation of health care dollars. The result has been a substantial decrease in annual physician incomes. Insurers have controlled health costs by arbitrarily refusing reimbursement for certain medical procedures and reducing payments for others.

This book is intended to serve as a text for introductory courses on the organization of health care for students in schools of public health, medicine, nursing, dentistry, and pharmacy and in schools and colleges that prepare physical therapists, occupational therapists, respiratory therapists, medical technologists, health administrators, and a host of other allied health professionals. It provides an introduction to the U.S. health care system and an overview of the professional, political, social, and economic forces that have shaped it and will continue to do so. Because the complex health care system in the United States is in a state of rapid change, this book is updated every two years to keep its readers abreast of new developments.

To facilitate its use as a teaching text, this book has been organized into a succession of chapters that both stand alone as balanced discussions of discrete subjects and, when read in sequence, provide incremental additions of information to complete the reader's understanding of the entire health care system. Although decisions about what subjects and material were essential to the book's content were relatively easy, decisions about the topics and content to be left out were very difficult. The encyclopedic nature of the subject and the finite length of the final manuscript were in constant conflict.

Thus the authors acknowledge in advance that nurses, dentists, pharmacists, physical and occupational therapists, and others may be disappointed that the text contains so little of the history and the political and professional struggles that characterize the evolution of their important professions. Given the centrality of those historical developments in students' educational preparation, it was assumed that appropriate attention to those subjects, using books written specifically for that purpose, would be included in courses in those professional curricula. To be consistent with that assumption, the authors tried to include only those elements in the history of public health, medicine, and hospitals that had a significant impact on how health care was delivered.

The authors made a similar set of difficult decisions regarding the depth of information to include about specific subjects. Topics such as epidemiology, history of medicine, program planning and evaluation, quality of care, and the like each have their own libraries of in-depth texts and, in many schools, dedicated courses. Thus it seemed appropriate in a text for an introductory course to provide only enough descriptive and interpretive detail about each topic to put it in the context of the overall subject of the book.

This book was written from a public health or population perspective and reflects the viewpoint of its authors. Both authors have public health and preventive medicine backgrounds and long histories of research into various aspects of the health care system, have planned and evaluated innovative projects for improving the quality and accessibility of care in both the public and voluntary sectors, and have served in key executive positions in the health field.

The authors have used much of the material contained in *Health Care USA: Understanding Its Organization and Delivery* to provide students, consumers, and neophyte professionals with an understanding of the unique interplay of the technology, workforce, research findings, financing, regulation, and personal and professional behaviors, values, and assumptions that determine what, how, why, where, and at what cost health care is delivered in the United States. In this seventh edition, as in each previous edition, we have included important additions and updates to provide a current perspective on the health care industry's continuously evolving trends.

The authors hope that as this book's readers plan and expand their educational horizons and, later, their professional experiences, they will have the advantage of a comprehensive understanding of the complex system in which they practice.

Reference

1. U.S. Bureau of the Census. The 2009 statistical abstract. National health expenditures—summary and projections. Available from http://www.census.gov/compendia/statab/2009/cats/health_nutrition/health_expenditures.html. Accessed November 16, 2009.

New to the Seventh Edition

In addition to updating all key financial, utilization, and other data with the latest available information, the seventh edition provides the following "new information."

Chapter 2: Benchmark Developments in U.S. Health Care

- Discussion of the growing influence of pharmaceutical and insurance companies on the costs and procedures of medical practice
- Public health's response to possible 2009–2010 swine flu epidemic
- Additional state legalization of physician-assisted suicide
- Obama administration's effort to complete a major reform of the U.S. health care system

Chapter 3: Hospitals: Origin, Organization, and Performance

- 2008–2010 economic recession effects on financial condition of hospitals
- New efforts of hospitals to reduce hospital-borne infections
- Updated information on hospital pharmaceutical and surgical errors
- New governmental effort to computerize hospital and pharmaceutical records

Chapter 4: Ambulatory Care

- Changes in physician office practice patterns
- New section describing the "patient-centered medical home"
- Updated trend in "urgent care center" growth and certification and continuing proliferation of retail clinics as a force in ambulatory care
- New information about the Federal Stimulus Package to increase numbers and size of federally qualified health centers

Chapter 5: Medical Education and the Changing Practice of Medicine

- New exposure of exorbitant payments to physicians to allow drug companies to ghost write medical journal articles and issue misleading reports on the safety and effectiveness of clinical trials

Chapter 7: Financing Health Care

- Latest national health expenditure data trends and projections and new graphic on national health expenditure data
- New comparison data between the U.S. and other developed countries' health expenditures in relation to population health status
- Information on new federal initiatives to combat fraud
- New data on health insurance coverage and costs
- New "disease management" initiatives by health plans
- New Medicare cost and quality initiatives
- Updates on Maine, Massachusetts, and Vermont universal coverage efforts

Chapter 9: Mental Health Services

- New data on prevalence, treatment, and diagnoses in the primary care sector
- Provisions of the 2008 Mental Health Parity and Addiction Equity Act
- Reports on two new, recent studies on states' Medicaid cost burden relative to the American Recovery and Reinvestment Act of 2009, noting funding reductions for psychiatric and behavioral health services, with accompanying new graphics

- Recent states' legislative activity relative to mental health insurance parity
- 2009 survey report from 50 states on effectiveness of services for the seriously mentally ill

Chapter 10: Public Health and the Role of Government in Health Care

- New changes in governmental cost and structure of its health service organizations
- 2009 public health's response to the swine flu epidemic in the context of epidemic preparedness

Chapter 12: Future of Health Care

- Updates on increasing difficulty smaller employers face in providing health insurance for employees
- New report on tax-favored health savings accounts, up 35% over the previous year
- New predictions about hospitals' competition with physician-owned facilities and privately owned diagnostic and ambulatory surgery centers
- New description of the Obama Health Reform Plan, questioning its survival in light of partisan political and popular opposition
- New summary on three states' successful implementation of universal health care reform legislation and the likelihood that other states will follow

CHAPTER 1

Overview of Health Care: A Population Perspective

This chapter provides a general overview of the U.S. health care industry, its policymakers, its values and priorities, and its various responses to changing conditions and problems. A template for understanding the natural histories of diseases and the levels of medical intervention is illustrated. Major influences in the advances and other changes to the health services system are briefly described in preparation for more extensive discussion in subsequent chapters. The conflicts of interest and ethical dilemmas resulting from medicine's technologic advances are also noted.

In recent years, health care has captured the interest of the public, political leaders, and an attentive media as never before. News of medical breakthroughs, deficiencies, rising costs, and congressional health care reform efforts attract a consistently high readership. For many, the fortunes and foibles of health care take on deeply serious meanings. There is a widespread sense of urgency among employers, insurers, consumer groups, and other policymakers about the seemingly unresolvable need to correct problems of access and cost without compromising the quality of care. The most recent debate about health care reform focused many Americans on the role health care plays in their lives and about the strengths and deficiencies of the complex labyrinth of health care providers, facilities, programs, and services.

There is growing concern that health care is a big, unmanageable business that consumes over 17% of the U.S. gross domestic product and exceeds $1.5 trillion in costs. Many health care providers and institutions have become commercial entrepreneurs beyond all expectations and to the concern of many. The commercialization of health care has created increasing conflicts between medical care providers on one side and policymakers and other third-party payers on the other.

Problems of Health Care

Although philosophical and political differences fuel the debates about health care policies and reforms, there is a general agreement that the health care system in the United States is fraught with problems and dilemmas. In spite of its impressive accomplishments, the U.S. health care system exhibits inexplicable contradictions in objectives; unwarranted variations in performance, effectiveness, and efficiency; and long-standing difficulties in its relationships with the public and with governments.

The strategies for addressing the problems of cost, access, and quality over the last 30 years reflect the periodic changes in political philosophies. The government-sponsored programs of the 1960s were designed to improve access for older adults and low-income populations without regard for the inflationary effects on costs. These programs were followed by regulatory attempts to address first the availability and price of health services, then the organization and distribution of health care, and then its quality. In the 1990s, the ineffective patchwork of government-sponsored health system reforms was superseded by the emergence of market-oriented changes, competition, and privately organized managed care organizations (MCOs).

The failure of government-initiated reforms created a vacuum that was filled quickly by the private sector. There is a difference, however, between recent governmental goals for health care reform and those of the market. Although the proposed government programs try to maintain some balance among costs, quality, and access, the primary goal of the market is to contain costs. As a result, there are serious concerns that market-driven reforms may not result in a health care system that equitably meets the needs of all Americans.

As the recent querulous debate over health care reform illustrated, when the dominant interest groups—government, employers, insurers, the public, and major provider groups—do not agree on how to change the system to accomplish widely desired reforms, the American people would rather continue temporizing. They are "unwilling to risk the strengths of our existing health care system in a radical effort to remedy admittedly serious deficiencies."[1]

Understanding Health Care

Health care policy usually reflects public opinion. Finding acceptable solutions to the perplexing problems of health care depends on public understanding and acceptance of both the existing circumstances and the benefits and risks of proposed remedies. Many communication problems regarding health policy stem from the public's inadequate understanding of health care and its delivery system.

Early practitioners purposely fostered the mystique surrounding medical care as a means to set themselves apart from the patients they served. Endowing health care with a certain amount of mystery encouraged patients to maintain blind faith in the capability of their physicians, even when the state of the science did not justify it. When advances in the understanding of the causes, processes, and cures of specific diseases revealed that previous therapies and methods of patient management were based on erroneous premises, physicians were not held responsible. Although the world's most advanced and proficient health care system provides a great deal of excellent care, the lack of public knowledge has allowed much care to be delivered that was less than beneficial and some that was inherently dangerous.

Now, however, the romantic naiveté with which health care and its practitioners were viewed has eroded significantly. Rather than a confidential contract between the provider and the consumer, the health care relationship now includes a voyeuristic collection of insurers, payers, managers, and quality assurers. Providers no longer have a monopoly on health care decisions and actions. Although the increasing scrutiny and accountability may be onerous and costly to physicians and other providers, it represents concerns of those paying for health care—governments, insurers, employers, and patients—about the value received for their expenditures. That these questions have been raised reflects the prevailing opinion that those who now chafe under the scrutiny are, at least indirectly, responsible for generating the excesses in the system while neglecting the problems of limited access to health care for many.

Cynicism about the health care system has grown as increasing information about the problems of costs, quality, and access has become public.

People who viewed medical care as a necessity provided by physicians who adhere to scientific standards based on tested and proven therapies have been disillusioned to learn that major knowledge gaps contribute to highly variable use rates for therapeutic and diagnostic procedures that have produced no measurable differences in outcomes. Nevertheless, as the recent discussions about system-wide reforms demonstrated, enormously complex issues underlie the health industry's problems, and the system's leadership has been inept in addressing them. "The quest for greater efficiency in the delivery of health care services is eternal in a country that spends far more on health care than any other, consistently has growth in spending that outstrips that of income, is unable to provide insurance coverage to at least 17% of its population, and ranks poorly among industrialized countries in system-wide measures such as life expectancy and infant mortality."[2]

Many health care system employees also have become discouraged. Institutional and agency administrators who say they care about patients but must reflect overriding budget considerations in every action confuse and demoralize health care workers. Most individuals in health care chose a health occupation not only because of the income potential, but also because they had a sense of caring and social justice. They made trade-offs and sacrifices for their values only to find that the reality is quite different. Nurses, the largest component of the health care workforce, are especially frustrated with their current role in hospitals. They feel overworked, unable to meet their own standards of quality care, and stressed to the point of leaving the profession. It is hoped that when the health care system again becomes stabilized in a more predictable economic environment, those contradictory messages from higher administrative levels will cease.

Why Patients and Providers Behave the Way They Do

In Chapter 3, the evolution of the U.S. system of hospitals makes clear the long tradition of physicians and other health care providers behaving in an authoritarian manner toward patients. In the past, hospitalized patients, removed from their usual places in society, were expected to be compliant and grateful to be in the hands of someone far more learned than themselves. More recently, however, recognizing the benefits of more proactive roles for patients and the improved outcomes that result, both health care providers and consumers are encouraging significant patient participation in every health care decision.

Indexes of Health and Disease

The body of statistical data about health and disease has grown enormously since the late 1960s, when the government began analyzing information obtained from Medicare and Medicaid claims, and computerized hospital and insurance data allowed the retrieval and exploration of huge files of clinical information. In addition, there have been continuing improvements in the collection, analysis, and reporting of vital statistics and communicable and malignant diseases by state and federal governments.

Data collected over time and international comparisons reveal common trends among developed countries. Birth rates have fallen, and life expectancies have lengthened so that older people make up an increasing proportion of total populations. The percentage of individuals who are disabled or dependent has grown as the health care professions have improved their capacity to rescue moribund individuals.

Infant mortality and maternal mortality, the international indicators of social and health care improvement, have continued to decline in the United States but have not reached the more commendable levels of countries with more demographically homogeneous populations. In the United States, the differences in infant mortality rates between inner-city neighborhoods and suburban communities may be greater than those between developed and undeveloped countries. The continuing inability of the health care system to address those discrepancies effectively reflects the system's ambiguous priorities.

Natural Histories of Disease and the Levels of Prevention

For many years, epidemiologists and health services planners have used a matrix for placing everything known about a particular disease or condition in the sequence of its origin and progression when untreated; this schema is called the natural history of disease. Many diseases, especially chronic diseases that may last for decades, have an irregular evolution and extend through a sequence of stages. When the causes and stages of a particular disease or condition are defined in its natural history, they can be matched against the health care interventions intended to prevent the condition's occurrence or to arrest its progress after its onset. Because these health care interventions are designed to prevent the condition from advancing to the next, and usually more serious, level in its natural history, the interventions are classified as the "levels of prevention." Figures 1-1, 1-2, and 1-3 illustrate the concept of the natural history of disease and levels of prevention.

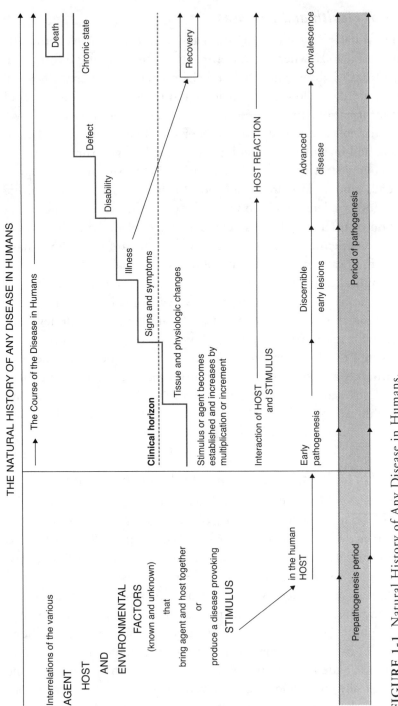

FIGURE 1-1 Natural History of Any Disease in Humans.
Source: Reprinted with permission from H. R. Leavell and E. G. Clark, *Preventative Medicine for the Doctor in His Community: An Epidemiologic Approach*, 3rd edition, p. 20, © 1965, The McGraw Hill Companies, Inc.

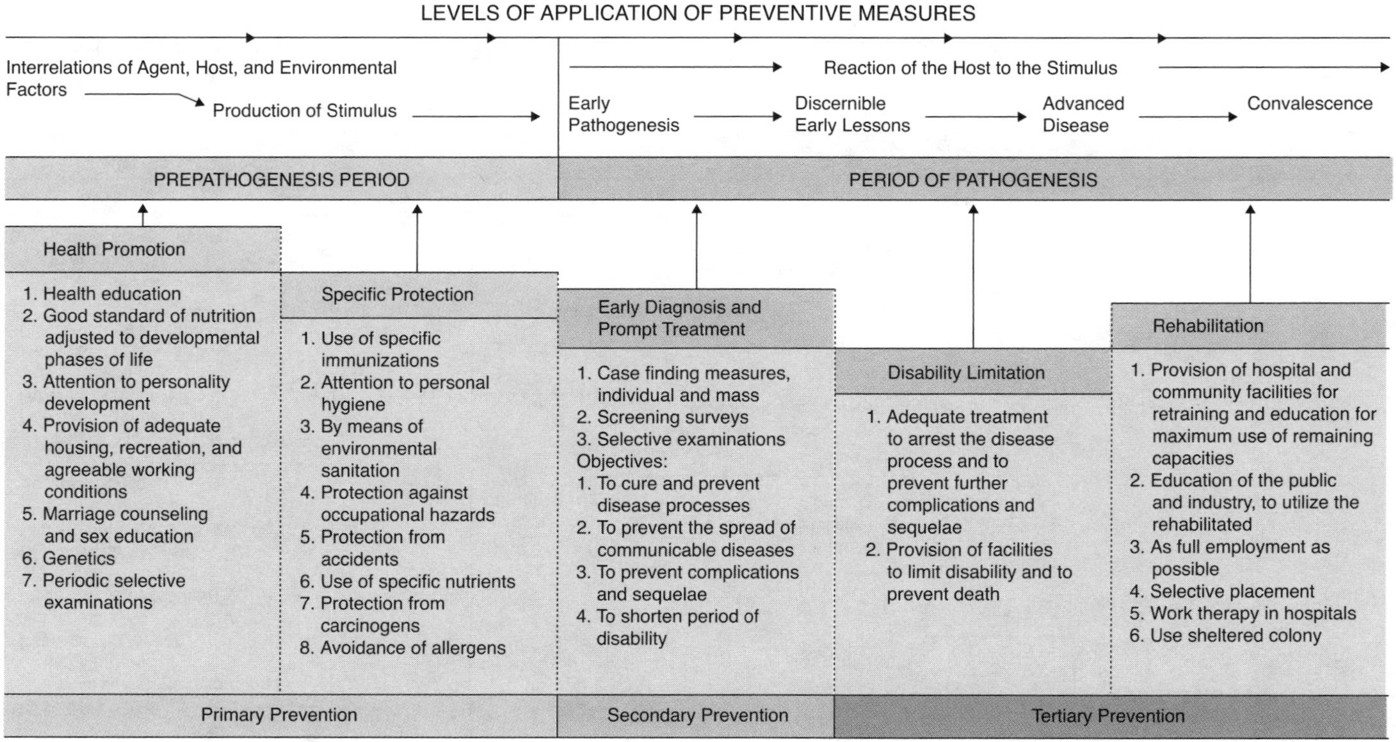

LEVELS OF APPLICATION OF PREVENTIVE MEASURES

	Reaction of the Host to the Stimulus		
Interrelations of Agent, Host, and Environmental Factors	Discernible Early Lessons	Advanced Disease	Convalescence
Production of Stimulus	Early Pathogenesis		

PREPATHOGENESIS PERIOD		PERIOD OF PATHOGENESIS		
Health Promotion	**Specific Protection**	**Early Diagnosis and Prompt Treatment**	**Disability Limitation**	**Rehabilitation**
1. Health education 2. Good standard of nutrition adjusted to developmental phases of life 3. Attention to personality development 4. Provision of adequate housing, recreation, and agreeable working conditions 5. Marriage counseling and sex education 6. Genetics 7. Periodic selective examinations	1. Use of specific immunizations 2. Attention to personal hygiene 3. By means of environmental sanitation 4. Protection against occupational hazards 5. Protection from accidents 6. Use of specific nutrients 7. Protection from carcinogens 8. Avoidance of allergens	1. Case finding measures, individual and mass 2. Screening surveys 3. Selective examinations Objectives: 1. To cure and prevent disease processes 2. To prevent the spread of communicable diseases 3. To prevent complications and sequelae 4. To shorten period of disability	1. Adequate treatment to arrest the disease process and to prevent further complications and sequelae 2. Provision of facilities to limit disability and to prevent death	1. Provision of hospital and community facilities for retraining and education for maximum use of remaining capacities 2. Education of the public and industry, to utilize the rehabilitated 3. As full employment as possible 4. Selective placement 5. Work therapy in hospitals 6. Use sheltered colony
Primary Prevention		**Secondary Prevention**		**Tertiary Prevention**

FIGURE 1-2 Levels of Application of Preventive Measures.
Source: Reprinted with permission from H. R. Leavell and E. G. Clark, *Preventative Medicine for the Doctor in His Community: An Epidemiologic Approach*, 3rd edition, p. 21, © 1965, The McGraw Hill Companies, Inc.

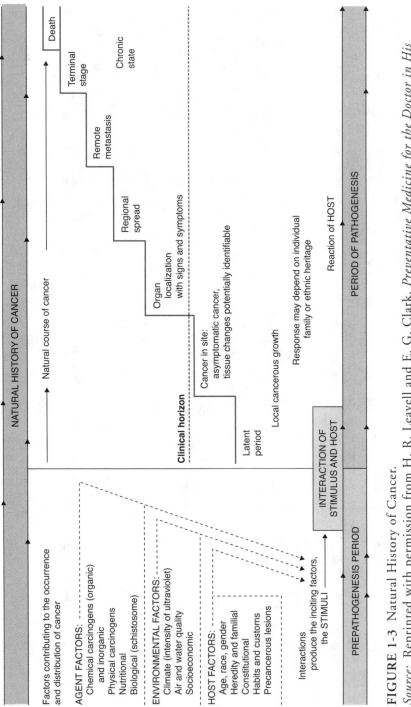

FIGURE 1-3 Natural History of Cancer.

Source: Reprinted with permission from H. R. Leavell and E. G. Clark, *Preventative Medicine for the Doctor in His Community: An Epidemiologic Approach,* 3rd edition, pp. 272–273, © 1965, The McGraw Hill Companies, Inc.

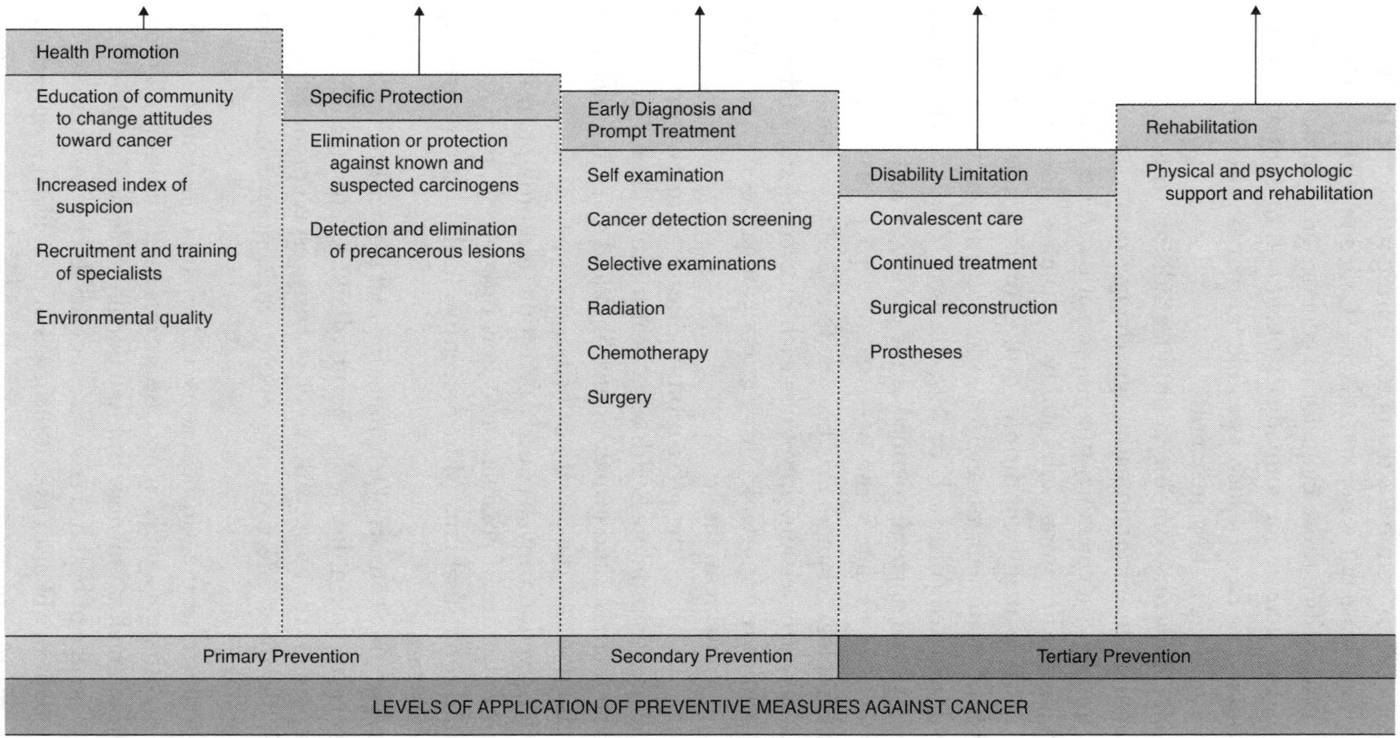

FIGURE 1-3 (continued) Natural History of Cancer.

Source: Reprinted with permission from H. R. Leavell and E. G. Clark, *Preventative Medicine for the Doctor in His Community: An Epidemiologic Approach*, 3rd edition, pp. 272–273, © 1965, The McGraw Hill Companies, Inc.

The first level of prevention is the period during which the individual is at risk for the disease but is not yet affected. Called the "prepathogenesis period," it identifies those behavioral, genetic, environmental, and other factors that increase the individual's likelihood of contracting the condition. Some risk factors, such as smoking, may be altered, whereas others, such as genetic factors, may not.

When such risk factors combine to produce a disease, the disease usually is not manifest until certain pathologic changes occur. This stage is a period of clinically undetectable, presymptomatic disease. Medical science is working hard to improve its ability to diagnose disease earlier in this stage. Because many conditions evolve in irregular and subtle processes, it is often difficult to determine the point at which an individual may be designated "diseased" or "not diseased." Thus, each natural history has a "clinical horizon," defined as the point at which medical science becomes able to detect the presence of a particular condition. Because the pathologic changes may become fixed and irreversible at each step in the disease progression, preventing each succeeding step of the disease is therapeutically important. This concept emphasizes the preventive aspect of clinical interventions.

Primary prevention, or the prevention of disease occurrence, refers to measures designed to promote health (e.g., health education to encourage good nutrition, exercise, and genetic counseling) and specific protections (e.g., immunization and the use of seat belts).

Secondary prevention involves early detection and prompt treatment to achieve an early cure, if possible, or to slow progression, prevent complications, and limit disability. Most preventive health care is currently focused on this area.

Tertiary prevention consists of rehabilitation and maximizing remaining functional capacity when disease has occurred and left residual damage. This stage represents the most costly, labor-intensive aspect of medical care and depends heavily on effective teamwork by representatives of a number of health care disciplines.

Figure 1-4 illustrates the natural history and levels of prevention for the aging process. Although aging is not a disease, it is a condition that is often accompanied by medical, mental, and functional problems that should be addressed by a range of health care services at each level of prevention.

The natural history of diseases and the levels of prevention are presented to illustrate two very important aspects of the U.S. health care system.

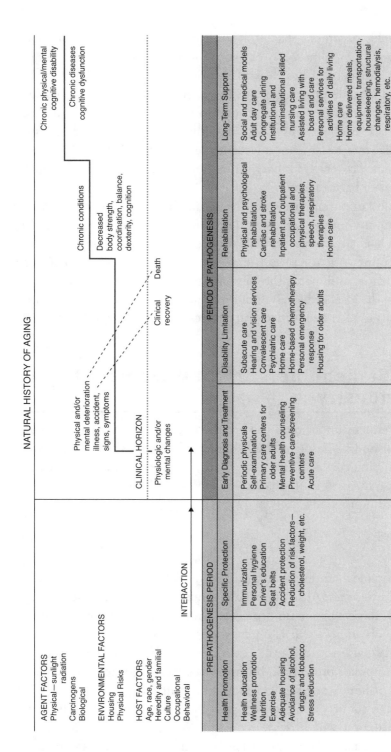

NATURAL HISTORY OF AGING

AGENT FACTORS
Physical—sunlight
  radiation
Carcinogens
Biological

ENVIRONMENTAL FACTORS
Housing
Physical Risks

HOST FACTORS
Age, race, gender
Heredity and familial
Culture
Occupational
Behavioral

INTERACTION

Chronic physical/mental
  cognitive disability

Chronic diseases
  cognitive dysfunction

Chronic conditions

Decreased
body strength,
coordination, balance,
dexterity, cognition

Physical and/or
mental deterioration
illness, accident,
signs, symptoms

CLINICAL HORIZON

Physiologic and/or
mental changes

Clinical
recovery

Death

PREPATHOGENESIS PERIOD		PERIOD OF PATHOGENESIS			
Health Promotion	Specific Protection	Early Diagnosis and Treatment	Disability Limitation	Rehabilitation	Long-Term Support
Health education Wellness promotion Nutrition Exercise Adequate housing Avoidance of alcohol, drugs, and tobacco Stress reduction	Immunization Personal hygiene Driver's education Seat belts Accident protection Reduction of risk factors—cholesterol, weight, etc.	Periodic physicals Self-examination Primary care centers for older adults Mental health counseling Preventive care/screening centers Acute care	Subacute care Hearing and vision services Convalescent care Psychiatric care Home care Home-based chemotherapy Personal emergency response Housing for older adults	Physical and psychological rehabilitation Cardiac and stroke rehabilitation Inpatient and outpatient occupational and physical therapies, speech, respiratory therapies Home care	Social and medical models Adult day care Congregate dining Institutional and noninstitutional skilled nursing care Assisted living with board and care Personal services for activities of daily living Home care Home delivered meals, equipment, transportation, housekeeping, structural changes, hemodialysis, respiratory, etc.

FIGURE 1-4 Natural History of Aging.
Source: Reprinted with permission from H. R. Leavell and E. G. Clark, *Preventative Medicine for the Doctor in His Community: An Epidemiologic Approach,* 3rd edition, pp. 272–273, © 1965, The McGraw Hill Companies, Inc.

First, it quickly becomes apparent in studying the natural history and levels of prevention for almost any of the common causes of disease and disability that the focus of health care historically has been directed at the curative and rehabilitative side of the disease continuum. Serious attention has been paid to refocusing the system on the health promotion/disease prevention side of those disease schemas only after the costs of diagnostic and remedial care became an unacceptable burden and the lack of adequate insurance coverage for over 40 million Americans became a public and political embarrassment.

The second important aspect of the natural history concept is its value in planning community services. The illustration on aging is a good example. That natural history and service level blueprint provides the planning framework for a multidisciplinary health services planning group to identify and match the community's existing services with those proposed in the idealized levels of prevention. Within this framework, the group begins to plan and initiate the services necessary to fill the gaps.

Major Stakeholders in the U.S. Health Care Industry

It is important to understand the health care industry and to recognize the number and variety of its stakeholders. The sometimes shared and often conflicting concerns, interests, and influences of these constituent groups cause them to shift alliances periodically to oppose or champion specific reform proposals.

The Public

First and foremost among health care stakeholders are the patients who consume the services. Although all are concerned with the issues of cost and quality, those who are uninsured or underinsured have an overriding uncertainty about access. It is unrealistic to assume that the U.S. public will some day wish to treat health care like other inherent rights, such as education or police protection, but there is general agreement that some basic array of health care services should be available to all U.S. citizens. Although the country waits to see what the recently passed health care reform legislation will provide, consumer organizations, such as the American Association of Retired Persons, and disease-specific groups, such as the American Cancer Society, the American Heart Association, and labor organizations, are politically active on behalf of various consumer constituencies.

Employers

Employers constitute an increasingly influential group of stakeholders in health care because they not only are paying for a high proportion of the costs but also are taking more proactive roles in determining what those costs should be. Large private employers, coalitions of smaller private employers, and public employers now wield significant authority in managed care and other insurance plan negotiations. In addition, employer organizations representing small and large businesses wield considerable political power in the halls of Congress.

Providers

Health care professionals are the core of the industry and have the most to do with the actual process and outcomes of the service provided. Physicians, dentists, nurses, nurse practitioners, physician assistants, pharmacists, podiatrists, chiropractors, and a large array of allied health providers working as individuals or in group practices and staffing health care institutions are responsible for the quality and, to a large extent, the cost of the health care system.

Hospitals and Other Health Care Facilities

Much of the provider activity, however, is shaped by the availability and nature of the health care institutions in which providers work. Hospitals of different types—general, specialty, teaching, rural, profit or not-for-profit, and independent or multifacility systems—are central to the existing health care system. However, they are becoming but one component of more complex integrated delivery system networks that also include nursing homes and other levels of care and various forms of medical practices.

Governments

Since the advent of Medicare and Medicaid, federal and state governments, already major stakeholders in health care, have become the dominant authorities over the system. Governments serve not only as payers but also as regulators and providers through public hospitals, state and local health departments, Veterans Affairs medical centers, and other facilities. In addition, of course, governments are the taxing authorities that generate the funds to support the system.

Alternative Therapies

Unconventional health therapies—those not usually taught in established medical and other health professional schools—contribute significantly to the amount, frequency, and cost of health care. In spite of the scientific logic and documented effectiveness of traditional, academically based health care, it is estimated that one in three adults uses alternative forms of health interventions each year and that more office visits are made to alternative care providers than to primary care physicians.

It is estimated that over $10 billion per year is spent on such alternative forms of health care as rolfing, yoga, spiritual healing, relaxation techniques, herbal remedies, energy healing, megavitamin therapy, the commonly recognized chiropractic arts, and a host of exotic mind–body healing techniques.[3]

The public's willingness to spend so much time and money on unconventional therapies suggests a substantial level of dissatisfaction with traditional scientific medicine. The popularity of alternative forms of therapy also indicates that its recipients confirm the effectiveness of the treatments by referring others to their practitioners. Whether or not these methods can be rationalized scientifically, if people feel better with their use and they do not deter individuals with treatable diseases from seeking conventional therapy, they serve a beneficial purpose. Insurance companies and MCOs are now considering alternative therapies as less expensive and probably equally effective options for keeping their beneficiaries feeling well.

In January 1995 the *Wall Street Journal* reported that several of the largest individual health insurance companies, including Mutual of Omaha and Prudential Insurance Company of America, began paying for selected unconventional therapies for heart disease and other chronic conditions.[4] In addition, the National Institutes of Health has established an Office of Alternative Medicine to fund studies of the efficacy of such therapies. Thus, as a somewhat paradoxical development, some of the most ancient concepts of alternative health care are gaining broader recognition and acceptance in an era of the most innovative and advanced high-technology medicine.

More for monetary than therapeutic reasons, a number of hospitals are now offering their patients some form of alternative medicine. According to an American Hospital Association survey, over 15% of U.S. hospitals opened alternative or complementary medicine centers by the year 2000. With a market estimated to be over $27 billion and patients willing to pay cash for alternative medicine treatments, hospitals are willing to rationalize the provision of several "unproven" services.[5]

Managed Care Organizations and Other Insurers

The insurance industry has long been a major and unrestrained stakeholder in the health care industry. Although the traditional, indemnity-type plans such as Blue Cross and Blue Shield are being replaced rapidly by managed care plans, they still are very much in evidence. Managed care plans may be owned by insurance companies just as the indemnity plans are, or they may be owned by hospitals, physicians, or consumer cooperatives. MCOs and the economic pressures they can apply through the negotiation of capitated fees have produced much of the change that has occurred in the regional systems of health care during the last few years.

Long-Term Care

The aging of the U.S. population will be a formidable challenge to the country's systems of acute and long-term care. Nursing homes, home care services, other adult care facilities, and rehabilitation facilities will become increasingly important components of the nation's health care system as they grow in number, size, and complexity. The creation of seamless systems of care that permit patients to move back and forth among ambulatory care offices, acute care hospitals, subacute care services, home care, and nursing homes within a single, integrated network of facilities and services will provide a continuum of services required for the more complex care of aging patients.

Mental Health

The mental health component of health care is often neglected in the debates on system reforms. Yet, psychiatric hospitals, community mental health facilities, and community-based ambulatory services serve large segments of the population and are critically important to the effectiveness of the health care system. Mental health and physical health are contiguous conditions and should, but do not, generate the same concern and unprejudiced funding.

Voluntary Facilities and Agencies

Voluntary not-for-profit facilities and agencies provide significant amounts of health counseling, care, and follow-up and research support and should be considered major stakeholders in the health care system. It is interesting that although the voluntary sector traditionally has not received the recognition it deserves for its contribution to the nation's health care, it is now suggested as the safety net to replace the services to be eliminated in cost-cutting proposals.

Health Professions Education and Training Institutions

Schools of public health, medicine, nursing, dentistry, pharmacy, optometry, allied health, and other health care professions have a significant impact on the nature, quality, and costs of health care. As they prepare generation after generation of competent health care providers, these schools also inculcate the values, attitudes, and ethics that govern the practices and behaviors of those providers as they function in the health care system. The influences of these schools, particularly as they contribute to the leadership of academic health care centers, are addressed in Chapter 5.

Professional Associations

National, state, and regional organizations representing health care professionals or institutions have considerable influence over legislative proposals, regulation, quality issues, and other political matters. The lobbying effectiveness of the American Medical Association, for example, is legendary. The national influence of the American Hospital Association and the regional power of its state and local affiliates are also impressive. Other organizations of health care professionals, such as the American Public Health Association, the Group Health Association of America, American Nurses Association, and the American Dental Association, play significant roles in health policy decisions.

Other Health Industry Organizations

The size and complexity of the health care industry encourage the involvement of a great number of commercial entities. Several, such as the insurance and pharmaceutical enterprises, are major industries themselves and have significant organizational influence. The medical supplies and equipment business and the various consulting and information and management system suppliers also are important players.

Research Communities

It is difficult to separate much of health care research from the educational institutions that provide for its implementation. Nevertheless, the national research enterprise must be included in any enumeration of stakeholders in the health care industry. Government entities, such as the National Institutes of Health and the Agency for Healthcare Research and Quality, and not-for-profit foundations, such as the Robert Wood Johnson Foundation and the Pew Charitable Trusts, exert tremendous influence over health care research and practice by encouraging investigations that serve policy decision making and defining the kinds of research that will be supported.

Development of Managed Care

Managed care refers to arrangements that link health care financing and service delivery and allows payers to exercise significant economic control over how and what services are delivered. Common features in managed care arrangements are as follows:

- *Provider panels:* Specific physicians and other providers are selected to care for plan members.
- *Limited choice:* Members must use the providers affiliated with the plan or pay an additional amount.
- *Gatekeeping:* Members must obtain a referral from a case manager for specialty or inpatient services.
- *Risk sharing:* Providers bear some of the health plan's financial risk through capitation and withholds.

- *Quality management and utilization review:* The plan monitors provider practice patterns and medical outcomes to identify deviations from quality and efficiency standards.

Health plans with these features are called managed care organizations, or MCOs. The most common MCOs are health maintenance organizations (HMOs) and preferred provider organizations. MCOs may directly employ medical staff, as in a staff model, or contract with independent providers or individual practice associations, or any combination of arrangements in between. Whatever the arrangement, however, in managed care, the provider is always economically accountable to the payer. Managed care is discussed at length in Chapter 7.

Rural Health Networks

Rural health systems are often incomplete, with shortages of various services and duplications of others. Federal and state programs have addressed this situation by promoting the development of rural health networks. Although relatively new, most of these networks strive to provide local access to primary, acute, and emergency care and to provide efficient links to more distant regional specialists and tertiary care services. Ideally, rural health networks assemble and coordinate a comprehensive array of services that include dental, mental health, long-term care, and other health and human services. Realistically, many of those services are lacking, and rural communities sometimes offer various incentives to attract or gain access to specific providers. When successful, however, rural health networks are a significant advantage to their communities. With sufficient structure and administrative capability, the networks can control the development of their service systems and negotiate effectively with MCOs.

With costs increasing and populations declining in many rural communities, it has been difficult for rural hospitals to continue their acute inpatient care services. Nevertheless, these hospitals are often critically important to their communities. Because a hospital is usually one of few major employers in rural communities, its closure has economic and health care consequences. Communities lacking alternative sources of health care within reasonable travel distance not only lose payroll and related business, but also lose physicians, nurses, and other health person-nel and suffer higher morbidity and mortality rates among those most vulnerable, such as infants and older adults.[6]

Some rural hospitals have remained viable by participating in some form of multi-institutional arrangement that permits them to benefit from the personnel, services, purchasing power, and financial stability of larger facilities. Many rural hospitals, however, have found it necessary to shift from inpatient to outpatient or ambulatory care. The development of ambulatory care services by rural and urban hospitals is a strong health care system trend, as is the increased use of less expensive ancillary per-sonnel. In many rural communities, the survival of a hospital depends on how quickly and effectively it can replace its inpatient services with a productive constellation of ambulatory care, and sometimes long-term care, services.

These rural hospital initiatives have been supported by federal legisla-tion since 1991. This legislation provided funding to promote the essen-tial access community hospital and the rural primary care hospital. Both are limited-service hospital models developed as alternatives for hospitals too small and geographically isolated to be full-service acute care facilities. Regulations regarding staffing and other service requirements are relaxed in keeping with the rural settings[7] and include allowing physician's assis-tants, nurse practitioners, and clinical nurse specialists to provide primary or inpatient care without a physician in the facility if medical consultation is available by phone.

The Balanced Budget Act of 1997 included a Rural Hospital Flexibility Program that replaced the essential access community hospital/rural pri-mary care hospital model with a critical access hospital (CAH) model. Any state with at least one CAH may qualify for the program, which exempts CAHs from strict regulation and allows them the flexibility to meet small, rural community needs by developing criteria for establishing network relationships. Although the new program maintains many of the same features and requirements as its predecessor, it adds more flexibility to limited-service hospitals by increasing the number of allowed occupied inpatient beds from 6 to 15 and the maximum length of stay before required discharge or transfer from 72 to 96 hours. The new program also allows maintenance of up to 25 total beds, with a swing bed program that allows flexibility in their use. The goal of the CAH program is to enable small rural hospitals to maximize reimbursement and meet community needs with responsiveness and flexibility.

The Balanced Budget Act also serves rural hospitals by providing Medicare reimbursement for "telemedicine" and other video arrangements that link isolated facilities with clinical specialists at large hospitals. Advances in telemedicine technology make it possible for a specialist to be in direct visual and voice contact with a patient and provider at a remote location.

Rural health care organization networks have been formed in response to market changes. They may be formally organized as not-for-profit corporations or informally linked for a defined set of mutually beneficial purposes. Typically, they advocate at local and state levels on rural health care issues, cooperate in joint community outreach activities, and seek opportunities to negotiate with MCOs to provide services to enrolled populations.

Priorities of Health Care

Certainly, the priorities of health care—the emphasis on dramatic tertiary care, the costly and intensive efforts to fend off the death of terminal patients for a few more days or weeks, the heroic and often futile attempts to save extremely premature infants at huge expense while thousands of women go without the prenatal care that would decrease prematurity—contribute to the obvious mismatch between the rising costs of health care and the failure to improve the measures of health status in the United States. It is difficult to rationalize the goals of a system that invests in the most sophisticated and expensive neonatal services to save premature, high-risk infants while cutting back on the relatively inexpensive and effective prenatal services that would have prevented many of those poor birth outcomes in the first place.

If health care were to be governed by rational policies, the benefits to society of investing in early prenatal care that is unquestionably cost-effective would be compared with trying to salvage extremely low-weight, high-risk infants who often need prolonged care because they are inadequately developed, dysfunctional human beings. Clearly, current priorities favor heroic medicine over the more mundane, far less costly preventive care that results in measurable economic and human benefits.

The Tyranny of Technology

In many respects, the health care system has done and is doing a remarkable job. Important advances have been made in medical science that have brought measurable improvements in the length and quality of life. The paradox is, however, that as our technology gets better and more expensive, more people are being deprived of its benefits. Health care providers can be so mesmerized by their own technologic ingenuity that things assume greater value than persons. For example, hospital administrations and medical staffs commonly dedicate their most competent practitioners and most sophisticated technology to the care of terminal patients while allocating far fewer resources to primary and preventive services for ambulatory clinic patients and other community populations in need of basic medical services.

Some community hospitals are recognizing this disparity by conducting outreach and education programs for the medically underserved. As long as reimbursement policies continue to favor illness intervention rather than prevention, however, most institutions will find it difficult to initiate and maintain prevention initiatives and allocate staff to the potentially more productive care of ambulatory clinic populations.

No better example of the pervasive influence of technology exists than that of the continuing advances in diagnostic imaging. Although clinicians still depend on the long-established and relatively simple radiograph technology, they now have at their disposal several new and highly sophisticated computer-assisted imaging techniques that vastly expand their capability to visualize body structures and functions. The total spent on new imaging procedures in the United States is in the billions of dollars and is rising annually.

The recurring theme among health services researchers assessing the value of technologic advances is a series of generally unanswered questions:

1. How does the new technology benefit the patient?
2. Is it worth the cost?
3. Are the new methods better than previous methods, and can they replace them?
4. Is treatment planning enhanced?
5. Is the outcome from disease better, or is the mortality rate improved?

Although many of the latest advances have gained great popularity and widespread acceptance, the rigorous assessments that address these basic questions have yet to be conducted.

Much of the philosophy underlying the values and priorities of the health care system today can be attributed to the unique culture of U.S. medicine. That philosophy owes much to the aggressive "can do" spirit of the frontier. The U.S. physicians want to do as much as possible. They order more diagnostic tests than their colleagues in other countries, prescribe drugs frequently and at relatively higher doses, and are more likely to resort to surgery whenever possible. Patients and their physicians regard the body as a machine, like a car, which helps explain their enthusiasm for annual checkups and devices such as pacemakers and artificial hearts.

Diseases are likened to enemies to be conquered. Physicians expect their patients to be aggressive, too. Those who undergo drastic treatments to "beat" cancer are held in higher regard than patients who resign themselves to the disease. Some physicians and nurses feel let down when dying patients indicate they do not want to be resuscitated or stipulate restrictions to palliative care only.

The treatment-oriented rather than prevention-oriented health care philosophy is encouraged by an insurance system that, before managed care, rarely paid for any disease prevention other than immunization. It is also understandable in an era of high-technology medicine that there is much more satisfaction and remuneration from saving the lives of the injured and diseased than in preventing those occurrences from happening in the first place.

The capitation concept and HMOs evolved from the expectation that health care could be improved if the financial incentives could be reversed. Rather than allowing providers to profit from treating sickness, managed care concepts reward providers for keeping patients well. However, the treatment orientation so pervades U.S. health care that even the widespread development and acceptance of HMOs have yet to result in a significant and effective national effort to accomplish health maintenance and disease prevention.

Social Choices of Health Care

The emphasis on cure also has disinclined the health care professions to address those situations over which they have had little control. Acquired dependence on cigarettes, alcohol, and drugs must be counted among the significant causes of impaired health in our population. The future effects on health and medical care associated with these addictions probably will exceed all expectations. Similarly, the AIDS epidemic is as much a social and behavioral phenomenon as it is a biologic one. Nevertheless, outside of the public health disciplines, the considerable influence and prestige of the health care professions have been noticeably absent in steering public opinion and governmental action toward an emphasis on health. Similarly, by comparison with resources expended on treatment after illness occurs, relatively little attention is given to changing high-risk behaviors even when the consequences are virtually certain and nearly always extreme.

The Aging Population

The aging of the U.S. population is of major significance among the health care system's emerging issues. It will increasingly affect every aspect of health care. The rate of aging is five times that of overall population growth. By the year 2050, it is estimated that 30% of the U.S. population will be over the age of 65 years. The number of persons over 85 years old will double, but the under-35 population will decline by 10%.

The growth of the population 65 years and older presents a serious challenge to health care providers and policymakers. Those 85 years and older are the fastest growing segment of the aging population. Projections by the U.S. Census Bureau suggest that the population 85 years and older will grow from about 4 million in 2000 to 19 million in 2050 (Figure 1-5).[8] The size of this age group is especially demanding of the health care system because these individuals tend to be in poorer health and require more services than the younger elderly.

Although the current population of older adults is predominately white, there will be more racial diversity and more persons of Hispanic origin within the U.S. older population in the coming years. There were relatively large population gains among older adults of Asian and Hispanic origin between 1980 and 1990, and those gains will increase substantially in subsequent decades.[8]

The older Hispanic population is projected to almost triple between 2000 and 2050. The older Hispanic population is growing much faster than the older black population. The number of older Hispanics was about two-thirds that of the black population in 2000. In 2050, older Hispanics will exceed the number of older blacks by 25%. A similar surge

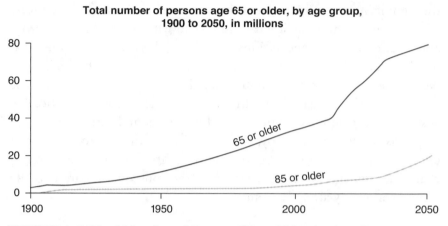

FIGURE 1-5 Total Number of Persons 65 or Older, by Age Group. *Source:* U.S. Bureau of the Census, decennial census data and population projections.

in the number of non-Hispanic Asian and Pacific Islanders is also projected during the period. The proportion of the non-Hispanic white population will drop significantly from 83.5% to 64.2% (Table 1-1).[9]

Although the older adults of the future will stay more active after retiring and be better educated, the burden of incurable chronic diseases of later life will be an enormous challenge to the health care system. As medical advances find more ways to maintain life, the duration of chronic illness and the number of chronically ill patients will increase. Consequently, the need for personal support will increase even more. The intensity of care required by frail older adults has the potential of affecting worker productivity. It is common for women to leave the workforce or to work part time to care for frail relatives at a time when they should build retirement benefits for their own old age.

The increased number of older persons with chronic physical ailments and long-term cognitive disorders raises significant questions about the capability of the U.S. health care system. Much has yet to be learned by practitioners serving the aged. Health care professionals are just beginning to recognize and gradually respond to the need to focus health care for older adults away from medications or other quick-fix remedies. The system is slowly acknowledging that the traditional medical service model is inappropriate to the care of those with multiple chronic conditions.

Table 1-1 Projected Population Age 65 and Older by Race and Hispanic Origin, 2000 and 2050

	Year 2000	Year 2050
Total	100.0	100.0
Non-Hispanic White	83.5	64.2
Non-Hispanic Black	8.1	12.2
Non-Hispanic American and Alaska Native	0.4	0.6
Non-Hispanic Asian and Pacific Islander	2.4	6.5
Hispanic	5.6	16.4

Note: Data are middle series projections of the populations. Hispanics may be of any race.

Source: U.S. Census Bureau, Population Projections of the United States by Age, Sex, Race, Hispanic Origin, and Nativity: 1999 to 2100. Published January 2000. http://www.census.gov/population/www/projections/natproj.html.

Chronically ill older patients need a multidisciplinary mix of services that must meet a broad spectrum of physical, medical, and psychosocial needs. This challenge requires a large increase in the number of health care providers trained in the special philosophies and skills of geriatric health care. The provisions of the Balanced Budget Act of 1997 that institutionalized the program of all-inclusive care for the older population in the revised Medicare reimbursement scheme symbolize growing acceptance of innovative ways to meet the needs of the older Americans.

The growing number of older adults faces serious gaps in financial coverage for long-term care needs. Unlike the broad Medicare program coverage for the acute health care problems of older Americans, the long-term care services needed to cope with the chronic disability and functional limitations of aging are largely unaddressed by either Medicare or private insurance plans. With the exception of the relatively small number of individuals with personal long-term care insurance, the major costs of long-term care services are borne by the individual older adults and their caregivers.

As a last resort, the Medicaid program has become the major public source of financing for nursing home care. Medicaid eligibility, however, requires that persons of means "spend down" their personal resources to meet the means-test criteria. For those disabled older adults who seek care in the community outside of nursing homes, Medicaid offers limited assistance. Thus the health policy issues associated with the multidisciplinary long-term care needs of older adults mount with every year's increase in the proportion of aged Americans and every upturn in the costs of health care.

Access to Health Care

Much attention has been paid to the economic problems of health care, and considerable investments of research funds have been made to address the issues of health care quality. The third major problem, however—that of limited access to health care among the estimated 45 million uninsured or underinsured Americans—continues to confound decision makers. The issue, of course, is more a moral than an economic one. Unlike most other developed nations, the United States has yet to decide on the ethical precepts that should underlie the distribution of health care. Although references frequently are made to those millions of citizens, including children, who are virtually locked out of the system, only a few professionals have had the courage to address this troublesome issue in open debate.

Polar positions have been taken by those who have addressed the question of whether society in general or governments in particular have an obligation to ensure that everyone has the right to health care and whether the health care system has a corresponding obligation to make such care available. Consider these opposing viewpoints by P. H. Elias and R. M. Sade, respectively:

> Physicians who limit their office practice to insured and paying patients declare themselves openly to be merchants rather than professionals. The mercantile approach has several consequences. First, it demeans the individual physician and cheapens the profession. Second, it puts the third-party payer, as a service purchaser, in a position of greater importance than the patient. Third, it fosters the myth that physicians as a group are greedy and self-serving rather than dedicated and altruistic. And most important, it deprives a large segment of our fellow humans of care. Physicians who value their professionalism should treat office patients on the basis of need, not remuneration.[10]
>
> The concept of medical care as the patient's right is immoral because it denies the most fundamental of all rights, that of a man to his own life and the freedom of action to support it. Medical care is neither a right nor a privilege: it is a service that is provided by doctors to others who wish to purchase it. It is the provision of this service that a doctor depends upon for his livelihood. . . . If the right to health care belongs to the patient, he starts out owning the services of a doctor without the necessity of either earning them or receiving them as a gift from the only man who has the right to give them; the doctor, himself.[11]

Although health care providers debate their individual and personal obligations to provide uncompensated care, the system itself finessed the problem for a long time by shifting the costs of care from the uninsured to the insured. This unofficial but practical approach to indigent care was ethically tolerable as long as the reimbursement system for paying patients was so open-ended that the cost of treating the uninsured could easily be passed on to paying patients. The cost shifting that worked under retrospective reimbursement, however, was not feasible under prospective payment and diagnostic reimbursement guidelines. Under the current price-competitive market pressures, health care providers are in the uncomfortable position of having to apply some kind of government intervention to address the problems of health care access.

Thus, the shifting winds of health care reform only underscore the confusion of the health policy of the United States. At the same time, U.S. health policymakers would like to assure the public that the health care system provides all citizens with comparable access to health care while maintaining the freedom of the providers from government interference in decisions about service production and delivery—and add for good measure that the system exercises budgetary and cost controls in the process.

It is obvious that these goals are contradictory and that attainment of any two leaves the third uncontrolled. Thus, policymakers have been forced to choose among pairs of these goals or fail to achieve all three. In the 1990s the government chose to let providers and insurers work out what care would be delivered and how, as long as they met government requirements for budgetary and cost controls. The third goal, equitable access, seems to have been deferred indefinitely. In spite of the recently passed health care reform legislation, the achievement of some kind of universal coverage that ensures that all Americans have access to a basic level of health care will not be resolved effectively until the system's stakeholders and the supporting public can formulate and reach consensus on the fundamental values underlying the problem.

Quality of Care

Another health care system problem area relates to variations in the quality and appropriateness of medical care. The uncertainty that pervades current clinical practice is far greater than most people realize. Problems in the quality and appropriateness of many diagnostic and therapeutic procedures impact heavily on costs.

Since the November 1999 report of the Institute of Medicine that estimated that medical errors take from 44,000 to 98,000 lives per year,
Congress, the president, medical institutions, and the public have been
stirred to respond to a problem that has existed for years. The increasing
complexity of the health care system, the potency of its pharmaceuticals,
the dangers inherent in invasive surgical procedures, and the potential for
error in the many information transfers that occur during hospital care
combine to put patients at serious risk. The strategies proposed to cope
with these problems, as well as the physician report cards, clinical guidelines, and other mechanisms designed to address inexplicable variations in
the provision of medical care are discussed in subsequent chapters.

It is important, however, to recognize the seriousness of the medical
error problem. Health care errors are the leading cause of preventable
deaths in the United States. Deaths resulting from medical mishaps in
acute care hospitals alone are between the fifth and eighth leading causes
of all deaths in the United States. The overall burden on society is much
greater when both fatal and nonfatal events are counted and when medical mishaps in medical offices, ambulatory centers, and long-term care
facilities are considered.[12]

Conflicts of Interest

One of the greatest advantages of the high-technology health care systems
that serve most metropolitan areas in the United States is the ability of
physicians and patients to benefit from referrals to a broad range of highly
specialized clinical, laboratory, rehabilitation, and other services. The
array of comprehensive diagnostic and therapeutic resources available in
most communities greatly enhances the clinical capability of health care
providers and the care of their patients.

In recent years, however, more and more providers have begun to
invest in laboratories, imaging centers, medical supply companies, and
other health care businesses. In many cases, these are joint ventures with
other institutions that conceal the identity of the investors. When
health care providers refer patients for tests or other services to health
care businesses that they own or in which they have a financial stake,
there is a serious potential for conflicts of interest. In fact, for the last
several years this referral for profit has been a sensitive medical issue

during congressional debates. Both federal and state governments and the American Medical Association have conducted studies that confirm that physician-owned laboratories, for example, perform more tests per patient at higher charges than those in which physicians have no invest-ments. These conflicts of interest undermine the traditional professional role of physicians and significantly increase health care expenditures. Government attempts to limit self-serving entrepreneurial activities of physicians are driven by economic concerns. The ethical implications should be of concern to the medical profession. A major contribution would be made to the code of conduct for health care providers if the American Medical Association provided physicians with a few clear guidelines regarding the growing encroachment of commercialism on medical practice.[13]

Health Care's Ethical Dilemmas

Once almost an exclusive province of physicians and other health care providers, moral and ethical issues underlying provider–patient relation-ships and the difficult decisions resulting from the vast increase in treat-ment options are now in the domains of law, politics, journalism, health institution administrations, and the public. During the last few decades, the list of ethical issues has expanded as discoveries in genetic identifica-tion and engineering, organ transplantation, a mounting armamentarium of highly specialized diagnostic and therapeutic interventions, and advances in technology have allowed the lives of otherwise terminal indi-viduals to be prolonged. In addition, an energized health care consumer movement advocating more personal control over health care decisions, economic realities, and the issues of the most appropriate use of limited resources are but a few of the topics propelling values and ethics to the top of the health care agenda. There is a social dimension to health care that never existed before and that the health professions, their educational institutions, their organizations, and their philosophical leadership are just beginning to address.

Clearly, the rapid pace of change in health care and the resulting issues have outpaced U.S. society's ability to reform the thinking, values, and expectations that were more appropriate to a bygone era. Legislative ini-tiatives are, correctly or not, filling the voids.

The 1997 decision of the U.S. 9th Circuit Court of Appeals permitting physician-assisted suicide for competent, terminally ill adults in the state of Oregon is an unprecedented example. New York State's 1990 passage of health care proxy legislation that allows competent adults to appoint agents to make health care decisions on their behalf if they become incapacitated is another. Living wills that provide advance directives regarding terminal care are now recognized in all 50 states.

Issue by issue, the country is trying to come to grips with the ethical dilemmas that modern medicine has created. The pluralistic nature of this society, however, and the Judeo-Christian concepts about caring for the sick and disabled that served so well for so long make sweeping reformation of the ethical precepts on which health care has been based very unlikely.

As Americans continue to live longer and new technologies vastly improve the treatment of disease, a new generation of health plans will evolve. The basic issues of cost, quality, and access, however, will undoubtedly persist, joined by a host of new concerns. How to improve Americans' health behaviors, how to involve consumers more effectively in health care decisions, and how to determine responsibility for medical management are among the challenges of this new decade.

References

1. Ginzberg E. Health care reform: why so slow? *N Engl J Med*. 1990;32: 1464–1465.
2. Nichols LM, Ginsburg BA, Christianson U, et al. Are market forces strong enough to deliver efficient health care systems? Confidence is waning. *Health Affairs*. 2004;23:8–21.
3. Blumberg DI, Grant WD, Hendricks SR, et al. The physician and unconventional medicine. *Alternative Ther*. 1995;1:31–35.
4. Carton B. Health insurers embrace eye-of-newt therapy. *Wall Street Journal*. January 30, 1995:B1.
5. Abelson R, Brown PL. Alternative medicine is finding its niche in nation's hospitals. *The New York Times*. April 13, 2002:B1, B3.
6. Fickenscher K, Voorman ML. An overview of rural health care. In: Shortell SM, Reinhardt UE, Eds. *Improving Health Policy and Management: Nine Critical Research Issues for the 1990s*. Ann Arbor, MI: Health Administration Press; 1992:111–149.
7. Fickenscher V. An overview of rural health care. *Ann Intern Med*. 1995;122: 111–149.

8. U.S. Bureau of the Census. *U.S. Population Estimates by Age, Sex, Race and Hispanic Origin: 1980–1991, Current Population Reports.* Washington, DC: Government Printing Office, 1993:15–10955, Table 1.

9. U.S. Bureau of the Census. Facts About Aging. Available from http://www.census.gov/population/www/projections/natproj.html. Accessed January 24, 2004.

10. Elias PH. Letter to editor. *N Engl J Med.* 1986;314:314–391.

11. Sade RM. Medical care as a right: a refutation. *N Engl J Med.* 1971;285:1281, 1289.

12. Kizer KW. Patient safety: a call to action: a consensus statement from the national quality forum. National Quality Forum for Health Care Measurement and Reporting. Available from http://www.qualityforum.org. Accessed September 16, 2002.

13. Relman AS. Self referral: what's at stake? *N Engl J Med.* 1992;327:1522–1524.

Benchmark Developments in U.S. Health Care

This chapter describes the important legislative, political, economic, organizational, and professional influences that transformed health care in the United States from a relatively simple professional service to a huge, complex, corporation-dominated industry. The effects of medical education, scientific advances, rising costs, changing population demographics, and American values and assumptions regarding health care are noted.

From its earliest history, health care, or, more accurately, medical care, was dominated by physicians and their hospitals. In the 19th and early 20th centuries, participation in U.S. medicine was generally limited to two parties—patients and physicians. Diagnosis, treatment, and fees for services were considered confidential between patients and physicians. Medical practice was relatively simple and usually involved long-standing relationships with patients and their families. Physicians set and usually adjusted their charges to their estimates of patients' ability to pay and collected their own bills. This was the intimate physician–patient relationship that the profession held sacred.

Free from outside scrutiny or interference, individual physicians had complete control over where, when, what, and how they practiced, and, not surprisingly, they preferred it that way. In 1934, the American Medical Association (AMA) published this statement: "No third party must be permitted to come between the patient and his physician in any medical matter."[1] The AMA was concerned about such issues as non–physician-controlled voluntary health insurance, compulsory health insurance, and the few capitated contracts for medical services negotiated by remote lumber or mining companies and a few workers' guilds. For decades, organized medicine repeatedly battled against these and other outside influences that altered "the old relations of perfect freedom between physicians and patients, with separate compensation for each separate service."[1]

As early as the 19th century, some Americans carried insurance against sickness through an employer, fraternal order, guild, trade union, or commercial insurance company. Most of the plans, however, were simply designed to make up for lost income during sickness or injury by providing a fixed cash payment.[1] Sickness insurance, as it was originally called, was the beginning of social insurance programs against the risks of income interruption by accident, sickness, or disability. Initially, it was provided only to wage earners. Later, it was extended to workers' dependents and other people.[2]

Around 1915 the drive for compulsory health insurance began to build in the United States, after most European countries had initiated either compulsory programs or subsidies for voluntary programs. The underlying concern was to protect workers against a loss of income resulting from industrial accidents that were common at the time. Families with only one breadwinner, often already at the edge of poverty, were devastated by loss of income caused by sickness or injury, even without the additional costs of medical care.

At the time, life insurance companies sold "industrial" policies that provided lump-sum payments at death, which amounted to $50 or $100. The money was used to pay for final medical expenses and funerals. Both Metropolitan Life and Prudential Insurance Company rose to the top of the insurance industry by successfully marketing industrial policies that required premium payments of 10 to 25 cents per week.[2]

In 1917, World War I interrupted the campaign for compulsory health insurance in the United States. In 1919, the AMA House of Delegates officially condemned compulsory health insurance with the following resolution[3]:

> The American Medical Association declares its opposition to the institution of any plan embodying the system of compulsory contributory insurance against illness or any other plan of compulsory insurance which provides for medical service to be rendered contributors or their dependents, provided, controlled, or regulated by any state or the federal government.

The majority of physician opposition to compulsory health insurance was attributed to an unfounded concern that insurance would decrease, rather than increase, physician incomes and to their negative experience with accident insurance that paid physicians according to arbitrary fee schedules.[1]

The Great Depression and the Birth of Blue Cross

The Depression of 1929 shook the financial security of both physicians and hospitals. Physician incomes and hospital receipts and admission rates dropped precipitously. As the situation grew worse, hospitals began experimenting with insurance plans. The Baylor University Hospital plan was not the first, but it became the most influential of those insurance experiments. By enrolling 1,250 public school teachers at 50 cents a month for a guaranteed 21 days of hospital care, Baylor created the model for and is credited with the genesis of Blue Cross Hospital Insurance. Baylor started a trend that developed into multihospital plans that included all hospitals in a given area. By 1937 there were 26 plans with more than 600,000 members, and the American Hospital Association started approving the plans. Physicians were pleased with the increased availability of hospital care and the cooperative manner in which their bills were paid. The AMA, however, was characteristically hostile and called the plans "economically unsound, unethical, and inimical to the public interest."[4]

The AMA contended that urging people "to save for sickness" could solve the problem of financing health care.[2] Organized medicine's consistently antagonistic reaction to the concept of health insurance, whether compulsory or voluntary, is well illustrated by medicine's response to the 1932 report of the Committee on the Costs of Medical Care. The establishment of the committee represented a shift of concern from lost wages to medical costs. Chaired by a former president of the AMA and financed by several philanthropic organizations, a group of 45 to 50 prominent Americans from the medical, public health, and social science fields worked for 5 years to address the problem of financing medical care. After an exhaustive study, a moderate majority recommended adoption of group practice and voluntary health insurance as the best way of solving the nation's health care problems; however, even this relatively modest recommendation was too much for some physicians on the panel. They prepared a minority report denouncing voluntary health insurance as more objectionable than compulsory insurance. Health insurance, predicted the minority, would lead to "destructive competition among professional groups, inferior medical service, loss of personal relationship of patient and physician, and demoralization of the profession."[5]

The dissenting physicians, however, did favor government intervention to alleviate the financial burden on physicians resulting from their obligation to provide free care to low-income populations. The AMA's House of Delegates reiterated its long-standing opposition to health insurance of any kind by declaring in 1933 that the minority report represented "the collective opinion of the medical profession."[6]

From the 1930s to the present there have been many efforts to enact various forms of compulsory health insurance. It was only when the proponents of government-sponsored insurance limited their efforts to older adults and the medically indigent, however, that they were able to succeed in passing Medicaid and Medicare legislation in 1965. Voluntary insurance against hospital care costs became the predominant health insurance in the United States during those decades. Although the advocates of government-sponsored health insurance had little success in improving the access of patients to medical care, the Blue Cross plans effectively improved hospitals' access to patients.

Sensitive to the power of the health care industry to defeat health insurance proposals by raising the battle cry of "socialized medicine," almost all proposed plans emphasized accommodations to the interest of physicians and hospitals. Especially after World War II, when the federal government began to heavily subsidize hospital construction and medical research, the expansion of the health care industry, particularly physician resources, became the overriding policy objective.

The government gave a huge boost to the private health insurance industry by excluding health insurance benefits from wage and price controls and by excluding workers' contributions to health insurance from taxable income. The effect was to encourage employees to take wage increases in the form of health insurance fringe benefits rather than cash.

Because insurance companies simply raised their own premium rates rather than tried to exert pressure on physicians and hospitals to contain costs, the post–World War II health insurance system pumped an ever-increasing proportion of the national income into health care. Clearly, contributing to the inflationary spiral was preferable to incurring the wrath of physicians and hospitals by infringing on their prerogatives to set prices and control the costs of their work. Medicare and Medicaid followed the same pattern. In fact, the preamble to the original legislative proposals specifically prohibited any interpretation of the legislation that would change the way health care was practiced.

Dominant Influence of Government

Although the health insurance industry contributed significantly to the spiraling costs of health care in the decades after World War II, it was only one of several influences. The federal government's coverage of health care for special populations played a prominent role. Over the years, the U.S. government developed, revised, and otherwise adjusted a host of categorical or disease-specific programs designed to address needs not otherwise met by state or local administrations or the private sector. Federally sponsored programs account for about 40% of this country's personal health care expenditures. Most physicians and other health professionals are trained at public expense. The government provides almost 6% of the funds available for research and development, and most not-for-profit hospitals have been built or expanded with government support. State and local governments also contribute, but in much smaller amounts.[7]

Although many of these programs are described in more detail in Chapter 7, it is important to recognize the health care policy implications of certain federal initiatives. Certainly, the Social Security Act of 1935 was the most significant social initiative passed by any Congress. The Act established the principle of federal aid to the states for public health and welfare assistance, maternal and child health, and children with disabilities services. It was the legislative basis for a number of significant health and welfare programs, including the all-important Medicaid and Medicare titles.

The government increased its support of biomedical research through the National Institutes of Health, which was established in 1930, and the categorical programs that addressed heart disease, cancer, stroke, mental illness, mental retardation, maternal and infant care, and many other conditions. Programs such as direct aid to schools of medicine, dentistry, pharmacy, nursing, and other professions and their students and support of health planning, health care regulation, and consumer protections, which were incorporated in the various 1962 amendments to the 1938 Food, Drug, and Cosmetic Act, were all part of the Kennedy-Johnson presidential policy era called Creative Federalism. The aggregate annual investment in those programs made the U.S. government the major player and payer in the field of health care.

Grants-in-aid programs alone, excluding Social Security and Medicare, grew from $7 billion at the start of the Kennedy administration in 1961 to $24 billion in 1970. President Nixon expressed his intent to undo the categorical programs and shift revenues to the state and local governments. For broad general purposes, this direction was labeled New Federalism. In spite of his efforts, grants-in-aid programs grew to almost $83 billion in 1980. Congress had resisted block grants and allowed only limited revenue sharing to take place.[7]

In the meantime, federal and state governments were underwriting the skyrocketing costs of Medicare and Medicaid with no effective controls over expenditures. The planners of the Medicare legislation made several misjudgments. They underestimated the growing number of older adults in the United States, the scope and burgeoning costs of the technologic revolution, and the public's rising expectations for the latest in every diagnostic and treatment modality.

The Medicare and Medicaid programs did provide access to many desperately needed health care services for older Americans, people with disabilities, and low-income populations. Because rising Medicare reimbursement rates set the standards for most insurance companies, however, their inflationary effect was momentous. In the mid-1960s, when Medicare was passed, the United States was spending about $42 billion on health care, or approximately 8.4% of the gross national product. The cost of U.S. health care now exceeds $2 trillion and consumes about 17% of the gross national product.

Three Major Health Care Concerns

The three major health care concerns—access, cost, and quality—are particularly problematic because attempts to control one or two of those problems exacerbate the one or two remaining. It is impossible to correct all three problems simultaneously. The government attempted to improve access through the Hill-Burton Act of 1946, which increased the number and size of health care facilities substantially. In addition, President Johnson's Medicare and Medicaid legislation ensured health care payment for older Americans and low-income populations and succeeded in bringing millions of patients into a now overbuilt system. These changes, however, were made at the cost of skyrocketing expenditures and questionable quality. The health care system's excess capacity and virtually unchecked funding improved access to competent and appropriate medical care for many but also resulted in untold numbers of clinical tests, prescriptions, surgery, and other expensive procedures that were often of questionable necessity. Almost all the federal health legislation since the passage of Medicare and Medicaid has been aimed at reducing the costs of health care but has focused little on the reciprocal effects of reducing both the availability and quality of health care.

Efforts at Planning and Quality Control

The federal government did not ignore the issues of cost and quality; the efforts to address those concerns were essentially doomed to be ineffectual by their very designs. To get legislation passed that might alter the existing constellation of health care services or that would scrutinize how well clinicians actually practiced, the powerful medical and hospital lobbies had to be accommodated. This meant that the legislation had to be "provider friendly," allowing physicians, hospital administrators, and other health professionals to maintain control over how the legislation was interpreted and enforced.

Two legislative initiatives of the 1960s typify the circumstances surrounding federal efforts to address the problems of the health care delivery system. In 1965, the Public Health Service Act was amended to establish a nationwide network of regional medical programs to address the leading causes of death: heart disease, cancer, and stroke. Throughout the country groups of physicians, most of whom were associated with academic medical centers, and a few nurses and other health professionals met to discuss innovative ways to bring the latest in clinical services to the bedside of the patients. As might have been predicted, representatives of each clinical specialty argued for funds to do more of what they were already doing. As a consequence, the regional medical programs improved the educational and clinical resources of their regions but did not dramatically improve the prevention or control of their target conditions.

A parallel program, the Comprehensive Health Planning Act, was passed in 1966 to promote comprehensive planning for more rational systems of health care personnel and facilities in each service region. The legislation required federal, state, and local partnerships. It also required that there be a majority of consumers on every decision-making body.[8]

Almost all the regional medical programs and Comprehensive Health Planning Act programs across the country soon were dominated by medical–hospital establishments in their regions. Although there were many productive outcomes from the money spent through the two programs, conflicts of interest regarding the allocation of research and development funds were common, and there was general agreement that the programs were ineffective in achieving their goals. The two programs were therefore combined by the National Health Planning and Resources Development Act of 1974.

Clearly, political rather than objective assessments led Congress to presume that combining two ineffective programs would result in one successful program. Nevertheless, the legislation called for a new organization, the Health Systems Agency (HSA), to have broad representation of health care providers and consumers on governing boards and committees.

After several years nothing had changed. Data submitted to the U.S. Department of Health, Education, and Welfare by the HSA indicated that provider board members were not representative of the overall provider workforce or the consumer population. The physician–hospital administrator establishment was over-represented, and other provider groups were under-represented. HSA board members were predominately white males, although nonwhites and females are heavily represented in the workforce and consumer population. The HSA function of recommending approvals of certificates of need for new or added facilities and equipment was compromised by the vested interests on the governing boards. The general ineffectiveness of HSA boards and committees in containing costs and preventing unnecessary duplication of services in their regions was recognized, and federal support ultimately was withdrawn.[9]

Several other programs beside Medicare and Medicaid were initiated during the Johnson administration to address the prevalence of mental illness and to support the education of health care professionals. The Health Professions Educational Assistance Act of 1963 provided direct federal aid to medical, dental, nursing, pharmacy, and other professional schools, as well as to their students. The Nurse Training Act supported special federal efforts for training professional nursing personnel, and during the same period the Maternal and Child Health and Mental Retardation Planning Amendments initiated comprehensive maternal and child health projects and centers to serve people with mental retardation. The Economic Opportunity Act supported the development of neighborhood health centers to serve low-income populations.[7]

The Johnson-era programs, especially Medicare and Medicaid, put the federal government deeply into the business of financing health care. President Johnson's ambitious activation of the concept of creative federalism enriched the country's health care system and improved the access of many impoverished citizens to continually improving medical care, but it also fueled the inflationary spiral of health care costs that has yet to be constrained. It is apparent that during the last three decades none of the attempts to correct the unnecessary duplication of facilities and services and their excessive or inappropriate use, or to contain their costs, has been successful.

Managed Care Organizations

In 1973, the Health Maintenance Organization Act supported the development of health maintenance organizations (HMOs) through grants for federal demonstration projects. An HMO is an organization responsible for the financing and delivery of comprehensive health services to an enrolled population for a prepaid, fixed fee. HMOs were expected to hold down costs by changing the profit incentive from fee for service to promoting health and preventing illness.

The concept was accepted widely, and between 1992 and 1999 HMOs and other types of managed care organizations experienced phenomenal growth, accounting for the majority of all privately insured persons.[10]

Subsequently, the fortunes of managed care organizations changed as both health care costs and consumer complaints increased.

Beginning in 2001, a derivative of managed care organizations, preferred provider organizations (PPOs), gained in popularity. Although PPOs encompass important managed care characteristics, they were organized by physicians and hospitals to meet the needs of private, third-party, and self-insured firms. By 2002 PPOs captured 52% of covered employees.[11]

Although most Americans are now receiving their health care through some sort of prepaid managed care arrangement, the evidence that significant savings will be realized is fragmentary. Stiff increases in HMO premium rates suggest that the widespread application of HMO concepts will not provide the long-sought containment of runaway health care costs. In addition, both consumers and providers are suggesting that the HMO controls on costs are compromising the quality of care. Consumer concerns about restrictions on choice of providers, limits on availability of services, and quality of health care have evoked a managed care backlash and have generated support for government regulation of managed care organizations.

In fact, the most recent available data from a large, nationally representative sample of privately insured persons under the age of 65 years found little difference between HMOs and other types of insurance.[12] Hospital use, emergency room visits, or surgeries did not differ significantly.

The limits placed by the administrative barriers on how much health care HMO enrollees can use are considered by many patients to be an unwarranted intrusion on traditional physician–patient relationships. Public opinion polls suggest that many consumers do not trust HMOs to provide the care they need if they become sick. It is therefore likely that pressure by consumers for less restrictive forms of managed care will make future care management strategies and cost savings more difficult for HMOs.

The Reagan Administration

Beginning with the Reagan administration and continuing to this day are attempts, some successful, to undo or shrink the federally supported programs begun in the 1960s and 1970s. Unlike Nixon and Ford, Reagan succeeded in implementing New Federalism policies that were all but stymied in previous administrations. A significant reduction in government expenditures for social programs occurred. Decentralization of program responsibility to the states was achieved primarily through block grants. Although his attempts at deregulation to stimulate competition had little success, Reagan's implementation of prospective payment to hospitals based on diagnosis-related groups (DRGs), rather than retrospective payment based on hospital charges, signaled the new effort to contain health care costs.[13]

Diagnosis-Related Groups

The DRG concept provides hospitals with a set dollar payment based on each patient's diagnosis on admission. If the hospital can discharge patients early and/or provide fewer services, it increases its profit. If patients require a longer hospital stay than the DRG allows or if more diagnostic or treatment services are needed, the hospital loses money.

The conversion of categorical and disease-specific programs to block grants, the withdrawal of federal support for professional education, and the creation of a Medicare resource-based relative value scale to adjust and contain physicians' fees are but a few examples of presidential or congressional actions to reduce the federal government's financial commitment to health care.

Biomedical Advances: Evolution of High-Technology Medicine

Health care in the United States dramatically improved during the 20th century. In the first half of the century the greatest advances led to the prevention or cure of many infectious diseases. The development of vaccines to prevent a wide range of communicable diseases, from yellow fever to measles, and the discovery of antibiotics saved vast numbers of Americans from early death or disability.

In the second half of the 20th century, however, technologic advances that characterize today's health care were developed. As so often happens with technologic change, after the scientific concepts that underlie the initial breakthroughs are understood, the pace of technologic development accelerates rapidly. Since the 1960s the rate of technologic advance has increased so quickly that the announcement of new discoveries or more sophisticated equipment has become commonplace.

The following are a few of the seminal medical advances that took place during the 1960s:

- The Sabin and Salk vaccines ended the annual epidemics of polio-myelitis.
- The mild tranquilizers Librium and Valium were introduced and widely prescribed, leading Americans to turn to medicine to cure their emotional as well as physical ills.
- The birth control pill was first prescribed and became the most widely used and effective contraceptive method.
- The heart–lung machine and major improvements in the efficacy and safety of general anesthesia techniques made possible the first successful heart bypass operation in 1964. Three years later, the first human heart transplant took place.

In 1972 computed tomography was invented. Computed tomography, which unlike x-rays can distinguish one soft tissue from another, is installed widely in U.S. hospitals and ambulatory centers. This valuable and profitable diagnostic imaging device started an extravagant competition among hospitals to develop lucrative patient services by making major capital investments in high-technology equipment. Later, noting the convenience and profit associated with diagnostic devices such as computed tomography and magnetic resonance imaging, medical groups purchased the devices and placed them in their own offices. This practice represents one example of how hospitals, physicians, and other health service providers have come to act as isolated economic entities rather than as members of a community of health care resources established to serve population needs. The profit-driven competition and resulting redundant capacity continue to drive up utilization and costs for hospitals, insurers, and the public.[14]

New technology, new drugs, and new and creative surgical procedures have made possible a wide variety of life-enhancing and life-extending medical accomplishments. Operations that once were complex and hazardous, requiring hospitalization and intense follow-up care, have become relatively common ambulatory surgical procedures. For example, the use of intraocular lens implants after the removal of cataracts has become one of the most popular surgical procedures (see Chapter 4). Performed on over a half million Americans annually, the procedure takes less than an hour and has very high success rates, and complications are rare. Although the ambulatory procedure costs less than it would in an inpatient setting, the aggregate costs for eye surgery will grow as the demand for the operation escalates among the increasing number of older Americans.

Technical Advances Bring New Problems

Almost every medical or technologic advance seems to be accompanied by new and vexing financial and ethical dilemmas. The greater ability to extend life raises questions about the quality of life and the right to die. New capabilities to use costly and limited resources to improve the quality of life for some and not others create other ethical problems.

Whatever its benefits, the increased use of new technology has contributed to higher health care costs. Some believe, however, that if the new technology were used properly and not overused for the sake of defensive medicine or to take advantage of its profit potential, it would actually lower health care costs.[15]

Both the AMA and the federal government have developed programs to explore these issues and to provide needed information for decision makers. The AMA has three programs to assess the ramifications of medical advancements: the Diagnostic and Therapeutic Technology Assessment Program, the Council on Scientific Affairs, and AMA Drug Evaluations.[16]

In the Technology Assessment Act of 1972 Congress recognized that "it is essential that, to the fullest extent possible, the consequences of technological applications be anticipated, understood, and considered in determination of public policy on existing and emerging national problems."[17] To address this goal, the Office of Technology Assessment, a nonpartisan support agency that works directly with and for congressional committees, was created. The Office of Technology Assessment relies on the technical and professional resources of the private sector, including universities, research organizations, industry, and public interest groups, to produce their assessments and provide congressional committees with analyses of highly technical issues. It was intended to help officials sort out the facts without advocating particular policies or actions.

The Agency for Health Care Policy and Research, created by Congress in 1989 and now called the Agency for Healthcare Policy and Quality, is intended to support research to understand better the outcomes of health care at both clinical and systems levels. It has a particularly challenging mission as technologic and scientific advances make it ever more difficult to sort out the complexities of health care and determine what works, for whom, when, and at what cost.

Roles of Medical Education and Specialization

Medical schools and teaching hospitals in the United States are the essential components of all academic health centers and are the principal architects of the medical care system. In addition to their research contributions to advancements in health care and their roles as major providers of health services, they are the principal places where physicians and other professional personnel are educated and trained. Year after year, professional schools graduate thousands of medical, nursing, and other professionals whose attitudes, values, and skills have been shaped by the educational and socialization process of their professional preparation. The annual infusion of new graduates of professional schools serves to reinforce continuously the values and policies of their teachers and role models.

During the last 30 years medical education and policies regarding the size and nature of the physician workforce have influenced the size, structure, and operation of the American health care industry. From post–World War II to the mid-1970s there were numerous projections of an impending shortage of physicians. The response at federal and state levels was to double the capacity of medical schools and to encourage the entry of foreign-trained physicians.[18]

The explosion of scientific knowledge in medicine and the technologic advances in diagnostic and treatment modalities encouraged specialization. In addition, the enhanced prestige and income of specialty practice attracted most medical school graduates to specialty residencies. It soon became evident that specialists were being produced in numbers that would lead to an oversupply. Also, they needed to be close to their referring doctors and to associate with major hospitals, which caused graduates to concentrate in urban medical centers. At the same time the shortage of nonspecialists among rural and inner-city populations became more serious.

Medical schools and hospitals, however, were not willing to address these related problems by giving up their high-demand, productive, and well-regarded specialist training emphases. Instead, they developed a more acceptable physician workforce policy to maintain or increase their training capacities. Schools erroneously assumed that producing an oversupply of physicians would force more physicians into primary care in underserved rural and inner-city areas. Unfortunately, this trickle-down workforce policy did little to change these problems and only added to the swelling ranks of specialists. Most new physicians still chose specialties in which the supply was already adequate and elected to practice where the surplus of physicians was increasing.

Hospitals added to the problem by developing residencies that met their own service needs without regard for oversupply. Supplemental Medicare payments for teaching hospitals and indirect medical education adjustments for hospital-based residents were and still are strong incentives for hospitals to add residents.[19]

The failure of past physician workforce policies is evident. In 1989, despite major increases in the physician supply, rural areas in the United States had fewer than 100 physicians per 100,000 persons, compared with up to six times that many in major cities. Furthermore, increasing the number of medical graduates did not correct the imbalance between specialists and generalists.[20]

The rapid growth of managed care plans in the 1990s was expected to produce profound changes in the use of the physician workforce. The emphasis on prevention and primary care and the employment of generalist physician "gatekeepers" to control inappropriate or unnecessary use of physician specialists were expected to cause a significant oversupply of specialists by the year 2000. To stave off the surplus, many medical schools and their teaching hospitals endeavored to produce equal numbers of primary care and specialist physicians instead of the one-third-to-two-third ratio that had existed for years.

As soon as the effort produced a sizable increase in the number of primary care physicians, new medical workforce projections refuted the prior predictions and forecast a shortage, rather than a surplus, of specialists. Current evidence indicates that the demand for certain specialists is exceeding the supply. Quite appropriately, most new medical school graduates are once again electing to prepare for practice in a medical specialty. Clearly, estimating a future physician shortage or surplus is a tenuous endeavor.

The forces of reform are exerting increasing pressures on schools of medicine and the other major health professions to change their curricula in keeping with the new emphasis on population-based thinking, prevention, and cost effectiveness. The inflexibility of traditional departmental organization and the relatively narrow areas of expertise required of faculty, however, present formidable obstacles to needed educational reforms.

Influence of Interest Groups

Many problems associated with U.S. health care result from a system shared among federal and state governments and the private health care industry. The development of fully or partially tax-funded health service proposals initiated waves of lobbying efforts by interest groups for or against the initiatives. Federal and state executives and legislators continue to receive intense pressure from supporters and opponents of health care system changes.[21] Lobbying efforts from special interest groups have become increasingly sophisticated and well financed. Since the 1970s, former congressional staffers appear on the payrolls of private interest groups, and former lobbyists assume positions on Capitol Hill. This strong connection between politicians and lobbyists is evidenced by the record number of dollars spent to defeat the Clinton Health Security Act of 1993 and both "for" and "against" President Obama's health care reform plans.

Five major groups have played key roles in debates on tax-funded health services: providers, insurers, consumers, business, and labor. Historically, physicians, the group most directly affected by reforms, developed the most powerful lobbies. Although the physician lobby is still among the best financed and most effective, it is recognized as not representing the values of large numbers of physicians detached from the AMA. In fact, several different medical lobbies exist as a result of political differences among physicians.

The American Medical Association

The AMA, founded in 1847, is the largest medical lobby, with a membership of 287,000 individuals, yet it represents less than half of the medical professionals. The AMA was at the height of its power from the 1940s to the 1970s, opposing government-provided insurance plans by every president from Truman through Carter. Compromises gained in the final Medicare bill still affect today's program. In the 1980s, however, the AMA steadfastly opposed cuts in Medicare proposed by the Reagan-Bush administration.

In 1989, the AMA changed its relationship with Congress. Initially locked out of White House discussions on the Clinton plan, the AMA was later included and supported, at least publicly, by the Obama plan for expanding health care access to all Americans. Nevertheless, cost containment, malpractice reform, and physician autonomy still remain as areas of contention.[22]

Insurance Companies

Even more than physicians, nurses, or hospitals, insurers' political efforts have been viewed as completely self-serving. The efforts of insurance companies to eliminate high-risk consumers from the insurance pools and their frequent premium rate hikes have contributed significantly to the focus on cost containment and the plight of the uninsured and underinsured in the debate on health care reform. Nevertheless, the Health Insurance Association of America, founded in 1956 and representing some 300 small companies, was responsible for that seemingly endless onslaught of television commercials featuring middle-class people worrying about the limited choice of physicians and other potential dangers of cost containment in the Clinton plan.

The insurance companies played an even stronger but more deceptive role in the debates about President Obama's health care reform effort by appearing to support the general idea while vigorously opposing the idea of a public option that would severely limit their otherwise unrestrained profits.[23] The amount of dollars spent in lobbying efforts by insurers and others with vested interests in the status quo and in misinforming the public to raise unwarranted fears about the proposed health care reform legislation hit a new high in deception and a new low in political machinations.

Consumer Groups

Although provider groups have been most effective in influencing health care legislation, the historically weak consumer movement has gained strength. Much of the impetus for health care reform on the national scene was linked to pressure on politicians from consumers concerned about rising costs and lack of security in health care coverage. Despite widespread disagreement among groups about the extent to which government involvement is needed, all are concerned about the questions of cost, access, and quality in the current health care system.

Better educated and more assertive citizens have become more cynical about the motives of leaders in both the political and health arenas and are much more effective in influencing legislative decisions. A prominent example is the American Association of Retired Persons (AARP). Founded in 1958, the AARP is one of the most influential consumer groups in the health care reform movement. Because of its size and research capability, it wields considerable clout among legislators who are very aware that the AARP's 40 million older citizens are among the most determined voters.

Although a single consumer group may have some influence in shaping a legislative proposal, consumer group coalitions that rally around specific issues are much more effective in generating political pressure. For example, a political battle over revamping the U.S. Food and Drug Administration (FDA) was initiated in 1995 when conservative think tanks and drug company officials urged a receptive Congress to make major changes in the agency's operations. These changes were intended to weaken the agency's investigative powers and reduce the time required for drug companies to introduce new drugs to the consumer market. The proposed changes would require the FDA to meet deadlines for investigating and approving new drugs and allow pharmaceutical companies to submit one, rather than two, well-controlled studies as proof of effectiveness.

Consumer groups entered the debate on both sides of the issue. The biggest and best organized was the Patients' Coalition, which is made up of more than 50 national nonprofit health groups. It includes such dissimilar organizations as the American Cancer Society, National Hemophilia Foundation, Arthritis Foundation, and several AIDS organizations such as the AIDS Action Council and Gay Men's Health Crisis. The coalition rushed to the FDA's defense and urged Congress to reject the proposals that could hurt consumers. Other consumer groups support the positions of the Pharmaceutical Research and Manufacturers Association, the main industry trade group that claims that FDA reforms could be accomplished without risking safety and effectiveness.[24]

The battle continues, however, between those who believe that keeping new drugs from the market while safety and effectiveness are carefully tested is denying help to those patients who might benefit from them and those who presume that drug manufacturers would take advantage of less rigorous testing to foist unproven or dangerous drugs on the market for profit. While the two sides continue to debate, administrative changes have taken place that shortened the assessment time for cancer-treating drugs in an effort to prolong life for dying patients.[25]

Business and Labor

The National Federation of Independent Businesses, founded in 1943, has almost 600,000 individual members and is the largest representative of small firms. The National Association of Manufacturers has about 4,000 members. Founded in 1895, it represents the interests of large employers. The U.S. Chamber of Commerce was founded in 1912 and represents 200,000 individuals and businesses. The Chamber and the National Association of Manufacturers have similar views on reform; they both generally welcome the equalizing effect of an employer mandate but are wary of intense government regulation and, particularly, of more government-run health care.[26]

Whenever business groups are involved in an issue, labor unions are sure to make their presence felt as well. The American Federation of Labor and Congress of Industrial Organization (AFL-CIO), once over 14 million individuals strong, has had a tremendous influence on national health policy. Although job losses during the current economic downturn have reduced membership by over a million members, the influence of organized labor is significant. Intimately connected with the AFL-CIO is the Service Employees International Union, founded in 1921. It is the largest union representing health care workers, with a membership of 1 million individuals, and its president is also chairman of the AFL-CIO's health care committee.

During the mid-1940s labor unions began to demand health care benefits as an alternative to wage increases not possible during postwar wage and price controls. The two major national unions, the AFL and the CIO, consolidated their power by merging in 1955. During the late 1960s they were able to address the issues of occupational safety and health and achieved passage of the Occupational Safety and Health Act of 1970.

Today, occupational safety and health hold a prominent place on the national agenda, and efforts to weaken the 1970 legislation or to reduce its enforcement are met with strong opposition from organized labor.

Pharmaceutical Industry

In recent years, the profit-laden pharmaceutical industry increased its spending on lobbying tactics and campaign contributions to unprecedented levels. With prescription drug prices and pharmaceutical company profits at record highs, the industry correctly anticipated public and congressional pressure to legislate controls on drug prices and drug coverage for older adults on Medicare.

Between 1997 and 1999, the drug industry spent $235.7 million to lobby Congress and the executive branch. As lawmakers moved to add a prescription drug benefit to Medicare that would include price controls, the drug industry hired 297 lobbyists—one for every two members of Congress.[27] Campaign contributions also rose to almost $14 million, a 147% increase over previous years. An industry that can spend that amount of money to block a comprehensive Medicare drug benefit that reins in sky-high drug costs is clearly costing the American public dearly. In fact, for the first time in the history of the U.S. health care system, insurers that cover prescription drug costs report that pharmaceutical costs now exceed the costs of hospital care.

More recently, the pharmaceutical industry made a calculated decision to throw its financial weight behind the Republican Party with $50 million in campaign contributions and an even larger army of lobbyists that has unlimited budgets to influence legislators. Before the Democratic sweep in 2009, the pharmaceutical industry succeeded in stifling any measure that would put a dent in its corporate earnings.

In addition, the pharmaceutical industry was given a large role in crafting the 2003 Medicare Part D prescription drug benefit plan, which in 2006 began providing huge profits to drug companies. Unfortunately, those Medicare recipients who enrolled in the plan were faced with a baffling array of choices. California, for example, offers 55 prescription drug plans from which to choose, and seniors find that it is very difficult to get accurate, unbiased information. Each plan has its own premium, its own deductible, and its own copayment for individual drugs.[28]

One of the most contentious elements in the Medicare Part D drug plan is the so-called doughnut hole. Beginning in 2006, the legislation calls for ending federal payment for a person's drug purchases after an annual spending limit is reached. Federal support resumes only after the beneficiary has spent $3,600 out-of-pocket for prescription drugs. The "doughnut hole" directly affects the middle class and disabled retirees who do not qualify for special poverty assistance yet still live on limited fixed incomes.

Public Health Focus on Prevention

Although the groups discussed in the previous section are primarily concerned with the diagnostic and treatment services that constitute over 95% of the U.S. health care system, there is an important public health lobby that speaks for health promotion and disease prevention. Often overlooked because of this country's historical emphasis on curative medicine, public health organizations have had to overcome several negative perceptions. Many health providers, politicians, and others associate public health with governmental bureaucracy or link the care of low-income populations with welfarism. Nevertheless, the American Public Health Association, founded in 1872 and having an aggregate membership of 50,000, has substantial influence on the national scene; however, because the positions of public health advocates are considered liberal in nature, the influence of the American Public Health Association wanes when the Republicans are in power and rises during Democratic administrations.[29]

The significant contributions of both governmental and voluntary organized public health agencies to the health of the American public and the political struggles that led to those accomplishments are described in Chapter 10.

Economic Influences of Rising Costs

The single most important impetus for health care reform throughout recent history has been rising health care costs and insurance premiums. Since the introduction of Medicare and Medicaid in 1965, almost all federal health law has been aimed at cost containment but without success. Overall, health care costs have risen from 5.3% of the U.S. gross domestic product in 1960 to over 17.6% in 2009. Growth in health spending has been advancing much faster than the rest of the U.S. economy. Aggregate health spending rose to over $2.5 trillion in 2009. Employer-sponsored health insurance premiums have increased 131%, and employee shares have increased at the same rate.[30] Chapter 7 presents a comprehensive overview of the complex and interlocking systems of fiscal incentives and constraints that contribute to the rising costs of health care and the difficulties inherent in attempts to exercise control over those costs.

The number of Americans without adequate or any health insurance was estimated at 37 million during the health care reform debates of 1994. More recent census bureau estimates put the number of uninsured at 46.7 million Americans or 17% of the total population.[30]

Of most importance when considering the magnitude of the problem is that the composition of that uninsured population is constantly changing. When those on Medicaid or other unemployed persons find jobs that provide group health insurance, those individuals leave the ranks of the uninsured. They are replaced, however, by those who become unemployed or lose Medicaid coverage. More and more employers, upset by the ever rising costs of employee health insurance, are reducing or eliminating health insurance as a fringe benefit.

Health Insurance Portability and Accountability Act

The Health Insurance Portability and Accountability Act, or HIPAA, signed into law in 1996, was intended to address the problem of the growing number of uninsured. The legislation permits individuals to continue insurance coverage after a loss or change of employment by mandating the renewal of insurance coverage except for specific reasons, such as the non-payment of premiums. The Act also regulates the circumstances in which an insurance plan may limit benefits because of preexisting conditions. It also mandates special enrollment periods for individuals who have experienced certain changes in family composition or employment status.

More sweeping in its effects is the part of the law called "Administrative Simplification." It required medical records to be computerized by October 2003. Although yet to be achieved, it is intended to reduce the costs and administrative burden of health care by standardizing the electronic transmission of many administrative and financial transactions. The standardization must also maintain the privacy of health information. As a result, the entire health care industry is involved in a costly high-tech upgrade of complex medical and financial documents to comply with the legislation.[31]

Aging of America

The elimination or control of many infectious diseases through immunization and antibiotics; the implementation of basic public health measures that contribute to the safety of food, water, and living and working conditions; a far more nutritious food supply; and constantly improving medical care have all combined to extend the life expectancy of people in the United States. Although AIDS, accidents, and violence are causing an increasing number of deaths among young people, the vast majority of Americans live to advanced ages. The proportion of Americans aged 65 and older is projected to grow from 13% in 2010 to 20% in 2035. That means that one in five Americans will be over age 65 and approximately half of those older people will be over 75 years of age. The population over 85 years is increasing even faster. By 2050, it is expected that one in four of those over age 65 years will be 85 years or older.[32]

The increased longevity of the population, particularly those with serious or disabling chronic illness, poses serious challenges to the U.S. health care system. The problems of financing and delivering an increasingly broad array of medical and other long-term care services are already serious and will become more critical as the proportion of dependent older adults grows in relation to the number still in the workforce.

Although the medical model of curing illness, maximizing function, and preventing premature death has been beneficial to many older Americans, it offers little to the growing number of older citizens who are not acutely or morbidly ill but who have irreversible physical or mental limitations that require diligent care by others. Although the number and kinds of institutionally and community-based long-term care services (described in Chapter 8) have increased, many are struggling to balance patient needs against their allowed benefits, rising costs, and limits imposed by third-party payers.

Of increasing importance is the need for mechanisms to support caregivers as older person care becomes the responsibility of more and more Americans. Changes in U.S. social structures have increased the stress on today's adults because they are required to provide financial, functional, or emotional support to aging family members. More women working outside the home, a high divorce rate, the geographic dispersion of family members, an increase in the number of adults simultaneously caring for both children and aging relatives, and the rise in the proportion of older adults taking care of even older relatives make respite services, adult day care, and other strategies to reduce stress and caregiver burnout mandatory.

Public Health's Lack of Preparedness

The terrorist attacks on September 11, 2001, and the 2005 Gulf Coast hurricanes revealed the lack of preparedness of this country's public health system to cope with emergency situations. Clearly, there were both "quality" and "quantity" deficits in public health preparedness. Both the number and the competencies of public health personnel available for emergency preparedness, as well as the systems in which they work, were revealed to be woefully inadequate.[33]

On the positive side, public exposure of the dwindling numbers of public health workers of highly variable competencies, employed in widely different public health organizations, was revealed as the consequences of decades of benign neglect. In Chapter 10, the extensive efforts to remedy the problems leading to the lack of emergency preparedness are discussed.

In a country facing epidemics of teenage pregnancy, sexually transmitted diseases, drug addiction, drive-by shootings, and crack-addicted infants, there seems to be a striking capacity for ignoring the truth about matters of public health and public good. Warren Bennis, author of *Why Leaders Can't Lead*, attributes this disregard in large part to the U.S.'s historical commitment to individual freedom. He explains why the decline in societal concern for the less fortunate that started in the 1980s was so well accepted[34]:

> The conflicts between individual rights and the common good are far older than the nation, but they have never been as sharp or as mean as they are today. In fact, as the upwardly mobile person has replaced the citizen, we have less and less that is good. The founding fathers based the constitution on the assumption that there was such a thing as public virtue. James Madison wrote, "The public good . . . the real welfare of the great body of people . . . is the supreme object to be pursued." At the moment, we not only cannot agree on what the public good is, we show no inclination to pursue it.

Even the institutions in which health care providers work reflect similar values. Rosemary Stevens, author of *In Sickness and in Wealth*, writes as follows[35]:

> By 1980 hospitals seemed obsessed with the language of management. Instead of an increased emphasis on chronic care and social services after the advent of Medicare and Medicaid—not an unreasonable expectation in programs dedicated to the older adult and low-income populations—hospital administrative training programs began to require courses in financial management. Administrators became managers, presidents, or CEOs; and the hospital journals rang with news of "product lines" (patient care), of capital financing, of diversification and innovation and of the "bottom line."

Under pressure to adjust to rapidly changing economic circumstances, many hospitals are engaging with providers in joint investments that raise serious questions about conflicts of interest. Ventures into the construction of privately owned high-technology diagnostic facilities by providers who refer patients for those services proliferate in competition with hospital facilities, apparently without concern for the ethical issues involved.

Oregon Death with Dignity Act

November 8, 1994, was a pivotal date in U.S. social legislation. Oregon voters approved Ballot Measure 16, the Oregon Death with Dignity Act, also known as the Oregon Physician-Assisted Suicide Act. The Act legalized physician-assisted suicide by allowing "an adult resident of Oregon, who is terminally ill to voluntarily request a prescription for medication to take his or her life."[36] The person must have "an incurable and irreversible disease that will, within reasonable medical judgment, produce death within six months." The Death with Dignity Act was a response to the growing concern among medical professionals and the public about the extended, painful, and demeaning nature of terminal medical care for patients with certain conditions. An additional consideration for some voters was the worry that the extraordinary costs associated with lengthy and futile medical care would exhaust their estates and leave their families with substantial debts.

A survey of Oregon physicians showed that two-thirds of those responding believe that physician-assisted suicide is ethical in appropriate cases.

Also, almost half of the responding physicians (46%) said that they might assist in a suicide if the patient met the criteria outlined in the act.[37]

The issue of euthanasia and physician-assisted suicide has been debated for years in other countries. Although among Westernized countries only Northern Australia has legalized physician-assisted suicide, the Netherlands has a long history of allowing euthanasia within the medical community.[38]

Provisions of the Oregon Death With Dignity Act

A physician must meet multiple requirements before he or she can write a prescription for a lethal combination of medications. The physician must ensure that the patient is fully informed about the diagnosis, the prognosis, the risks, and likely result of the medications and the alternatives, including comfort care, pain control, and hospice care. Then a consulting physician must confirm that the patient's judgment is not impaired by a mental condition and that the decision is fully informed and voluntary. The patient is then asked to notify next of kin. Family notification is not mandatory, however. After a 15-day waiting period, the patient must again repeat the request. If the patient does so, the physician is then permitted to write the fatal prescription. Although it varies from year to year, fewer than half of the terminally ill patients who receive prescriptions actually ingest the lethal medications.[39]

In November 2008, the State of Washington initiated its own Death with Dignity Act along the same lines as that of Oregon.[40] On the last day of 2009 the Supreme Court of the State of Montana ruled to maintain the state law that protects doctors from prosecution for helping terminally patients die.[41] It will be interesting to observe if the concept of physician-assisted suicide becomes a legislative issue elsewhere in the United States as well.

Internet and Health Care

Data collection and information transfer are critical elements of the health care system, and thus it is not surprising that the Internet has become a major influence in U.S. health care. More than half of Americans accessed health information on the Internet in 2009.[42] Consumers have access to vast resources of health and wellness information, have the ability to communicate with others sharing similar health problems, and are able to gain valuable data about medical institutions and providers that permit well-informed choices about services and procedures. Internet users are becoming more educated and participatory in clinical decision making. Physicians and other providers are now challenged by the need to deal with a more knowledgeable and involved patient population.

Health care consumers turn to the Internet, at least in part, because of dissatisfaction with the amount of information available from traditional sources. A host of websites offers everything from interactive health assessments to personalized diet and fitness programs. Internet use also provides the benefit of anonymity, convenience, and freedom from inhibitions. For those reasons it is becoming a growing alternative to traditional in-office counseling, particularly in the field of mental health. The mental health field has initiated a variety of forms of online therapy for consumers who are more comfortable with the impersonal nature of Internet communication.

Providers also are entering the online world of health care communication. After a slow start, provider-sponsored websites are proliferating at a rapid pace. In addition to information for consumers about the provider's training, competencies, and experience, many providers encourage e-mail exchanges that invite queries and provide opportunities to respond to consumer informational needs.

A wide variety of other web-based entrepreneurial ventures have also begun to take advantage of the huge and growing market of Internet surfers. Both dependable and questionable entrepreneurs are offering consumers opportunities to cybershop for pharmaceuticals, insurance plans, medical supplies and equipment, specific physician services, and other health-related commodities. The public is well advised to be cautious in making commitments on the Internet. Appendix B provides a listing of some of the most reliable consumer-oriented websites.

Basic Issues

The basic issues underlying efforts to improve the U.S. health care system remain, as they have for decades, concerns for costs, access, and quality. Although knowledge, technology, and resources have developed so that superb and dramatic medical care can be provided to meet even the most formidable needs of this country's population, such care is provided at unacceptable cost, with unnecessary duplications of effort, and to the exclusion of the health maintenance and preventive activities that might have reduced the incidence of the medical conditions that required those curative efforts. It is, by every assessment, a health care system focused on providing excellent care for the individuals within it while virtually ignoring the more basic health service needs of the larger populations outside of it.

Landmark Health Legislation: Patient Protection and Affordable Care Act of 2010

Given that a number of previous presidents had tried and failed to accomplish similar health care reform, the Patient Protection and Affordable Care Act of 2010 (PPACA) enacted by the Obama administration over vociferous Republican opposition is an historic achievement.

The PPACA is groundbreaking as it addresses consumer protections, the pivotal role of employer-provided insurance coverage and government's role in providing health care access for the most vulnerable populations. As examples[43]

- For consumers, the Act removes financial barriers to preventive care, bars insurance policy rejections due to pre-existing conditions, and prohibits lifetime insurance coverage limits and coverage cancellations due to serious illness.
- For employers, the Act authorizes tax credits of up to 35% of premiums to make employee coverage more affordable and authorizes a temporary reinsurance program to offset the costs of expensive health claims for employers that provide health benefits for retirees 55–64 years of age.
- For the most vulnerable populations, the Act expands Medicaid coverage to all non-Medicare eligible individuals under 65 years of age with incomes up to 133% of the federal poverty level.

Major objectives of the PPACA addressing groundbreaking efforts include[44]

- Requirement that all individuals have health insurance by 2014 with some exceptions

- Expansion of public programs' eligibility including Medicaid, Children's Health Insurance and payment increases to primary care physicians for Medicaid services to equal Medicare payments
- States' creation of Health Benefit Exchanges for individuals and small employers to provide consumers with information that enables their choosing among alternative health insurance policies
- Insurance market regulations that prevent insurers from denying coverage for any reason, and from charging higher premiums based on health status and gender
- Assessment of a $2000 per employee fee to employers of more than 50 employees if they do not offer health insurance coverage and if they have at least one employee receiving a premium credit through an Exchange. Additional rules apply for employers who do not offer health insurance.

The current estimate of the net cost of the PPACA by the Congressional Budget Office is $938 billion, based on a predicted decrease of 32 million uninsured individuals by 2019 with a concomitant reduction of $124 billion in the federal deficit. The costs of the PPACA are expected to be borne by a combination of savings from the Medicare and Medicaid programs and new taxes and fees, including an excise tax on high-cost insurance.[44]

The new law is widely contested as lawmakers in 39 state legislatures have, or plan to introduce bills to block the law's implementation. Also, arguing that the new law infringes on states' rights, Republican attorneys general in 13 states have filed suit in Florida federal court.[45]

At this very early point following passage of the PPACA, predicting its success in achieving major changes in the organization, delivery, efficiency, and effectiveness of health care services is highly speculative. As implementation rules are published and challenges are navigated in the courts, outcomes will be determined over the next several years.

References

1. Numbers RL. The third party: health insurance in America. In: Vogel MJ, Rosenburg CE, Eds. *The Therapeutic Revolution: Essays in the Social History of American Medicine*. Philadelphia: University of Pennsylvania Press; 1979.
2. Starr P. Transformation in defeat: the changing objectives of national health insurance, 1915–1980. In: Kindig DA, Sullivan RB, Eds. *Understanding*

Universal Health Programs, Issues and Options. Ann Arbor, MI: Health Administration Press; 1992.

3. Minutes of the House of Delegates. *JAMA.* 1920;74:1317–1328.
4. Leland RG. Prepayment plans for hospital care. *JAMA.* 1933;100:113–117.
5. Committee on the Costs of Medical Care. *Medical Care for the American People: The Final Report of the Costs of Medical Care.* Chicago: University of Chicago Press; 1932.
6. Minutes of the Eighty-Fourth Session, 12–16 June 1933. *JAMA.* 1933;100: 44–53.
7. Lee PR, Benjamin AE. Health policy and the politics of health care. In: Lee PR, Estes CL, Eds. *The Nation's Health,* 4th ed. Sudbury, MA: Jones and Bartlett; 1994.
8. Litman TJ, Robins LS. *Health Politics and Policy,* 2nd ed. Albany, NY: Delmar Publishers; 1991.
9. Cheekoway B, O'Rourke T, Macrima DM, et al. Representation of providers on health planning boards. *Int J Health Serv.* 1981;11:573–581.
10. McGinley L. HMO fracas moves to who makes medical decisions. *Wall Street Journal.* February 18, 1999:A24.
11. Hurley RE, Strunk BC, White JJ, et al. The puzzling popularity of the PPO. *Health Affairs.* 2004;23:56–68.
12. Reschovsky JD, Kemper P. Do HMOs make a difference? *Inquiry.* 1999/2000; 36:374–377.
13. Lee PR, Estes CL. *The Nation's Health,* 4th ed. Sudbury, MA: Jones and Bartlett; 1994.
14. Ropes LB. *Health Care Crisis in America.* Santa Barbara, CA: ABC-CLIO;1991.
15. Gallwas G. The technological explosion: its impact on laboratory and hospital costs. *Pathologist.* 1980;31:86–91.
16. McGivney WT, Hendee WR. Technology Assessment in medicine: the role of the American Medical Association. *Arch Pathol Lab Med.* 1988;112: 1181–1185.
17. Office of Technology Assessment. *Assessing the Efficacy and Safety of Medical Technologies.* Washington, DC: Government Printing Office; 1978.
18. Reinhardt UE. Reinhardt on reform (interview done by Donna Vavala). *Physician Executive.* 1995;21:10–12.
19. Eisenberg JM. If trickle-down physician workforce policy failed, is the choice now between the market and government regulation? *Inquiry.* 1994;31: 241–249.
20. Schroeder SA. Academic medicine as a public trust. *JAMA.* 1989;262:803–812.
21. Oberlander J. The politics of paying for health reform: zombies, payroll taxes, and the Holy Grail. *Health Affairs.* 2008;27:w544–w555.
22. Fuchs VR. Health reform: getting the essentials right. *Health Affairs.* 2009;28:w180–w183.
23. McGinley L. Patients' groups jump into battle over proposals to restructure FDA. *Wall Street Journal.* February 22, 1996:B5.

24. USHHS, U.S. Food and Drug Administration. FDA Sees Rebound in Approval of Innovative Drugs in 2003. FDA News Release, January 15, 2004. Available at http://test.fda.gov/NewsEvents/Newsroom/PressAnnouncements/2004/ucm108225.htm. Accessed March 18, 2010.

25. Murray A. Trade group fight against drug review is self-defeating. *Wall Street Journal.* November 30, 2004:A4.

26 National Association of Manufacturers. Available from http://www.nam.org. Accessed October 7, 2009.

27. "Drug firms" political outlays skyrocket. *Wall Street Journal.* July 7, 2000:A14.

28. Centers for Medicare & Medicaid Services, U.S. Department of Health and Human Services. Medicare prescription drug plans. Available from http://www.medicare.gov/Choices/PDP.asp. Accessed October 27, 2009.

29. American Public Health Association. Available from http://www.apha.org. Accessed October 10, 2009.

30. National Coalition on Health Care. Economic cost fact sheets. Available from http://nchc.org/facts-resources/fact-sheet-coverage. Accessed October 22, 2009.

31. David Brailer on a private-public health information technology infrastructure. Interview by Susan V. White. *J Healthc Qual.* 2004;26(6):20–24.

32. U.S. Census Bureau. National Population Projections, Interim Projections 2000–2050. Based on Census 2000 (Released 2004). Available from http://www.census.gov/population/www/projections/usinterimproj/. Accessed October 28, 2009.

33. Lurie N, Wasserman J, Nelson CD. Public health preparedness: evolution or revolution? *Health Affairs.* 2006;25:935–945.

34. Bennis W. *Why Leaders Can't Lead: The Unconscious Conspiracy Continues.* San Francisco: Jossey-Bass; 1989:40.

35. Stevens R. *In Sickness and in Wealth: American Hospitals in the Twentieth Century.* New York: Basic Books; 1989.

36. Emanuel EJ, Daniels E. Oregon's physician-assisted suicide law: provisions and problems. *Arch Intern Med.* 1996;156:46, 50.

37. Lee MA, Nelson HD, Triden UP, et al. Legalizing assisted suicide: view of physicians in Oregon. *N Engl J Med.* 1996;334:310–315.

38. De Wachter MAM. Active euthanasia in the Netherlands. *JAMA.* 1989; 262:3316–3319.

39. Hedberg K, Tolle S. Putting Oregon's Death with Dignity Act in Perspective: Characteristics of Decedents Who Did Not Participate. *J Clin Ethics.* Summer 2009:20(2)133–135.

40. Washington State Department of Health. Death with Dignity Act. Available from http://www.doh.wa.gov/dwda/. Accessed November 9, 2009.

41. Johnson K. Ruling by Montana Supreme Court bolsters physician-assisted suicide. *The New York Times.* January 1, 2010:A16.

42. Reuters Health Information. More than half of Americans use Internet for health. Available from http://www.nlm.nih.gov/medlineplus/print/news/fullstory_94892.html. Accessed April 24, 2010.

43. The Henry J. Kaiser Family Foundation. Summary of New Health Reform Law. Available from http://www.kff.org/healthreform/upload/8061.pdf. Accessed April 24, 2010.
44. The Henry J. Kaiser Family Foundation. Summary of coverage provisions in the Patient Protection and Affordable Care Act and the Health Care and Education Reconciliation Act of 2010. Available from http://www.kff.org/healthreform/upload/8023-R.pdf. Accessed April 24, 2010.
45. Lowes R. Obama signs historic healthcare reform bill. Medscape Medical News. Available from http://www.medscape.com/viewarticle/719012. Accessed April 24, 2010.

Hospitals: Origin, Organization, and Performance

This chapter's overview of the genesis of U.S. hospitals provides a basis for understanding their characteristics and organization. The major private and governmental insurance initiatives that contributed to the growth and centrality of hospitals in the health care system are defined. The chapter also discusses the diverse functions of hospitals and their staff and management structures. Important aspects of the relationship between staff and patients are reviewed, with particular emphasis on the rights and responsibilities of patients in that often intimidating environment. The chapter concludes with a discussion of the quality of care provided in hospitals and an explanation of the forces of health care system reform that influenced hospital economics, service patterns, and provider relationships.

Of all the familiar institutions in U.S. society, the hospital is, at the same time, the most appreciated, most maligned, and least understood. Besides serving as a place for the treatment of the sick and injured, it may function as a research laboratory, an educational institution, and a major employer within the community.

Being a hospital patient is usually at best an unpleasant personal trial and at worst a serious, perhaps life-threatening, event. Where else in the free world, outside of a prison, does an individual voluntarily submit to being confined to a room in scanty institutional garb and to being poked, prodded, jabbed with needles, questioned, fed, toileted, and alternately ignored and attended, seemingly at the whim of a legion of strangers?

Historical Perspective

The often strained relationship between patients and hospital personnel such as doctors, nurses, aides, technicians, and therapists dates back to the earliest history of health care in the United States. The indifference to patients' needs for information, comfort, and humane contact that is a common complaint about hospital care is rooted not only in the overall history of medical care but also—and especially—in the history of hospitals.

Hospitals in early America served quite different purposes from those of today. They were founded to shelter older adults, the dying, orphans, and vagrants and to protect the inhabitants of a community from the contagiously sick and the dangerously insane.

During the 18th century Boston was the largest city in the new democracy, with about 7,000 citizens. Philadelphia and New York each had about 4,000 people. Whatever passed for medical care in those days was provided in the home. It was necessary, however, in these and other seaport towns to provide refuge for sailors and other shipboard victims of contagious diseases who often were unceremoniously left ashore when the ships departed. The town responded by organizing pest houses, quarantine stations, or isolation hospitals to segregate the sick from the town inhabitants and to prevent the spread of disease. Because these facilities were not intended to be used by the local citizenry, they were usually located well outside the city limits.

As populations grew, mental illness became an additional problem. Individuals whose behavior offended or frightened the townspeople came to the attention of the town board. It was common in those days for the town board to order relatives or friends to build a small stronghouse, or cell, on their property to contain a person with mental illness. If the individual had no relatives or friends, the town might lease him or her at an auction to the lowest bidder, who would take responsibility for confining that individual for 1 year, usually in exchange for his or her labor.

The existence of pest houses, or isolation hospitals, also provided the towns with what seemed an ideal solution for dealing with other individuals whose presence posed a risk to or offended its inhabitants. Over time, people with mental illness or those in poor health, the homeless, and the petty criminal joined the contagious ill that occupied those facilities.

Bellevue Hospital was originally the Poor House of New York City, established in 1736 to house the "poor, aged, insane, and disreputable." In 1789 the Public Hospital of Baltimore was established for low-income populations, people with mental or physical illness, and the seafaring of Maryland. One hundred years later, in 1889, it became the now prestigious Johns Hopkins Hospital.

Eventually, almost every city of any size in early America had a pest house to isolate patients during epidemics. Most cities also had an almshouse for low-income populations, sometimes with an added infirmary. Many of today's county or municipal hospitals were originally combinations of almshouses and infirmaries.

The largest county institution, Eloise Hospital in Wayne County, Michigan, was started in 1835 to serve the "old, young, deaf, dumb, blind, insane, and destitute." It grew to 6,000 beds to care for acute and chronic illness and mental diseases and to provide domiciliary services to low-income populations. The Kings County Hospital in Brooklyn, Philadelphia General Hospital, and Cleveland City Hospital are similar examples.

Most hospitals in the United States in the 19th century were disgraceful, the antithesis of what their patients needed. They were dirty, unventilated, and contaminated with infections. They were overcrowded and offered little or no medical care. The only nurses available were former inmates or women who could get no other work. As a result, they only accelerated the spread of disease. The public, however, knew little of these conditions. Because visiting was restricted, patients were effectively cut off from the outside world. Persons with family or the means to obtain home medical or nursing care shunned hospitals.

Certain religious orders saw the hospitals' clients as so helpless, so miserable with incurable disease, or so maimed by accident that they presented an opportunity for spiritual outlet for those seeking salvation through good works. Thus began the close relationships of the Protestant and Catholic religions with hospitals and hospital nursing. Religious nursing groups played a major role in the evolution of hospital care. Catholic religious orders were the first groups responsible for kindly and humane nursing performed by fairly well-educated, sincere, and devoted disciples. The American branch of St. Vincent de Paul Sisters of Charity, founded by Mother Elizabeth Seton in 1809, established hospitals that still stand in major cities across the United States.

The Protestant nursing movement began in Germany and was brought to Pennsylvania in 1850. It was based on the formal training of nurses in religion, nursing, and nursing education. The nurse teachers were called deaconesses. The Protestant church hospital, or deaconess movement, had an important influence on nursing.

Ironically, it was the Civil War of the 1860s that brought about public appreciation of the work of women in nursing. When sick or wounded soldiers were returned to their hometowns attended by obviously dedicated and capable nurses, it was the first time that relatives of those soldiers encountered women as nurses outside of their own homes. Nursing gained a much more positive image and came to be viewed as a respectable career option for women.

All this early hospital care was focused on only the most unfortunate of the population with physical and mental illness. Although provided in the most deplorable conditions, hospital care reflected the early American concept of charity and public responsibility, which required that provision be made for low-income populations, people with physical or mental illness, vagrants, and criminals. Institutions originally classified as almshouses provided refuge for all of them. Later, physicians realized the efficacy of separating the sick population from the rest of the needy and putting them in facilities more properly called hospitals. The Pennsylvania Hospital in Philadelphia, the New York Hospital in New York City, and the Massachusetts General Hospital in Boston were founded by physicians who obtained citizen funding for charitable hospitals. Their motives, however, were not altogether in the interests of the patients. They wanted a place to practice surgery and obstetrics, to obtain patients to serve for the instruction of medical students, and to protect the well population from people with physical or mental illness.

Sources That Shaped the Hospital Industry

Health Insurance

The transformation of hospitals from simple, charitable institutions to complex, technical organizations was accompanied by a parallel growth of private hospital insurance. In 1940, 9% of the U.S. population had hospital insurance. By 1986, that figure exceeded 74%.[1]

By the 1960s billions of dollars were flowing into hospitals from insurance companies, such as Blue Cross/Blue Shield, medical society plans, and other plans sponsored by unions, industry, physicians, and cooperatives. The availability of hospital insurance removed an important cost constraint from hospital charges. The ability of insurers to cope with ever-rising hospital costs by distributing relatively small premium increases over large numbers of subscribers opened the floodgates to hospital admissions. Expanding hospital services and relatively unrestrained reimbursement rates created an inflationary spiral that was to persist for decades.

In addition, medical advances and medical specialization encouraged hospitalization, and the hospital industry expanded to meet the demand. After World War II the American Hospital Association (AHA) convinced Senators Lister Hill and Harold Burton to sponsor legislation that provided federal monies to the states to survey hospitals and other health care facilities and to plan and assist construction of additional facilities. The Hill-Burton Hospital Construction Act was signed as Public Law 79-75 in 1946 and became a major influence in the expansion of the hospital industry.[1] Over 4,600 projects to expand existing facilities or construct new ones were initiated within 20 years after its passage. That federal support of hospital construction was critically important to the location of hospitals in underserved rural areas.

Medicare and Medicaid

In 1966 the hospital industry was the recipient of another major legislative contribution to its fiscal well-being by the passage of Medicare, Title XVIII of the Social Security Act. The legislation provided the growing population of Americans over age 65 years with significant hospital and medical benefits. In one decisive legislative action, the large population of older Americans, the group most likely to need hospitalization, was ensured hospital care, and the hospitals were ensured to be reimbursed on the basis of "reasonable costs."

The companion program, Medicaid, Title XIX of the Social Security Act, was established at the same time to support medical and hospital care for persons classified as medically indigent. Unlike Medicare, Medicaid required the states to establish joint federal–state programs that covered persons receiving public assistance and, if they wished, others of low income. Because the states had broad discretion over eligibility, benefits, and reimbursement rates, the programs that developed differed widely among the 50 states.

Medicare, and to a lesser extent Medicaid, had enormous impact on hospitalization rates in the United States. In a little over 10 years after the implementation of Medicare, persons over 65 years old were spending well over twice as many days in the hospital as those aged 45 to 64 years.[1] Because the rising Medicare rates became the standards for establishing hospital reimbursement rates in general, Medicare probably did more to fuel the rising costs of hospital care than any other factor.

The Medicare and Medicaid programs also had another effect. Because these programs provided government funding for the hospital care of low-income population and older adults, they altered the long-standing nature or mission of hospitals by diminishing the traditional charitable or social role of those voluntary institutions. It was not long after the implementation of those programs that hospitals became increasingly focused on profit, maximizing the more lucrative activities, and closing or reducing services that operated at a loss. In the 1980s hospitals, along with most of U.S. industry, became market oriented and aggressively enterprising. The monetary incentives built into the Medicare system favored entrepreneurial, short-term financial interests.

Rosemary Stevens, author of *In Sickness and in Wealth: American Hospitals in the Twentieth Century*,[1] wrote this: "One effect was to bring hospitals into prominence as enterprises motivated by organizational self-interest, by the excitement of the game, by greed." She concluded with this:

> Medicare and Medicaid, supposedly designed to promote egalitarianism, fostered sharp inequities in the health-care system while disarming criticism from low-paid American workers and the poverty population. The stage was set for today's struggles to rethink, once again, the American health-care system—and to redefine the relative roles of voluntarism, government, and business for the last few years of the twentieth century.

Growth and Decline in Numbers of Hospitals

The number of hospitals in the United States increased from 178 in 1873 to 4,300 in 1909. In 1946, at the close of World War II, there were 6,000 American hospitals, with 3.2 beds available for every 1,000 persons. That year, Congress passed the Hill-Burton Hospital Construction Act to fund expansion of the hospital system to achieve the goal of 4.5 beds per 1,000 persons.[2] The system grew thereafter to reach a high of approximately 7,200 acute-care hospitals.

During the 1980s, however, medical advances and cost-containment measures caused many procedures that once required inpatient hospitalization to be performed on an outpatient basis. Outpatient hospital visits increased by 40% with a resultant decrease in hospital admissions. Fewer admissions and shortened lengths of stay for patients resulted in a significant reduction in the number of hospitals and hospital beds. Health care reform efforts and the acceptance of managed care as the major medical practice style of U.S. health care resulted in enough hospital closings and mergers to reduce the number of governmental and community-based hospitals in the United States to approximately 5,700.

Types of Hospitals

Acute-care hospitals are distinguished from long-term care facilities such as nursing homes, rehabilitation centers, and psychiatric hospitals by the fact that the average stay of their patients is less than 30 days. Such hospitals have one of three basic sponsorships:

1. Voluntary not-for-profit entities
2. Owned and managed by profit-making corporations
3. Public facilities, supported and managed by governmental jurisdictions

Hospitals may also be divided into teaching and nonteaching hospitals. Teaching hospitals are affiliated with medical schools and provide clinical education for medical students and medical and dental residents. They, and many hospitals not affiliated with medical schools, also provide clinical education for nurses, allied health personnel, and a wide variety of technical specialists.

Only about one-fifth of hospitals are teaching facilities affiliated with one or more of the allopathic and osteopathic medical schools in the United States. Most teaching hospitals are voluntary not-for-profit institutions or government-sponsored public hospitals. The last survey of this country's hospitals conducted by the AHA concluded that there were

2,923 voluntary not-for-profit hospitals sponsored by religious groups or other community-based organizations. They constitute over 80% of the 5,815 registered hospitals in the United States.[3]

They include large numbers of small community general hospitals and smaller numbers of large tertiary-care facilities. These large tertiary-care facilities are usually affiliated with medical schools. The presence of medical school faculty with strong research interests and the availability of medical residents to assist in the collection of clinical data put teaching hospitals in the forefront of clinical research on medical conditions and treatments.

The federal government, through the U.S. Department of Veterans Affairs (VA) or the U.S. Public Health Service, operates 213 public hospitals. In addition, state and local governments maintain over 1,100 public hospitals. These public hospitals are usually large and well staffed with full-time attending physicians and residents. Such hospitals are usually teaching hospitals, with a heavy preponderance of economically disadvantaged patients.

Public hospitals in many localities deliver the fiscally problematic, but essential, community services that other hospitals are reluctant to provide. These high-cost, low-return services include sophisticated trauma centers, psychiatric emergency services, alcohol detoxification services, other substance abuse treatment, and burn treatment. In addition, there are 447 nonfederal psychiatric hospitals.

Investor-owned, for-profit hospitals grew from a few physician-owned facilities before the 1965 Medicare and Medicaid legislation to 982 in 2009.[3] Most for-profit hospitals belong to one of the large hospital management companies that dominate the for-profit hospital network. An increasing number, however, are physician-owned specialty hospitals. Such hospitals usually limit their services to treatments in one of three major specialty categories: orthopedics, surgery, or cardiology.

Although these new specialty hospitals are typically upscale facilities with many patient luxuries, they usually operate with greater efficiency and provide excellent care in their few targeted services. Nevertheless, they have raised a series of concerns about their performance and their effect on community hospitals.

First, it is clear that specialty hospitals treat the less complex, more profitable cases, leaving the more difficult, less profitable, or uninsured patients to be served by community hospitals. Second, because physician-owners of specialty hospitals profit directly by the value of services provided by their hospitals, there are concerns that clinical decisions may be influenced by financial incentives.[4]

Supporters of physician-owned specialty hospitals point out that the physician-owners take great pride in the quality of care provided in their hospitals, that they also work in community hospitals, and that their facilities enhance their communities by paying taxes as for-profit agencies.[5]

The number of beds in not-for-profit, state and local government, and federal hospitals decreased in the last decade, whereas the much smaller number of beds in for-profit facilities increased slightly. The last annual survey of the AHA counted about 951,045 staffed beds among all U.S. registered hospitals in the United States.[3]

Financial Condition of Hospitals

Beginning in the mid-1990s, thousands of hospitals were involved in mergers, acquisitions, and other multihospital deals in an effort to capture and solidify market shares and gain economies of scale. In 1996 alone, 235 deals involved 768 hospitals.[3] Although the service and financial outcomes of the mergers and other deals vary from location to location, there is little evidence that the multihospital strategies are meeting expectations. In fact, some of the mergers that combined facilities with differing administrative and clinical cultures have only added to their economic problems.

Those economic problems result from a combination of factors over which the hospitals have little control. The Balanced Budget Act of 1997, which reduced payments for Medicare patients below the costs of treating them, wreaked havoc on U.S. hospitals. At the same time hospital changes were held in check by hard-bargaining managed care organizations.

In contrast to the restraints on revenues, costs were rising at an unprecedented pace. Costly new technology, pharmaceuticals, and services, as well as significant inflationary increases, combined with declining occupancy to significantly reduce operating margins. During a recent survey of the AHA, 90% of the responding hospitals reported serious financial problems that required cost-cutting measures, and many had reduced staff.[6] The development of private specialty hospitals and diagnostic centers owned by physicians that compete with community hospitals for their most profitable services only add to the continuing losses of community hospitals.

Academic Health Centers, Medical Education, and Specialization

Medical, dental, nursing, pharmacy, and allied health schools and their teaching hospitals are the principal sources of education and training for most health care providers. Major universities with several or all of those different schools join them in organizational entities called academic medical centers or academic health centers.

Much of the basic and clinical research in medicine and other health care disciplines is conducted in these health centers and their related hospitals. The teaching hospitals usually provide the most technologically advanced care in their communities and also offer inpatient and ambulatory care for economically disadvantaged populations. Thus, the three objectives of academic health centers—education, research, and service—are fulfilled most adequately by teaching hospitals.

The influence of these medical centers on health care during the last few decades has been extraordinary. The advances that occurred in the medical sciences and technology that resulted in the introduction of life-saving drugs, anesthetics, surgical procedures, and other therapies and the development and use of sophisticated computerized diagnostic techniques increased both the use and the costs of hospital services. Physicians could intervene more successfully in the course of an ever-increasing array of conditions of disease and injury, and they enthusiastically exercised those capabilities. This increased intervention resulted in increases in both the life expectancy of most Americans and the proportion of the gross national product devoted to health care; however, these advances also significantly expanded the knowledge base and performance skills required of physicians to practice up-to-date clinical medicine.

Academic medical centers responded by increasing the number of physicians with in-depth expertise in increasingly narrow fields of clinical practice. Specialization and subspecialization grew, subdivided, and grew more. More and more physicians limited their activities to narrower and narrower fields of practice. In doing so they greatly increased the overall technologic sophistication of hospital practice along with the number of costly consultations that take place among specialist hospital physicians; the amount of expensive equipment, supplies, and space maintained by hospitals to serve specialist needs; and, in general, the complexity of patient care. The contributions of highly specialized clinical practice to the quality of hospital care have been both extraordinarily beneficial and regrettably negative. Although the superspecialists of U.S. medicine have given the profession its justified reputation for heroic medical and surgical achievements, specialization also has fragmented and depersonalized patient care and produced a plethora of often questionable tests, procedures, and clinical interventions.

Although academic medical centers have contributed admirably to the advancement of medicine, and especially hospital-delivered medical and surgical care, they have not brought their impressive expertise to bear effectively on solving the delivery system problems that have plagued their industry. Rather, the commitments of academic medicine to high-technology research and patient care and its adherence to traditional organizational structures and professional roles have prevented it from taking the lead in correcting health care system problems. As a result, medical education and medical organizations in general are reacting to, rather than guiding, the changes taking place.

Hospital System of the Department of Veterans Affairs

The tax-supported, centrally directed Veterans Health Administration of the VA is the country's largest health care system and a significant component of America's medical education system. The VA owns and operates 156 hospitals, most of which are affiliated with medical schools. The VA also operates 136 nursing homes, 43 residential rehabilitation facilities, and over 800 outpatient clinics. With its large number of hospitals and other facilities, over 12,000 full-time salaried physicians, over 900 dentists, and 33,000 nurses, the medical care program of the VA would be expected to be a prime target for the congressional cost cutters of large and expensive federal programs. With the current conflicts in Iraq and Afghanistan, however, the VA has regularly escaped the competitive pressures of the rest of the system. Instead, with broad bipartisan political support, the VA has received an annual congressional appropriation consistently higher each year than requested in the president's budget. Apparently, the strong political advocacy for veterans in the United States restrains any congressional initiative to give up VA hospitals in favor of subsidizing the care of veterans in the private sector.[7]

Like the rest of the hospital industry, the VA is reorganizing its facilities to lower costs, improve the quality of its care, and better integrate its patients throughout the system. Its major change has been the creation of 22 networks called Veterans Integrated Service Networks, each of which functions as a vertically integrated delivery system.[8]

An important part of the VA's organizational transition is its Health Services Research and Development Service. It works to improve the quality of health care for veterans by examining the impact of the organization, financing, and management of health services on their quality, cost, access, and outcomes. The latter activities are especially important because the VA is not only facing rising costs but also an influx of more severely traumatized patients and an aging and sicker veteran population of past wars.

In April 2007, however, the previously well-earned reputation for excellent care provided by the VA system was undone by public exposure of the dreadful circumstances of care at Walter Reed Army Medical Center in Washington, DC. Apparently, the hospital was unprepared, understaffed, and overwhelmed by the numbers, severity, and patterns of blast-related injuries to the military in Iraq. Such individuals require extremely complex and lengthy rehabilitation services to ensure maximum functional and psychosocial outcomes. Neither the staff nor the physical facilities of the hospital were judged adequate to meet the challenge.[9]

Instead of increasing the number of VA employees and services to meet the needs of those severely injured, the Bush administration chose to contract with outside agencies. An independent panel, headed by two former secretaries of the Army, issued a sweeping indictment of the leadership, training, staffing, and physical facilities. The conditions they reported included unkempt physical facilities and a bureaucratic maze that left severely injured soldiers in limbo for months.[10]

Another major subcontracting mistake became public knowledge in June 2009. A contracted physician, board certified in radiation oncology, was the contributing member of a team that botched the treatment of 92 veterans with prostate cancer.[11]

Structure and Organization of Hospitals

The organizational structure of today's hospital is a complex maze of committees, departments, personnel, and services. In addition to being a caring, people-oriented institution, it is at the same time a many-faceted, high-tech business. It operates just like any other large business, with a hierarchy of personnel, channels of authority and responsibility, and constant concern about its bottom line.

Likewise, the people who work in hospitals exhibit the same range of human characteristics as their counterparts in other businesses. Patients and their families trying to obtain the best possible results from the services of a hospital, therefore, should base their approach on the same principles they use in dealing with other service entities. They need to determine who is in charge, what services to expect from whom and when, with what results, and at what cost to them.

The following general description of hospital structure and organization uses the voluntary not-for-profit community hospital as the example because this type of institution has historically provided the model for hospital organization. The direction, control, and governance of the hospital are divided among three influential entities: the medical staff, the administration, and the board of directors or trustees. The major operating divisions of a hospital represent areas of the hospital's functions. Although they may use different names, the usual units are medical, nursing, patient therapy, diagnosis, fiscal, human resources, hotel services, and community relations.

Medical Division

The medical staff is a formally organized unit within the larger hospital organization. The president or chief of staff is the liaison between the hospital administration and members of the medical staff. Typically, the medical staff consists primarily of medical physicians, but it also may include other doctoral-level professionals, such as dentists and psychologists.

A major role of the medical staff organization is to recommend to the hospital board of directors the appointment of physicians to the medical staff. The board of directors approves and grants various levels of hospital privileges to physicians. Such privileges commonly include the right to admit patients to the hospital, to perform surgery, and to provide consultation to other physicians on the hospital staff. Another medical staff function is to provide oversight and peer review of the quality of medical care in the hospital. It performs this function through a number of medical staff committees, which coordinate their efforts closely with the hospital's administration and committees of the hospital's board of directors.

Members of the medical staff who have completed their training and are in practice are referred to as attending physicians. In addition, the hospital usually has a house staff of physicians who are engaged in postmedical school training programs under the supervision of attending staff members. These members of the house staff are referred to as residents. They rotate shifts to provide 24-hour coverage for the attending medical staff's patients in the specialty departments to which they are assigned.

There is no universal rule as to how a hospital's medical departments or divisions are organized. Most often, the types of practice of the hospital's medical staff determine the specialty components within the medical division. Medicine, surgery, obstetrics and gynecology, and pediatrics are usually major departments. In larger hospitals and in most teaching hospitals, the subspecialty areas of medical practice are represented by departments as well. In the internal medicine specialty, subspecialty departments might include cardiology or cardiac care, ophthalmology, urology, oncology, gastroenterology, pulmonary medicine, endocrinology, otolaryngology, and a variety of others. In the surgical area subspecialties might include orthopedics, thoracic, neurosurgery, cardiac surgery, and plastic and reconstructive surgery. Each medical department or division in a hospital is headed by a physician department head or chairman who is charged with overseeing the practice and quality of medical services delivered in the department. In a teaching hospital, either the department head or another designated attending physician is responsible for coordinating the required educational experiences of medical students and residents.

Nursing Division

The nursing division usually comprises the single largest component of the hospital's organization. It is subdivided by the type of patient care delivered in the various medical specialties. These nursing units are composed of a number of patient beds grouped within a certain area to allow centralization of the special facilities, supplies, equipment, and personnel pertinent to the needs of patients with particular conditions. For example, the kinds of equipment and skills and the level of patient care needs vary considerably between an orthopedic unit and a medical intensive care unit.

A head nurse, often carrying the title of "nurse manager," has overall responsibility for all nursing care in his or her unit. Such care includes carrying out the attending physician's and house staff physician's orders for medications, diet, and various types of therapy. In addition, the nurse manager supervises the unit's staff, which may include nurses' aides and orderlies. The nurse manager is also responsible for coordinating all aspects of patient care, which may include services provided by other hospital units, such as the dietary department, physical therapy department, pharmacy, and laboratories. The nurse manager also has the responsibility of coordinating the services of departments such as social work, discharge planning, and pastoral care for the patients in the unit.

Because nursing services are required in the hospital at all times, staff is usually employed in three 8-hour shifts. Normally, the nurse manager of a unit works during the day shift, and two other members of the nursing staff assume what is referred to as charge duty on the other two shifts of the day. Charge nurses report to the nurse manager.

A nursing supervisor may have management responsibility for a number of nursing units. These nursing supervisors in turn report to a member of the hospital's administration, who is usually a vice president for nursing or an assistant administrator.

It is also common to find an individual with the title of ward clerk or unit secretary on each nursing unit. The ward clerk assists the head nurse with paperwork and helps to coordinate the other hospital services related to patient care.

Allied Health Professionals

Not as well known as the physicians and nurses who are central to the care and treatment of patients in hospitals is the wide array of personnel who provide other hospital services that support the work of the physicians and nurses and the others who operate behind the scenes to make the facility run smoothly.

Staff members in an increasingly diverse array of health care disciplines are now classified as allied health personnel, and their roles in the complex health care system are often not recognized or well understood by the public. Allied health personnel support, complement, or supplement the functions of physicians, dentists, nurses, and other professionals in delivering health care to patients. They contribute to environmental management, health promotion, and disease prevention.

There are now over 200 allied health occupations and specialties, and advancing medical technology is likely to create the need for even more personnel with highly specialized training and relatively unique skills. Those who are responsible for highly specialized or technical services that have a significant impact on health care are prepared for practice through a wide variety of educational programs offered at colleges and universities.

The range of allied health professions may be best understood by classifying them by the functions they serve in the delivery of health care. Some disciplines may serve more than one of these functions:

1. Laboratory technologists and technicians play a major role in the diagnosis of disease, the monitoring of physiologic function, and the effectiveness of medical interventions. Medical technologists, nuclear medical technologists, radiologic technologists, and cytotechnologists are but a few of the specialists on whom hospitals depend.

2. Allied health practitioners of the therapeutic sciences are essential to the treatment and rehabilitation of patients with a wide variety of injuries and medical conditions. Examples include physical, occupational, and speech therapists and physician assistants.

3. Behavioral scientists are crucial to the social, psychological, and patient education activities related to health maintenance, disease prevention, and accommodation to disability. Professionals in this category include social workers, health educators, and rehabilitation counselors in mental health, alcoholism, and drug abuse.

4. Specialist support service personnel include those who perform administrative and management functions and others with special expertise that often work closely with the actual providers of patient care. Health information administrators, formerly called medical record administrators, food service administrators, dietitians, and nutritionists, are examples of personnel in this category.

The following descriptions of some of the key hospital services reflect the close functional relationships among the various kinds of highly specialized individuals required to staff hospital services.

Diagnostic Services

Every hospital either maintains or contracts with laboratories to perform a wide array of tests to help physicians diagnose illness or injury and monitor the progress of treatment. One such laboratory is the pathology laboratory, which examines and analyzes specimens of body tissues, fluids, and excretions to aid in diagnosis and treatment. These laboratories are usually supervised by the hospital's pathologist, who is a physician specialist.

The radiology department, directed by a physician specialist called a radiologist, provides radiographs for a variety of diagnostic purposes and may also provide radiation therapy for the treatment of certain disorders. Grouped under the rubric "diagnostic imaging services," a wide array of more sophisticated imaging equipment has been developed that incorporates computer technology. This includes computed tomography (CT), magnetic resonance imaging (MRI), and positron emission tomography (PET). Unlike radiograph technology, which is limited to providing images of the body's anatomic structures, these imaging advances have unique abilities to visualize structures in several planes and, with positron emission tomography, even quantify complex physiologic processes occurring in the human body. Thus they add immeasurably to the understanding and treatment of major ailments, including heart disease, stroke, cancer, epilepsy, and Alzheimer's disease.

A variety of other diagnostic services also may be available through specific medical specialty or subspecialty departments, such as cardiology and neurology. For example, a noninvasive cardiac laboratory administers cardiac stress testing to assess a patient's heart function during exercise. Obstetricians commonly use an imaging capability called ultrasonography to visualize the unborn fetus.

Rehabilitation Services

Rehabilitation or patient support departments provide specialized care to assist patients in achieving optimal physical, mental, and social functioning after resolution of an illness or injury. One such department is physical medicine, where diagnosis and treatment of patients with physical injuries or disabilities are conducted. This department is headed by a specialist physician called a physiatrist who usually works with a team of physical therapists, occupational therapists, and speech therapists. Other health-related specialists, such as social workers, may provide additional services to support the rehabilitation of patients with complex problems.

Other Patient Support Services

The hospital pharmacy purchases and dispenses all drugs used to treat hospitalized patients. The department is headed by a licensed pharmacist, who is also responsible for pharmacy technicians and others who work under his or her supervision.

Among other functions, the social services department helps patients about to be discharged to arrange financial support and coordinate needed community-based services. Generally, the social services department assists patients and their families achieve the best possible social and domestic environment for the patients' care and recovery. Such services are available to all hospital patients and their families.

Discharge planning services (discussed in more detail later in this chapter) may or may not be a part of the social services department. Frequently, staffing includes both nurses and social workers who are responsible for planning posthospital patient care in conjunction with the patients and their families. The discharge planning department becomes involved when the patient requires referral for one or more community services or placement in a special care facility after discharge.

Nutritional Services

The nutritional services department includes food preparation facilities and personnel for the provision of inpatient meals, food storage, and purchasing and catering for hospital events. It may also operate a cafeteria for employees and, in larger hospitals, may sponsor educational programs for student dietitians. An important function of this department's staff is educating patients on dietary needs and restrictions. This department usually is headed by a chief dietitian who has a degree in nutritional science, and it may be staffed by any number of other dietitians and clinical nutrition specialists with specific expertise in dietary assessment and food preparation.

Administrative Departments

Hospitals contain other professional units that provide a wide variety of nonmedical services essential to the management of the hospital's physical plant and business services. Patients are certainly aware of two of them: the admissions department, through which a hospital stay is initiated, and the business office, through which a hospital stay is terminated. These units are two of the many components of the hospital's complex management structure.

The general administrative services of the hospital are headed by a chief executive officer or president who has the day-to-day responsibility for managing all hospital business. He or she is the highest ranking administrative officer and oversees an array of administrative departments concerned with financial operations, public relations, and personnel. Most larger hospitals have a chief operating officer, who oversees the operation of specific departments, and a chief financial officer, who directs the many and varied fiscal activities of the hospital. Those key administrative officers are commonly positioned as corporate vice presidents. The large number of employees and the wide array of individual skills required to staff a hospital competently call for a personnel or human resources department with highly specialized labor expertise. That department is also usually headed by a vice president for human resources. Because nursing is such a large component of the hospital's service operations, the larger facilities also maintain a chief nursing executive at the vice-president level.

Hotel Services

Hotel services are generally associated with the hospitality functions common to hotels. They include building maintenance, security, laundry, television, and telephone services.

Information Technology's Impact on Hospitals

Although overall rates of adoption of health information technology throughout the health care industry have been slow, hospitals have implemented technologies at faster rates than physician offices. Recent Healthcare Information Management and Systems Society (HIMSS) reports show that most hospitals have adopted some level of the technology, although most are well below full electronic medical record implementation.[12]

Hospitals were motivated to adopt new health information technology to lower costs, reduce medical errors, and meet The Joint Commission requirements.[13] The technology allowed hospitals to reduce information duplication and improve the utilization of lab and radiology results.[14] Administratively, new health information technology increased the efficiency of coding and billing[15,16] and provided health care personnel with quicker access to patient records.[17]

In 2004, President Bush signed an Executive Order that called for "the development and nationwide implementation of an interoperable health information technology infrastructure to improve efficiency, reduce medical errors, raise the quality of care, and provide better information for patients, physicians, and other health care providers."[18] The long-range sequence of goals is to establish

1. Electronic medical records in medical offices and hospitals
2. Regional health information organizations for information analysis and exchange
3. Statewide information networks for data mining, knowledge gains, and information exchange
4. A national information network for public health monitoring and population statistics

Congress continued to encourage health information technology with a steady flow of bills promoting a national health information network, overall health information technology adoption, physician grants for electronic medical records purchases, and, recently, the Hitech Trust Act. Under this Act the Centers for Medicare & Medicaid Services will provide reimbursement incentives for eligible professionals and hospitals who are successful in becoming "meaningful users" of certified electronic health record technology. "Meaningful use" was defined as "not only the adoption of the technology, but the implementation and exchange of health information to improve clinical decision making at the point of care." The incentive payments will begin in 2011 with penalties under Medicare for noncompliance beginning in 2015.[19]

Complexity of the System

Almost two-thirds of U.S. hospitals employ more than 1,000 workers.[20] Major hospital systems may have thousands of employees, significant turnover of personnel requiring training and indoctrination of new employees to the complicated procedures of the organization, and a maze of information transmission requirements with high potential for miscommunication. The newer diagnostic and therapeutic methods that are increasingly effective are also increasingly complex.

Thus, even this very limited description of the hospital's complex structure and organization should make it clear that with so many different kinds of employees and so many interrelated systems and functions, it is a small wonder that hospitals work at all, much less as well as they do. With the multitude of tasks performed every day by the hundreds of employees in a busy hospital, misunderstandings and information breakdowns in patient care are inevitable. In acknowledgment of the fact that their organizations are too complex and their employees too compartmentalized in their responsibilities to solve system problems, the majority of this country's hospitals have patient representatives, sometimes called patient advocates, to serve as ombudspersons for the patients. They are prepared to intervene on behalf of the patients in a wide variety of situations. The phone numbers of those patient representatives are usually provided to patients in the material given them during the admission process or left conspicuously in their rooms.

Types and Roles of Patients

In the early development of hospitals, the patient was considered an unavoidable burden to society. In its mercy, society provided the hospital as a refuge—and incidentally, a workplace for the physician and his disciple, the medical student. Patients receiving this charity were expected to be grateful for the shelter and nursing care and even for the opportunity to lend their bodies and illnesses for medical practice. On the other hand, patients who could afford to pay for their medical and nursing care continued to receive it in the comfort and dignity of their homes.

By 1900 proper training in nursing, effective anesthetic agents, modern methods of antisepsis and sterilization, and other medical advances had revolutionized hospital practices. Hospitals changed from merely supplying food, shelter, and meager medical care to the unfortunate needy and contagious to providing skilled medical, surgical, and nursing care to everyone; however, the belief persisted that patients in the hospital, removed from their usual social environment, were in a dependent relationship with charitable authorities. Remnants of the idea that these professionals have the knowledge and authority to decide what is best for grateful and uncomplaining patients persist to this day, regardless of the expense to the patient or the merit of the services.

Unfortunately, the behavior of many patients and their families has been conditioned to reinforce this philosophy. In the hospital otherwise assertive, independent individuals tend to assume a passive and dependent "sick role." Numerous sociologic studies of patient behavior have concluded that the patients who behave in the traditional submissive sick role help to preserve the authoritarian attitude of health care providers that most consumers now consider patronizing and inappropriate.[21]

Rights and Responsibilities of Hospitalized Patients

Patients in hospitals have individual rights, many of which are protected by state statutes and regulations. The constitution of the United States and, in particular, its Bill of Rights are not suspended when a citizen enters a hospital. In fact, since 1972 the AHA has published a "Statement on a Patient's Bill of Rights" that is displayed prominently in every hospital in the country. In addition, hospitals are required by their accrediting body to make this information known to every patient admitted. Very importantly, the statement recognizes that the hospital, in addition to the physician, has a responsibility for the patient's welfare. In fact, the ultimate responsibility for everything that happens within the hospital, including the medical care provided, lies with the hospital institution and its board of directors.

Many hospitals, other institutions, and government agencies have modified the language of the original AHA Statement on a Patient's Bill of Rights to represent more accurately their individual interpretations of their responsibilities or to communicate better with special populations. In addition to posting these statements on the walls of the facility, hospitals also distribute their modified versions under their own organization title with the admission documents provided to patients.

The following description of major patients' rights is a synthesis of the statements posted by several hospitals. Patients have the right to

1. Receive respectful and considerate treatment, including respect for their personal privacy, during examinations, tests, and all forms of interaction with their physicians, staff members, and others involved in their care.

2. Know the names and titles of all individuals providing their care and the name of the physician responsible.
3. Complete and understandable explanations of their diagnosis, treatment, and prognosis. They also have the right to designate another individual to receive such explanations on their behalf.
4. Receive from the physician all the information necessary to give informed consent before any procedure or treatment. Such information should include a description of the procedure or treatment, the estimated period of convalescence, the risks involved, the risk of not accepting the treatment or procedure, and any alternative options.
5. Request and receive consultation on their diagnosis and treatment or obtain a second opinion.
6. Set limits on the scope of treatment that they will permit, or refuse, treatment and be informed of the consequences of such refusal.
7. Leave the hospital, unless unlawful, even against the advice of their physicians and receive an explanation of their responsibilities in exercising that right.
8. Request and receive information and assistance in discharging financial obligations to the hospital, and review a complete bill, regardless of the source of payment.
9. Access to their records on demand as well as access to someone capable of explaining anything that is confusing or difficult to understand (since April 2004 a requirement of the federal HIPAA law for hospitals, physicians, and clinics).
10. Receive assistance in planning and obtaining necessary support after discharge.

Those endowed with individual rights are always expected to assume certain reciprocal individual responsibilities. Patients are obligated to act responsibly toward physicians and hospitals by cooperating with all reasonable requests for personal and family information. It is to their own benefit that patients inform medical or hospital personnel if they do not understand or do not wish to follow instructions. If a patient would like a family member or other advocate to be involved in treatment decisions, that individual should be identified to the physician, and the hospital and contact information should be provided.

It is also incumbent on patients to recognize that hospitals are highly stressful institutional settings and that other patients, as well as the hospital personnel, deserve consideration and respect. Courtesy to others in the close confines of hospital quarters is most appreciated.

In no other institutional setting are individual rights at greater risk of being compromised than in a hospital; however, the risks do not arise from a purposeful disregard for patients by physicians or the hospital staff or from their individual or collective determination to subject patients to treatment against their will. The personal integrity of patients may be unintentionally violated as a result of certain institutional circumstances and factors unique to the hospital setting. These institutional circumstances arise from the fact that the hospital, like most large complex organizations, has a life of its own, which pulses with an infinite array of daily scheduled events that pervade every aspect of its functioning. There are schedules for changing beds, bathing patients, serving meals, administering medications, obtaining specimens, providing therapy, checking vital signs, performing surgery, housekeeping, admitting, discharging, doing rounds, receiving visitors, performing examinations, and, finally, preparing patients for the night.

The vast number of tasks that evolve from the care needs of up to several hundred people who are ill each day requires the planning and scheduling of every activity if they are all to be accomplished within a 24-hour period. The pressure of the daily schedule often makes it difficult for hospital personnel to pay attention to the special needs of individual patients. Even though a patient's particular schedule of tests, procedures, treatments, and examinations is uniquely related to his or her condition and the physician's orders, it also is influenced by the needs of fellow patients and the schedules of the physicians, technicians, technologists, nurses, nurses' aides, therapists, students, and numerous others involved directly or indirectly in the patient's care.

A patient's treatment may also be modified by the schedule of those daily institutional events, which although unrelated to his or her treatment can have an impact on what does or does not happen on any given day. Such institutional events include inspections, grand rounds, nursing in-services, unplanned staffing shortages, and an array of technical problems with any of the hundreds of the pieces of medical equipment used to perform the daily functions of a sophisticated hospital.

As it becomes clearer that the schedule, rather than the patients' needs, drives the caregivers, the second major reason why patient rights may be in jeopardy in the hospital setting emerges. Physicians may not be aware of the many aspects of daily care in the hospital that determine whether patients are comfortable and reasonably satisfied during their hospital stay. Physicians are likely to spend only a few minutes a day with each patient. That means that patients nearly always depend on the nursing staff and other support personnel for the medical and personal care they should receive. Very importantly, nurses are supposed to be continuously monitoring each patient's condition and alerting the physician to any change in a patient's status; however, the number of patients for whom a nurse is responsible and the number of tasks that the nurse is required to perform during the course of a single work shift make it extremely difficult, or sometimes impossible, to fulfill that obligation. In addition, the increasing number of caregivers involved with each patient provides additional opportunities for failures of communication and subsequent mistakes in the treatment programs for individual patients. Although hospitals do their best to develop fail-safe systems to protect patients against the possibility of human error in the delivery of their care, mistakes can happen. One patient can receive a medication intended for another. The report of a laboratory test can get lost and require the repeat of an uncomfortable procedure. A physician's instructions can be overlooked, and the patient may be deprived of something that he or she was supposed to receive. The patient may continue receiving something that was supposed to be stopped. A nurse's note alerting the physician to a change in the patient's condition may be missed, and the patient may fail to receive something that he or she requires.

Progressive hospital systems encourage patients to recognize their vulnerability during hospitalization and urge them or their family members to function as active participants in, rather than passive recipients or observers of, hospital care. In addition, state health departments, which certify hospitals to operate, ensure the right of patients to press complaints about hospital care and services. Hospitals are required by law to investigate patient complaints and respond to them. In fact, a hospital must provide a written response if a patient so requests.

Important Decisions, Informed Consent, and Second Opinions

No description of the structure and processes of hospitals is complete without mention of the very important personal decisions regarding medical care that patients are asked to make, often, unfortunately, under circumstances that are stressful if not intimidating. A cornerstone of the personal rights of hospitalized patients is the right to know

- What is being done to them and why
- What the procedure entails
- How the procedure can be expected to benefit them
- What risks or consequences are associated with a procedure
- What is the probability of risks and consequences

In short, in almost all cases the doctrine of informed consent ensures that patients have ultimate control over their own bodies. This doctrine, first recognized legally in 1914, has been reaffirmed repeatedly over the years and is now generally recognized to encompass not only all the previously mentioned elements but also the right to receive information about alternative forms of treatment to the one recommended.

A physician has no legal right to substitute his or her judgment for the patient's in matters of consent. This principle means that even though a physician may believe a certain intervention is in the patient's best interest, the patient has the absolute right to reject that recommendation. The right of patients to refuse a certain procedure or treatment until they are satisfied that it is in their best interest allows them to stay in control of their health care.

That is why it is considered appropriate for patients to obtain second opinions to satisfy concerns about the necessity for various tests and other procedures. Because there is evidence that seeking the opinion of a second physician regarding the need for surgical and other invasive procedures often results in a decision to reject the original advice, many insurers now require a confirming second opinion before agreeing to pay for surgical procedures.

In many medical situations the wisest course of action is uncertain or debatable. The need for certain surgical procedures is one good example. Few people realize that the medical needs for some common operations have never been clearly defined by scientific studies. When such studies have been performed, many procedures, even those that surgeons once favored, have turned out to offer no real benefit or improvement over alternative treatments. Unlike the introduction of new drugs, which must be extensively tested to document safety and benefits before they can be marketed, new operations have been introduced and become popular based on clinical impressions rather than on the systematically collected information necessary to determine in what circumstances the benefits justify the risks. Because the best estimates are that only 20% of the more than 20 million operations performed in the United States each year involve critical, life-threatening emergencies in which the physician must operate immediately, patients usually have time to deliberate carefully over the need for surgery and its potential risks and benefits.

Diagnosis-Related Group Hospital Reimbursement System

Until 1983 a patient stayed in the hospital until the physician decided that he or she was well enough to leave. If the patient was going to a nursing home or some other institution, sometimes that patient had to remain in the hospital until a bed became available in the other institution. In most cases, however, physicians had a considerable amount of leeway in making decisions about the length of a patient's stay in the hospital, and they usually tried to balance the best interests of the patients with those of the hospital.

For this and other reasons, the length of time patients stayed in the hospital varied, even among those being treated for the same condition. In fact, the patterns of medical care varied considerably from one geographic location to another. For many years physicians on the West Coast of the United States discharged patients from hospitals 2 or more days earlier than their counterparts in the Northeast for patients with the same conditions. Apparently, differing regional medical practice patterns guide physician behaviors.

In any case each hospital monitored its own situation. Each had a utilization review committee made up of physicians and administrators who were required to review the lengths of stay of hospitalized patients and to ensure that neither the quality of care nor the efficiency of the hospital was being compromised by physicians' decisions.

During the 1970s and early 1980s, however, the cost of hospital care rose so fast that health insurance companies and big corporations that paid huge insurance premiums to cover the hospitalization costs of their workers dramatically increased the pressure on federal agencies to find a way to stem the rising tide of hospital expenses.

Two factors made change imperative. Hospitals were paid a set amount for each day that a patient stayed in the facility. That amount was determined retrospectively by determining what it cost per day per bed to operate the hospital the year before. Under that arrangement the hospital had no incentive to keep costs down. In fact, if it did, it would receive a smaller daily reimbursement rate the next year than if it spent freely. Furthermore, it became clear to the government and the insurance companies that they were paying not only for uncontrolled costs per hospital day but also for hospital days that were not necessary. On a national scale hundreds of thousands of hospital days that did not benefit the patients, at a cost of several hundred dollars per day, amounted to a huge and valueless financial burden. Hospital costs were forcing the federal Medicare program, which served older Americans, to exceed all financial projections.

There was another worry as well. Not only are unnecessarily long hospital stays expensive, but they also can be dangerous to the patients' health. Older patients are especially vulnerable. Patients are exposed to infections and diseases in hospitals that they would not face at home. In addition, many older patients lose the ability to do some of the basic activities of daily living, such as dress, feed, or toilet themselves, during a long stay in a hospital. Those patients come out of the hospital less able to function than when they went in. Shortened stays in hospitals, especially for older patients, can often be beneficial as well as less expensive.

In 1983 the federal government radically changed the way hospitals would be reimbursed for the costs of treating Medicare patients. The new payment system, referred to as diagnosis-related groups (DRGs), is designed to provide hospitals with a financial incentive to discharge patients as soon as possible. It is a prospective payment system, which means that the patient's diagnosis determines how much the hospital is paid, and the hospital knows that amount in advance. The payment is a set amount based on the average cost of treating that particular illness or condition. If the patient requires less care or fewer days in the hospital than the DRG average, the hospital is paid the average cost regardless, and the hospital makes money. If the patient requires a longer stay or more care than the DRG average, the hospital loses money.

This carrot-and-stick system was adopted quickly by almost all states and hospital insurance companies and now affects all hospital patients, not just Medicare patients. It quickly changed hospital behavior. The built-in system of financial rewards and punishments caused hospitals to discharge patients more quickly and sometimes before they were completely recovered, a practice that has increased the need for home-delivered health care

services. In addition, medical staff is much more conservative about order-
ing tests and procedures that are of marginal value in diagnosis and treatment. Now hospitals do everything they can to ensure that their average
cost in a particular DRG category stays within the reimbursement limit. In
most cases the incentive to discharge patients as soon as possible does not
cause problems. In some cases, however, it does, and patients have to be
readmitted for further treatment. A more detailed discussion of the impact
of this reimbursement method on the financial viability of hospitals is provided in Chapter 7, which deals with the financing of health care.

Discharge Planning

The hospital is responsible for employing discharge planners to help
patients arrange for safe and appropriate accommodations after a hospital
stay. Using information provided by the patient or the patient's family, a
discharge planner must see to it that the patient who needs follow-up
services, such as home care, obtains them. The planner must then help
make the necessary, specific arrangements. If the patient requires a transfer to another level of institutional care, such as a nursing home, it is the
responsibility of the discharge planner to arrange that transfer before the
patient can be discharged from the hospital.

The hospital's financial incentive to discharge patients as soon as possible should never cause patients to be discharged before they are medically
ready to leave and before arrangements have been made to ensure that they
will receive the necessary posthospital care. Patients who believe that either
of these two conditions will not be met by their anticipated discharge date
have the right to appeal that date. If they cannot persuade their physician
or discharge planner to reconsider the discharge decision, they can ask the
hospital for a written notice of discharge. For those receiving Medicare, the
written notice will allow two free Medicare-covered days in the hospital,
whether or not they decide to appeal.

The hospital's discharge notice must include instructions on how the
patient can have the hospital's decision reviewed by the peer review organization (PRO). The PRO is under contract with the federal government
to ensure that hospitals and physicians follow Medicare rules. Every geographic area in the United States is covered by a federally designated
PRO. Patients have 3 calendar days after receiving written notice to ask

the hospital to refer their case to the PRO. The PRO then has 3 working days to return its decision.

The PRO will reverse the decision to discharge and require Medicare to cover the costs of the additional days if it is convinced the patient is in need of continuing hospital care. If the PRO does not reverse the decision, the hospital can bill the patient directly for any stay after 2 days following its written notice to the patient. There is also a mechanism to appeal the PRO's decision and a further process for a Medicare appeal.

Subacute Care

It was inevitable under recent economic pressures that hospitals would find ways to increase utilization, fill empty beds, and increase revenues. Subacute care, a level of care that falls between inpatient hospitalization and long-term or nursing home care, provided one such opportunity.

Subacute care is a mix of rehabilitation and convalescent services that requires 10 to 100 days of care. It is a level and duration of care inappropriate to either acute-care hospitals or most skilled nursing facilities. Thus, both hospitals and nursing homes have created special units within their facilities to provide for subacute care. Because that care level falls between well-established reimbursement formulas, setting up acute-care facilities has allowed hospitals and nursing homes to find different ways to capture the highest reimbursement rates.

Some hospitals have licensed their subacute-care facilities separately from the rest of the hospital to exempt them from the prospective payment system. Others have converted a hospital-based skilled nursing facility to subacute care. Still others have transformed an entire acute-care facility to a long-term care facility. Unlike acute-care facilities these long-term care hospitals receive higher cost-based reimbursement from Medicare.[22]

In any case subacute care, viewed as a new financial opportunity for health care institutions, is one of the fastest growing developments in the hospital and nursing home industries. Managed care providers welcome the opportunity to direct patients to subacute-care facilities that can treat them effectively for a fraction of the cost of traditional hospital care.

The rapid development of subacute care and the accompanying switch from prospective payment to cost-based reimbursement, however, has prompted the federal government's Health Care Financing Administration and agencies in several states to take steps to halt the spread of subacute-care units within both hospitals and nursing homes until the value of subacute care can be determined. Questions about whether hospitals or nursing homes are more suitable to administer subacute care have been raised. In addition, because the focus of subacute care is more on new forms of reimbursement than on a new type of service, studies are under way to determine the cost effectiveness and usefulness to patients of this type of care. Clearly, it is a high-stakes development in the hospital industry.

Market-Driven Reforms Affecting Hospitals

With consumers, employers, government, and commercial payers intensifying their demands for lower costs, higher quality, better access, and more information about outcomes, most hospitals undertook a series of competitive efforts to retain and, if possible, improve their market positions. Many engaged in mergers and consolidations intended to effect economies of scale and place them in a better position to negotiate with managed care organizations and other payers. Others, in communities with excess hospital capacity, either closed or converted to other uses, such as ambulatory or long-term care facilities.

Since 1980, approximately 2,000 hospitals closed in the United States, and hospital inpatient days declined by one-third. Furthermore, with an increasing number of medical services occurring in ambulatory settings, hospitals are facing the need to reduce inpatient capacity and refocus their service efforts on intensive care and other inpatient essentials.[23]

Patient-Focused Care

One of the consequences of high-technology hospital care was the industrialization of patient care activities. The corporate thinking that swept the hospital industry in the 1970s and 1980s brought production-line concepts to what formerly had been very personal, high-touch, rather than high-tech, relationships between patients and caregivers, primarily nurses.

Rather than being patient oriented, the care became task oriented, with every chore identified and delegated to the person at the lowest skill level who was capable of carrying it out. Thus a nurse might be assigned the task of going from patient to patient just taking vital signs, temperatures, blood pressures, and pulses. Another individual, not necessarily a nurse, might be only bathing those same patients, another drawing blood, another handing out medications, and so forth. The result for patients was a succession of relatively anonymous caregivers, none of whom had a knowledgeable relationship with the patients they served. Responsibility and accountability for the total care of patients became increasingly diffuse. Opportunities for patients to fall into the cracks between the many caregivers increased, and more midlevel managers were necessary to oversee operations. Any questionable gains in efficiency were achieved at the costs of patient satisfaction, communication, and personal care.

Patient satisfaction studies reflected an increase in patient complaints about the loss of identity, dignity, and respect for them as individuals that characterized their hospital stay. Particularly frustrating to many hospital patients and their families was the difficulty they experienced in obtaining information or even identifying someone capable of answering questions. For most, the lack of communication between hospital staff, including physicians, and the patients and their families was the most irritating aspect of the hospital experience.

After an extensive survey of over 6,000 hospital patients and 2,000 individuals who accompanied patients during their hospital stays as well as research drawn from field visits and focus groups, the Picker/Commonwealth Program for Patient-Centered Care, established in 1987, was able to identify a series of patient care failings common among hospitals.[24] Unquestionably, the diffusion of clinical responsibility that complicates communication among caregivers and the flow of information between caregivers and patients affect the quality of clinical care. In addition to making patient experiences unpleasant and stressful, communication and coordination breakdowns needlessly duplicate effort and delay or omit important procedures and tasks. One devastating finding was that as many as 20% of patients concluded that no one was in charge of their hospital care.[25]

It is significant in the Picker/Commonwealth findings that the most technologically sophisticated teaching hospitals with the most specialized medical staffs also are viewed as the least sensitive to the personal and cultural values, concerns, and perceptions of their patient populations. Conversely, the cultural homogeneity of staff and patients and the relative simplicity of small community hospitals are viewed as more conducive to patient-sensitive care. Clearly, the advances in medical care and the industrialization of many, if not most, hospitals have caused the medical system to lose touch with its essential constituency—its patients—and its essential mission to serve their needs.[25]

Of course, some very large and sophisticated hospitals did not follow the crowd, and they stand out as highly mission oriented, innovative, and sensitive to patient needs and wants. They reshaped their patient care systems on the strengths of their highly skilled nursing personnel to be extremely responsive to patient concerns and to measure precisely how patients experience the process and outcomes of the care they receive.

Beth Israel Hospital in Boston and Cedars-Sinai Medical Center in Los Angeles are two excellent examples of patient-focused hospital care. The quality of nursing care is deemed as important to the safety and well-being of patients in those hospitals as it is to the progress of their medical care. Excellent hospitals give nurses a meaningful role in the care and treatment of patients, and Beth Israel Hospital has been cited many times as the model for other hospitals. Its primary care nursing program, developed in 1974, has one of the most successful histories of patient-centered care. Each patient is assigned a registered nurse responsible for designing a coordinated individual plan of care. The primary care nurse assumes 24-hour responsibility for maintaining continuity of care from admission to discharge and coordinates all other caregivers in the process.[26]

Similarly, Cedars-Sinai Medical Center pioneered the concept of patient-focused care with organizational redesigns, clinical practice guidelines, and firm accountability for the quality of patient care. The dedication and effectiveness of the nursing staff are reflected in its reputation as one of the world's most diversified and sophisticated medical centers and its repeated 95% patient satisfaction ratings.[26]

Clearly, the trend is moving away from the industrial model of hospital care that eroded public trust and confidence in hospital care and toward small team responsibility for the quality of patient services. To lure patients who now have more options, hospitals are focusing on friendlier staff, better food, and more amenities. Many hospitals have done away with visiting hours and invite patients' family members to stay as long as they like. Hospitals even accommodate visitors who stay the night with reclining chairs and delivered breakfasts.[27]

Horizontal Integration

Under the general business definition, horizontally integrated organizations are aggregations that produce the same goods or services. They may be separately or jointly owned and governed, operated as subsidiary corporations of a parent organization, or exist in a variety of other legal or quasi-legal relationships. According to Roger Kropf[28]:

> In the hospital industry, horizontal integration was viewed as potentially advantageous because a chain of hospitals might be able to purchase supplies and services at a volume discount, would be able to hire specialized staff at the corporate level to increase expertise, would be able to raise capital less expensively on the securities markets, and would be able to market hospital services under a single brand name in a number of communities.

Both for-profit and not-for-profit hospitals engaged in horizontal integration in an effort to meet the economic imperatives of the changing industry climate. The horizontal integration strategy spawned large numbers of hospital mergers and acquisitions and significant growth in the number of multihospital systems during the 1980s. As the trend in inpatient utilization and lengths of stay continued their declines throughout the 1980s, managed care organizations and other large purchasers of health care were increasing demands for the availability of comprehensive, continuous care housed within discrete, accountable systems. For this and other reasons, horizontal integration as a primary strategic initiative declined in favor.

Mergers and acquisitions have continued to the present, but often for reasons different from the advantages initially identified. Now, in communities across the United States, with managed care saturating markets more than penetrating them, consolidation of facilities, staff, and other resources of previously separate organizations has become critical to the survival of a rational health care delivery system.

Vertical Integration

Vertically integrated organizations are ones that operate a variety of business entities, each of which is related to the other. In health care, a vertically integrated system includes several service components, each of which addresses some dimension of a population's health care needs. The system may be fully comprehensive, with a complete continuum of services ranging from prenatal to terminal care. Other systems may contain some, but not all, of the services required by a population. A fully comprehensive vertically integrated system in its ideal form includes all facilities, personnel, and technologic resources to render the complete continuum of care, which comprises (1) all outpatient primary care and specialty diagnostic and therapeutic services, (2) inpatient medical and surgical services, (3) short- and long-term rehabilitative services, (4) long-term chronic institutional and in-home care, and (5) terminal care. Such a system also includes all required support services such as social work and health education. In theory, vertically integrated systems offer attractive benefits to their sponsoring organizations, patients, physicians, and other providers, as well as payers.

Sponsors of vertically integrated organizations gain the advantage of an increased market share across a mixture of high-profit, loss-generating, and break-even revenue sources. They benefit from an increased likelihood of retaining patients for many or all their service needs. In addition, they are advantageously positioned to negotiate with managed care organizations by ensuring the availability of comprehensive, continuous care for an insured population at competitive prices. For patients, the most obvious benefit is continuity of care throughout the various system components and improved case management. Physicians and other providers benefit from both greater certainty about the flow of patients to their practices and improved ease of referrals. Managed care organizations and other large purchasers view integrated organizations favorably because of the relative ease of negotiating pricing with one organization instead of several. In addition, quality monitoring, patient case management, and physician and other provider activity can be managed and monitored more efficiently when they are all part of the same organization.

Quality of Hospital Care

It has always been easier to evaluate the quality of the medical care provided in hospitals than that provided in medical offices or other delivery sites because of the availability of comprehensive medical records and other sources of clinical information, systematically collected and stored for later recovery. The definition of quality, however, derives from both various operational factors and the measures or indicators of quality selected and the value judgments attached to them. For many years, quality was defined as "the degree of conformity with preset standards" and encompassed all the elements, procedures, and consequences of individual patient–provider encounters. Most often, however, the standards against which care was judged were implicit rather than explicit and existed only in the minds of peer evaluators.

The peer-review technique had both benefits and failings. A common peer-review quality-assurance process used in hospitals until the 1970s was the chart audit. Periodically, an audit committee made up of several providers appointed by the hospital medical staff would review a small sample of patient records and make judgments as to the quality of care provided.

Such audits were ineffective for several reasons. First, the evaluators used internalized or implicit standards to make qualitative judgments. Second, there was no rational basis for chart selection that would permit the evaluators to extrapolate the sample findings to the broader patient population. Third, even if deficiencies were identified, the auditors were reluctant to take corrective action because their deficient colleagues might be on the next audit committee reviewing their patient care.

Avedis Donabedian of the University of Michigan made an important contribution to quality-of-care studies by defining the three basic components of medical care—structure, process, and outcome. Structural components are the qualifications of the providers, the physical facility, equipment, and other resources and the characteristics of the organization and its financing.[29] Until the 1960s the contribution of structure to quality was the primary, if not the only, quality-assurance mechanism in health care. Traditionally, the health care system relied on credentialing mechanisms, such as licensure, registration, and certification by professional societies and specialty boards, to ensure the quality of clinical care.

Hospital reviews for accreditation by the then Joint Commission on Accreditation of Hospitals were also based almost exclusively on structural criteria. Judgments were made about physical facilities, the equipment, the ratios of professional staff to patients, and the qualifications of the various personnel. The underlying assumption of structural quality reviews was that the better the facilities and the qualifications of the providers, the better the quality of the care rendered.

The past focus on structural criteria assumed quite erroneously that enough was known about the relationship of the structural aspects of care to its processes and outcomes to identify the critical or appropriate structural indicators. It was much later that hospital accreditation involved process criteria and, more recently, outcomes.

The process components are what occur during the encounters between patients and providers. Process judgments include what was done, how appropriate it was, and how well performed, as well as what was omitted that should have been done. The assumption underlying the use of process criteria is that the quality of the actions taken during patient encounters determines or influences the outcomes.

The outcomes of care are all the things that do or do not happen as a result of the medical intervention. Only recently has quality assurance in the hospital field focused on the relationships among structure, process, and outcomes. In the past it had always been argued by providers that so many different variables influence the outcomes of medical care that it is inappropriate and unfair to providers to attribute patient outcomes solely to medical interventions. That argument was dismissed, however, with the introduction of computerized information systems and sophisticated analytical techniques that permit the collection and analysis of data on most or all the potential intervening influences and allow the findings to be adjusted for patient differences. Now, quality-of-care data are routinely standardized to account for age, gender, severity of illness, accompanying conditions, and other variables that might influence outcomes.

Variations in Medical Care

In 1973 two researchers, John Wennberg and Alan Gittlesohn, published what would be the first of a series of papers documenting the variations in the amounts and types of medical care provided to patients with the same diagnoses living in different geographic areas.[30] Those publications emphasized that the amount and cost of hospital treatment in a community had more to do with the number, specialties, and individual preferences of the physicians than the medical conditions of the patients.

At the same time concerns about the variability of hospital care and the conclusions from studies on its quality prompted federal action. The Social Security Act was amended to create a national network of local professional standards review organizations charged with ensuring that health care services purchased in whole or in part by the Medicare, Medicaid, or maternal and child health programs conform to appropriate professional standards and are delivered effectively and efficiently.

With persistent concerns about improving the quality of hospital care and containing soaring costs, various groups have formed to survey and report on the quality of hospital care. Chief among them has been the Leapfrog Group. It was founded in November 2000 by the Business Roundtable with support from The Robert Wood Johnson Foundation. Members include more than 160 Fortune 500 corporations and other large private and public sector health benefits purchasers that represent more than 36 million enrollees.

The Leapfrog Group fields the Leapfrog Hospital Quality and Safety Survey, a voluntary online survey that tracks hospitals' progress toward implementing all 30 of the safety practices endorsed by the National Quality Forum. The Leapfrog website, www.leapfroggroup.org, displays each hospital's results and is updated each month with data from additional hospitals; anyone can review the results at no charge. Leapfrog has compiled the first free online database of programs across the country that offer financial or nonfinancial rewards and incentives for improved performance. The Leapfrog Incentive and Reward Compendium also is available at www.leapfroggroup.org.[31]

Hazards of Hospitalization

Medical errors have been a serious problem in hospitals for years, but improving patient safety did not become a serious national concern until recently. Although those in the health professions and more knowledgeable members of the public have long been aware of the error-prone nature of hospital care, it was not until the November 1999 release of a report prepared by the prestigious National Academy of Science's Institute of Medicine (IOM) on medical mistakes that the magnitude of the risks to patients receiving hospital care became common public knowledge.

By extrapolating the findings of several well-conducted studies of adverse events occurring in hospitals to the 33.5 million hospital admissions in the United States during 1997, the IOM report concluded that as few as 44,000 and as many as 98,000 deaths occur annually because of medical errors.[32] The report put the magnitude of the problem in the context of other comparable concerns by noting that more people die from medical errors in a year than motor vehicle accidents or breast cancer and that medication errors alone kill more people than workplace injuries.

Errors are defined as "the failure to complete a planned action as intended or the use of a wrong to achieve an aim."[31] Those errors may be attributed to failures in diagnostic, treatment, or surgical procedures; selection or doses of medication; delays in diagnosis or treatment; and a host of other procedural lapses, including communication or equipment failures.

There is general agreement that system deficiencies are the most important factor in the problem and not incompetent or negligent physicians and other caregivers. Modern medicine with its highly effective but extremely complex diagnostic and therapeutic methods can be formidably risky. Extensive surgical procedures are error prone, as are increasingly powerful therapeutic drugs. Miscommunication among overstressed employees is common in busy hospitals. With so many steps and so many people involved in the care of hospital patients, the potential for error grows with every patient day, and small lapses develop into large tragedies.[32]

The IOM report presents a series of recommendations to improve the quality of care during the next 10 years. The report lays out a comprehensive strategy for reducing medical errors through a combination of technologic, policy, regulatory, and financial strategies intended to make health care safer. Better use of information technology such as bedside computers, avoidance of similar-sounding and look-alike names and packages of medications, and standardization of treatment policies and protocols would help to avoid confusion and reliance on memory and handwritten communications. The most controversial of the recommendations, however, is the call for a nationwide mandatory reporting system that would require states to report all "adverse events that result in death or serious harm" (p. 75).[32]

The health care system and its practicing physicians need to make radical changes in cultural attitudes and individual prerogatives, however, before the necessary system changes and reporting requirements can be institutionalized. The IOM report, which moved awareness of the magnitude of medical errors from the anonymity of the hospitals to the nation's media and subsequently to the halls of Congress, has already produced vociferous debate over issues of mandatory or voluntary reporting. Questions of liability, confidentiality, and avoidance of punishment must be settled before any reporting legislation can be passed. In the meantime, other recommendations for more focus on patient safety by professional groups, medical societies, health care licensing organizations, and hospital administrations could be followed with more immediate benefits.

Shortage of Nurses Created Staffing Crisis

Three factors combined to drive a hospital nursing shortage to crisis proportions. First, increasing dissatisfaction with staffing reductions, overwork, and too little time to maintain the quality of patient care drove nurses out of hospitals into early retirement or into home or ambulatory care. Second, with the heavy work responsibilities of nursing as a career and many other more attractive options, fewer young people were entering that clinical field. Last, aging of the current nurse workforce accelerated staffing losses. With one-third of the employed nurses over 50 years of age, only an increasing pool of new nurses entering the pipeline could rescue hospital nursing from its critical shortage.[33]

The consequences are serious. There is increasing evidence that nurse staffing is related to patient outcomes in both medical and surgical cases. Studies indicate a direct link between the number of registered nurses and the time they spend with patients and the number of serious complications and patient deaths. Low nurse staffing increases the likelihood that some patients will suffer pneumonia, shock and cardiac arrest, and gastrointestinal bleeding, and some patients will die as a result.[34]

Although the nursing shortage is far from over, the situation has improved. In the last few years pay increases, relatively high national unemployment rates, and private initiatives aimed at encouraging men and women to become nurses have resulted in employment growth among registered nurses. The influx of foreign-born registered nurses and the return to nursing of older women accounted for a large share of the increase in nurse employment. Unfortunately, faculty shortages in schools of nursing have limited class size even when applications have increased.[35]

Current Research Efforts in Quality Improvement

After The Joint Commission recognized the development of multi-institutional hospital networks, it produced a new and quantitatively measurable definition of quality with a results focus. The new definition characterizes the quality of a provider's care as the degree to which the care delivered increases the likelihood of desired patient outcomes and reduces the likelihood of undesired outcomes, given the current state of medical knowledge.

This objective and quantitative definition of quality contrasted sharply with the previous subjective and qualitative definition that required estimates of adherence to somewhat nebulous performance standards. It also left room for nonclinical outcomes, such as accessibility (the ease with which patients can avail themselves of services) and acceptability (the degree to which health care satisfies patients).

Hospitals now conduct regular patient satisfaction studies to obtain patients' views about the services they receive. Such studies encompass several aspects of care, including access, convenience, information received, financial coverage, and perceived quality. It is particularly important for hospital executives to monitor how well their patients' comfort and communication needs were met. Patient satisfaction studies add a new dimension to the definition of quality. "Quality" becomes what the patient receives as judged by the patient rather than what the facility provides as judged by the providers.

Closely related to the cost and quality dilemma associated with high technology was the problem that some patients received too many procedures, tests, and/or medications that were inappropriate, useless, or even harmful. Although some of those procedures were probably performed to protect the physician or hospital from potential malpractice litigation, some reflected unexplainable regional variations in medical practice, and some were clearly driven by the reimbursement system at the time that rewarded physicians for doing more, not less.

A large number of studies examined the appropriateness of the use of various medical tests and procedures. Using similar methods, researchers compared medical records against well-established criteria for performing specific medical procedures. Those procedures were then rated as performed for "appropriate," "inappropriate," or "equivocal" reasons. The RAND Corporation summarized the findings of a number of RAND-supported research studies, as shown in Figure 3-1.[36]

Overall, it appears that a significant proportion of hospital procedures is performed for inappropriate reasons. The proportion of all procedures judged to be questionable or equivocal also shows wide-ranging variation. "On average, it appears that one-third or more of all procedures performed in the United States are of questionable benefit" (p. 3).[32]

Hospitals That Join Newest Quality Initiative Save Lives

For several years after the IOM's shocking report about the number of deaths caused by hospital errors, Dr. Donald Berwick, a Harvard professor and president of the nonprofit Institute for Healthcare Improvement, challenged hospitals to improve their quality of care and save lives. By June 2006 over 3,100 hospitals had signed on to his "100,000 Lives Campaign." They agreed to implement six types of changes designed to prevent lethal mistakes. The changes were aimed at preventing medication errors, preventing hospital-acquired infections, deploying rapid-response teams to cope with emergency situations, and the like. Although all participating hospitals did not initiate all six changes, after 18 months Dr. Berwick estimated that about 122,300 patient lives were saved.[37]

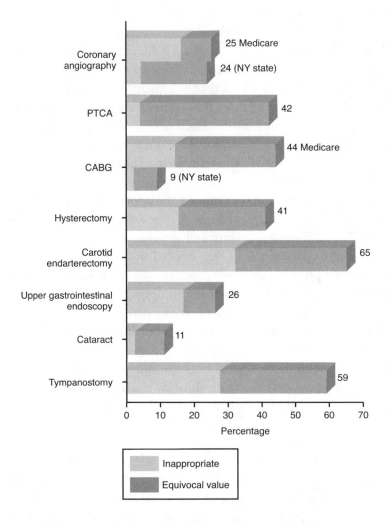

FIGURE 3-1 Proportion of Procedures Judged Either "Clinically Inappropriate" or "Of Equivocal Value": Summary of Selected Studies. *Source:* Reprinted with permission from: Rand Health Research Highlights, "Assessing the Appropriateness of Care: How Much is Too Much?" RB-4522, © RAND.

Responsibility of Governing Boards for Quality of Care

Although the medical staffs and other professional providers of patient care in hospitals make the decisions and carry out the procedures that lead to the patient care outcomes, it is the governing boards of hospitals that are ultimately responsible for the quality of the care provided. The board is responsible for the hospital's quality assurance and risk management programs, all quality-improvement programs, and the oversight of the medical staff. The latter responsibility is discharged primarily through its oversight of and final decisions regarding appointments and privilege delineations of medical staff members. Otherwise, oversight of the medical staff is delegated to the various committees of the medical staff organization.

The board oversees the hospital's quality assurance programs and related functions by monitoring specific information regarding program effectiveness in the identification and resolution of patient care problems and of the medical staff in quality assurance. Some of the indicators that hospital boards regularly review are as follows:

- Mortality rates by department or service
- Hospital-acquired infections
- Patient complaints
- Patient falls
- Adverse drug reactions
- Unplanned returns to surgery
- Hospital-incurred traumas

Needless to say, only the most diligent and dedicated lay board members are capable of interpreting these data and then formulating clear and understandable explanations for their occurrence. Health care reforms are intended to address these problems specifically.

Hospitalists: A Rapidly Growing Innovation

As discussed in more detail in Chapter 5, physicians called "hospitalists" are rapidly taking over the care of inpatients in U.S. hospitals. Hospitalists, usually internists by training, assume responsibility for the care of inpatients from admission to discharge. They substitute for the patient's primary physician for the period of the hospital stay and provide and/or coordinate all patient care by staff and specialists. Because hospitalists are based in the hospitals, they are able to provide more responsive and continuous care than patients' primary physicians, whose hospital visits are brief and less frequent.

Because it is generally accepted that the presence of hospitalists shortens lengths of stay, improves the continuity and quality of hospital care, and has economic advantages to hospitals, hospitalist medicine is rapidly becoming the preferred model of inpatient care.[38]

Forces of Reform: Cost, Quality, and Access

The performance benchmarks of cost, quality, and access that, with few exceptions, hospitals addressed for decades with moderate enthusiasm and little, if any, effect have now become the survival criteria for the future. Because the scientific breakthroughs and technology advancements have made hospitals the complex institutions they have become, hospital care has been both admired for its diagnostic and therapeutic accomplishments and criticized for its costly inefficiencies, duplications, and inequities in access and quality. Ironically, the same high technology that contributed so much to hospitals' medical achievements also has been used to reveal their performance shortcomings in uncompromising detail. The sophisticated computerized clinical information systems that supported the research that focused on the cost effectiveness or outcomes of expensive medical interventions have increasingly documented and given public recognition of system deficiencies. Studies similar to that of the IOM,[39] which took 2 years of reviewing scientific articles, conducting hearings, and making site visits at health care institutions, came to the conclusion that the poor quality of health care is a major problem in the United States. Citing widespread overuse of expensive technologies, underuse of inexpensive "caring" services, and error-prone application of health care services, these studies concluded that the system deficiencies not only wasted money but also actually harmed patients.[40]

The public debate over the escalating costs of health care and the need for major health care reforms have raised the level of awareness of most Americans. Whatever the final form of U.S. health care after the industry-wide reformation takes place, there is general agreement that hospitals will no longer be the axis on which the rest of the system turns. Reduced in both capacity and importance, hospitals will simply be essential components of community-based and integrated systems of primary, tertiary, long-term, and home health care with significant public health and disease prevention functions.

There will be great variation in the capability of America's thousands of hospitals to adjust to what they will interpret as radical reversals of form and function. In the new hospital market economy, however, it appears likely that the Darwinian law of nature, survival of the fittest, will determine which hospitals remain to serve the American public in the 21st century.

References

1. Stevens R. *In Sickness and in Wealth: American Hospitals in the Twentieth Century*. New York: Basic Books; 1989.
2. Teisberg EO, Vayle EJ. *The Hospital Sector in 1992*. Boston: Harvard Business School; 1991.
3. Fast Facts on U.S. Hospitals. Available from http://www.aha.org/aha/resource-center/Statistics-and-Studies/fast-facts.html. Accessed December 8, 2009.
4. Rohr R. The paradox of specialty hospitals, hospitalist leadership. Available from http://www.HCPRO.com. Accessed December 8, 2009.
5. Greenwald L, Cromwell J, Adamache W, et al. Specialty versus community hospitals: referrals, quality, and community benefits. *Health Affairs*. 2006;25:106–118.
6. Bellandi D. Spinoffs, big deals dominate in '99. *Modern Healthcare*. 2000;30:36.
7. Facts About the Department of Veterans Affairs. Available from http://www.va.gov/about_va/. Accessed December 10, 2009.
8. Gilles RR, Shortell SM, Young GJ, et al. Best practices in managed organized delivery systems. *Hosp Health Serv Admin*. 1997;42:299–321.
9. Peake JB. Beyond the Purple Heart: continuity of care for the wounded in Iraq. *N Engl J Med*. 2005;352:219–222.
10. Panel on problems at Walter Reed issues strong rebuke. *New York Times*. April 12, 2007:A-11.
11. Bogdanich W. At V.A. hospital, a rogue cancer unit. *New York Times*. June 21, 2009:A1, A22.
12. Healthcare IT. Healthcare Providers. Available from http://www.himssanalytics.org/hc_providers/index.asp. Accessed November 18, 2009.
13. Ewing T, Cusick D. Knowing what to measure. *Health Financ Manage*. 2004;58:60–63.
14. Wang SJ, Middleton B, Prosser LA, et al. A cost-benefit analysis of electronic medical records in primary care. *Am J Med*. 2003;114:397–403.
15. Shmitt KF, Wofford DA. Financial analysis projects clear returns from electronic medical records. *Health Financ Manage*. 2002;56:52–57.

16. Manchemi N, Brooks RG. Reviewing the benefits of electronic health records and associated patient safety technologies. *J Med Syst.* 2006;30: 159–168.
17. Sandrick K. Calculating ROI for CPRs. *Health Manage Technol.* 1998;19:16.
18. White SV. Interview of David Brailer. *J Healthc Qual.* 2004;26:20–24.
19. U.S. Department of Health and Human Services. Health IT home. Available from http://healthit.hhs.gov/. Accessed January 6, 2009.
20. U.S. Department of Commerce. *County Business Patterns, 1997.* Washington, DC: U.S. Government Printing Office.
21. Faulkner M, Anyard B. Is the hospital sick role a barrier to patient participation? *Nursing Times.* 2002:35–36.
22. Anders G. Hospitals rush to remodel to offer subacute care—and get paid twice. *Wall Street Journal.* October 3, 1996:A1, A8.
23. Shortell SM. *The Future of Hospitals and Health Care Management.* Washington, DC: VA Office of Research and Development; 1996.
24. Delbanco TL, Stokes DM, Cleary PD, et al. Medical patients' assessments of their care during hospitalization: insights for internists. *J Gen Intern Med.* 1995;10:679–685.
25. Gerteis M, Leviton SE, Daily J, et al. *Through the Patient's Eyes: Understanding and Promoting Patient-Centered Care.* San Francisco: Jossey-Bass; 1993.
26. Sunshine L, Wright JW. *The Best Hospitals in America.* New York: Henry Holt and Company; 1987.
27. Rundle RL. We hope you enjoy your stay. *Wall Street Journal.* November 22, 2004:R5.
28. Kropf R. Planning for health services. In: Kovner AR, Ed. *Health Care Delivery in the United States.* New York: Springer; 1995:353.
29. Donabedian A. Evaluating the quality of medical care. *Millbank Mem Fund Q.* 1966;44:166–206.
30. Wennberg JE, Gittlesohn A. Small area variation in health care delivery. *Science.* 1973;182:1102–1108.
31. The Leapfrog Group. The Leapfrog Incentive and Reward Compendium. Available from http://www.leapfroggroup.org/. Accessed January 5, 2005.
32. Kohn LT, Corrigan JM, Donaldson MS, et al. *To Err Is Human: Building a Safer Health System.* Washington, DC: Institute of Medicine; 1999.
33. Dworkin RW. Where have all the nurses gone? *Public Interest.* 2002: 23–36.
34. Needleman J, Buerhaus PI, Stewart M, et al. Nurse staffing in hospitals: is there a business case for quality. *Health Affairs.* 2006;25:204–211.
35. Buerhaus PI, Staiger DO, Averbach DI, et al. Trends: new signs of a strengthening U.S. nurse labor market? *Health Affairs.* 2004;10.1377/ hlthaff.w4.526. Available from http://www.healthaffairs.org. Accessed October 9, 2009.
36. RAND Health Research Highlights. *Assessing the Appropriateness of Care: How Much Is Too Much?* Santa Monica, CA: Rand Corporation; 1998.

37. Hospital initiative to cut errors finds about 122,300 lives were saved. *Wall Street Journal.* June 15, 2006:D6.

38. Glabman M. *Hospitalists: The Next Big Thing.* American Hospital Association, Center for Healthcare Governance, Trustee. Chicago: Health Forum, Inc.; 2005:7–11.

39. Lohr KN. *Medicare: A Strategy for Quality Assurance,* Vol. I. Washington, DC: National Academy Press; 1990.

40. Palmer RH, Adams ME. Quality improvement/quality assurance taxonomy: a framework. In: Grady ML, Bernstein J, Robinson S., Eds. *Putting Research to Work in Quality Improvement and Quality Assurance.* Washington, DC: U.S. Department of Health and Human Services; 1993:13–37.

CHAPTER 4

Ambulatory Care

This chapter reviews the major elements of ambulatory (outpatient) care. Ambulatory care encompasses a diverse and growing sector of the health care delivery system. Physician services are the chief component; however, hospital outpatient and emergency departments, community health centers, departments of health, and voluntary agencies also contribute important services, particularly for the uninsured and vulnerable populations. Ambulatory surgery is a continuously expanding component of ambulatory care, as new technology allows an increasing number of procedures to be performed safely and economically outside the hospital.

Overview and Trends

Ambulatory care comprises health care services that do not require overnight hospitalization. Ambulatory care is the predominant mode of health care delivery in the United States. Once largely consisting of visits to private physicians' offices and hospital outpatient clinics and emergency departments, ambulatory care today encompasses a broad and expanding array of services.

New medical and diagnostic procedures and technologic advancements allow procedures previously requiring hospitalization to be performed on an outpatient basis. As early as a decade ago, surgical procedures that commonly warranted a hospital stay are now routinely performed on a same-day, ambulatory basis.

In addition to the numerous new diagnostic and treatment tools available in the outpatient setting and the advanced technology that makes outpatient treatment safe and effective, financial mandates also have driven services into the ambulatory arena. Beginning in the 1980s, prospective hospital reimbursement replaced retrospective payment on a national scale through Medicare's initiation of the diagnosis-related group (DRG) payment system. The new payment system provided financial incentives to decrease the duration of inpatient stays and to increase service delivery efficiency. Hospitals responded to the new payment system by shifting procedures and services amenable to outpatient delivery from the more expensive inpatient environment to less expensive and more efficient ambulatory delivery systems.

Both DRGs and increasing pressures from health care purchasers to control costs contributed to the rapid expansion of health maintenance organizations and other forms of managed care. With an emphasis on providing services in the least expensive, most effective manner possible, managed care organizations exerted a powerful influence that compelled a shift toward the appropriate use of ambulatory services to replace more expensive inpatient care.

Ambulatory care capacity has expanded in both the hospital-based and non–hospital-based, or "freestanding," settings. Historically, hospitals operated virtually all ambulatory or outpatient clinics within the hospital's main facilities or in contiguous facilities on the hospital campuses. Many hospitals still operate clinic services on site, and many have retained ambulatory surgical services within the main facility in response to community need, physician demand, and teaching activity. The conversion of underused inpatient units also provided a cost-effective means for hospitals to accommodate the shift to ambulatory surgical services and other ambulatory procedures within the hospital.

Beginning in the 1980s, hospitals expanded their service networks to include geographically distributed freestanding facilities throughout their service areas, both for routine diagnosis and treatment and for ambulatory surgical services. In addition to cost considerations, two other factors influenced this trend for hospitals. First, the 1980s and 1990s saw increased consumer demand for conveniently located, easily accessible facilities and services, two factors frequently lacking on hospital campuses. This is particularly true for large teaching hospitals, which are often located in congested urban centers and are perceived as inconvenient by patients. Second, with the growing concerns of inner-city hospitals about competition with other institutions for market share of profitable outpatient services and referrals for inpatient care, hospitals recognized the need to expand their service distribution network to larger segments of the community by establishing conveniently located facilities. Hospitals also recognized that some ambulatory services, such as surgery, could be operated most efficiently off site and be removed from the scheduling complexities and other requirements of a system that must accommodate a vast array of physician and patient needs.

Independent of hospital organizations, for-profit corporations' freestanding facilities providing ambulatory, primary, specialty, and surgical services have proliferated. In addition to profitability and cost-control features attractive to insurers, responsiveness to consumer preferences was also a primary driver in these developments.

The decade of the 1990s saw a continuing upward trend in the total number of ambulatory care facilities owned and operated by hospitals, physicians, and independent chains. Services provided by these facilities are diverse and represent a response to population demographics in their respective service areas as well as reimbursement opportunities. A partial listing of the array of ambulatory care facilities includes cancer treatment, diagnostic imaging of many different types, renal dialysis, pain management, physical therapy, cardiac and other types of rehabilitation, outpatient surgery, occupational health, women's health, and wound care.

A significant corollary to developments in ambulatory care delivery for hospital-operated and independent organizations has been the entry of physicians into the business of outpatient diagnostic, treatment, and surgical services previously available to their practices in only the hospital setting. The same factors operative in the larger industry—technologic advances making the purchase, maintenance, and operation of the required equipment feasible and cost effective in freestanding facilities; consumer demand for convenient, user-friendly environments; and profitability—have compelled this development.

Physician involvement in this arena has paralleled that of hospitals in practice areas, such as ophthalmologic surgery for lens replacement and laser therapy, certain types of gynecologic surgery, fiber-optic gastrointestinal diagnosis, chemotherapy, renal dialysis, computed tomography, magnetic resonance imaging, and more. The implications of this trend for hospitals' business volume and revenue have been significant as physicians and hospitals emerge as competitors engaged in the same lines of business. These developments are permanently, and in the view of some, negatively altering the long-standing relationships between physicians and their affiliated hospitals.[1–3]

The ambulatory care delivery system is changing and growing rapidly as its various organization models evolve, including new efforts to measure quality relative to costs. The service constellation also is growing rapidly and becoming more diverse. As the reimbursement system continues to evolve and new treatment modalities are developed, ambulatory service provider roles continue to refine. Numerous service delivery hybrids continue to develop in the ambulatory care arena. This chapter provides a framework for understanding the origins, development, and future direction of this important sector of the health care delivery system that continues on the growth trajectory illustrated by Figures 4-1 and 4-2.[4]

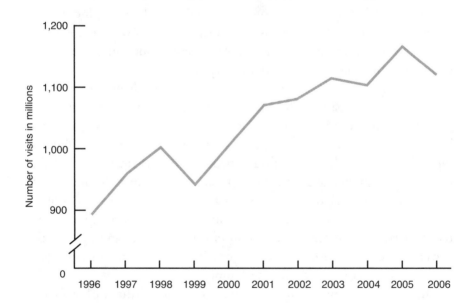

FIGURE 4-1 Number of Outpatient Visits in Millions, 1996-2006.
Sources: CDC/NCHS, National Ambulatory Medical Care Survey; National Health Statistics Reports, No. 8, August 6, 2008.

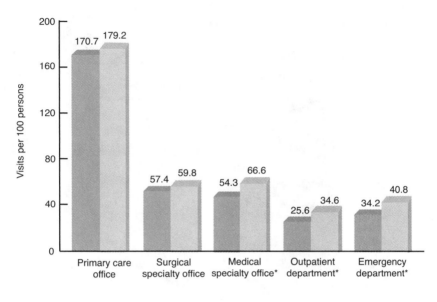

*Significant change (p < 0.05).

FIGURE 4-2 Age-adjusted Ambulatory Care Visit Rates by Setting: United States, 1996 and 2006.
Source: CDC/NCHS, National Ambulatory Medical Care Survey and National Hospital Ambulatory Medical Care Survey; National Health Statistics Reports, No. 8, August 6, 2006.

Private Medical Office Practice

It is common to think of ambulatory services organized and delivered under some institutional aegis, such as a hospital or the community-based clinics of public health departments; however, private physician office practices constitute the predominant mode of ambulatory care in the United States. In 2006, the most recent year for which data are available, the National Center for Health Statistics estimates that patients made 902 million visits to physician offices: 526 million to primary care physicians, 198 million to medical specialists, and 178 million to surgical specialists.[5] Figure 4-3 provides a snapshot of physician office visits by specialty. Over one-fourth of office visits used electronic medical records. Claims for payment were submitted electronically at 85.5% of visits. [5]

The way physicians organize and operate their private practices has evolved from a variety of factors. The single most significant development

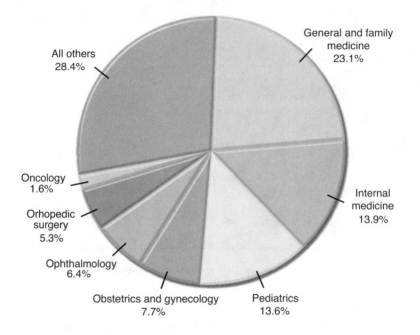

FIGURE 4-3 Percent Distribution of Office Visits by Physician Specialty: United States, 2006.
Sources: CDC/NCHS, National Ambulatory Medical Care Survey, 2006.

has been a continuing increase in the number of group practice arrangements and their size. An increasing number of physicians are partners or salaried employees of group practices.[6]

The origins of group practice can be traced to the Mayo Clinic in the late 19th century. The Mayo Clinic group practice generated considerable controversy among physicians. A 1932 report by the Committee on the Costs of Medical Care endorsed organized group practices and the use of insurance payments. The American Medical Association (AMA) condemned the report, declaring that group and salaried physicians were unethical. The controversy erupted into a legal battle when Group Health Insurance was organized in Washington, DC, in 1937. The AMA informed physicians that the plan was unethical and expelled all Group Health Insurance–salaried physicians. Hospitals received lists of "reputable physicians." "The Washington, DC Medical Society and the AMA were subsequently indicted, found guilty, and fined for having conspired to monopolize medical practice."[7] Around the country local medical societies lost attempts to obstruct the formation of group practices. For the next few decades negative confrontations occurred as physicians sought participation in developing group health plans. Participating physicians were socially ostracized and denied hospital privileges. By the 1950s, because of effective legal challenges against organized medicine and a physician shortage, opposition to group practice subsided.

Before 1950, most physicians operated solo practices. Since then, rising specialization, changing economics, and the desire for more control over their lifestyles caused physicians to group together, either in single fields, such as primary care, or into multispecialty groups. Group practice involves several physicians practicing together in some type of coordinated arrangement. In contrast to an individual physician, fee-for-service payment basis, most groups pay their members a salary augmented with a percentage of practice net profits.

The old solo-practice model made the physician responsible for his or her entire patient caseload 24 hours a day, every day of the year. Before the proliferation of specialties, these physicians normally provided all medical care required by their patients, with the exception of surgery or occasional consultation. The demands on their time and stamina were enormous. Aside from occasional coverage arrangements with a colleague to allow for brief time off, their schedules were relentless and unpredictable.

Beginning in the 1960s, several factors influenced a major shift from the solo mode of private practice to group practice. Social movements in the United States produced a heightened awareness of lifestyle adaptations that allowed healthy accommodation for personal growth and balance between professional and personal responsibilities. In the same period, medical specialization burgeoned as the growth in medical knowledge and technologic advances increased exponentially. Rapidly advancing knowledge in every field of medicine and the resulting specialization created new challenges for the solo generalist and the specialist. Most obvious were increasing demands on physicians to maintain a command of a body of knowledge that was continuously yielding new diagnostic and therapeutic breakthroughs in virtually every field of practice.

The introduction of Medicare reimbursement in 1966 dramatically altered the private medical office and its financial, billing, and reimbursement processes. Before the government's entry into financing private practice services, physician reimbursement came from largely two sources: personal patient payments or third-party private insurance. Blue Cross/Blue Shield and a relatively small number of other private indemnity carriers comprised most of the third-party payments. Billing and collection were relatively simple. When Medicare began providing primary coverage for everyone over the age of 65 years, private physicians' offices found themselves dealing with a new insurance carrier and a vast array of new government regulations and fee schedules. In addition, many Medicare recipients also carried supplemental private insurance contracts to reimburse the balance that Medicare did not cover. For the private physician's office the regulation, complexity, and volume of billing requirements burgeoned. Solo-practice office administration, once the province of the physicians themselves, with possibly a receptionist and bookkeeper, now required an increased level of sophistication and a great deal more time.

Other factors also influenced the shift to group practice. Malpractice insurance costs began to rise dramatically in the 1970s. Inflation fueled rising office lease and rental expenses. The need for more sophisticated administrative support services increased with advancing technology and more complex billing and record-keeping requirements. As technology advanced and diagnostic equipment became available for in-office use, groups could benefit from sharing equipment acquisition costs and ensuring the volume necessary to justify ongoing staffing and maintenance. Physicians recognized that group practice could provide other economies of scale through shared administrative overhead.

Group practice evolved in two forms. One consisted of groups of physicians in the same discipline, usually primary care, surgery, obstetrics, or pediatrics. The other form was multidisciplinary specialty practices, usually including primary care physicians in collaboration with several major specialties or subspecialties. There were important features that both generalist and specialist physicians found more attractive in group practice than solo practice. First, although typically each physician carried his or her own caseload of patients, physicians could arrange a routine, preplanned schedule of after-hours call and weekend and vacation coverage. Another attractive dimension of group practice was that it provided a professionally supportive environment.

With the continuing growth of medical information and knowledge required to maintain state-of-the-art competencies and an ever-expanding range of diagnostic and therapeutic alternatives available, group practice enables physicians to access each other's knowledge and experience in an informal consultative environment. This interchange of information not only provided professional support but also introduced an informal system of peer review to each physician's practice, which, in theory, could contribute to patient care quality. Group practice also enabled patient orientation to alternative coverage arrangements, and thus, their expectation of seeing or contacting another physician in the absence of their own could be established in advance.

Multispecialty group practices evolved for many of the same reasons as single-specialty groups. For specialists a major benefit was that group membership reduced reliance on patient referrals from other community physicians because economic incentives made keeping the business inside the group beneficial to all members. Patients also benefited by having diagnosis, treatment, and consultation services available at one location. The arrangement also facilitated communication and coordination of results and findings and sped up the turnaround of information.

Surgical group practices evolved similarly to those in the general and other specialty medical fields for similar reasons; however, surgeons have tended to avoid multispecialty grouping. Instead, most are either general surgeons or specialists in such areas as gastrointestinal, cardiothoracic, vascular, or orthopedic surgery. Economies of scale afford the same advantages in these practices as those in general medical and multispecialty practices with respect to sharing operating costs. Today, nearly one-third of physicians work in solo or 2-physician practices, 15% work in groups of 3 to 5 physicians, and 19% work in practices of 6 to 50 physicians.[8] Approximately 20% of medical practices with three or more physicians contains about one-half of all office-based physicians.[9]

Currently, 87.6% of physicians contract with managed care organizations and almost 70% of physicians indicate that they have five or more managed care contracts.[8] On average, approximately one-half of all physicians' practice revenue derives from public sources, with about 31% from Medicare and 17% from Medicaid.[8]

Patient-Centered Medical Home

The patient-centered medical home (PCMH) "is a team-based model of care led by a personal physician who provides continuous and coordinated care throughout a patient's lifetime to maximize health outcomes. The PCMH practice is responsible for providing all of a patient's health care needs or appropriately arranging care with other qualified professionals. This includes the provision of preventive services, treatment of acute and chronic illness, and assistance with end-of-life issues."[10] The PCMH applies to all ages of patients with a distinctive orientation toward individual patients' partnership with the provider team, in all aspects of their care. The model recognizes that the current reimbursement system fails to meaningfully address multiple patient needs and provider demands for a comprehensive, coordinated, and integrated approach to managing all aspects of an individual's health. As such, the PCMH embodies recommendations for major reimbursement reforms that compensate physicians for the time required to provide and arrange for the holistic care necessary to meet the full spectrum of patient needs. As described in "Joint Principles of the Patient-Centered Medical Home" by the American Academy of Family Physicians, American Academy of Pediatrics, American College of Physicians, and American Osteopathic Association, the PCMH embodies seven principles, summarized below[11]:

1. Every patient has an ongoing relationship with a personal physician trained to provide first-contact, continuous care.
2. The personal physician leads a team of individuals in the practice who take responsibility for the ongoing care of patients.
3. The personal physician is responsible to provide for all the patient's health care needs or takes responsibility for appropriately arranging care with other qualified professionals, including acute care, chronic care, preventive services, and end-of-life care.
4. Care is coordinated and/or integrated across all elements of the complex health care system (subspecialty, hospital, home, nursing home) and is facilitated by transferable electronic registries to ensure patients get care where and when they need it.
5. Quality and safety are hallmarks: Physicians create care plans with their patients, engage in voluntary quality improvement activities, and use information technology to support optimal care; patients actively engage in decision making, and physicians seek feedback to ensure that expectations are being met; and practices voluntarily obtain recognition by a nongovernment entity to demonstrate

capabilities to provide patient-centered services consistent with the medical home model.

6. Enhanced patient access includes open scheduling, expanded hours, and new options for communication between practice staff and patients (e.g., e-mail).

7. Payment for services recognizes the added value provided to patients in the PCMH and includes reimbursement for time required by physicians and other team members for face-to-face and other types of interactions with patients, care coordination, follow-up, documentation, and other responsibilities central to holistic health care for every patient.

The PCMH model is not new; it was described in 1967 by the American Academy of Pediatrics and in 2004 by the American College of Physicians and the American Academy of Family Physicians.[12] However, in the past few years with increasing, broad-based recognition of the health care delivery systems' stark inadequacies of care continuity, safety, and quality and increasing pressures on all providers to reduce costs and waste, the model has gained widespread support from physicians, health plans, government payers, and corporate purchasers of health insurance and consumer advocates. The model presently has formal support from all major primary physician groups and 18 additional physician organizations.[13] In 2006, the Patient-Centered Primary Care Collaborative was created to advocate for improvement in the primary care delivery model and now consists of over 260 members, including patient advocate groups, a number of large national employers, most of the nation's primary care physician associations, health benefits companies, trade associations, academic centers, and health care quality improvement associations.[13] Several pilot and demonstration projects testing the quality and efficiency of the PCMH model are currently underway or planned, supported by private foundations and the Centers for Medicare & Medicaid Services.[14]

Although assessments of the success of the PCMH await further study and analyses, a preliminary review of four primary care sites reported in 2009 is encouraging. Results in applying the model in the four practices revealed annual average per capita out-of-pocket and combined payer spending 15% below their regional peers, and scores on publicly released or payer-collected quality and patient experience measures equaled or exceeded average regional scores.[15]

Other Ambulatory Care Practitioners

In addition to physicians, a number of other licensed health care professionals conduct practices in ambulatory settings. Among the most common are dentists, podiatrists, social workers, psychologists, physical therapists, and optometrists. Like physicians, they may practice singly or in single-specialty or multispecialty groups. For example, there are general solo-practice dentists and multispecialty dental groups who provide general preventive and curative services, as well as services in specialties such as periodontics and orthodontics. Likewise, psychologists in a group may include both generalists and specialists in forensic, child, and other types of psychological interventions. Chapter 6 discusses other ambulatory care practitioners in detail.

Ambulatory Care Services of Hospitals: History and Trends

Acute-care voluntary hospitals have operated outpatient clinics since the 19th century. The early ones were located predominantly in urban centers whose indigent populations lacked access to private medical care. At that time the provision of outpatient services was largely a function of government-sponsored public hospitals. With the proliferation of the voluntary not-for-profit hospitals beginning in the early 20th century, outpatient clinics provided a means for those hospitals to fulfill part of their charitable mission by serving low-income populations who had little, if any, access to private physicians. Hospital outpatient clinics also provided a teaching setting for university-affiliated hospitals, which trained physicians as part of their community mission.

Historically, hospital outpatient clinics were a low-status component of the constellation of hospital care. J. H. Knowles, who was then director of the Massachusetts General Hospital, wrote in 1965, "Turning to the outpatient department of the urban hospital, we find the stepchild of the institution. Traditionally, this has been the least popular area in which to work, and as a result, few advances in medical care and teaching have been harvested here for the benefit of the community."[16] Because they cared for a low-income population, hospital outpatient clinics addressed complex medical and social problems, poor compliance with treatment, and discontinuity in care. Hospitals did not support the outpatient clinics with equipment and staff. Medical students and hospital-affiliated physicians of lowest rank, who agreed to see clinic patients in return for admitting privileges, staffed the clinics.

Today, hospital outpatient clinics in urban and rural areas still function as the community's safety net for the medically needy population; however, the status of those services within the hospital and the roles and positions of physicians working in them have changed radically. The change has been most dramatic since the early 1980s when an array of factors converged to increase both the volume and scope of available hospital outpatient services. Far from the stepchild image characterized by Knowles, hospitals view outpatient clinical services as helping to ensure a source of inpatient admissions and generating revenue from the use of hospital ancillary services.

No longer the repository for reluctant physicians and students obligated to work there, now hospital outpatient clinics are organized along the lines of private physician group practices and are aesthetically pleasant, well equipped, and customer oriented. With respect to the hospitals' financial picture, the direction is clear. In 1980 outpatient services revenue constituted only 13% of total voluntary hospital revenues in the United States.[17] This figure has continued to rise over succeeding decades, with the outpatient share of total hospital revenue currently ranging between 30% and 45% depending on hospital type and size.[18]

Because clinic services traditionally were organized both for the social goal of caring for the needy and for providing teaching and research opportunities, they have tended to be organized by human organ systems and the diseases affecting them. For example, medical clinics, in addition to general medicine, might include clinics for dermatology (skin), cardiology (heart), gastroenterology (digestive tract), rheumatology (bone and connective tissue), and other specialties. In addition to general surgery, surgical clinics might include such specialties as orthopedics (bone), vascular (circulatory system), and others. This type of organization was attractive to attending specialists, researchers, and educators because it allowed narrowly focused concentration on particular patient complaints and illnesses. Beyond this benefit, however, the complex interactions among physicians and patients inherent in this anatomic organization of services have both positive and negative implications for both.

For patients, specialty clinics provide a specialized approach to diagnosis and treatment by physicians with interests and training in their conditions.

Also, clinic teaching functions often result in thorough and exhaustive examination and case review for the students' benefit that might not otherwise occur in a nonteaching setting.

Treatment in hospital specialty clinics also has drawbacks for patients. Often, specialty clinics treat patients only on certain days each week or on 2 or 3 days per month, depending on the demand for the service. Patients with multiple conditions may have to visit several specialty clinics, necessitating many return visits at which different physicians see them. Because communication among physicians in different specialty clinics can be uncertain, patients may receive conflicting advice or instruction, may be medicated inappropriately with drugs prescribed by several different specialists, and may "fall through the cracks" when a complaint arises that does not seem to fit the specialty area of one of their providers. Similarly, for the physician this type of categorical treatment environment requires a high degree of initiative to maintain accurate, current information on patients treated by multiple specialists. Such communication challenges among clinical settings are an area ripe for the initiation of electronic health records.

Beginning in the 1950s, as medical specialization continued, additional subdivision of the teaching hospitals' outpatient clinic services was required to support medical training needs, further exacerbating these problems of continuity and coordination of care. The training requirements of medical students and residents, who could be required to rotate through different specialty clinics as often as monthly, created still more rifts in continuity for patients who, in the course of one illness, might be seen by several different practitioners in the same clinic.

Beginning in the early 1980s, several influences began to have an impact on how hospital outpatient clinic services were organized and delivered. One major influence was the adoption of the DRG hospital reimbursement method, which emphasized decreased lengths of stay. For hospitals, an anticipated result was declining inpatient revenues. Another major factor was the growing importance of managed care organizations and their emphasis on the role of primary medical care. These issues also brought a heightened realism to several years of growing concern on the part of medical educators. The uncontrolled proliferation of specialists at the expense of maintaining a balanced supply of general physicians would have to be addressed to respond to payer and rising consumer demands for more cost-effective, efficient, and coordinated care.

Facing declining inpatient revenue, increasing influences of managed care, and shifting medical education emphasis to primary medicine, hospitals initiated reorganization and expansion plans for outpatient clinic services that focused heavily on primary care areas. Teaching hospitals planned jointly with their affiliated medical schools, and nonteaching facilities followed suit to pursue expansion of both the volume and array of outpatient services with primary care as the core. Teaching hospitals also undertook outpatient clinic reorganizations, creating primary care centers under the direction of paid, full-time faculty department heads with administrative, clinical, and teaching oversight responsibility.

Hospitals hired full-time and part-time physicians as employees who, with medical school faculty appointments, undertook ongoing responsibility for day-to-day patient care, teaching, and supervision of students and residents. Primary care physician employees were organized into practice group models along the lines of private group practices. This primary care model provided a rational structure for the general medical care of clinic patients and helped ensure appropriate referrals and coordination of patient care within and among outpatient clinic specialty units.

The group model of outpatient primary care also supported the hospitals' teaching mission by alleviating reliance on voluntary physician staffing of clinic sessions and student supervision responsibilities. Medical students and residents were provided a more supportive and consistent learning environment by continuously interacting with members of the practice group instead of interacting with different mentors over the course of their rotation. Patients benefited from improved coordination of their care and the opportunity to develop a relationship with an individual provider, who functioned as their private attending physician. Although the distribution and organization of most specialty clinic services have not changed appreciably in teaching hospitals, developments in the organization of primary care in hospital-based clinics have made a major contribution to the coordination and appropriate delivery of services to hospital-based outpatient clinic consumers.

Outpatient business continued to expand, and although hospital admissions and lengths of stay decreased, similar reorganizations were undertaken in certain consumer-sensitive service areas. As one example during the 1980s, the upscale, childbearing-age female population was seen as a major consumer group. Hospitals seized an opportunity to attract new business by reorganizing obstetrics and gynecology services.

The old, hospital-based clinics were relabeled with attractive titles such as "Women's Centers," and facilities were renovated, decorated, and equipped to mimic state-of-the-art private medical offices. The purely clinical services were augmented by free or low-cost health information and education services, with emphasis on prevention, wellness, and personal service. Hospitals undertook extensive public relations and media campaigns to attract the privately insured and self-paying population with many initiatives in outpatient clinical areas that appeared to hold promise for new business and enhanced revenue streams.

Although major changes have occurred in the organization and delivery of hospital outpatient clinics over the past 30 years, fiscal and operational challenges remain for hospitals' outpatient clinics. Some have enjoyed considerable success in attracting new patients with private insurance and self-pay capability and have succeeded in achieving a healthier balance in their previously predominant caseload of Medicaid or charity-care patients. Trends in the volume of hospital outpatient clinic caseloads and payment sources will be subjects of interest as the 2010 health care reform legislation is implemented over the next several years.

Hospital Emergency Services

In 2006 U.S. hospitals operated 3,833 hospital emergency departments, 186 fewer than in 1996.[19] During the same 10-year period the annual number of emergency department visits increased by 32%, from 90.3 million to 119.2 million, on average about 227 visits every minute.[19] The increase in emergency department visits is attributed to overall population growth, a decrease in the number of available emergency departments, increases in the numbers of older Americans, constrained capacity in other outpatient settings, and increasing numbers of uninsured.[19]

Approximately 15.4% of patients arrive at emergency departments by ambulance, and about 13% of visits result in hospitalization.[19] Per capita emergency department use is heaviest for infants under 1 year of age; persons 75 years of age and older have the next highest per capita rate of visits.[19] The visit rate by uninsured individuals is approximately 43% higher than the rate of persons with private insurance, reflecting emergency departments' safety net function.[19] The reasons for emergency department visits encompass a broad spectrum, ranging from life-threatening conditions to those treatable in primary care settings. The Centers for Disease Control and Prevention reports that almost half of metropolitan center hospitals routinely experience emergency department crowding and that one-third of hospitals report the need to divert ambulances to other emergency departments because of a lack of capacity.[20–22]

Emergency departments in most hospitals are high-technology facilities staffed by emergency medicine specialists 24 hours a day, 365 days a year. Although designed to care for life-threatening illness or injury, the public increasingly looks to them for medical care that ranges from the unnecessary to the routine. A high proportion of emergency department visits is deemed to be nonurgent (Figure 4-4).[19] One contributing factor to inappropriate emergency department use is patients' self-interpretation of symptoms. Also, when physicians receive after-hours calls or calls regarding potentially serious complaints and it is neither practical nor seems appropriate for the patient to be seen in the private office, physicians may direct patients to the emergency department for immediate care. Physicians may also use the emergency departments to perform certain tests or examinations requiring equipment not available in their offices. Because state and federal regulations require that hospitals turn no

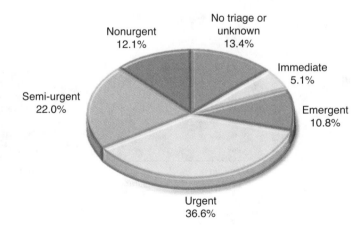

FIGURE 4-4 Percent Distribution of Emergency Department Visits by Immediacy with Which Patients Should Be Seen.
Source: CDC/NCHS, National Ambulatory Medical Care Survey, 2006.

one away, patients know that emergency departments are a guaranteed source of care regardless of their ability to pay or the nature of their complaint. In terms of payment source, Medicaid patients represent the highest emergency department visit rate and privately insured persons the lowest (Figure 4-5).[19]

Over one-third of annual emergency room visits (42.4 million visits) are for injuries, poisoning, and adverse effects of prior medical treatment. The latter include complications of medical and surgical procedures and adverse effects of medication.[19] Approximately 2.5 million visits (2.1%) are made by individuals discharged from the hospital in the previous 7 days.[19]

Emergency departments are organized to treat episodes of serious illness and injury and are therefore not a good choice for routine care. First, care is much more expensive than in an appropriate ambulatory setting because it consumes the time of specialist personnel for conditions in which that level of personnel is unnecessary. Second, waiting times are often long because life-threatening cases appropriately have priority. Third, the emergency department, by its nature, is not organized or staffed to provide follow-up care for routine illnesses. To promote appropriate care for patients who

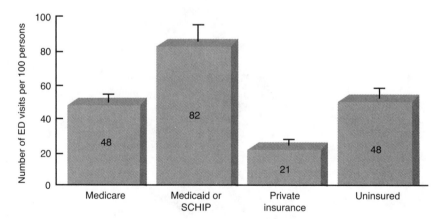

Note: Error bars are 95% confidence intervals. The denominator for each rate is the population total for each type of insurance obtained from the 2006 Nation Health Interview Survey. More than one source of payment may be recorded per visit. SCHIP is State Children's Health Insurance Program.

FIGURE 4-5 Number of Emergency Department Visits per 100 persons by Expected Source of Payment: United States, 2006.
Source: CDC/NCHS National Ambulatory Medical Care Survey, 2006.

inappropriately present at the emergency department, staff will refer them, when possible, to ambulatory primary care services. Initially, managed care organizations attempted to curb inappropriate emergency department use by requiring their members to obtain telephone preauthorization before going to the emergency department and by imposing financial disincentives through copays of emergency department fees when the visit did not result in hospitalization; however, the consumer backlash against such restrictions resulted in most states passing "prudent layperson" legislation, which requires insurance companies to reimburse costs based on care that a reasonable layperson would consider necessary.[23]

Despite the recognition that inappropriate emergency department use drives up costs and results in inadequate continuity of care, many individuals who lack resources to pay for care or are unaware of other sources of care find the emergency department the most accessible source of care when private physicians are unavailable. Until the health care system successfully reduces financial barriers to care and achieves a universal, basic level of access to routine medical care, a large volume of inappropriate emergency department use can be expected to persist.

In the past, like other teaching hospital outpatient clinics, the emergency department was a place of indenture for medical interns or residents who were required to provide coverage as a component of their training. Often, to earn extra income, residents would contract to "moonlight" extra hours for their assigned hospital or for other hospital emergency departments. Nonteaching hospitals also often hired residents on a contracted basis to cover the emergency department or required attending staff to provide rotating coverage.

From both the physicians' and patients' perspective, this staffing configuration was less than ideal. Physicians working in emergency departments under these arrangements often had little training or experience with the illnesses and injuries encountered there. Over the past 20 years, the greatly expanded knowledge, techniques, and equipment available for the care of critically ill and injured patients and concerns about liability resulting from deploying physicians without specific training and experience in emergency care have resulted in dramatic changes in how emergency departments are staffed and organized and services are delivered.

Since 1979, emergency medicine has been recognized as a medical specialty with accompanying requirements for extended specialty training and experience to attain board-certified status, as in the other medical specialty fields.[24] Now, physicians qualified by training and experience in emergency medicine staff most hospital emergency departments. Several corporations employ groups of board-qualified or board-certified emergency medicine physicians and contract their services to hospitals. Medical schools with accredited training programs in emergency medicine may staff their affiliated hospitals' emergency departments as a faculty practice group and provide clinical training for department residents, similar to the organization of other outpatient clinics.

In addition to physicians, emergency departments are staffed by nurses with advanced education and training in the triage and care of critically ill or injured patients. Emergency departments also employ an array of other personnel who provide medical and nursing assistance and clerical support. Depending on the needs of the population served by the hospital, emergency department staff may also include mental health professionals and social workers. On-call arrangements with hospital staff members of other departments or with contracted professionals assist emergency department staff to meet other needs of patients presenting at the emergency department.

Freestanding Services

Non–hospital-based, or freestanding, ambulatory care facilities may be owned and operated by hospitals, hospital systems, or physician groups or by independent, for-profit, or not-for-profit single entities or chains. Many hospital systems, independent entities, and chains operate multiple ambulatory care facilities that provide a wide array of services, including ambulatory surgery, occupational health services, physical rehabilitation, substance abuse treatment, renal dialysis, cancer treatment, diagnostic imaging, cardiovascular diagnosis, sports medicine, and urgent/emergent care. Technology advances, entrepreneurial business opportunities, the drive to reduce costs, and consumer preferences for convenient services continue to advance freestanding services as major components of the health care delivery system.

The diversity of services available in freestanding facilities prevents a comprehensive discussion of their organizational features in this text; however, the following provides an overview of the major types of freestanding facilities that play roles in the rapid expansion of ambulatory care services.

Primary Care Centers

As an outgrowth of many of the same factors that fueled the reorganization, expansion, and enhancement of hospital-based clinic services, freestanding primary care centers proliferated rapidly since the 1980s. For hospitals, the desire to capture new market share, to ensure the flow of inpatient admissions, to bring new volume to ancillary departments such as laboratory and radiology, to enhance revenues, and to improve service delivery efficiency to meet the demands of managed care have all contributed to the move toward off-site facility development. For teaching hospitals these facilities, like hospital-based clinics, continue to play important roles in providing a teaching environment for students and residents in internal medicine, family medicine, obstetrics and gynecology, and pediatrics. Depending on state licensure requirements, they may be operated as extension clinics of the hospital or as hospital-affiliated corporate entities. Increasingly, physicians are investing in development and ownership of freestanding facilities as business opportunities that provide high-quality, practitioner- and patient-friendly sites in which to carry on their practices.

Freestanding primary care facilities approximate the appearance and organization of a private physician's office. Staff physicians may themselves be the owners, or they may be employees of the owner entity. In hospital-operated facilities staff physicians are commonly employees of the owner hospital; in the case of a teaching facility physicians may be jointly compensated through a medical school–affiliated faculty practice group and the hospital.

In addition to primary care physicians, staff may include registered nurses, nurse practitioners, physician assistants, medical office assistants, laboratory personnel, receptionists and clerical support, information technology personnel, social workers, and case management staff. In many ambulatory care facilities, nurse practitioners and physician assistants are the mainstays of the day-to-day operation, providing a broad range of services, including physical assessments, diagnosis, patient histories, education, and counseling. Nurse practitioners, often with specialized training in specific areas such as pediatrics, women's health, geriatrics, and adult medicine, are generally acknowledged as effective in carrying out their responsibilities and are well accepted by patients. Registered nurses, nurse practitioners, and physician assistants also triage patients and counsel and educate patients via phone contact.

Urgent Care Centers

The first urgent care centers opened in the 1970s. The Urgent Care Association of American (UCAOA) describes urgent care center services as "providing walk-in, extended hour access for acute illness and injury care that is either beyond the scope or availability of the typical primary care practice or retail clinic."[25] Urgent care centers may also provide other health care services such as occupational medicine, travel medicine, and sports and school physicals. In most states urgent care centers do not require licensure separate from that of a typical physician office that operates under the physician's license auspices.[25] The UCAOA emphasizes that urgent care centers neither treat the life-threatening emergencies appropriate for hospital emergency departments nor assist with labor and delivery. The UCAOA also distinguishes urgent care centers from in-store retail clinics, in that urgent care centers provide a broader scope of services to a wider age range and use a staffing model of primarily physicians rather than nurse practitioners.[25] (See discussion of retail clinics below.)

The American Academy of Urgent Care Medicine defines this medical discipline as "provision of immediate medical service (no appointment necessary) offering outpatient care for the treatment of acute and chronic illness and injury."[26] The UCAOA estimates there to be more than 8,000 such facilities in the United States providing over 100 million annual visits, with about 100 or more new centers opening each year.[25] The UCAOA reports that 55% of centers are located in suburban communities, 25% in urban areas, and 20% in rural areas.[25] Ownership is diverse, including for-profit corporate chains, single entities, hospitals, private physician groups, and managed care organizations. By operating for extended hours, including evenings, weekends, and holidays, and accepting patients on a walk-in basis, they meet consumer needs for convenient care for episodic illness or injury. Some centers enable patients to register online with a brief medical history in advance to expedite their visit. Physician staff members are usually specialists in internal, family, or emergency medicine.

Established in 1997, the American Board of Urgent Care Medicine offers certification in the field of urgent care medicine to qualified candidates who have successfully completed an Accreditation Council for Graduate Medical Education residency in emergency medicine, family practice, general surgery, internal medicine, obstetrics and gynecology or pediatrics; meet several other requirements for experience in the field and continuing medical education; and pass a certification examination.[27]

In addition to physicians, urgent care centers may employ registered nurses, nurse practitioners, physician assistants, reception, or other support staff and may provide radiology and basic laboratory services. Acceptable payment typically includes all forms of insurance, cash, and credit cards. Individual urgent care centers may be granted certification by the UCAOA upon meeting specific criteria for staffing models, facility equipment, hours of operation, and other requirements.[28]

From the consumer standpoint, urgent care centers fill gaps in the delivery system created by the inflexibility of private physician appointment scheduling and unavailability during nonbusiness hours. The centers provide a much more convenient and user-friendly alternative to a hospital emergency department during hours when private physicians are unavailable. In addition, for individuals who are new to a community and have not had the opportunity to establish a physician relationship, the centers can meet immediate needs in a convenient, economical manner without incurring the long waits and expense of the hospital emergency department. Typically located in highly visible facilities, such as storefronts in commercial areas, they offer valued convenience and ease of accessibility to their consumers. Because they are a less expensive alternative to the hospital emergency department, managed care organizations usually fully reimburse members' use of urgent care facilities when their physicians are not available.

Urgent care centers make clear to patients that they do not provide ongoing care for chronic conditions, although they may be the site where a chronic condition such as diabetes or hypertension is initially diagnosed. If patients do not have a routine source of care, center personnel may encourage them to obtain one and may provide information about area physicians or primary care centers that are accepting new patients to encourage continuity. The UCAOA recommends that "all individuals have a primary care physician and supports the American Academy of Family Physician's concept of a 'medical home.'"[25] To maintain positive relationships with physicians whose patients they have treated, the centers may forward records of treatment to the patients' physicians.

Hospitals have expressed concern that urgent care centers may cull significant numbers of paying patients, leaving to their emergency departments a disproportionate share of the most ill and expensive-to-treat patients. In areas where the centers have proliferated, the private physician community also has voiced concerns about the availability of such facilities affecting patients' motivation to develop a relationship with a primary physician. Nonetheless, the growth in numbers of urgent care centers is a clear indication that consumers perceive them as a positive alternative to the hospital emergency department, and for those without a primary physician's availability, they can meet nonemergency needs in a convenient and consumer-friendly manner.

Retail Clinics

Clinics operated at retail sites such as pharmacies and supermarkets are a rapidly emerging form of ambulatory care. The first retail clinics opened in 2000 in the Minneapolis-St. Paul area in grocery stores.[29] Expanding from approximately 60 retail clinic sites in 2005, there are now approximately 1,000 retail sites managed by more than 40 different clinic operators functioning nationwide.[30] Known by consumer-friendly names, such as "MinuteClinic" and "TakeCare," the clinics operate in CVS pharmacies, Walgreens, Wal-Mart and Target stores, and many other retail locations. The "MinuteClinic," owned by the CVS drugstore chain, accounts for more than half of all clinic sites.[30] Retail clinics represent an entrepreneurial response to consumer demand for fast, affordable treatment of easy-to-diagnose, acute conditions. Market reports in 2009 identify drug stores, retailers, and hospitals as the top operators of retail clinics.[31] Staffed by nurse practitioners or physician assistants, a physician is not required on site, although many clinics have physician consultation available by phone. Patient polls to date indicate a high degree of satisfaction with the availability and use of the clinics.[30]

The clinics' lower cost has captured insurers' attention, particularly as employers require workers to pay larger premium shares and increased copayments and deductibles. Many insurance companies are contracting with retail clinics to allow patients to pay only copays. Some employers are encouraging retail clinic use by waiving the copay entirely.[32] In the start-up phase of retail clinics, payment for services was directly by consumers without insurance company participation, a model avoiding the expense of working with insurers but resulting in higher out-of-pocket consumer expenses than a visit copay for a primary physician visit. Now, approximately 85% of clinic sites accept insurance and copayments; a recent survey noted that 62% of all visits derived some part of payment from an insurance carrier.[30]

Retail clinics' scope of practice is narrower than that of urgent care centers. A 2006 report for the California HealthCare Foundation, "Health Care in the Express Lane: Retail Clinics Go Mainstream," notes there are strategic, practical, and regulatory reasons for the narrow scope.[29] The report cites the strategic importance of maintaining low prices, minimal staffing, rapid patient turnaround, and the use of software to manage a predetermined range of potential diagnoses. Practically, the practice scope is limited to conditions that do not require private spaces for disrobing and that can be diagnosed with simple laboratory procedures that do not fall under state or federal regulatory requirements.

Reactions to the clinics from the organized medical community vary from acceptance of this development as a consumer choice to strong opposition. Primary care physicians have many concerns about quality and continuity of care as well as competition. The American Academy of Family Physicians has the retail clinic phenomenon under continued study and in 2006 issued a list of desirable clinic attributes that include the definition of service scope, evidence-based medicine, a team approach with primary physicians, referral arrangements, and electronic health records. Some physicians concede that retail clinics are filling a need for rapid access that their offices do not offer. A past president of a state medical society noted, "MinuteClinic has exposed an Achilles' heel of office-based practice; there is an access problem. If there were not, care options such as MinuteClinic or similar counterparts would not be venturing in for-profit medicine."[32]

In 2007, the AMA petitioned federal and state regulators to investigate retail clinics for possible conflicts of interest, noting that its petitions were prompted by stores' claims that the clinics increase prescription drug sales and help increase other sales. The AMA alleged potential conflicts of interest on the basis that clinics are not independent of the stores selling the drugs and prescriptions that retail clinics recommend or prescribe. Among other misgivings, "The AMA says retail clinics undermine and disrupt the relationship between patients and their doctors, and make it much harder to decide who is responsible when things go wrong."[33] The AMA also took issue with health insurers allowing retail clinics to waive or lower patient copayments while continuing to require physicians to collect the fees, arguing that this practice may actively influence patients to choose the clinic over a physician visit on the basis of cost rather than quality.[32]

As retail clinics continue proliferating, much more research is required to learn about the quality, profitability, and impacts on the health care delivery system. For the present this growing ambulatory care business is under close observation by employers, insurers, retailers, investors, and the medical and consumer communities. It is clear, however, that retail clinics have moved into the mainstream of primary health care delivery and will likely influence the future primary care delivery system.

Ambulatory Surgery Centers

Ambulatory or outpatient surgery accounted for almost two-thirds of all surgeries performed in 2006.[34] In the decade between 1996 and 2006 the rate of visits to freestanding ambulatory surgery centers (ASCs) increased approximately 300% while the rate in hospital-based centers was flat[34] (Figure 4-6). In 2006 an estimated 53.3 million surgical and nonsurgical procedures were performed during 34.7 million ambulatory surgery visits.[34] Approximately 19.9 million ambulatory surgery visits occurred in hospitals, and 14.9 million occurred in freestanding settings.[34] The National Center for Health Statistics defines ambulatory surgery as "surgical and non-surgical procedures performed on an ambulatory (outpatient) basis in a hospital or free-standing center's general operating rooms, dedicated ambulatory surgery rooms, and other specialized rooms such as endoscopy units and cardiac catheterization labs."[34] Outpatient surgery continues to be a major contributor to the overall growth trend in ambulatory care.

In the 1970s physicians led the development of freestanding ASCs because they saw opportunities created by advancing technology to establish quality and cost-effective alternatives to inpatient surgery. ASCs were physicians' solutions to frustration with in-hospital bureaucracy, operating room schedule difficulties, and patient inconvenience.[28] Today, physicians have ownership of approximately 90% of freestanding ASCs, hospitals have ownership interest in 21% of all ASCs, and 3% are owned entirely by hospitals.[35] Between 2000 and 2007 the number of Medicare-certified ASCs increased at an average annual rate of 7.3%; in 2008 there were approximately 5,149 Medicare-certified ASCs in the United States.[36]

Hospitals responded to the demand for outpatient surgery, faced with competition from physician-run freestanding facilities and insurer demands

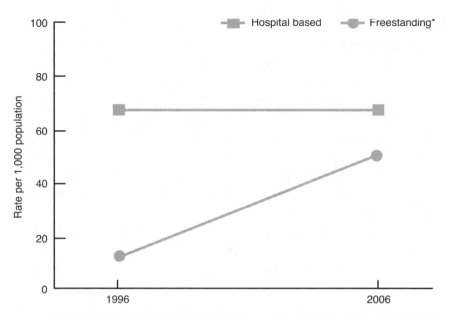

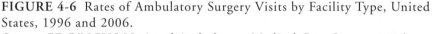

*The rate of ambulatory visits includes ambulatory surgery patients admitted to hospitals as inpatients for both 1996 and 2006. As a result, the data differ from those presented in the 1996 report.

FIGURE 4-6 Rates of Ambulatory Surgery Visits by Facility Type, United States, 1996 and 2006.
Source: CDC/NCHS National Ambulatory Medical Care Survey, 2006.

for lower costs. In 1982 Medicare expanded coverage to include ambulatory surgical procedures, and the Medicare hospital prospective payment system subsequently created strong incentives for hospitals to shift surgery to outpatient settings.[35] Between 1982 and 1992 outpatient surgeries in community hospitals increased over 200%, whereas inpatient procedures declined by more than 32%.[37]

Several advancements in medical technology and changes in payment arrangements were the two primary drivers promoting the increase in ambulatory surgical procedures as alternatives to inpatient surgery. One of the most significant factors was the development of general anesthetics that resolved safely and quickly, enabling patients to return to normal functioning within a few hours. Advancements in surgical equipment and techniques reduced or eliminated the invasiveness of many procedures and their complications and risks. With these and other technologic advances making outpatient surgery increasingly feasible and safe, mounting financial pressures resulted in Medicare, insurance companies, and managed care organizations requiring that certain procedures be performed in the less costly ambulatory setting unless physicians were able to demonstrate the necessity of hospitalization. The initial years of the shift from inpatient to ambulatory surgery provided opportunities for hospitals to convert space into efficient, cost-effective care delivery areas, encouraging the development of separate surgical management systems for ambulatory and complicated cases. Although initially this conversion entailed capital expenditures and staffing additions, well-managed ASCs quickly became profitable.

Freestanding ambulatory surgical facilities owned and operated by hospitals, physicians, or independent entities offer several advantages over the in-hospital services, including enhanced aesthetics, ease of accessibility, and the opportunity to customize the scheduling and organization of service delivery independent of hospital bureaucracy. It is not surprising that they were embraced rapidly by physicians who were freed from the rigors of operating room scheduling, staff, and equipment availability typical in the hospital setting. Patients view freestanding facilities as far more user friendly and responsive to their needs than their hospital-based counterparts, with 98% reporting a high degree of satisfaction with services.[38]

ASCs are among the most highly regulated health care providers. Forty-three states require licensure of ASCs with explicit criteria for licensure approval.[39] Medicare also requires rigorous inspection of ASCs to qualify for reimbursement. Approximately 85% of all ASCs are Medicare approved.[39] Many ambulatory surgery centers also voluntarily submit to accreditation reviews by The Joint Commission, the Accreditation Association for Ambulatory Health Care, the American Association for the Accreditation of Ambulatory Surgery Facilities, or the American Osteopathic Association.[39]

Patient care quality has benefited significantly from improved technology and advanced, less traumatic surgical techniques applied in the ambulatory setting. Patients experience fewer complications, much faster recovery, and less disruption to normal activity from ambulatory than from hospital inpatient surgery. Continuing advances in surgical and anesthetic procedures, postoperative pain management, and other technology provide future opportunities to move even more types of inpatient surgery into the ambulatory setting.

Community Health Centers

Federally funded, community-based primary care centers originated during Lyndon Johnson's presidency in the mid-1960s and represented a facet of that administration's social reform movement labeled the "war on poverty." Originally authorized by the Office of Economic Opportunity, coordinating responsibility was transferred to the Public Health Service in the mid-1970s. Funded under Section 330 of the Public Health Service Act, the organization and staffing patterns of these facilities draw from earlier models of public health services oriented toward the needs of underserved communities.[40] Centers were initially established in cities and in rural communities across the country, and although they differed from each other with respect to size and the scope of available services, they had common characteristics rooted in federal funding requirements, including focus on needs of the underserved, comprehensive primary care, professional staffing, community involvement, and partnerships between the public and private sectors. Subsequent amendments to Section 330 established specialized primary care programs for migrant workers, the homeless, and residents of public housing.[40]

Community health centers are typically staffed by multidisciplinary teams that include physicians, nurses, social workers, nutrition science professionals, and support personnel. The staffing pattern reflects a commitment to a comprehensive service approach to address the multidimensional nature of health and health-related needs of underserved populations. Target patients are minorities, childbearing-age women, infants, persons with HIV/AIDS, substance abusers, and individuals and families who experience health service access barriers for any reason. In addition to primary care, preventive care, and dental services, community health centers assist patients to link with other supportive programs and services such as public assistance, Medicaid, the Women, Infant, and Children supplemental nutrition program, and the Children's Health Insurance Program. Many community health centers also offer onsite laboratory testing, pharmacy services, and radiology services and may provide transportation, translation, and health education services as specific needs dictate. To facilitate access to services, community health centers may also employ outreach workers drawn from the centers' service areas. These workers receive training in health and social service needs assessment and advocacy for early intervention and continuity of care.

Today, community health center grants are administered by the Bureau of Primary Care, Health Resources and Services Administration of the U.S. Department of Health and Human Services. Fees for services are based on income and are offered without charge to the neediest patients. The program has grown substantially over the years from 104 centers in the early 1970s. In 2008 over 1,200 centers with over 7,500 delivery sites in every state and U.S. territory delivered services to 20 million individuals.[41,42] Revenue sources include federal grants, state and local governments, Medicare and Medicaid, and private insurance. Medicaid reimbursement provides the largest share of the centers' patient revenue[42] (Figure 4-7). Community health centers may be organized under the aegis of local health departments, as part of larger not-for-profit human service organizations, or as stand-alone, not-for-profit corporations. All Federally Qualified Community Health Centers must meet fundamental parameters that include[40]

- Location in a high-need community designated as a medically underserved area or population
- Governance by a community board of directors composed of 51% or more health center patients who represent the population served
- Provision of comprehensive primary health care services and supportive services (education, translation, transportation, etc.) that promote access to health care
- Provision of services available to all with fees adjusted on ability to pay
- Meeting other performance and accountability requirements regarding administrative, clinical, and financial operations

Community health centers continue to be a critically important source of primary care for the nation's most vulnerable and underserved citizens. In recognition of their crucial role, in December 2009 the Obama administration earmarked $600 million in Recovery Act funds to support major construction and renovation projects at 85 community health centers and to support health centers' adoption of electronic health records and other health information technology systems.[43]

Public Health Ambulatory Services

The delivery of ambulatory health services by state, county, or municipally supported governmental entities has its roots in the early American

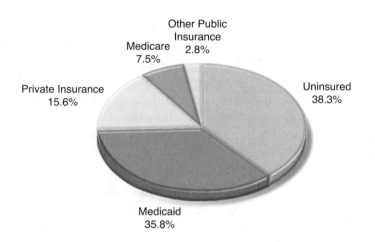

Other Public
Insurance
2.8%
Medicare
7.5%
Private Insurance
15.6%
Uninsured
38.3%
Medicaid
35.8%

FIGURE 4-7 Payment Sources for Community Health Center Patients. *Source:* Department of Health and Human Services, Health Resources Administration Uniform Data System.

ethic of community responsibility for care of needy community residents. Since the colonial period, altruistic citizens sought the charity of the community to provide for the less fortunate by supporting the development of almshouses or "poor houses" to care for the needy and orphaned children. Many of these institutions became the precursors of community hospitals.

With the evolution of state and local governments' roles in providing welfare services and the development of the public health discipline in the late 19th and early 20th centuries, tax-supported state and local health departments began providing ambulatory personal health services. The public health community's successful campaigns in controlling childhood and other communicable diseases were rapidly followed by the recognition of the emergence of chronic disease by the medical care community. This recognition resulted in major shifts of resources toward specialized medical care, to the detriment of public health's preventive agenda.[44] In addition to maintaining its basic mission to promote and protect the public's health and safety, the public health community was expected to mount new initiatives to promote healthy lifestyles, provide safety-net services to growing needy populations, and expand regulatory oversight to accommodate the rapidly expanding medical care industry.[44]

Ambulatory health services that became the domain of health departments included the administration of preventive public health measures, such as cancer and chronic disease screening, immunization, high-risk maternal and infant care, family planning, tobacco control, and tuberculosis and sexually transmitted disease screening and treatment. Some local health departments also established federally qualified or other types of community health centers to provide a range of primary care services to needy individuals of all ages.

Today, the scope of ambulatory care services delivered by public health departments ranges across a wide spectrum from prevention-oriented programs, such as immunizations, well-baby care, smoking cessation, and cancer and chronic disease screening and education, to a full range of personal health services offered through ambulatory care centers. Historically, support for ambulatory public health services has included combinations of city, county, and state funding, plus federal and state disease-specific or block grant funds.

Public health ambulatory services staff may include physicians, nurses, aides, social workers, public health educators, community health workers, and clerical and administrative staff, who function under the overall administrative direction of a local health officer. This health officer may or may not be a physician, depending on the population size of the jurisdiction and individual state or municipal requirements. Depending on the geographic area, the governmental aegis may be state, county, or city.

Findings of two separate 2005 surveys of all state departments of health by the Association of State and Territorial Health Officials and of 2,865 local public health agencies conducted by the National Association of County and City Health Officials revealed the extent to which local public health agencies are providing or contracting for ambulatory services.[45] Only 11.8% reported delivering "primary care" services per se; however, significant percentages of local public health agencies continue to provide an array of other ambulatory services, with adult and child immunizations topping the list.

The September 11, 2001, terrorist attacks and threats of bioterrorism brought a renewed focus to the role of the federal, state, and local public health agencies in providing public protection and supporting national security. In response, in 2002 the federal government transferred $5 billion to the states to improve public health and medical emergency preparedness to strengthen the existing public health infrastructure.[46]

Experts acknowledge that the infusion of federal funds improved local and state level emergency preparedness across several parameters.[46] However, the new funding occurred when states were encountering the sharpest revenue shortfalls in recent decades. "Instead of building more capacity, public health agencies found themselves having to support ongoing services and the new preparedness mission with very little extra funding."[46] The 2009 threat of an H1N1 (swine flu) influenza pandemic tested the capacity of state and local public health agencies to identify and mobilize personnel and other resources to meet ambulatory services demands for mass immunizations. Analysis and reports on public health agencies' performance in meeting immunization demands are not yet available. However, a report on state and local health departments' timeliness of communication using websites following the declaration of a national public health emergency in response to the H1N1 outbreak found considerable variability in local level performance. Further study is needed to determine the causes of variability, including Internet access, staffing constraints, and patterns in media use.[47]

Not-for-Profit Agencies

Not-for-profit agencies operate a variety of ambulatory health care services throughout the United States. Services have evolved from many sources, often cause related, to address needs of population groups afflicted by specific diseases or types of conditions. Asthma, diabetes, multiple sclerosis, and cerebral palsy are a few of the conditions addressed. As not-for-profit organizations, many are chartered by states as charitable organizations and maintain tax-exempt status with the Internal Revenue Service. These designations allow them to solicit charitable contributions for which their donors may receive tax deductions. Governed by boards of directors who receive no compensation for their services, these organizations may be operated by a totally volunteer staff or employ numerous paid professionals and have annual operating budgets of several million dollars.

Characteristically, voluntary ambulatory health care agencies were established through the advocacy of special interest groups that desired to address the health care or health-related needs of a population group whose needs were not being adequately met by existing community services. Some operate as single entities, others as independent affiliated agencies of national organizations. Planned Parenthood Federation of America is an example of one such organization. Its clinics provide preventive care, education, and direct services for gynecologic care and contraception in numerous locations throughout the United States. Another example is the Alzheimer's Association, which provides or assists affected individuals and their caregivers with specialized education and social support and promotes research into causes and treatment for the disease. Frequently, legislative advocacy related to the organization's interests at the federal, state, and local levels is a major component of not-for-profit organization activity.

Financial support for voluntary ambulatory health care agencies is diverse. Sources may include charitable contributions, private payment, third-party insurance reimbursement (including Medicare and Medicaid), and federal, state, or local government grants. In many agencies a large proportion of clients is uninsured or underinsured and lacks personal resources, making financial subsidies crucial to continued viability. Agencies with missions to serve the neediest members of the community continue meeting challenges posed by the ebb and flow of government grant dollars and community economic conditions that affect philanthropic support through efficient business practices and a variety of private fundraising activities.[48] Although voluntary agencies provide only a small fraction of the ambulatory care services, as compared with hospitals and other ambulatory care organizations, they are important as repositories of community values, as symbols of community charity and volunteerism, and as advocates for populations with special needs.

Continued Future Expansion and Experimentation

The focus of the U.S. health care delivery system has shifted from hospitals to expanded use of ambulatory care services. Major forces continuing to drive this shift will be advances in medical technology and diagnostic and treatment modalities that allow more services to be provided safely and effectively in the outpatient setting, cost-reduction initiatives by private and government payers, and consumer demands for more convenient, accessible services. The roles of urgent care centers and retail clinics in the ambulatory care landscape will continue to evolve as experience is acquired and evidence accumulates and is analyzed about patient outcomes, satisfaction, costs, and profitability. Involvement of the organized medical community in establishing standards of care and quality can also be expected to bear on this emerging component of the ambulatory care industry. The PCMH concept will continue to gain traction with major players in the health delivery system. Results of pilot and demonstration projects with this model of ambulatory care will inform practitioners and policymakers on future model applications in the evolving ambulatory services environment.

References

1. Goldsmith J. Hospitals and physicians: not a pretty picture. *Health Affairs.* 2007;26:w72–w75. Available from http://content.healthaffairs.org/cgi/content/full/26/1/w72. Accessed December 12, 2009.

2. Berenson RA, Ginsburg PB, May JH. Hospital-physician relations: cooperation, competition, or separation? *Health Affairs.* 2006;26:w31–w43. Available from http://content.healthaffairs.org/cgi/reprint/26/1/w31.pdf?ck=nck. Accessed December 12, 2009.

3. MacNulty A, Reich J. Surveys and interviews examine relationships between physicians and hospitals. The Physician Executive, September–October 2008. Available from http://www.noblis.org/MissionAreas/HI/ThoughtLeadership/Documents/articleACPESurvey.pdf. Accessed December 14, 2009.

4. Schappert SM, Rechtsteiner EA. Ambulatory medical care utilization estimates for 2006. National Health Statistics Reports. Available from http://www.cdc.gov/nchs/data/nhsr/nhsr008.pdf. Accessed December 14, 2009.

5. Cherry DK, Hing E, Woodwell DA, et al. National Ambulatory Medical Care Survey: 2006 summary. National Health Statistics Reports. Available from http://www.cdc.gov/nchs/data/nhsr/nhsr003.pdf. Accessed December 14, 2009.

6. U.S. Department of Labor, Bureau of Labor Statistics. Physicians and surgeons: occupational outlook handbook: 2010–2011 edition. Available from http://www.bls.gov/oco/ocos074.htm#emply. Accessed December 14, 2009.

7. Raffel MW, Raffel NK. *The U.S. Health System: Origins and Functions,* 4th ed. Albany, NY: Delmar Publishers; 1994:36–44.

8. Center for Studying Health System Change. A snapshot of U.S. physicians: key findings from the 2008 Health Tracking Study Physician Survey. Available from http://www.hschange.com/CONTENT/1078/. Accessed December 14, 2009.

9. Hing E, Burt CW. Office-based medical practices: methods and estimates from the National Ambulatory Medical Care Survey: advance data, No. 383. Available from http://www.cdc.gov/nchs/data/ad/ad383.pdf. Accessed December 14, 2009.

10. American College of Physicians. What is the patient-centered medical home? Available from http://www.acponline.org/running_practice/pcmh/understanding/what.htm. Accessed January 5, 2010.

11. American Academy of Family Physicians. Joint principles of the patient-centered medical home, 2007. Available from http://www.aafp.org/online/etc/medialib/aafp_org/documents/policy/fed/jointprinciplespcmh0207.Par.0001.File.tmp/022107medicalhome.pdf. Accessed January 5, 2010.

12. American College of Physicians. The advanced medical home: a patient-centered, physician-guided model of health care. Position Paper. Philadelphia: American College of Physicians; 2005. Available from http://www.acponline.org/advocacy/where_we_stand/policy/adv_med.pdf. Accessed January 5, 2010.

13. American College of Physicians. Who supports the PCMH model? Available from http://www.acponline.org/running_practice/pcmh/understanding/who.htm. Accessed January 5, 2010.

14. American College of Physicians. Grant-funded activities. Available from http://www.acponline.org/running_practice/pcmh/understanding/grant_activities.htm. Accessed January 5, 2010.

15. Milstein A, Gilbertson E. American medical home runs. *Health Affairs*. 2009;28:1317–1325.

16. Knowles JH. The role of the hospital: the ambulatory clinic. *Bull NY Acad Med*. 1965;41:68–70.

17. Fraser I, Lane L, Linne E. Ambulatory care: a decade of change in health care delivery. *J Ambul Care Manage*. 1993;16:1–8.

18. Healthcare Financial Management Association. Outpatient revenue percentage of net patient revenue depends on hospital size. November 2008. Available from http://thomsonreuters.com/content/healthcare/pdf/394449/1108DT.pdf. Accessed December 30, 2009.

19. Pitts SR, Niska RW, Xu J, et al. National hospital ambulatory medical care survey: 2006, emergency department summary. National Health Statistics Reports no. 7, August 6, 2008. Hyattsville, MD: National Center for Health Statistics. Available from http://www.cdc.gov/nchs/data/nhsr/nhsr007.pdf. Accessed December 15, 2009.

20. Cunningham PJ. What accounts for differences in the use of hospital emergency departments across U.S. communities? *Health Affairs*. 2006;25:w324–w336.

21. U.S. Government Accounting Office. Report to the Chairman, Committee on Finance, U.S. Senate. Hospital emergency departments: crowding continues to occur and some patients wait longer than recommended time frames. Available from http://www.gao.gov/new.items/d09347.pdf. Accessed December 18, 2009.

22. Centers for Disease Control and Prevention. Media brief. Almost half of hospitals experience crowded emergency departments. Available from http://www.cdc.gov/nchs/pressroom/06facts/hospitals.htm. Accessed December 30, 2009.

23. Kongstvedt PR. *Essentials of Managed Health Care,* 5th ed. Sudbury, MA: Jones and Bartlett; 2007:14.

24. American Board of Emergency Medicine. ABEM history. Available from https://www.abem.org/PUBLIC/portal/alias_Rainbow/lang_en-US/tabID_3573/DesktopDefault.aspx. Accessed December 31, 2009.

25. Urgent Care Association of America. Urgent care industry information kit, 2009. Available from http://www.ucaoa.org. Accessed January 1, 2010.

26. American Academy of Urgent Care Medicine. Available from http://aaucm.org/default.aspx. Accessed January 1, 2010.

27. American Board of Urgent Care Medicine Certification. Available from http://aaucm.org/Resources/370/FileRepository/ABUCM%20Brochure.pdf. Accessed January 1, 2010.

28. Urgent Care Association of America. Certified urgent care criteria. Available from http://www.ucaoa.org/recognition_certification_criteria.php. Accessed January 1, 2010.

29. Scott MK. Health care in the express lane: retail clinics go mainstream. Oakland, CA: HealthCare Foundation, July 2006. Available from http://www.mcms.org/downloads/Healthcareintheexpresslaneretailclinics.pdf. Accessed January 2, 2010.

30. Laws M, Scott MK. The emergence of retail-based clinics in the United States: early observations. *Health Affairs.* 2008;27:1293–1297.

31. Merchant Medicine. ConvUrgentCare report: U.S. walk-in clinic industry snapshot, November 1, 2009. Available from http://www.merchantmedicine.com/uploadeddocuments/Merchant%20Medicine%20Industry%20Snapshot%20November%202009.pdf. Accessed January 2, 2010.

32. American Academy of Family Physicians. Retail health clinics are rolling your way. Available from http://www.aafp.org/fpm/20060500/65reta.html. Accessed January 2, 2010.

33. Medical News Today. AMA calls for investigation of retail health clinics. Available from http://www.medicalnewstoday.com/healthnews.php?newsid=75308&nfid=crss. Accessed January 2, 2010.

34. Cullen KA, Hall MJ, Golosinskiy A. Ambulatory surgery in the United States, 2006. National Health Statistics Reports; no. 11. Revised. Hyattsville, MD: National Center for Health Statistics. 2009. Available from http://www.cdc.gov/nchs/data/nhsr/nhsr011.pdf. Accessed December 19, 2009.

35. Ambulatory Surgery Center Coalition. Ambulatory surgery centers: a positive trend in health care. Available from http://www.ascassociation.org/advocacy/AmbulatorySurgeryCentersPositiveTrendHealthCare.pdf. Accessed January 2, 2009.

36. KNG Health Consulting LLC. An analysis of recent growth of ambulatory surgical centers prepared for the Ambulatory Surgery Coalition, June 2009. Available from http://ascassociation.org/study.pdf. Accessed January 2, 2010.

37. Casalino LP, Devers KJ, Brewster LR, et al. Focused factories? Physician-owned specialty facilities. *Health Affairs.* 2003;22:56–67.

38. Ambulatory Surgery Center Association. The history of ASCs. Available from http://www.ascassociation.org/faqs/aschistory/. Accessed January 2, 2010.

39. Ambulatory Surgery Center Association. The regulation of ambulatory surgery centers. Available from http://www.ascassociation.org/faqs/ascregulations/. Accessed January 2, 2010.

40. U.S. Department of Health and Human Services, Health Resources and Services Administration, Bureau of Primary Health Care. The health center program: an overview. Available from http://bphc.hrsa.gov. Accessed January 3, 2010.

41. U.S. Department of Health and Human Services, Health Resources and Services Administration, Bureau of Primary Health Care. Health centers: America's primary care safety net, reflections on success, 2002–2007. Rockville, MD. June 2008. Available from http://bphc.hrsa.gov/success/index.htm. Accessed January 3, 2009.

42. National Association of Community Health Centers, Inc. America's health centers, October 2009. Available from http://www.nachc.org/client/documents/America's_%20Health_Centers_updated_11_09.pdf. Accessed January 3, 2010.

43. The White House Office of the Press Secretary. President Obama announces recovery act awards to build, renovate community health centers in more than 30 states. December 9, 2009. Available from http://www.whitehouse.gov/the-press-office/president-obama-announces-recovery-act-awards-build-renovate-community-health-cente. Accessed January 3, 2009.

44. McGinnis M. Can public health and medicine partner in the public interest? *Health Affairs.* 2006;25:1048–1049.

45. Beitsch LM, Brooks RG, Menachemi N, et al. Public health at center stage: new roles, old props. *Health Affairs.* 2006;25:913–921.

46. Salinsky E. Gursky E. The case for transforming governmental public health. *Health Affairs.* 2006;25:1019–1028.

47. Ringel JS, Trentacost E, Lurie N. How well did health departments communicate about risk at the start of the swine flu epidemic in 2009? *Health Affairs.* 2009;28:w743–w759.

48. Alliance for Advancing Nonprofit Health Care. The value of nonprofit health care. Available from http://www.nonprofithealthcare.org/reports/5_value.pdf. Accessed January 5, 2010.

CHAPTER 5

Medical Education and the Changing Practice of Medicine

This chapter provides an overview of the growth and change in medical education from the colonial apprentice system to today's high-technology, specialty-oriented instruction in the basic sciences and clinical fields. The evolution of specialty and subspecialty practice is discussed, as is the funding of graduate medical education. Developments such as clinical practice guidelines, the introduction of specialty physicians called "hospitalists," physician report cards, health information technology, and new ethical issues are defined. The chapter concludes with a discussion of the future of medical practice.

Medical Education: Colonial America to the 19th Century

There were no medical schools in colonial America. Women treated the sick at home with the help of medicinal herbs, the advice of friends, and some self-help publications of questionable credibility. Only a few of the university-trained physicians in Europe came to the colonies. Those European physicians trained other physicians in an apprentice relationship. Because there was no formal method of testing or licensing new physicians after they concluded their apprenticeship, they were free to practice with no outside control.

The first medical school in America was established in 1756 at the College of Philadelphia (later the University of Pennsylvania). Shortly after that, in 1768, a second was founded at King's College (later Columbia University). Both schools graduated only a handful of students each year.

Training under a single physician remained the most common method of physician education until the founding of hospitals in the mid-18th century. Physicians not only brought their own apprentices to the hospital, but they encouraged other students to observe patient treatment. This practice became so popular that the Philadelphia Hospital began to charge students who were not apprenticed to physicians on the staff. By 1773 the hospital decided to regulate this system so that an aspiring physician could pay a fee to the hospital and be formally apprenticed to the institution for 5 years.[1] Physicians were granted a certificate on the completion of their apprenticeship.

By 1800 only four new medical schools had been added to the ones in Pennsylvania and New York, and Harvard University had opened one in 1783 and Dartmouth College in 1797. The schools were small, with three or four faculty members teaching all courses. At the time there were still very few restrictions on who could practice medicine. The first law concerning medicine in the colonies was enacted in Virginia in 1639 to control physician fees.[2] Various states attempted to enact medical licensing legislation during the 18th and early 19th centuries, but "by the time of the Civil War, not a single state had a medical licensure act in effect" (p. 424).[2] Moreover, as the number of medical schools grew, their diplomas came to be viewed as licenses to practice.

In 1821 Georgia became the first state to restrict medical licenses to graduates of medical schools.[1] Opposition was strong, especially from the apprentice-trained physicians. However, as physicians from medical schools began to outnumber those from the apprentice system, the MD degree became the standard of competence. The endorsement of formal medical education over apprenticeship training encouraged an increase in the number of medical schools.

Many of the new medical schools had weak programs and no hospital affiliations. In 1892 Harvard became the first medical school to require 4 years of training. In 1893 Johns Hopkins initiated a 4-year curriculum as part of a pioneering effort to improve medical education. The Johns

Hopkins model became the standard for subsequent reform of all medical education.[1]

Many medical schools during this period operated without strict admission requirements, a well-trained faculty, or a place for clinical observation and practice. As a consequence the quality of the medical degree varied greatly from school to school. Medical societies were organized largely to improve the quality of education and practice. The first such society was the Medical Society of Boston, organized in 1736.[2]

By the turn of the 19th century most states had medical societies. In 1847 most of those state societies affiliated with the newly formed American Medical Association (AMA). "Though the goal of the AMA at the time was to improve medical education, its early attempts to reform or close some of the weaker medical schools were ineffective" (p. 6).[1] Many of the AMA members opposed closing the weaker schools because they were associated with them and had a vested interest in keeping them open. As a result, attempts to establish a national standard for medical teaching floundered for a few decades.

The Association of American Medical Colleges (AAMC), founded in 1876 by 22 medical schools, also supported a 4-year curriculum such as the one introduced by the medical schools of Harvard and Johns Hopkins. However, it lacked the influence to accomplish the desired reforms.

Flexner Report and Medical School Reforms

In 1904 the AMA created a new Council on Medical Education and also began the *Journal of the American Medical Association*. The AMA used the journal to publish medical school failure statistics on state board licensing examinations and to group schools by their failure rates.

The most important educational reform accomplishment of the AMA, however, began in 1905 when it obtained the help of the Carnegie Foundation to investigate and rate medical schools. Abraham Flexner of the Foundation headed a study of the medical schools in the United States and Canada. He proposed to examine the entrance requirements at each institution, the size and training of the faculty, endowment fees, the quality of laboratories, and the relationship between the medical schools and hospitals.

In 1909 Flexner started his educational survey of all 155 medical schools in the United States and Canada. He visited each school, interviewing the dean and a few faculty members and inspecting laboratories and equipment. After each visit he summarized the facts observed during his visit and mailed the summary to the dean for verification. The deans and faculty of each school cooperated happily with Flexner in the mistaken belief that Carnegie was contemplating a contribution to their school.

Flexner's full report, *Medical Education in the United States and Canada*, was published by the Carnegie Foundation in 1910. The report was an accurate and searing description of abuses in the medical schools. Schools were referred to as a "disgrace" and a "plague spot." The assets and liabilities of each school were described in detail, and corrective measures were offered. In the aftermath of this criticism some schools closed and others consolidated. Flexner had recommended that the number of schools be reduced from 155 to 31, but a decade later the number was only down to 85.[1]

Not all observations in Flexner's report were negative. Dartmouth, Yale, and Columbia were able to make alterations that improved the quality of their programs. Schools that received praise for excellent performance included Harvard, Western Reserve, McGill, Toronto, and especially Johns Hopkins, which was described as a "model for medical education."[1]

Coming from an independent body, the Flexner Report gave increased leverage to medical reformers. Licensing legislation was pursued more vigorously, and new requirements for the length of medical training and for the quality of laboratories and other facilities were established. The AMA and the AAMC accelerated efforts at reform and, in 1942, established the Liaison Committee on Medical Education to serve as the official accrediting body of medical schools.

One of the most important outcomes of Flexner's report was that it stimulated support for medical education from foundations and wealthy individuals. Schools that received the most favorable ratings from Flexner shared most of the money. Because most were associated with universities, the university-affiliated medical schools gained significant influence over the direction of medical education.[1]

Academic Medical Centers

Federal research grants of the 1950s and 1960s encouraged the research-oriented medical schools and their teaching hospitals to become the country's centers of scientific and technologic advances in health care. Most of the large tertiary-care hospitals affiliated with the approximately 80 medical schools were attracting patients with complicated medical conditions and getting better results than their smaller unaffiliated counterparts.

Because university medical complexes were increasingly recognized as leading the way toward a more sophisticated and effective health care system, the federal government assisted in extending that expertise through the regional medical program legislation of 1965. One of many federal grant programs of that decade, it funded the development of regional medical programs across the United States to upgrade medical knowledge about the leading causes of death: heart disease, cancer, and stroke. The regional medical programs supported research, continuing professional education, service innovation, and regional networking among hospitals and other health care facilities. By 1974, however, the university-based regional medical programs had lost their political support and soon disappeared.

By then, however, the university medical centers were well established as the proponents of cutting-edge advances in research and clinical medicine. By the early 1980s federal support had increased the number of medical schools to 127.

Academic medical centers broadened into academic health centers by adding to their complexes such professional schools as nursing, pharmacy, dentistry, and allied health. Together with their large teaching hospitals and other clinical facilities, these academic medical centers became a powerful force in the health care arena.

Academic health centers have become the principal places of education and training for physicians and other health care personnel, the sites for most basic research in medicine, and the clinical settings in which many of the advances in diagnosis and treatment are tested and perfected. The teaching hospitals of academic health centers are also the major providers of the more sophisticated patient care required by trauma centers, burn centers, neonatal intensive care centers, and the technologically advanced treatment of cancer, heart disease, and neurologic and other conditions. In addition to their complex tertiary-care services, teaching hospitals in most cities provide much of the primary care for economically disadvantaged populations.

The highly specialized, high-technology nature of academic health centers makes them the most expensive type of facility in America's health care system. In addition, care at teaching hospitals is, of necessity, less efficient. Because student physicians order more diagnostic tests and procedures and often have to consult with senior doctors regarding diagnoses and treatment procedures, lengths of stay are longer and therefore more costly. Available data suggest that hospitals affiliated with academic health centers are 20% to 30% more expensive than other hospitals.[3] Now, however, because health care has shifted from an era of abundant resources to one of stringent economic constraints, academic medical centers are under increasing pressure to cut back on high-cost activities or face ballooning deficits and questionable survival.[4]

Medical schools depend on a variety of sources for revenue. A major source is the clinical practice of faculty. In 2008, 37% of the total income of U.S. medical schools came from their faculty practice plans. Federally supported research grants and contracts contributed about 19%. Medical schools receive relatively small proportions of their total revenue from state and local government appropriations, hospital programs, tuition and fees, and endowments.[5] Their diverse funding requires them to assemble the necessary revenues from multiple sources.

The federal government has subsidized the training of resident physicians through the Medicare program. Because over half of the total patient revenues of academic health center hospitals came from Medicare and Medicaid, reductions in the support from those programs affect academic hospitals in two ways. By scaling back subsidies for graduate medical education and by encouraging beneficiaries to enroll in managed care plans, the government decreased the revenue of academic medical centers and reduced the number of patients available for clinical training and research.[6]

Graduate Medical Education Consortia

There are two types of physicians: the MD (Doctor of Medicine) and the DO (Doctor of Osteopathic Medicine). MDs are also known as allopathic physicians. Although both MDs and DOs may use all accepted methods of treatment, including drugs and surgery, DOs place special emphasis on the body's musculoskeletal system. In 2009 there were 131 accredited schools of medicine[7] and 25 accredited colleges for degrees in osteopathy.[8]

No national agency grants licenses to practice medicine. Instead, after completing a residency a physician must obtain a license from the medical board of the state where he or she plans to practice. Each state is independent in determining who may practice within the state and may have special requirements or restrictions for licensure. To provide direct patient care, physicians are required to complete a 3- to 7-year graduate medical program accredited by the Accreditation Council for Graduate Medical Education (ACGME) in one of the recognized medical specialties.[9]

There are nearly 7,000 residency programs, loosely held together by accreditation and certification processes, medical schools, program directors, and hospital executives. Given the large number of programs and their loose-knit organization, questions about the quality of the programs and their pertinence to issues of personnel supply and specialty distribution inevitably have been raised. U.S. residency programs were described at the 1992 Macy Foundation conference, "Taking Charge of Graduate Medical Education: To Meet the Nation's Needs in the 21st Century," as "responsive principally to the service needs of hospitals, the interests of the medical specialty societies, the objectives of the residency program directors, and the career preferences of the medical students."[10]

The situation has been addressed with varying success by a number of graduate medical education consortia. These consortia are formal associations of medical schools, teaching hospitals, and other organizations involved in the training of residents. The consortia have central coordination and direction that encourage the members to function collectively. The major aims of graduate medical education consortia are to improve the structure and governance of residency programs, to increase the ambulatory care training experiences, and to address imbalances in physician specialty and location.[11]

Whether these consortia succeed in addressing the imbalances in medical specialty workforce to be more accountable to society's needs or whether medicine's historical reluctance to take decisive actions that alter the status quo will bring government intervention are open questions. As in so many other aspects of health care, it is likely that market forces, rather than policy decisions, will determine the outcomes.

Delineation and Growth of Medical Specialties

In the mid-1980s the AMA resisted the development of medical specialties. Questions were raised about whether specialists would fragment care by not treating the whole patient and whether surgeons, trained to operate, would disregard noninvasive alternative medical treatments.

The AMA's slow response to specialty interests prompted specialists to form their own societies and associations. In the last half of the 19th century, organizations arose for physicians interested in ophthalmology, otology, gynecology, obstetrics, and pediatrics. After World War I, with specialization increasing among physicians, specialty hospitals were founded in some cities, and general practitioners found themselves eased out of hospitals by specialists. In response the American Academy of General Practice was formed in 1947 to advocate for general practice departments in hospitals. It was not until 1969, however, that general practice, now called family medicine, became a recognized specialty.

Questionable Early Training of Medical Specialists

Despite the growth in the number of specialists, at the time of the Flexner Report there was no standard for adequate specialty training. The length of specialty training required by various medical schools and hospitals ranged from just a few weeks to 3 years, and the quality of graduating specialists varied from excellent to incompetent. A physician with almost any amount of training could practice as a specialist.

In 1917 the U.S. Army, in need of physicians, examined the qualifications of those physicians who wished to be classified as specialists. Even though many had practiced for years as specialists, the results were shocking. Very high percentages of physician specialists were rejected by the service as unfit to practice as specialists, and some were deemed unfit to practice in any branch of medicine at all.

As improved technology and the development of safer and more effective anesthesia and antiseptic techniques made surgery a more acceptable medical option, the demand grew, and the numbers of surgeons and hospitals increased in response. The American College of Surgeons, established in 1912, set up standards and a board in 1917 for certifying specialists. At the same time the AMA started inspecting internship sites and produced a listing of approved internship hospitals.

Although both the AMA and the American College of Surgeons began to rate the quality of postgraduate training, they quickly realized they could not make their findings public. "Conditions were so bad the results were suppressed" (p. 16).[1] In 1924 the Council on Medicine Education began to approve hospitals for residency specialty training programs. For the next 40 years residency programs were initiated in all kinds of hospitals with little regard for the quality of the training experience. Often poorly planned and supervised, residents' educational experiences were secondary to their obligations as house staff to serve whatever patient load they were assigned. Assigned to single departments, the opportunities for developing expert clinical knowledge and skills depended on how much interest a few attending physicians had in teaching and the type of patient admitted to that specialty service.

Problems in the quality of training resulting from the lack of standards abounded. Reform was needed, and a half century after the Flexner Report the AMA again requested an outside examination of the medical education process. The AMA commissioned a Citizens Committee on Graduate Medical Education, chaired by John S. Mills, who issued his report in 1966. Key recommendations of the report included the elimination of independent internships and giving the accreditation of residency training programs to institutions rather than to individual medical departments. In 1970 the AMA endorsed the inclusion of the first year of graduate medical education in a program approved by an appropriate residency review committee (RRC). The term "internship" was dropped, and by 1980 the AMA had issued recommendations for broad training in the first postdoctoral year.

The current curriculum requirements for becoming a specialist are well defined and standardized. The physician must graduate from medical school, serve in a residency program in an approved setting, and pass a qualifying examination. The appropriate specialty board then certifies the physician. The boards are sponsored by the major specialty society in the area of study and the appropriate specialty section of the AMA.

Specialty Boards and Residency Performance

Boards were formed for each specialty to ensure a proper instructional program and training period followed by an examination and certification to practice. The American Board of Ophthalmology, established in 1933, was the first specialty board. In the same year an advisory board for medical specialties was organized. Shortly thereafter, the American Board of Medical Specialties achieved official recognition of specialty boards in medicine. By 1991 there were 24 member boards.

Within the 24 medical specialties, there are now over 100 subspecialties, and the number is increasing as different kinds of specialists train in similar subspecialties. For instance, the specialties of family medicine, internal medicine, and pediatrics all have subspecialties in sports medicine. In addition, advancing technology is creating new subspecialties each year. The specialty areas and a partial list of the growing subspecialties of medicine are presented in Table 5-1.[12]

The usual procedure for subspecialization is for specialists to complete their residency training and become board certified. Then they take another period of training, called a fellowship, which prepares them to subspecialize or conduct research in a specific area.

Each specialty board has an RRC charged with the responsibility of preserving the quality of graduate medical education. In 1928 the AMA published the guidelines for approved residencies and fellowships that set educational standards for residencies. The ACGME, formed in 1972 by the American Board of Medical Specialties, the American Hospital Association, the AMA, AAMC, and the Council of Medical Specialty Societies, extends authority to RRCs to determine the standards for its residencies.

The ACGME supervises and receives reports from each RRC. Thus, "the RRC and all specialties establish guidelines for acceptable standards for graduate medical education. . . . The RRC also controls the number of residents allowed in each program and in general oversees the conduct of the residencies."[2]

In addition to the controls of ACGME and its five parent organizations, numerous influences affect different aspects of residency content and training. These include 24 specialty boards and RRCs, hospital directors, medical school deans, program directors, training directors, faculty, house staff, and specialty societies. The problems inherent in this disjointed system of control will intensify as health care reforms force consideration of changes to accommodate specialty imbalance, physician supply, reductions in funding, shifts from inpatient to ambulatory care, and the general reconfiguration taking place in the health care industry.

The fastest growing field of medical practice has been developing outside of the aforementioned systems of control over specialty training. Hospitalists are physicians whose sole responsibility is the care of hospitalized patients, and their number is growing. There are now more than 12,000 hospitalists in the United States, and the number is expected to reach 30,000 at the end of 2010.

Hospitalists spend all their time in hospitals taking care of patients from admission to discharge. They are present to monitor patients several times

Table 5-1 Medical Specialty and Subspecialty Areas

ABMS Member Boards certify physicians in more than 145 specialties and subspecialties. The following chart lists the current specialty and subspecialty certificates offered by ABMS Member Boards.

American Board of Allergy and Immunology

Allergy and Immunology	No Subspecialties

American Board of Anesthesiology

Anesthesiology	Critical Care Medicine
	Hospice and Palliative Medicine
	Pain Medicine

American Board of Colon and Rectal Surgery

Colon and Rectal Surgery	No Subspecialties

American Board of Dermatology

Dermatology	Clinical and Laboratory Dermatological Immunology
	Dermatopathology
	Pediatric Dermatology

American Board of Emergency Medicine

Emergency Medicine	Hospice and Palliative Medicine
	Medical Toxicology
	Pediatric Emergency Medicine
	Sports Medicine
	Undersea and Hyperbaric Medicine

American Board of Family Medicine

Family Medicine	Adolescent Medicine
	Geriatric Medicine
	Hospice and Palliative Medicine
	Sleep Medicine
	Sports Medicine

American Board of Internal Medicine

Internal Medicine	Adolescent Medicine
	Advanced Heart Failure and Transplant Cardiology[1]
	Cardiovascular Disease
	Clinical Cardiac Electrophysiology
	Critical Care Medicine
	Endocrinology, Diabetes, and Metabolism
	Gastroenterology
	Geriatric Medicine
	Hematology
	Hospice and Palliative Medicine
	Infectious Disease
	Interventional Cardiology
	Medical Oncology
	Nephrology
	Pulmonary Disease
	Rheumatology
	Sleep Medicine
	Sports Medicine
	Transplant Hepatology

(continues)

Table 5-1 Medical Specialty and Subspecialty Areas *(continued)*

American Board of Medical Genetics

Clinical Biochemical Genetics*	Medical Biochemical Genetics[2]
Clinical Cytogenetics*	Molecular Genetic Pathology
Clinical Genetics (MD)*	
Clinical Molecular Genetics*	

American Board of Neurological Surgery

Neurological Surgery	No Subspecialties

American Board of Nuclear Medicine

Nuclear Medicine	No Subspecialties

American Board of Obstetrics and Gynecology

Obstetrics and Gynecology	Critical Care Medicine
	Gynecologic Oncology
	Hospice and Palliative Medicine
	Maternal and Fetal Medicine
	Reproductive Endocrinology/Infertility

American Board of Ophthalmology

Ophthalmology	No Subspecialties

American Board of Orthopaedic Surgery

Orthopaedic Surgery	Orthopaedic Sports Medicine
	Surgery of the Hand

American Board of Otolaryngology

Otolaryngology	Neurotology
	Pediatric Otolaryngology
	Plastic Surgery Within the Head and Neck
	Sleep Medicine

American Board of Pathology

Anatomic Pathology and Clinical Pathology*	Blood Banking/Transfusion Medicine
Pathology—Anatomic*	Cytopathology
Pathology—Clinical*	Dermatopathology
	Pathology—Chemical
	Pathology—Forensic
	Pathology—Hematology
	Pathology—Medical Microbiology
	Pathology—Molecular Genetic
	Pathology—Pediatric
	Neuropathology

American Board of Pediatrics

Pediatrics	Adolescent Medicine
	Child Abuse Pediatrics[3]
	Developmental-Behavioral Pediatrics
	Hospice and Palliative Medicine
	Medical Toxicology
	Neonatal-Perinatal Medicine
	Neurodevelopmental Disabilities
	Pediatric Cardiology
	Pediatric Critical Care Medicine
	Pediatric Emergency Medicine
	Pediatric Endocrinology
	Pediatric Gastroenterology
	Pediatric Hematology-Oncology
	Pediatric Infectious Diseases
	Pediatric Nephrology
	Pediatric Pulmonology

Table 5-1 Medical Specialty and Subspecialty Areas *(continued)*

Pediatrics (continued)	Pediatric Rheumatology
	Pediatric Transplant Hepatology
	Sleep Medicine
	Sports Medicine

American Board of Physical Medicine and Rehabilitation

Physical Medicine and Rehabilitation	Hospice and Palliative Medicine
	Neuromuscular Medicine
	Pain Medicine
	Pediatric Rehabilitation Medicine
	Spinal Cord Injury Medicine
	Sports Medicine

American Board of Plastic Surgery

| Plastic Surgery | Plastic Surgery Within the Head and Neck |
| | Surgery of the Hand |

American Board of Preventive Medicine

Aerospace Medicine*	Medical Toxicology
Occupational Medicine*	Undersea and Hyperbaric Medicine
Public Health and General Preventive Medicine*	

American Board of Psychiatry and Neurology

Psychiatry*	Addiction Psychiatry
Neurology*	Child and Adolescent Psychiatry
Neurology with Special Qualification In Child Neurology*	Clinical Neurophysiology
	Forensic Psychiatry
	Geriatric Psychiatry
	Hospice and Palliative Medicine
	Neurodevelopmental Disabilities
	Neuromuscular Medicine
	Pain Medicine
	Psychosomatic Medicine
	Sleep Medicine
	Vascular Neurology

American Board of Radiology

Diagnostic Radiology*	Hospice and Palliative Medicine
Radiation Oncology*	Neuroradiology
Radiologic Physics*	Nuclear Radiology
	Pediatric Radiology
	Vascular and Interventional Radiology

American Board of Surgery

Surgery	Hospice and Palliative Medicine
Vascular Surgery	Pediatric Surgery
	Surgery of the Hand
	Surgical Critical Care

American Board of Thoracic Surgery

| Thoracic Surgery | Congenital Cardiac Surgery[2] |

American Board of Urology

| Urology | Pediatric Urology |

*Specific disciplines within the specialty where certification is offered.
[1]Approved 2008; first issue yet to be determined
[2]Approved 2007; first issue 2009
[3]Approved 2006; first issue November 2009
Source: Reprinted with permission from Approved ABMS Specialty Boards and Certificate Categories, pp. 111–114, (c) 2009, www.abms.org (This is not a complete list of specialties and subspecialties.)

a day, order tests, involve consultants as necessary, and, in general, coordinate all care during hospital stays. They are expected to care for hospitalized patients in consultation with each patient's primary care physician.

Because there are no specific training requirements for hospitalists, most are trained in internal medicine or, in the case of children's services, pediatrics. For personal reasons they have chosen to give up private practice and become employees of one or more hospitals or of companies that contract to provide hospitalist services to several hospitals.[13]

Physician Workforce and U.S. Medical Schools

In the mid-1960s the federal government expected a national shortage of physicians in the United States. New policies and programs were established to increase the number of physicians. In the 20 years between 1980 and 2000, the total number of physicians in the United States increased from 467,679 to 813,770—an increase of 74%. The physician-to-population ratio increased from 207 to 296 per 100,000 people. More recently, that number has grown to about 900,000 physicians in the United States.

At the same time there are continuing debates between those who predict physician shortages and those who warn of a physician oversupply. Whether there is a shortage or not, it is the wide geographic variation in physician location rather than the number of physicians that remains a problem. Physicians per 10,000 population actually providing patient care vary from over 35 in Massachusetts to under 16 in Iowa.[14] Regardless of the number of physicians per overall population, the low supply in the less attractive rural and inner-city areas continues to deny adequate medical care to those populations.

Between 1990 and 1997 the total number of medical residents in accredited residency programs rose from 82,902 to 98,143.[15] Much of that increase was due to the influx of international medical graduates. Nearly one-fourth of the physicians practicing in the United States graduated from medical schools in other countries. Most of those graduates gained entry to the U.S. health care system by completing an accredited medical residency. For more than a decade the total number of residency positions has continued to increase, with graduates of foreign medical schools making up a larger percentage of the total number.[16]

Between 1990 and 2000 more than 45,000 international medical school graduates (IMGs) entered practice in the United States after serving residencies in U.S. hospitals.[17] In fact, most of the hospitals in the United States depend on IMGs to fill their residency positions. About one-fourth of all hospital residencies are filled by IMGs, and consequently, they represent approximately one-fourth of the physician workforce in the United States.[17]

In 1998, in response to complaints about the lack of basic clinical and communication skills among some IMGs, a requirement was initiated that they must pass a clinical skill assessment before entering a residency. Although there was a surge of IMG entrants immediately before the requirement went into effect, there has been a significant drop in IMG entrants since the requirement was initiated. As a result the quality of the applicants has improved while still providing enough IMGs to fill the residency positions not taken by U.S. medical graduates.[18]

Ratios of Generalist to Specialist Physicians and the Changing Demand

Primary care or generalist physicians are widely defined as those who practice family medicine, general internal medicine, and general pediatrics. Physicians practicing obstetrics and gynecology are also sometimes included as primary care practitioners. For years the numbers of generalist physicians have been considered too low to meet the basic health care needs of large segments of the general population. Additionally, the emphasis on medical diagnosis and treatment by combinations of specialist and subspecialist physicians has been criticized as contributing significantly to the complexity and rising costs of medical care.[19]

In the early 1990s the growth of managed care raised concerns that the long-standing 60:40 ratio of medical specialists to primary care physicians would leave the United States with an inadequate number of primary care physicians and an oversupply of specialists. Those forecasts led to a number of federal and state policies that encouraged the training of more primary care practitioners. There followed a significant increase in the number of physicians practicing in the primary care fields of family medicine and pediatrics.

In contrast to the early predictions, however, the marketplace demand for medical specialists did not decrease, and the increased supply of primary care physicians appears adequate to meet population needs. In fact, rather than the predicted national oversupply of specialist physicians, many areas of the country are experiencing an inadequate supply of specialists to meet community needs.[20]

The preponderance of medical specialists among all practicing physicians in the United States was not brought about by design. There never has been a master plan to create a more ideal, or even specific, distribution of specialties within the physician workforce. The number, types, and preparation of physicians have been left to the often independent actions of medical schools, their teaching hospitals, the American Board of Medical Specialties, and the ACGME.

The current ratio of specialists to generalist physicians, about 65:35,[21] is the result of individual career choices made by medical students before graduation. Thus one of the most important influences of academic health centers is the socialization process that shapes the skills, values, and attitudes of generation after generation of physicians and other health care professionals. It is the educational and training exposures to the different specialty practices and to the practitioners of those specialties that influence a student's personal career objectives and subsequent practice pattern. It is significant in considering the origins of the specialist/generalist imbalance that, until very recently, almost every aspect of most medical school and teaching hospital experiences favored the practice of specialty medicine. Many medical students who had every intention of becoming generalist physicians were induced by exposure to the medical education environment to change their minds.

The hierarchy of respect in the cultures of most academic medical centers tends to denigrate primary care as less intellectually demanding, less prestigious, and requiring less skill than the subspecialties. Although untrue, specialists in medical schools convey the message indirectly—and sometimes directly—to patients, medical students, and other physicians that generalists are not competent to handle the wide range of problems they face. Although generalists cannot have the same expertise in every field that a specialist has in one field, generalists develop a very high level of knowledge in all aspects of primary care and are capable of making appropriate and judicious use of the expertise of specialists when the need arises.

The primary care experience in most medical schools also is skewed when medical students and residents see most patients in tertiary-care hospitals, work in clinics that are considered of low priority, and rarely find a preeminent primary care faculty person to serve as a role model. In addition, the differences in working hours, being on-call, income, and public recognition that favor specialists cause many medical students and residents to rethink initial interests in primary care medicine.[22]

Nevertheless, most medical schools encourage medical graduates to accept residencies in one of the primary care fields. Admission committees give preference to candidates for admission that evidence interest in primary care medicine. Family practice departments cultivate promising students, and most medical schools have moved some of their clinical training sites from tertiary-care hospitals to ambulatory service settings and private group practice offices to give students more primary care experience.

Among the most persuasive influences on the practice specialty decisions of graduating medical students are the market conditions that determine the need for and success of potential various medical specialists. Medical students are very much aware of the demand and supply for specialists and subspecialists in urban communities and the opportunities for generalists in managed care environments. They also know they will have the option to seek further training in a subspecialty at a later date if they aspire to more specialized practice.

Preventive Medicine

In 1991 the Pew Charitable Trusts published a report that outlined what was expected to drive future health care. They concluded that a health-oriented approach that stresses disease prevention will characterize future health care systems. The report emphasized "that health concerns will be addressed at a community level and that medical schools will require that learning in a community environment be part of physician training. Physicians will need to be well versed in social and environmental health determinants. Focusing on preventive care and treatment techniques that use technology to the patient's advantage is the challenge facing the new physician."[23]

Medicine and medical education, however, have a history of being incredibly inept in establishing health promotion and disease prevention as a high priority in the U.S. health care system. "Although practicing preventive medicine is a cost saving mechanism, nationwide we spend most health care dollars treating preventable disease."[24] Parameters for prevention are clearly established in many areas, but past studies have shown that only a small percentage of physicians actually adhere to the guidelines.[24]

More recently, however, rising public awareness, media pressure, and enlightened leadership have produced some innovative and productive collaborations between clinical and preventive medicine. In addition to their long history of participating in the public health measures to prevent vaccine-preventable childhood diseases, sexually transmitted diseases, and HIV infection that depend on physician case reporting, immunization, and education, practicing physicians have collaborated in community campaigns for problems such as childhood obesity, diabetes, smoking cessation, cholesterol education, and early cancer detection. For these alliances to expand and grow, however, there needs to be significant changes in all areas of medical education, practice incentives, accountability measures, and financing.[25]

Changing Physician–Hospital Relationships

Until recently, physicians and hospitals maintained unique, commensal relationships that brought both of them profits from a single source—patient admissions. The independence and autonomy of physicians were respected, and their relationship to the hospital in the care of patients was overlooked by paying the physician separately on a fee-for-service basis and the hospital on the basis of costs incurred. Because hospitals were dependent on physicians to admit patients and make use of the hospitals' resources, hospitals courted physicians by providing them with time, equipment, staff, and other perquisites with little regard for the effects on hospital costs. Additionally, hospitals were challenged to keep their physical facilities attractive, their hotel services efficient, their support services responsive, and their medical staffs as reputable as possible to attract patients and encourage physicians to select their facilities.

In turn, physicians had responsibilities to the institution itself and to the patients they admitted to the hospital. As a component of a hospital's tripartite governance structure, the medical staff organization was responsible to the board of trustees and the administration for a host of organizational activities that require medical expertise. Through the medical staff organization and its committees, physicians have been obligated to provide the knowledge and authority to establish clinical policies and procedures, perform utilization review, ensure quality, and determine the credentialing standards for admission to the hospital's medical staff.[26]

The roles and responsibilities of physicians, however, are changing from when they were the sole determinants of hospital admissions, diagnostic tests and therapeutic procedures, the length of hospital stays, the use of hospital-owned services and other resources, and referrals. The spiraling costs of unchecked and mutually beneficial financial and practice relationships of physicians and hospitals have incurred demands by all concerned that have radically altered the business of hospitals and their physician connections. In an environment of constrained resources, the relationships between physicians and hospitals are now different and often far more stressful.

Under the prospective payment system, hospitals are at financial risk if the lengths of patient stays or the costs of resource use exceed that allowed for specific patient diagnoses. As a result, hospitals are constantly monitoring and sometimes questioning physician decisions in providing patient care. Albeit indirectly, the administration of the hospital now has a role in clinical decision making, and it is an interaction in which neither party engages enthusiastically.

There are other reasons physicians can no longer ignore the financial consequences of their clinical decisions. Managed care plans that contract with hospitals to provide services to their members select those hospitals that demonstrate operating efficiency and cost effectiveness. Physicians who are not sensitive to the impact of their practice patterns on the financial burden of their hospitals and do not cooperate in keeping them competitive will find themselves increasingly unwelcome on hospitals' medical staffs.

In addition to these stresses on the internal relationships of hospitals and physicians, there are external conflicts. The new economic environment is causing hospitals and physicians to strain their traditional, long, and fruitful relationship by going into competition with each other. Group practice growth and new technologies that permit many procedures that formerly required inpatient hospitalization to be performed in ambulatory settings have given physicians the financial resources and patient volume to acquire and use these technologies. These entrepreneurial activities have placed physicians in direct competition with hospitals.

In an analogous move, as their inpatient admissions decreased, hospitals have shifted a great many of their activities to community-based ambulatory settings that competed, in some instances, with their own medical staff. Clearly, the competition for patients in the reformed environment has changed traditional hospital–physician relationships.[27]

As was mentioned earlier, one significant change has been the introduction of new hospital-based subspecialty physicians called hospitalists. In the United States the hospitalist movement and the term "hospitalist" were introduced in the mid-1990s. In Europe and Canada the role of a hospital-based specialist who managed only inpatients has been well established for years.

Unlike hospital-based emergency or critical care specialists, hospitalists may manage patients in any of the inpatient units. Primary care physicians "hand off" their hospitalized patients to hospitalists who serve as physicians of record while those patients are in the hospital. Hospitalists then return the patients to their primary care physician at the time of hospital discharge.

There are several benefits attributed to the use of hospitalists. Hospitalists spend a great deal of time in the hospital and thus are familiar with the hospital systems and can expedite care. They can provide more continuous observation of patients and respond more rapidly to crises and changes in patient condition. Hospitalists also become more expert in recognizing and caring for common inpatient disorders.

The burgeoning hospitalist movement reflects efforts by hospitals to reduce both costs and medical errors as well as to improve the general quality of care. Studies confirm that hospitalists reduce costs by shortening hospital stays, preventing complications, and reducing readmissions. In addition, patients seem more satisfied with hospitalist care than with primary physicians who are able to spend only a few minutes a day with each patient as they fit hospital visits into their busy office schedules.[13]

Cost Containment and the Restructuring of Medical Practice

Historically, physicians were self-employed, engaged in solo practice or with a small number of associates, and received payment on a fee-for-service basis. With the exception of litigated circumstances of alleged malpractice, there was little or no outside accountability for the medical decisions and procedures that occurred during the diagnosis and treatment of patients. It was not until concerns over the rising cost of health care resulted in cost-containment initiatives that changed the method of reimbursement for medical services. Physicians were subjected to practice parameters and evaluations. Insurance companies, which for decades had simply increased premiums to compensate for escalating charges, began to use various strategies to hold down costs and stabilize premiums by monitoring physician services rendered.

The introduction of combined, capitated, or other risk-sharing financing and delivery had a dramatic impact on the health care system. Under capitation, health maintenance organizations reimbursed health care providers a set amount per patient. In return, providers were required to provide a comprehensive set of health care services. Capitation payments provided physicians with a base income that could include bonuses or other financial incentives.

In addition to affecting income and methods of payment, managed care, whether or not a health maintenance organization, subjected physicians to utilization reviews. Testing, treatment, and surgery decisions were monitored and evaluated. Physicians rallied against the loss of authority and income, and some have countered by forming their own preferred provider organizations and independent practitioner organizations. The vast majority of physicians, however, continue to subject themselves to the drastically discounted fee-for-service payments and other restrictions of managed care insurers.

Physicians have good reasons to complain. From 1995 to 2003 the average net income of physicians declined 7% after adjusting for inflation, whereas the incomes of their counterparts in other professions rose by 7%. Primary care physicians, already the lowest paid, saw a 10% decline in their earnings—another reason why medical graduates shun primary care.[28] As might be expected, many physicians compensated for the decline in income by booking as many patients as possible into each working day—a practice that decreases both the quality of care and patient satisfaction.

Clinical Practice Guidelines

Just as managed care has impinged on physician practice autonomy, so has the development of practice guidelines. Their growing acceptance as the means to more cost-effective and efficient health care has raised concerns about further intrusions by outside forces into the process of clinical decision making. Practice guidelines are defined as "systematically developed statements to assist practitioner and patient decisions about appropriate health care for specific clinical circumstances."[29]

Clinical practice guidelines evolved in the late 1970s and early 1980s after publication of data showing wide variations in the applications of medical procedures in regions in the United States and increased use of questionable, inappropriate, and unnecessary services that added significantly to the spiraling costs of health care. These studies are discussed in detail in Chapter 11, but it is important to note here that the variations in the level of health care interventions were so great as to suggest that physicians were unaware of the relative effectiveness of various procedures and that patients were not benefiting from much of the care they received.

Health care researchers conjectured that assessments of the outcomes or relative effectiveness of various medical procedures would lead to practice guidelines and eliminate ineffective, unnecessary, or inappropriate procedures and their related costs. To this end Congress created the Agency for Health Care Policy and Research in 1989. The agency was directed to fund outcomes research and start developing practice guidelines. After a slow start the agency started releasing practice guidelines for specific conditions. Although fewer than two dozen guidelines had been released by 1995, the agency's efforts sparked a great deal of guideline development by other institutions and agencies.[30] The RAND Corporation, medical specialty societies, health maintenance organizations, insurers, and others have now produced over 1,600 practice parameters.[31]

Although a number of specialty societies have developed and promoted practice guidelines as a service to their members, many physicians believe practice guidelines threaten their autonomy. After years of making clinical decisions without outside scrutiny or interference, practice guidelines appear to be yet another means for third-party payers and policymakers to make physicians document their performance and demonstrate their cost effectiveness.

Acceptance of practice guidelines seems to be dependent on who developed them and how they are presented. The guidelines that are trusted the most have been developed by the physicians' own organizations, such as the AMA or a specialty society. Guidelines developed by insurers or pharmaceutical firms are trusted the least.

The widespread application of clinical practice guidelines is expected to have a significant effect on medical practice. The nature of that effect is difficult to predict, however. Guidelines are considered by some to be the means to prevent unnecessary and negligent events and to clarify when negligence has occurred. Others believe that employers, insurers, providers, and others who base treatment and payment decisions on practice guidelines are likely to face complicated legal questions if harm results. In any case, with government agencies, health systems, third-party payers, specialty societies, and managed care organizations promoting the use of guidelines, it is certain they will become an integral part of medical practice.

Physician Report Cards

In the mid-1970s the code of ethics of the AMA explicitly prohibited "information that would point out differences between doctors." Thirty-two states passed laws supporting the AMA's position. The laws were intended to prevent misleading or competitive advertising of office hours, charges, or services. The position of organized medicine, however, reflected a long history of protecting physician performance from public scrutiny.[32]

Subsequently, the state laws supporting the AMA's position were determined to be violations of the First Amendment. Passage of freedom of information acts that prohibited governments from hiding information from the public removed the barriers that prevented the public from comparing the performance of physicians. In 1986, when the Health Care Financing Administration released hospital-specific mortality rates for Medicare patients, the dam was broken. In December 1991 *Newsday* published the first information regarding physician performance ever made public.[32] Never again would the public be denied access to government data about the quality of medical care. The publication was based on New York State's pioneering effort to compare and publish hospital-specific, severity-adjusted heart surgery mortality rates. Although New York State had intended to publish the names of only the hospitals involved, a *Newsday* freedom of information request, supported by the State Supreme Court, forced release of the rankings of the heart surgeons involved.[32]

Within less than a decade the contentious matter of exposing the comparative performance of physicians on a wide spectrum of variables has been resolved in favor of the consumers of medical care. Although physicians have protested and lobbied against each additional revelation as inaccurate, unfair, and misleading, consumer groups are winning out. A dozen states have passed legislation that gives the public access to physician information, including disciplinary records, malpractice actions, and whether a physician has lost privileges at a hospital. Florida has gone so far as to release the exact amount of every malpractice payment going back to the 1980s and allows the public to request a summary of each case that includes the patient's allegations.[33]

Medical societies in general support physician-profiling programs that report a physician's education, training, licensure, and membership in professional societies, state disciplinary actions, and serious misdemeanor convictions. They object strongly to medical malpractice and hospital disciplinary information as not true indicators of the quality of care.

Information technology has made it possible to assemble and adjust performance data so that service entities, be they physicians, hospitals, or managed care plans, can be compared on a wide variety of parameters of importance to consumers. Concise and relevant information on the quality of services provided can be invaluable to patients reviewing their options. Report cards allow the public to see information regarding the comparative performance of physicians and hospitals. It is also important to recognize that report cards have introduced incentives that encourage providers to improve their performance. Physicians want good report cards, and their behavior changes rapidly when they realize their colleagues are doing better than they are.

Internet sites have greatly facilitated access to report card information. Health Grades, Inc. provides a consumer website, www.healthgrades.com, that provides quality ratings and profiles for over 5,000 hospitals, 620,000 physicians, and 16,000 nursing homes. In addition, information is available on other health care providers such as home health agencies, chiropractors, fertility clinics, and assisted living residences.[34]

Introduction of Health Information Technology

The introduction of health information technology into the practice of medicine means that both new and established physicians will enter a new era in clinical practice. The impact is evident as physicians struggle with decisions about how much computer technology they can successfully incorporate into their practices.

Medical schools have responded by introducing medical informatics training into their coursework. Students may be trained on electronic medical records, wireless technologies, and the use of personal digital assistants (also called palmtop computers) for medical information, prescription notes, and alerts. Medical schools may have difficulties, however, finding suitable tenure-track faculty with both clinical backgrounds and technology skills. Nevertheless, the development of new health information technology is making it easier to educate physicians, transfer medical knowledge, investigate medical outliers, and communicate with other physicians.

Medical schools and teaching hospitals have adapted their curricula to include technology-enabled team communication and care, centralized electronic medical records, access to relevant data sources and medical libraries, real-time reporting of data, and support for decisions through evidence-driven care protocols. Telehealth, defined by the American Telemedicine Association as remote health care, is enabling remote monitoring of patients and making possible real-time surgical interventions from remote sites.

As the technology becomes established in medical practice, traditional diagnostic mechanisms will rely more on assisted decision making for physician and nurses through computer decision support systems, evidence-based medicine, computerized physician order entry, and e-prescribing as the norm. Health information technology will become a necessary component of the entire patient care continuum, in direct patient care, in audits and quality reporting, in long-term care, and in health information exchange. Beyond the hospital, personal health records can be used to interact with the patient in pre- and postcare situations.

The recent focus on the role of health information technologies to improve health quality and lower costs and some financial assistance has created momentum for its adoption. Nevertheless, there is still a long way to go to overcome the paucity of medical informatics and information technology courses in undergraduate medical curricula and a lack of research to assess the effectiveness of medical informatics in undergraduate medical education.[35] However, a study of third-year medical students reported generally positive attitudes toward using the electronic health record in the ambulatory setting. They noted that they received more feedback on their electronic charts than on paper charts. Students were concerned, however, about the potential impact of the electronic health record on their ability to conduct the doctor–patient encounter.[36]

A New Medical Practice Concept: The "Medical Home"

A new model of medical practice, known as the "medical home," is being promoted as a more viable alternative to the current system's focus on a variety of acute-care specialists. The medical home, at least theoretically, proposes that patients benefit from simpler, more personalized health care experiences. The major problem, however, is that the concept depends heavily on the role of the primary physician as the central hub of the medical home. In the absence of a strong primary component, already a major deficiency of the current health care system, the medical home concept, no matter how desirable, is not likely to prosper.[37]

Escalating Costs of Malpractice Insurance

The steeply rising costs of medical liability insurance are a growing concern for practicing physicians, medical schools, and teaching hospitals. In the last decade schools of medicine and hospitals have seen their liability premium costs increase from 6 to 10 times—from thousands to millions. In some states physicians, especially specialists, have seen their premiums triple or quadruple in just a few years.

Rising liability insurance costs reflect steep increases in the amount of malpractice jury awards. Also, during an economic downturn insurance companies that depended on investment income are forced to raise premiums to keep their businesses viable.

In any case the effect has been demoralizing to many physicians. Physicians are leaving high-premium states, choosing to retire early, or reducing high-risk aspects of their practice to lower their insurance costs. Many communities are deprived of certain medical services, such as obstetrics, as a result. It appears that legislative limits placed on jury awards are required to resolve the problem.

Growing Concern About Ethical Issues

Two developments have focused attention on a number of issues of medical ethics. Rather than concerns about unethical or unprofessional conduct, these ethical issues reflect the practice dilemmas faced by physicians working in the rapidly changing health care environment. The first set of ethical concerns relates to the various policies promoted by managed care organizations. Efforts of such organizations to manage the financing, costs, accessibility, or quality of the care delivered cause them to subject physicians to a range of guidelines, treatment parameters, peer reviews, and financial incentives and penalties. Cost-avoidance policies that require preauthorization for the more expensive procedures, substitution of less expensive tests, and restraint of hospitalization in favor of alternative ambulatory services raise questions about increased risks to patients.

Interestingly, an opposite set of ethical concerns could be raised about the risk to patients subjected to the practices of fee-for-service traditional medicine, which the managed care policies try to avoid—unnecessary hospitalizations, needless or inappropriate tests and procedures, ineffective treatments, and uncoordinated care by multiple providers. There is no question, however, that particular control strategies of managed care present related ethical issues. Increasingly, physicians admit that they exaggerate the severity of an illness to help patients get necessary care. Systems that encourage deceitful practices, be they fee-for-service or managed care, diminish the professional standards of medicine.

The second development that is creating vexing ethical issues is the remarkable advance in technologic capability that has occurred in the last few years. Medicine's ability to save more severely brain-injured patients, increasingly premature infants, terminally ill or brain-dead patients, and others with no promise of functional survival has increased the need for ethical guidelines. At present, individual physicians can decide how they advise families of such patients. If the family and the physician cannot agree about treatment, there is no set procedure for deciding what to do. These and other ethical dilemmas brought about by the technologic advances in medicine present formidable challenges to the ethics committees of hospitals and professional organizations.

Among the most critical of future ethical issues are those related to advances in the field of molecular biology and gene manipulation and therapy. International research efforts, such as the Human Genome Project and the discovery and characterization of molecular correlates of human health and disease, with all their potential use and abuse ramifications, present a mind-boggling ethical challenge. The future use of individual genetic blueprints for diagnosis and treatment as well as for predicting future medical events has scientists, policymakers, and ethicists concerned about potential runaway applications of the technology. Amid all the potential benefits of this amazing scientific advance are fears of the unethical application of the technology.

Physicians and the Internet

Patients are not the only ones using the Internet to obtain online health information. Recent studies found that after a slow start, 70% of U.S. physicians are now using the Internet to access the sites of peer-reviewed research, medical publishers, medical societies, and health care provider organizations.[38] The number of new medical websites has been growing at the rate of 10% per month, listing information about everything from medical meetings around the world to the disease-specific displays of pharmaceutical companies to quality information provided by national medical organizations. In addition, physicians themselves have developed personal websites to establish their credentials, explain their practice specialties, and attract patients and referrals.

In addition to information on professional meetings and seminars and the latest developments in clinical practice, physicians can obtain the latest data from more than 4,000 clinical trials. The National Institutes of Health website, www.ClinicalTrials.gov, allows physicians as well as the public to learn about federal, university, and private medical studies at more than 47,000 locations nationwide. Information is provided about the research locations, designs, purpose, criteria for participation, and diseases or treatments under study.

The Internet release of that information long before it can be evaluated as suitable for publication through established methods and published in one of the traditional peer-reviewed medical journals has set off a heated debate between the leading figures in academic medicine and advocates of open access.

Future of Medical Practice

Medicine has made astounding progress in the last half century. An increasing number of highly specialized physicians and support personnel, working in concert, achieve marvels of technical accomplishment. Yet the overall success of American medicine as measured by overall health system performance place the United States 37th in the world according to the World Health Organization.[38] These rankings are usually explained away by pointing to the heterogeneity of the U.S. population as compared with those of other developed countries. Nevertheless, underlying the impressive motivation and clinical competence of American physicians and the outstanding technology available to them is a system that was organized for a much earlier period in medical history. For instance, the incredibly complex character of current American medicine, with a few notable exceptions, still relies on the slow hand-offs of personal and clinical information from one physician to another or between and among other care providers. Sometimes the information does not move at all or gets misplaced. It is an incongruity of a highly sophisticated diagnostic and treatment structure that many physicians and hospitals still rely on barely legible handwritten notes to record patient assessments, treatment modalities, and patient responses.

Communication among providers and between providers and patients remains problematic as medical technology progresses and time pressures on physicians increase. The National Board of Medical Examiners addressed one aspect of the patient communication problem. Starting with the 2005 class of graduating medical students, a requirement of graduation is passing a "clinical skills assessment" test. The day-long test, with actors playing the part of patients with common illnesses, examines a graduate's ability to communicate with patients, gather information, perform physical examinations, and diagnose illnesses.[39]

It is ironic that just at the time when scientific and technologic advances have prepared the U.S. health care system to make its greatest contributions to the prevention and treatment of disease, the financing and delivery problems of the system are in frustrating disorder. Unfortunately, until those problems are solved, health care never will be able to achieve the full potential of its scientific and technical capacity. In the midst of all the changes taking place, one circumstance seems abundantly clear: Physicians and their professional organizations are incapable of resolving the problems they now face.

Physicians can work closely with the hospitals to serve their mutual needs. They can contract with managed care organizations to continue to serve the enrollees who were previously their fee-for-service patients. They can join the various provider networks to retain some negotiating power among the shifting market forces, but they cannot solve the problems that affect them the most because those are the problems of the larger society. Even if all participants in the system—providers, consumers, payers, insurers, and managed care organizations—try to solve the health system problems, they cannot do it. This situation is occurring at a crucial time in the evolution of medical care: The components of the system are struggling for long-term viability, if not survival, in an environment that is changing rapidly.

The imbalance among the access, cost, and quality of health care that provoked the market-driven reforms evolved from an entrepreneurial system that tried constantly to improve an already superb ability to diagnose and treat the ills of individual patients while failing dismally to address the needs of the larger society. The more sophisticated the medical care technology became, the more indifferent providers seemed to become toward meeting the health needs of populations rather than individuals.

Now, the health care system's problems of cost, access, and quality have demonstrated, at great expense, that it is not enough for physicians and other health professionals to serve the individuals they choose, one patient at a time. The education and socialization of health professionals have failed when many, if not most, feel no obligation to address the health needs of groups of people in ways that benefit public health and decrease the need for costly medical interventions.

Most physicians and other health care professionals in clinical practice have not been adequately prepared to exercise their potential to prevent disease, address the problems of unequal access to competent care, and assume accountability for the effectiveness of their therapies. The high level of autonomy physicians enjoyed for decades is rapidly disappearing because they failed to bring their salient knowledge and skills to bear on relevant societal problems. The power to direct the course of health care in the United States has rapidly shifted from the providers to the insurers and purchasers.

Instead of fighting to retain the status quo in battles already lost, physicians and other health care professionals should be making it clear to the larger society that the dynamics driving the health care revolution cannot be dealt with separately by vested interests. Medicine is not solely responsible for inventing more health care than people want to pay for. Medicine responded to the public desire to have the best and the most of medical services, but medicine now has a responsibility to make the public understand that the problem is beyond those within the system. As politically onerous as it might be, U.S. citizens and their representatives have to assume the responsibility for carefully and deliberately creating a new form of health care organization that ensures a coherent, efficient, and effective health care delivery system. Until that happens, physicians will continue to lose the authority, autonomy, and status that formerly characterized the practice of medicine.

References

1. Raffel MW, Raffel NK. *The U.S. Health System: Origins and Functions,* 4th ed. Albany, NY: Delmar Publishers; 1994.
2. Jones RS. Organized medicine in the United States. *Ann Surg.* 1993;217:423.
3. Anderson GF, Greenberg G, Lisk CK, et al. Academic health centers: exploring a financial paradox. *Health Affairs.* 1999;18:163.
4. The National Academic Press. Academic health centers: leading change in the 21st century. In: *The Consequences of Current Financing Methods for the Future Roles AHCs.* 2004:92–109. Available from http://www.aahcd.org. Accessed September 27, 2009.
5. Association of American Medical Colleges. Tables and graphs for fiscal year 2008-U.S. medical schools, p. 42. Available from http://www.aamc.org/data/finance/start.htm. Accessed September 28, 2009.
6. Association of Academic Health Centers, Washington, D.C. About Academic Health Centers. Available from http://www.aahcdc.org/about/. Accessed August 14, 2000.
7. Association of American Medical Colleges. AAMC accredited medical schools. Available from http://www.aamc.org/medicalschools.htm. Accessed October 4, 2009.
8. American Association of Colleges of Osteopathic Medicine. AACOM accredited colleges of osteopathic medicine. Available http://www.aacom.org/people/colleges/pages/default.aspx. Accessed October 4, 2009.
9. National Resident Matching Program. About residency. Available from http://www.nrmp.org/about_nrmp/index.html. Accessed August 7, 2000.
10. Morris TQ, Sirica CM. Taking charge of graduate medical education: to meet the nation's needs in the 21st century. Proceedings of a conference sponsored by the Josiah Macy, Jr. Foundation. New York, June 1992.
11. Kelly JV, Larned FS, Smits HL, et al. Graduate medical education consortia: expectations and experiences. *Acad Med.* 1994;12:931–943.
12. American Board of Medical Specialties. Specialties and subspecialties. Available from http://www.abms.org/Who_We_Help/Physicians/specialties.aspx. Accessed October 2, 2009.
13. The Hospitalist Model of Care. A knoll by Robert Wachter. July 14, 2009. Available from http://knol.google.com/k/the-hospitalist-model-of-care#. Accessed October 3, 2009.

14. National Center for Health Statistics. *United States 2004 with Chartbook on Trends in Health of Americans.* Hyattsville, MD: Centers for Disease Control and Prevention; 2004.

15. Daugherty RM Jr. Health Care and the Market. Hastings Center Report. 1998;28:(4)4.

16. National Center for Health Statistics, Bureau of Health Professions. Table 107, first-year enrollment and graduates of health professions schools and number of schools according to profession: United States, selected years 1980–98. Available from /www.cdc.gov/nchs/products/pubs/pubd/hus/tables/99hus107.pdf. Accessed August 14, 2000.

17. Whelan GP, Gary NE, Kostis J, et al. The changing pool of international medical graduates seeking certification training in US graduate medical education programs. *JAMA.* 2002;288:1079–1084.

18. U.S. Department of Labor, Bureau of Labor Statistics. Occupation outlook handbook, 2010–2011, physicians and surgeons. Available from http://www.bls.gov/oco/ocos074.htm. Accessed December 27, 2004.

19. Cooper RA. Seeking a balanced physician work force for the 21st century. *JAMA.* 1994;272:680–687.

20. Salsberg ES, Forte GJ. Trends in the physicians workforce, 1980–2000. *Health Affairs.* 2002;21:165–173.

21. U.S. Department of Labor, Bureau of Labor Statistics. Occupational outlook handbook, 2010–2011, physicians and surgeons. Available from http://www.bls.gov/oco/ocos074.htm. Accessed July 22, 2000.

22. Steiner E, Stoken JM. Overcoming barriers to generalism in medicine: the residents' perspective. *Acad Med.* 1995;70:589–594.

23. O'Neil EH. Education as part of the health care solution. *JAMA.* 1992; 268:1146.

24. Inwald SA, Winters FD. Emphasizing a preventive medicine orientation during primary care/family practice residency training. *J Am Osteopath Assoc.* 1995;95:268.

25. McGinnis JM. Can public health and medicine partner in the public interest? *Health Affairs.* 2006;25:1044, 1052.

26. Kovner AR. *Health Care Delivery in the United States,* 5th ed. New York: Springer; 1995:429–430.

27. Goldsmith J. Hospitals and physicians: not a pretty picture. *Health Affairs.* 2007;26:72–75.

28. Tu HT, Ginsburg PB. Losing ground: physician income, 1995–2003. Tracking Report No. 15, June 2006, Center for Studying Health System Change. Available from http://www.hschange.org. Accessed October 5, 2009.

29. Institute of Medicine. United States Committee on Clinical Practice Guidelines. In: Field MJ, Lohr KN, Eds. *Guidelines for Clinical Practice: From Development to Use.* Washington, DC: National Academy Press; 1992:63.

30. Agency for Health Care Policy and Research. AHCPR clinical practice guideline topics. Agency for Health Care Policy and Research News Report. March 1994.

31. Toepp MC, Kuznets N. *Directory of Practice Parameters: Titles, Sources, and Updates.* Chicago: American Medical Association Office of Quality Assurance and Medical Review; 1994:vi.

32. Millenson ML. *Demanding Medical Excellence.* Chicago: University of Chicago Press; 1997:173.

33. Special report, docs fight to hide lawsuits. *New York Daily News, Sports Final.* April 17, 2000:12.

34. The Healthcare Report Cards, Inc. Web site grades 5,000 U.S. hospitals in critical medical specialties. *Health Industry Today.* 1999;62:10.

35. Kushniruk OT. Incorporation of medical informatics and information technology as core components of undergraduate medical education—time to change! *Stud Health Technol Inform.* 2009;143:62–67.

36. Chumley RE, Dobbie AE. Electronic health records in outpatient clinics: perspectives of third year medical students. *BMC Med Educ.* 2008;8.

37. AAMC Reporter. Medical home concept gains momentum. March 2008. Available from http://www.aamc.org. Accessed March 10, 2009.

38. Physician use of internet explodes. *Health Manage Technol.* 1999;20:8–9.

39. American Medical Association. Advocacy & policy. Clinical skills assessment exam. Available at http.www.ama-clinical-skills-assessment-exam. Accessed October 5, 2009.

CHAPTER 6

Health Care Personnel

This chapter defines the major health care professions, with particular emphasis on their educational preparation, credentials, numbers, and roles in the health service system. The factors that influence demand for the various health care providers are also reviewed. The chapter concludes with a discussion of the development of health workforce policy and some expectations for the future.

As one of the nation's largest and most important industries, health care is also one of the largest employment sectors. The Department of Labor estimates that 13.8 million people, or approximately 10% of the U.S. workforce, are employed in the health care industry. In the next decade, more new jobs, about 4 million, will be created in health care than in any other industry.[1]

Although hospitals are still a major employer, recent employment growth has been among health maintenance organizations, ambulatory clinics and services, home health providers, and offices of health practitioners.

Health Professions

There are more than 200 occupations and professions among the over 13 million workers in the health care field. As the system continues to change, making use of new technology, expanding in some sectors and contracting in others, additional occupations and professions will appear. The personnel of those new occupations and professions will be required to possess more specialized knowledge and more sophisticated skills.

Specialization to attain higher levels of technical competence also reduces the flexibility of providers to develop more efficient staffing patterns. Specialization among the workforce increases personnel costs as additional employees are required to perform specific tasks. Smaller service facilities, especially in rural areas, are burdened most by the need for infrequently used specialists.

As a result, there is growing acceptance of multiskilled health practitioners. Hospitals, in particular, are employing individuals trained in more than one skill. A large number of combinations are feasible: Occupational therapy assistants are also serving as physical therapy assistants, radiologic technologists are performing ultrasound, and a variety of nonclinical personnel is performing phlebotomy.

The expansion of home health care services is also contributing to job growth. Technologic advances now permit sophisticated medical procedures to be performed in home settings. Cost constraints force people to forego or shorten hospital stays, and the larger number and increased longevity of aging Americans will increase the need for the home care services of nurses, therapists, and aides. Table 6-1 shows the distribution of health care workers.

Table 6-1 Percent Distribution of Health Care Employment by Setting

Offices and clinics of:	Percent Distribution
Physicians	12.3
Dentists	5.7
Other Practitioners	3.5
Outpatient care centers	6.4
Home health care services	5.4
Other health care services*	6.9
Hospitals	41.5
Nursing care facilities	13.8
Residential care without nursing	4.4
All health service sites	100.0

*Includes ambulance services, blood banks, diagnostic centers, and others.
Source: Reprinted from U.S. Department of Labor, Bureau of Labor Statistics.

Credentialing and Regulating Health Professionals

Government regulation of the health professions is considered necessary to protect the public from incompetent and unethical practitioners. Because each state assumes and exercises most of that responsibility for itself, how health care occupations are regulated and the manner in which regulation is carried out vary from state to state. About 50 health occupations are regulated throughout the United States.

Regulatory restrictions limit health care service agencies in how they may use personnel and limit their ability to explore innovative ways to provide patient care. Similarly, regulatory restrictions influence educational programs to focus curricula on what has been prescribed by regulatory boards and their related accrediting bodies. Many states have taken steps to revise their credentialing systems to provide greater flexibility and responsiveness to fast-changing health care technology.[2]

The health care occupations have been regulated by one of three procedures: state licensure, state or national certification, or state or national registration. In licensure, the state law defines the scope of practice to be regulated and the educational and testing requirements that must be met to engage in that practice. Licensure, the most restrictive of the three types of regulation, is intended to restrict entry or practice in certain occupations and to prevent the use of professional titles by those without predetermined qualifications. For example, it is illegal for individuals to perform procedures defined in the statutes as medicine or dentistry or to call themselves physicians or dentists without the appropriate license.

Most licensure boards are composed primarily of practitioners whose concern is for setting standards and assessing competence for initial entrance into the field. Except by requiring attendance at continuing education courses, licensure boards have done very little about ensuring continuing competence, dealing with impaired practitioners, or disciplining wayward members of their professions; however, they do have the power to censure, warn members, or even revoke licenses.

Certification is the regulating process under which a state or voluntary professional organization, such as a national board, attests to the educational achievements and performance abilities of persons in a health care field of practice. It is a much less restrictive regulation than licensing and means that the individual has obtained advanced or specialized training in that area of practice. When applied to such fields as psychology and social work, certification does not make it illegal for unqualified individuals to engage in activities within the scope of practice in those fields as long as they do not claim or use the titles of certified psychologist or social worker. Certification allows the public, employers, and third-party payers to determine which practitioners are appropriately qualified in their specialty or occupation.

Certification generally has no provision for regulating impaired or misbehaving practitioners other than putting them on probation or dropping them from certification. Unlike the licensed professions, the certified occupations have no legal basis for preventing an impaired or professionally delinquent individual who is uncertified from practicing. It is left to third-party payers or employers to insist on only certified practitioners.

Registration began as a mechanism to facilitate contacts and relationships among members of a profession and potential employers or the public. It is the least rigorous of regulatory processes, ranging from simple listings or registries of persons offering a service, such as private duty nurses, to national registration programs of professional or occupational groups that require educational and testing qualifications. Because most registration programs are voluntary, they have little to do with continuing competence or disciplinary actions.[3]

Health Care Occupations

Space does not allow for the description of all or even most of the occupations in health care, but several major health care occupations are outlined here. Because Chapter 5 is devoted to medical education and practice, the information regarding physicians in this chapter is purposely limited.

Physicians

There are 131 accredited medical schools in the United States that award the Doctor of Medicine (MD) degree. Although current enrollment has increased slightly, the 16,167 graduates of U.S. medical schools in 2008 reflects a decrease of 203 graduates from the previous year. The number of women enrolled in U.S. medical schools has more than doubled in the last 20 years. In 2008, the graduating medical class was 49% female.

The number of minority students enrolled in medical schools nearly tripled during the same period and now constitutes one-third of medical school enrollees. In 2008, 64% of the medical school graduates were white, 7% black, 7.3% Hispanic, 21% Asian, and 3.8% either foreign, Native American, or of mixed or unknown race.[4]

There are 25 accredited colleges of osteopathy that offer the Doctor of Osteopathy (DO) degree. In the last two decades their enrollment has nearly doubled, and they now graduate about 2,400 students per year. Doctors of medicine and doctors of osteopathy share the same privileges in most U.S. hospitals. The 55,000 doctors of osteopathy practicing in the United States make up about 8% of all the physicians in the country.[5]

Although medical education in the United States begins in undergraduate medical school, it continues intensively for as many as 8 years of graduate medical training. Most states require 1 year of graduate medical education before a physician can be licensed. That year, which used to be called an internship, is now considered the first of 3 years of residency training regarded by the medical profession as the minimum needed to practice medicine.

Residency training prepares a physician to practice a medical specialty. In a period of 3 to 8 years, depending on the specialty, residency qualifies a physician for certification in 1 of 24 medical specialty boards. Further residency training, often called a fellowship, can lead to a certificate in 1 of over 100 subspecialties. Chapter 5 lists these medical specialties and subspecialties (see Table 5-1).

Because U.S. medical schools consistently graduate about 5,000 fewer new physicians per year than are employed as first-year residents, the gap is filled by physicians trained in medical schools outside of the United States. The responsibility for evaluating the credentials of international medical graduates (IMGs) entering the United States to enter residency programs lies with the Educational Commission for Foreign Medical Graduates, a private nonprofit organization sponsored by major U.S. medical organizations, including the American Association of Medical Colleges.

Although a more stringent certification process and the heightened security concerns after the tragic events of September 11 may have deterred some IMGs from pursuing the opportunity to train in the United States, the number entering this country annually, about 6,000, is more than adequate to meet the annual shortfall of U.S. medical school graduates.[6]

The impetus for this influx is the demand for resident house officers in both teaching and nonteaching hospitals. All but the most prestigious hospitals, particularly those in rural or inner-city areas, depend heavily on foreign medical graduates to staff their clinical services.

After finishing their residency training, most of these IMGs remain in the United States to practice. As a result, IMGs now constitute about one-fourth of the active U.S. physician workforce. Also, a relatively stable group of about 1,350 U.S. citizens attend medical schools outside the country and return to practice each year.

About 35% of the over 700,000 practicing physicians in the United States are in primary care, general pediatrics, general or family practice, or general internal medicine practice. Almost two-thirds of this country's physicians limit their practice to one of the many medical specialties.[7]

Nevertheless, there are serious shortages in certain medical specialties that affect the efficiency and quality of medical care in some geographic areas. Depending on the region of the country, several of a wide range of medical specialists may be in short supply.[8]

Nursing

Nursing was a common employment position for women during the 19th century through association with a religious or benevolent group. A physician, Ann Preston, organized the first training program for nurses in the United States in 1861 at Philadelphia's Woman's Hospital. Training was open to all women "who wished greater proficiency in their domestic responsibilities."[9]

At the turn of the century hundreds of new hospitals were built under the aegis of religious orders, ethnic groups, industrialists, and elite groups of civic-minded individuals. Because student nurses were a constantly renewable source of low-cost workers to staff the wards, even some of the smallest hospitals maintained nursing schools.[10] Hospital nursing school programs, therefore, were primarily sequences of on-the-job training rather than academic courses. As the programs evolved, stronger academic components were introduced, eventually leading to baccalaureate degrees instead of hospital diplomas.

World War I had a profound effect on the nursing profession. Before the war nursing was divided into three domains—public health, private duty, and hospital. Public health nursing was the elite pursuit and was recognized as instrumental in the campaign against tuberculosis and promoting infant welfare. Only a few nurses worked for hospitals. In 1920, over 70% of nurses worked in private duty, about half in patients' homes and half for private patients in hospitals.

The war emphasized the drama and effectiveness of hospitals, and it soon became the center of nursing education in the increasingly special-ized acute-care medical environment. The social medicine and public health aspects of nursing were subjugated to the image of nursing as a symbol of patriotism, national sacrifice, and efficiency. The war experi-ence established nurses as dedicated associates in hospital science. Nursing leaders promoted the idea of upgrading nursing through high-quality hospital nursing schools, preferably associated with universities. The choice to idealize the role of the nurse as dedicated and deferential to the physician specialist in the hospital marginalized the independent role of the nurse in social medicine and public health.[11]

Different levels of nursing education were developed at a variety of educational institutions. A registered nurse (RN) could be trained in a 2-year associate degree program at a community college or a junior col-lege, a 2- to 3-year diploma program offered through a hospital, or a 4- to 5-year bachelor's of science degree program at a university or college.

The increasing complexity in health care forced specialization in nurs-ing as it did in medicine. Nurses with a bachelor's degree may undertake advanced studies in several clinical areas to develop the needed compe-tence for teaching, supervision, or advanced practice. Clinical nurse spe-cialists in hospitals play important liaison roles between the medical practitioners in narrow and highly technical subspecialties, the patients, and supportive nursing services. By the 1960s, master's degree and doc-toral programs were developed for nurses who wished to specialize.

The number of RNs in the United States increased by over 1 million between 1980 and 2000. The increase slowed considerably during the last 4 years of that period as nurse dissatisfaction with working conditions became widely known. The latest survey of the RN population conducted in 2004 and reported in 2006 indicated a new high of 2.9 million RNs in the United States and that 83% of those nurses were actively employed. The average age had climbed to 46.8 years, the highest average age since record keeping began in 1960. Only 8% were less than 30 years old com-pared with 25% in 1980.[12]

It has been estimated that about one-third of the increase in the num-ber of nurses in the United States since the 1990s was due to the influx of nurses born outside of the United States.[13] Nurses are encouraged to leave their home countries and work in the United States for the opportunity to earn more money, enjoy a higher standard of living, and advance their education.

One of the major changes occurring in nursing is in the type of program that nurses enter to obtain their basic education. Almost 90% of nurses now receive their basic education in an institution of higher education compared with 20% in 1960. RNs with master's or doctorate degrees rose to 376,901, an increase of 37% since 1980.[12]

Nurses began to specialize during the 1950s. After World War II, nurses were in short supply, and hospitals began to group the least physiologically stable patients in one nursing unit for intensive care. The more competent nurses cared for the sickest patients, but instead of lowering the need for nurses the critical care nurse specialty began, and the need for staff nurses continued to grow.

There are now more than 50 U.S. schools that have at least one of the three types of doctoral programs in nursing. The doctor of nursing is the first professional doctoral degree building on liberal arts or scientific education and preparing the student to take the state licensing exam to practice as an RN. The doctor of nursing science (DNS and DNSc) degrees are professional doctorates that prepare the nurse for advanced clinical practice. The nursing PhD is an academic degree with requirements similar to the PhD in other fields—extensive preparation in a narrow field and a dissertation.[14] Table 6-2 shows the distribution of employed RNs nurses by setting. During the 1980s the importance of nursing research was recognized by the addition of the National Center for Nursing Research within the National Institutes of Health.

Men comprise a small percentage of the nurse population, although their numbers are increasing. In 2000 only about 5.4% of RNs were men. By 2004 the number of men in nursing reached 9.5% of all nurses. Rapid increases are also occurring in the numbers of RNs identifying themselves as members of a minority group. By 2002 one of every five nurses was of a minority group.[15]

Hospital consolidations in response to market pressures and the widespread acceptance of managed care affect nursing employment in several ways. Hospital workforces have been reorganized to adjust to fiscal restraints, reductions in the number of admissions, and shortened lengths of stay. At the same time, increases in the intensity of nursing care required by the more complicated illnesses of the patients who are

Table 6-2 Percent Distribution of Employed Registered Nurses by Setting in 2000

Setting	Percent Distribution
Hospital	62.1
Nursing home	8.4
Ambulatory care setting	8.1
Home health	6.5
Community/Public Health	4.8
Student health service	2.9
Nursing education	2.3
Occupational health	1.0
Other	3.9
Total	100.0

Source: Data from U.S. Department of Health and Human Services, Health Resources and Service Administration, Bureau of Health Professions, National Center for Health Workforce Analysis, 2000 National Sample Survey of Registered Nurses.

admitted to hospitals suggest the need for higher nurse-to-patient ratios. Thus, although many hospitals employ fewer nurses for inpatient care, those retained are expected to maintain clinically sophisticated nursing skills, monitor lesser trained persons employed to provide direct patient care, and manage nursing units filled with seriously ill patients.

Fewer nurses taking care of more severely ill patients during even shorter hospital stays, combined with the need to supervise nonprofessional and unlicensed personnel performing nursing tasks, has increased nursing workloads, lowered morale, and raised serious concerns about the declining quality of care.[14]

Not surprisingly, concerns for the quality of care, frustration with unresponsive hospital managers, and burnout from working in understaffed facilities have made hospital nursing a less attractive career. As a result, many competent nurses have retired or sought employment in non-inpatient settings. Nurses formerly employed in hospitals have been absorbed in ambulatory service facilities such as surgery centers and group practices. Others have chosen to reorient themselves to the quite different job requirements of nurses in home care organizations and long-term care facilities.[15]

Although there remain important concerns about the continued aging of the currently employed RN population and the difficulty schools of nursing are experiencing in expanding nursing enrollment due to lack of faculty, there are promising developments. There has been a recent increase in the number of nursing graduates taking the licensure exam, and hospitals are developing innovative ways to increase enrollment in schools of nursing. For instance, North Carolina Baptist Hospital in Winston-Salem has created a steady supply of nurses by paying all educational expenses for 45 nursing students each year in return for a 3-year commitment to the hospital. Other facilities are offering attractive sign-on bonuses to recruit new graduates. In addition, many schools of nursing are adding accelerated programs as a way to bring nurses to the workforce more quickly.[16] The Robert Wood Johnson Foundation, which has a long history of supporting nurses, is addressing one of the roots of the problem. Its projects are directed at changing the frustrating nursing work environment through alterations of both physical facilities and hospital cultures. The changes are intended to decrease the amount of time nurses spend on non-nursing tasks to permit them to focus on the more satisfying responsibilities of maintaining the quality of patient care.[17] Figure 6-1 illustrates the supply and demand projections for the nursing profession.

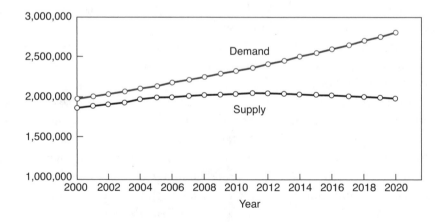

FIGURE 6-1 National Supply and Demand Projections of FTE Registered Nurses, 2000 to 2020.
Source: U.S. Department of Health and Human Services, Health Resources and Service Administration, Bureau of Health Professions, RN Supply and Demand Projections.

Licensed Practical Nurses

A licensed practical nurse (LPN) works under the direct supervision of an RN or physician. One-year LPN training is offered at about 1,100 state-approved technical or vocational schools or community or junior colleges. Programs include both classroom study and supervised clinical practice. Like RNs, LPNs must pass a state licensing examination.

Since 2002, when 28% of the over 700,000 LPNs worked in hospitals, employment in hospitals is decreasing. The reduction in inpatient days and the substitution of unlicensed personnel have decreased the number of LPNs in hospitals by almost 10,000 per year. The demand for LPNs in the other work settings, however, is increasing. Nursing homes employ 26% of the LPNs, and another 12% are employed in physician offices and clinics. The remainder works in home health care, residential care facilities, schools, and government agencies.[18]

Nurse Practitioners

Nurse practitioners are RNs with advanced education and clinical experience. Most nurse practitioners specialize. Neonatal nurse practitioners work with newborns. Pediatric nurse practitioners treat children from infancy through adolescence. School nurse practitioners serve students in elementary and secondary schools, colleges, and universities. Adult and family nurse practitioners are generalists who serve adults and families. Occupational health nurse practitioners work in industry providing on-the-job care. Psychiatric nurse practitioners serve people with mental or emotional problems. Geriatric nurse practitioners care for older adults.[19]

The earliest nurse practitioners were nurse midwives and nurse anesthetists. A nurse midwife usually is an RN who completes a 1- or 2-year master's degree program in nurse midwifery. They are licensed by the state and may also be required to be certified by the American College of Nurse Midwives. Currently, almost all midwife-assisted births take place in a hospital or birthing clinic.

The roots for the nurse anesthetist specialty go back over a century, when nurses administered anesthesia in Catholic hospitals. Early training was provided in hospitals, but in 1945 the American Association of Nurse Anesthetists established a certification program. Nurse anesthetists are now required to have a master's degree from an accredited school and must pass the national certification examination. Most nurse anesthetists work with physician anesthesiologists in hospitals, ambulatory surgery centers, and urgent care centers providing comprehensive care to patients who need anesthesia.[20]

The current nurse practitioner movement began in the 1960s because of the shortage of physicians. The goal was to have specially prepared nurses augment the supply of physicians by working as primary care providers in pediatrics, adult health, geriatrics, and obstetrics. Nurse practitioners had to overcome some resistance from organized medicine and legal difficulties caused by restrictions in most state nurse practice acts, which included a prohibition against nurses diagnosing and treating patients. Nurse practitioners sought state-by-state changes in nurse practice acts, and by 1975 most states had started certifying or accepting the national certification of nurse practitioners, nurse midwives, and nurse anesthetists.[21]

Two-thirds of the first 131 nurse practitioner programs were relatively short certificate programs, and one-third were master's programs. The programs specialized primarily in training for practice in pediatrics, midwifery, maternity, family medicine, adult health, or psychiatry. As in most ventures into uncharted territory, several approaches to nurse practitioner preparation were tested. Eventually, it was accepted that a nurse practitioner should be an RN with a master's degree. National certification and recertification are necessary.[22]

Efforts at health care cost containment have increased the demand for cost-effective nurse practitioners. Rural hospitals, with limited reserves of physicians, make substantial use of nurse practitioners and physician assistants and consider them to be a cost-effective means to an expanded scope of service to primary care.[23]

Nurse practitioners and physician assistants also are heavily involved in emergency department care, managing a wide range of conditions in about 4% of all emergency department visits.[24]

The high regard for nurse practitioners among both other medical personnel and the public is evidenced by the fact that there are now over 300 master's and post-master's programs in the United States for the preparation of nurse practitioners.[25]

Clinical Nurse Specialist

A different, but related, type of advanced nursing practice is the clinical nurse specialist. The specialty role was developed in response to the specific nursing care needs of increasingly complex patients.[26] Like specialist physicians, clinical nurse specialists are advanced practice specialists with in-depth knowledge and skills that make them valuable adjunct practitioners in specialized clinical settings. As a result, there are now more than 230 master's programs for the advanced preparation of clinical nurse specialists.[27]

Dentistry

Dentistry in early America was primitive. Tooth extraction was performed by itinerant tooth drawers, the neighborhood doctor or barber, or, in many cases, the local blacksmith. Because there were no regulations, anyone could practice dentistry, and skilled craftsmen and artisans turned their talents to dental practice.

Until about 1850 almost all prominent dentists were medical doctors who had chosen dentistry rather than general medicine as their vocation.[28] It was also in the 19th century that dentistry began its emergence from a trade to a profession. Dental schools were established to replace preceptorships, and dental practitioners participated in developing laws to regulate the profession.[29]

In 1840, the State of Maryland chartered the first dental school, the Baltimore College of Dental Surgery. The course of study lasted 2 years, the same as that required for a medical degree. By 1884, 28 dental colleges existed. Although a few were affiliated with universities, most were privately owned. New York took the lead in regulating the profession by licensure. The state's dental society was empowered in 1868 to establish a board of censors to examine candidates. In time, it became the State Board of Dental Examiners. By the end of the century, most other states also had passed licensure laws.

The mix of university-affiliated and independent dental schools resulted in significant variations in the quality of dental education. In 1922, 12 years after the Carnegie Foundation for the Advancement of Teaching had issued the Flexner Report evaluating U.S. medical education, the foundation created a commission to examine dental education. The commission's report appeared in 1926 and resulted in a complete reorganization of dental education in the United States.[30]

World War II brought about profound changes in Americans' attitudes toward dentistry. Citizens were shocked to learn that the dental health of the nation's young men was deplorable. Among the first 2 million draftees summoned by the Selective Service System, one of five lacked even the minimum standard of 12 functioning teeth. The Selective Service had to eliminate all dental standards to avoid mass disqualification of selectees. As a consequence, after the war the United States made a vigorous effort to improve the dental health of the country's population.

Before World War II, dentists were not involved in public health, and few dental schools taught anything on the subject. A decade after the first graduate course of study in dental public health was established in the 1940s by the University of Michigan, the new field of public health dentistry emerged in the United States. Today, a number of schools have established courses leading to advanced degrees in the field, and there is an American Board of Dental Public Health to certify them as specialists.

The U.S. Public Health Service established the National Institute of Dental Research in 1948. Ultimately incorporated into the National Institutes of Health, the National Institute of Dental Research played a major role in furthering basic and applied dental research.

Also beneficial to dentistry during the postwar years was the increase in insurance group plans that provide payment for routine dental care and, in certain instances, more extensive dentistry at an additional premium. By 1980, almost 100 million Americans were covered, to some degree, by a dental insurance plan; today, it is a common employee benefit.

The overall number of dentists per U.S. citizen reached its highest point in 1987 but will continue to decrease in the coming decades. There have been major decreases in the annual number of dental graduates, whereas the general population continues to increase.

Nine practice specialties have developed in dentistry:

1. Dental public health
2. Endodontics
3. Oral and maxillofacial pathology
4. Oral and maxillofacial radiology
5. Oral and maxillofacial surgery
6. Orthodontics and dentofacial orthopedics
7. Pediatric dentistry
8. Periodontics
9. Prosthodontics

Unlike in medicine, more than 85% of the 150,000 practicing dentists in the United States are general practitioners.[31] There are 56 U.S. dental schools in the United States, a decrease of 5 since 1980. These dental schools graduate about 4,300 dentists per year, a drop of over 1,200 per year in the last two decades. Graduates receive a Doctor of Dental Surgery (DDS) degree or its equivalent, a Doctor of Dental Medicine (DMD).

The demographic composition of America's dental profession is also changing. From a low of 13% in 1980, minorities now constitute one-third of the annual enrollment in dental schools. Women are also more prominent in dental school enrollment. Female dental students, once a rarity in dental schools, now comprise nearly one-half of first-year enrollments.[32]

Overall, dentists are working fewer hours for increased earnings. Dentistry has successfully resisted managed care and capitated payments and remains a "cottage industry." With most dentists in solo practice choosing to serve only those with dental insurance or the fiscal means to pay prevailing fees, many of the population groups with the greatest need for dental services continue to be underserved. Neither dental education nor the current practice model places high priority on the creation of a dental safety net for underserved populations.[33]

Pharmacy

Pharmaceutical practice dates back to ancient Egypt, Rome, and Greece. The first apothecaries appeared in Europe during the 12th century. By 1546 the Senate of the city of Nuremberg, Germany, recognized the value of standardizing drugs to ensure uniformity in filling prescriptions.[34]

Hospital pharmacists were apprentice physicians in early America. In 1765 John Morgan proposed that medicine and pharmacy be separate, and by 1811 the New York Hospital had a full-time pharmaceutical practitioner. The American Pharmaceutical Association was organized on October 7, 1852. Professional training programs were developed for pharmacists, and by 1864 there were eight colleges of pharmacy in the United States.[35]

Eighty-nine colleges of pharmacy are now accredited to confer degrees by the American Council on Pharmaceutical Education. Pharmacy programs grant a Doctor of Pharmacy (PharmD) degree after at least 6 years of postsecondary study. The PharmD degree has replaced the Bachelor of Pharmacy degree, which is no longer awarded. Sixty-seven colleges of pharmacy also offer a master's or PhD degree after completion of a PharmD program for pharmacists who want more laboratory or research experience to do research for a drug company or teach at a university. After graduation each pharmacist is licensed by passing a state examination and completing an internship with a licensed pharmacist. Schools of pharmacy graduate about 8,000 students annually. The number of active pharmacists in the United States is now well over 200,000, an increase of over 50,000 since 1980.[36]

In 1976 the American Pharmaceutical Association created the Board of Pharmaceutical Specialties. It has since approved nuclear pharmacy, nutrition support pharmacy, oncology pharmacy, pharmacotherapy, and psychiatric pharmacy as specialties in which pharmacists may be certified.[37]

Sixty percent of pharmacists work in community pharmacies, many of which are owned by large commercial chains. There, they may supervise other employees, manage overall business needs, computerize patients' records, and advise physicians and patients about drug dosage, side effects, and interaction with other medications. Twenty-five percent of pharmacists work in hospitals, and the balance are employed by clinics, nursing homes, health maintenance organizations, and the federal government.

Employment of pharmacists is expected to grow faster than the average for all occupations because of the increased pharmaceutical needs of an aging population and the increased use of medications. The need for pharmacists is increasing as they become more involved in drug therapy decision making and patient counseling. Although enrollment in pharmacy programs is growing as students are attracted by high salaries and good job prospects, employment opportunities are expected to exceed applicants through the year 2012.[36]

Podiatric Medicine

Podiatric medicine is concerned with the diagnosis and treatment of diseases and injuries of the lower leg and foot. Podiatrists can prescribe drugs; order radiographs, laboratory tests, and physical therapy; set fractures; and perform surgery. They also fit corrective inserts called orthotics, design plaster casts and strappings to correct deformities, and design custom-made shoes.

There are seven accredited schools in the United States where students can apply after graduating from college. Graduates obtain a Doctor of Podiatric Medicine (DPM) degree. The 4 years of professional training is similar to that for physicians. A residency is not required, but most podiatrists spend 2 or more years completing a residency in a hospital after they graduate. Podiatrists may also take postgraduate training and become board certified in the specialties of orthopedics, primary medicine, or surgery. All doctors of podiatric medicine must be licensed by the state in which they practice. It is probably in the care of older adults, enabling people to live at home and function independently as long as possible, that podiatric medicine makes its greatest public health contribution.

Podiatric care is more dependent on disposable income than other medical services. Medicare and most private health insurance programs cover acute medical and surgical foot services, as well as diagnostic radiographs and leg braces; however, routine foot care ordinarily is not covered.[38]

Chiropractors

Chiropractors treat the whole body without the use of drugs or surgery. Special care is given to the spine, because chiropractors believe that misalignment or irritations of spinal nerves interfere with normal body functions. Today, there are 15 chiropractic programs and 2 chiropractic institutions. Students need at least an associate degree before applying to one of the accredited programs or colleges. After completion of the Doctor of Chiropractic (DC) Degree, all states require chiropractors to be licensed to practice. About 2,500 graduates of chiropractic programs enter the growing profession each year, bringing the number of active practitioners to over 70,000.[39] Patients are generally satisfied with chiropractic care, and for specific conditions causing back pain, chiropractors achieve outcomes comparable with those of physicians.[40]

Chiropractic practice has strong public support, and chiropractors have used that patronage to make significant gains in legal and legislative areas. Regardless of medicine's questions about chiropractic's lack of scientifically proven effectiveness, chiropractors achieved Medicare coverage and participate in most managed care, and many other insurance policies contain some form of chiropractic coverage.

Optometry

A Doctor of Optometry (OD) examines patients' eyes to diagnose vision problems and eye disease, prescribes drugs for treatment, and prescribes and fits eyeglasses and contact lenses. An optometrist should not be confused with an ophthalmologist or an optician. An ophthalmologist is a physician who specializes in the treatment of eye diseases and injuries and uses drugs, surgery, or the prescription of corrective lenses to correct vision deficiencies. An optician is a licensed health professional who fits eyeglasses or contact lenses to individual patients as prescribed by ophthalmologists.

Optometrists must graduate from 1 of the 17 accredited 4-year colleges of optometry and pass both written and clinical state board examinations to obtain a license to practice. More than 1,300 students graduate each year to swell the current number of active optometrists to over 34,000.

One-year residency programs are available for optometrists who wish to specialize in family practice optometry, pediatric optometry, geriatric optometry, occupational vision care, low-vision rehabilitation, vision therapy, contact lenses, hospital-based optometry, or sports vision.

Optometrists usually work in private practice, but many are now forming small group practices. Optometrists can hire opticians and optometric assistants to help them increase their productivity and thus care for more patients. Persons over age 45 years visit optometrists and ophthalmologists more frequently because of the onset of vision problems in middle age and the increased likelihood of cataracts, glaucoma, diabetes, and hypertension in old age. Because more than half of the people in the United States wear glasses or contact lenses and there is a constant need for eye care by the majority of the aging population, growth in the field of optometry is expected to remain consistent.[41]

Health Care Administrators

Like any other business, health care needs good management to keep it running smoothly. Health care administrators are managers who plan, organize, direct, control, or coordinate medicine and health services in hospitals, clinics, nursing care facilities, and physicians' offices. Most health care administrators are employed in hospital settings, but others work for insurers, clinics, or medical group practices. Employment opportunities are numerous because there are over a quarter of a million jobs for health care administrators.

Bachelor's, master's, and doctoral degree programs in health care administration are offered by a wide variety of colleges and universities. At least 70 schools have accredited programs leading to a master's degree in health services administration. There also are short certificate or diploma programs, usually lasting less than 1 year, in health services administration or in medical office management.[42]

Allied Health Personnel

Unlike professionals in medicine, dentistry, nursing, and pharmacy, allied health personnel represent a varied and complex array of health care disciplines. Allied health personnel support, complement, or supplement the professional functions of physicians, dentists, or other health professionals in delivering health care to patients, and they assist in environmental health control, health promotion, and disease prevention. A number of more recent categories of health care specialists were created to implement the new procedures, equipment, and diagnostic, surgical, and therapeutic techniques that proliferated during the last three decades. There are now well over 100 allied health occupations.[43]

The range of allied health professions may be understood best by classifying them according to the functions they serve. They may be grouped into the following four categories:

1. Laboratory technologists and technicians
2. Therapeutic science practitioners
3. Behavioral scientists
4. Support services

It should be recognized, however, that some allied health disciplines should be included in more than one of these functional classifications.

There are a rapidly growing number of technicians and technologists, including such major categories as cardiovascular technicians and technologists, clinical laboratory technicians, emergency medical technicians, health information technicians, nuclear medicine technologists, cytotechnologists, histologic technicians and technologists, surgical technologists, occupational safety and health technicians, pharmacy technicians, and many more. Because space does not allow for a discussion of all or even most of these important health vocations, the following descriptions include only several representative disciplines in this allied health category.

Laboratory Technologists and Technicians

Clinical laboratory technologists and technicians have a critically important role in the diagnosis of disease, monitoring of physiologic function and the effectiveness of intervention, and application of highly technical procedures. Technologists, also known as clinical laboratory scientists or medical technologists, usually have a bachelor's degree in one of the life sciences. Clinical laboratory technicians, also known as medical technicians or medical laboratory technicians, generally need an associate's degree or a certificate.

Among their roles, clinical laboratory personnel analyze body fluids, tissues, and cells checking for bacteria and other microorganisms; analyze chemical content; test drug levels in blood to monitor the effectiveness of treatment; and match blood for transfusion.

The National Accrediting Agency for Clinical Laboratory Sciences accredits 467 programs for clinical laboratory technologists and technicians. Employed graduates of those programs number over 300,000. More than 50% of those employed work in hospitals. Most of the others work in physician offices or diagnostic laboratories. Faster than average employment growth is expected because of population growth and development of new laboratory tests.[44]

Radiologic Technology. A radiologic technologist works under the supervision of a radiologist, a physician who specializes in the use and interpretation of radiographs. The radiologic technologist uses radiographs, fluoroscopic equipment, and high-tech imaging machines such as ultrasonography, computed tomography, magnetic resonance imaging, and positron emission tomography to produce films that allow physicians to study the internal organs and bones of their patients. Formal training programs in radiography range in length from 1 to 4 years and lead to a certificate, associate's degree, or bachelor's degree. Two-year associate's degrees are most prevalent. The Joint Review Committee on Education in Radiology has accredited over 600 formal programs in 2007.

Technologic advances and the growth and aging of the nation's population continue to increase the demand for diagnostic imaging. As a result the vacancy rate for radiologic technologists is the highest in any field of health care. The U.S. Department of Labor predicts that employment opportunities for radiologic technologists will grow faster than the average for all health care occupations through 2014.[45]

Nuclear Medicine Technology. Nuclear medicine technologists use diagnostic imaging techniques to detect and map radioactive drugs in the human body. They administer radioactive pharmaceuticals to patients and then monitor the characteristics and functions of tissues or organs in which they localize. Abnormal areas show higher or lower concentrations of radioactivity than do normal ones.

Nuclear medicine technologists are prepared in 1-year certificate programs offered by hospitals to those who are already radiologic technologists, medical technologists, or RNs or who are in 2- to 4-year programs offered in university schools of allied health. Nuclear medicine technologists must meet the minimum federal standards on the administration of radioactive drugs and the operation of radiation detection equipment. In addition, about half of all states require technologists to be licensed. Technologists also may obtain voluntary professional certification or registration.[46]

Therapeutic Science Practitioners

Practitioners of the therapeutic sciences are essential to the treatment and rehabilitation of patients with diseases and injuries of all kinds. Physical therapists, occupational therapists, speech pathology and audiology therapists, radiation therapists, and respiratory therapists are only some of the allied health disciplines in this category.

Physical Therapy. Physical therapists provide services that help restore function, improve mobility, relieve pain, and prevent or limit physical disabilities of patients suffering from injuries or disease. They restore, maintain, and promote overall fitness and health. They review patients' medical histories and measure patients' strength, range of motion, balance, coordination, muscle performance, and motor function. They then develop and implement treatment plans that include exercises to develop flexibility, strength, and endurance. They also may give patients exercises to do at home.

Physical therapists may also use electrical stimulation, hot or cold compresses, and ultrasound to relieve pain and reduce swelling. They also teach patients to use assistive and adaptive devices, such as crutches, prostheses, and wheelchairs. Physical therapists supervise physical therapy assistants to aid them in meeting the needs of an increasing number of patients. Physical therapy assistants earn associate's degrees and take a national certifying examination. Physical therapists may practice as generalists or specialize in areas such as pediatrics, geriatrics, orthopedics, sports medicine, neurology, or cardiopulmonary physical therapy.

There were 209 accredited physical therapy programs in 2007. Of those, 43 offered master's degrees and 166 offered doctoral degrees.[47] The Commission on Accreditation in Physical Therapy Education no longer accredits physical therapy programs that do not provide at least master's-level degrees. Employment opportunities have grown rapidly in the physical therapy field, and the demand now exceeds the supply.

Occupational Therapy

Occupational therapists assist patients in recovering from accidents, injuries, or diseases to improve their ability to perform tasks in their daily living and working environments. A wide range of patients work with occupational therapists, from those with irreversible physical disabilities to those with mental disabilities or disorders. Occupational therapists assist patients in caring for their daily needs such as dressing, cooking, and eating. They also use physical exercises and other activities to increase strength and dexterity, visual acuity, and hand–eye coordination. Occupational therapists instruct in the use of adaptive equipment such as wheelchairs, splints, and aids for eating and dressing. They may also design or make special equipment needed at home or at work. Therapists may collaborate with clients and employers to modify work environments so that clients can maintain employment.

A bachelor's degree in occupational therapy was the minimum requirement for entry into this field, but beginning in 2007 a master's degree or higher is now required.

Occupational therapists work in offices, nursing homes, community mental health centers, adult daycare programs, rehabilitation centers, and residential care facilities. Private practice is currently the fastest growing sector of this profession. As the population ages and patients with critical problems survive more frequently, the demand for occupational therapists will continue to increase.[48]

Speech-Language Pathology

Speech-language pathologists, sometimes called speech therapists, treat patients with speech problems, swallowing, and other disorders in hospitals, schools, clinics, and private practice. About one-half of all speech pathologists are employed in the education system—from preschools to universities.

About 233 colleges and universities offer graduate programs in speech-language pathology. A master's degree is the standard practice requirement. Speech-language pathologists use written and oral tests and special instruments to diagnose the nature of the impairment and develop an individualized plan of care. They may teach the use of alternative communication methods, including automated devices and sign language.

The number of speech-language pathologists, now numbering about 130,000, is expected to grow rapidly as the population ages.[49]

Physician Assistant

The emergence of physician assistants (PAs) closely parallels the creation of nurse practitioners. In the 1960s there was a shortage of health care providers. Duke University initiated the first PA program in 1961. It was a new provider model designed to benefit from the experience and expertise of the many hospital corpsmen and medics that were discharged from the armed forces. As the flow of returning corpsmen and medics tapered off, individuals without prior health care training were accepted into PA programs. The Medex program, which began at the University of Washington and was later adopted at a number of other universities, is well known. It was designed to train general assistants to family medicine physicians and internists.

Today there are at least 135 education programs for PAs. Sixty-eight offer a master's degree, and the rest offer a bachelor's or associate's degree. PAs provide health care services under the supervision of a physician. Unlike medical assistants who perform routine clinical and clerical tasks, PAs are formally trained to provide diagnostic, preventive, and therapeutic health care services as delegated by the physician. PAs take medical histories, order and interpret laboratory tests and x-rays, make diagnoses, and prescribe medications as allowed in 47 states and the District of Columbia.

Many PAs are employed in specialties such as internal medicine, pediatrics, family medicine, orthopedics, and emergency medicine. Others specialize in surgery and may provide preoperative and postoperative care and act as first or second assistants during major surgery.

The U.S. Department of Labor projects a significant increase in the employment of PAs because of an expected expansion of the health care industry and an emphasis on cost containment.[50]

Behavioral Scientists

Behavioral scientists are crucial in the social, psychological, and community and patient educational activities related to health maintenance, prevention of disease, and accommodation of patients to disability. They include professionals in social work, health education, community mental health, alcoholism and drug abuse services, and other health and human service areas.[51]

Social Work

Social workers counsel patients and families and assist them in addressing the personal, economic, and social problems associated with illness and disability. They arrange for community-based services as necessary to meet patient needs after discharge from a health facility. A bachelor's degree is required; however, a master's degree from an accredited graduate school of social work is often the standard for employment.

Social workers provide social services in hospitals and other health-related settings. Medical and public health social workers provide patients and families with psychosocial support in cases of acute, chronic, or terminal illnesses. Mental health and substance abuse social workers assess and treat persons with mental illness or those who abuse alcohol, tobacco, or other drugs.

The most recent tally (2006) by the Council on Social Work Education listed 458 bachelor's programs, 181 master's in social work degree programs, and 74 doctoral programs. Employment of social workers is expected to grow faster than the average of other occupations, especially for those with backgrounds in gerontology and substance abuse treatment.[52]

Rehabilitation Counselor

A rehabilitation counselor gives personalized counseling, emotional support, and rehabilitation therapy to patients limited by physical or emotional disabilities. Patients may be recovering from illness or injury, have psychiatric problems, or have intellectual deficits. After an injury or illness is stabilized, the rehabilitation counselor tests the patient's motor ability, skill level, interests, and psychologic makeup and develops an appropriate training or retraining plan. The goal is to maximize the patient's ability to function in society.

A master's degree is often required to be licensed or certified as a rehabilitation counselor. The Commission on Rehabilitation Counselor

Certification offers voluntary certification. The need for rehabilitation counselors is expected to grow as the population ages and medical technology saves more lives. In addition, legislation requiring equal employment rights for persons with disabilities will increase the demand for counselors to prepare such people for employment.[53]

Support Services

Support services are necessary for the highly complex and sophisticated system of health care to function. Service specialists perform administrative and management duties and often work closely with the actual providers of health care services. Health information administrators, dental laboratory technologists, electroencephalographic technologists, food service administrators, surgical technologists, and environmental health technologists are some of the allied health professionals in this category, and they serve to illustrate the diverse nature of the required support disciplines in allied health.

Health Information Administrators

Health information administrators are responsible for the activities of the medical records departments of hospitals, skilled nursing facilities, managed care organizations, rehabilitation centers, ambulatory care facilities, and a number of other health care operations. They plan and maintain information systems that permit patient data to be received, recorded, stored, and retrieved easily to assist in diagnosis and treatment. These data may also be used to track disease patterns, provide information for medical research, assist staff in evaluating the quality of patient care, and verify insurance claims. Health information administrators supervise the staff in the medical records department and are responsible for the confidentiality of all the information within their departments.

A bachelor's degree in health information administration is the entry-level credential. The Council of Certification of the American Health Information Management Association gives a national accreditation examination for Registered Health Information Administrator. Currently, there are over 50 programs preparing health information administrators and over 150 programs training medical records and health information technologists/technicians. The U.S. Department of Labor estimates further vigorous growth in the employment of these health information personnel by 2016.[54]

Career Advancement in Allied Health

Because the allied health fields offer so diverse an array of programs, the opportunity for career advancement through educational "laddering" is probably without equal.

It is commonplace for graduates of allied health programs to practice for a period of time and then advance their careers by entering higher level programs and achieving more advanced degrees.

Alternative Therapists

Rather than diminishing the public's interest in alternative forms of health care, the increasing sophistication of scientific medicine seems to have fostered a more receptive climate for alternative forms of therapy. Across the country, notably on the West Coast and in the Midwest, there is widespread interest in complementary and alternative medicine (CAM). CAM is defined as "a group of diverse medical and health care systems, practices, and products that are not presently considered to be part of conventional medicine." Complementary medicine and alternative medicine differ from each other. Complementary medicine is used together with conventional medicine. Alternative medicine is used in place of conventional medicine.[55]

In 1992, with one-third of Americans resorting to alternative medical therapies, the National Institutes of Health created an Office of Alternative Medicine to examine whether alternative therapies work. The more perplexing question of how they work was to be investigated later. In 1998, when more than 40% of Americans reported the use of alternative or complementary therapies, the Office of Alternative Medicine was elevated to the National Center for Complementary and Alternative Medicine and its mandate expanded.

A 2004 press release of the National Center provided the findings of a 2002 national health interview survey that queried respondents about 27 types of complementary and alternative treatments—10 requiring the services of a provider, such as an acupuncturist or chiropractor, and 17 nonprovider types, such as herbs, megavitamins, and special diets. The survey found that the U.S. public spent $36 to $47 billion that year on CAM therapies. Of that amount, $12 to $20 billion was spent "out of pocket" to professional CAM providers; $5 billion was spent on herbal products alone.[56]

The Center also engaged in the first international study of traditional medicines, including ancient Chinese and Native American methods. The plan proposed the first National Institutes of Health study of botanicals to sort through 1,500 medicinal herbs for evaluation. Unusual therapies, such as telepathic distance healing, considered to be on the far fringes of medical practice, were also investigated.[57]

Many alternative therapies involve lifestyle programs, such as macrobiotics, natural food diets, yoga, and other stress-reducing techniques. Others focus on mind–body techniques, including biofeedback, visualization, music therapy, and prayer. Still others are traditional practices of other cultures—acupuncture, homeopathy, and microdose pharmacology.

Along with alternative techniques comes a new class of alternative practitioners. To name a few, there are certified trager practitioners, who rock and cradle the patient's body for relaxation and mental clarity; doctors of naturopathy, who use natural healing methods that include diet, herbal medicine, and homeopathy; advanced certified rolfers, who use deep massage to restore the body's natural alignment; and registered polarity practitioners, who use touch and advice on diet, self-awareness, and exercise to balance energy flow. In spite of the fact that medical societies strongly oppose naturopathy, considering the practice "unscientific" and "irrational," naturopathic doctors have made great strides in the last few years. Although they do not have medical degrees and are trained in loosely monitored schools, they are able to generate strong public support within state legislatures.[58]

The gains of naturopaths and other alternative practitioners reflect the public's frustration with much of conventional medicine, high drug prices, and media reports of disproved treatments. The interest of insurance companies in alternative forms of medicine is also important. Insurers say that when traditional medicine is ineffective and an alternative form of therapy, such as acupuncture for a condition such as chronic pain, costs less and satisfies the patient, they will pay for it. As a result several states now require insurance companies to cover naturopathic procedures and others, such as acupuncture.[59]

Factors That Influence Demand for Health Personnel

Without attempting to include all interrelated factors that influence demand for various types of health personnel, it is important to recognize some major determinants of the size and nature of the health care employment sector. Regardless of the potential for legislatively mandated reforms of the health care system, the number and skill requirements of each discipline within the health care workforce depend on the interdependence of the following factors.

Changing Nature of Disease, Disability, and Treatment

The aging of the population and advances in the treatment of acute and life-threatening conditions result in an increasing survival of people with chronic illness or disabilities. The growing number of patients with deteriorating mental capacities, cardiac conditions, cancer, stroke, head and spinal cord injuries, neonatal deficits, and congenital disorders significantly increase the demand for workers who provide and support prolonged medical treatment, rehabilitation, and nursing home or custodial care.

Physician Supply

Although many categories of health personnel perform independently of physicians, most of the decisions regarding the use of health care resources, acceptance of other therapeutic modalities, and treatment provided by nonphysicians are made by physicians. It is therefore important to recognize that the anticipated changes in the numbers and types of physicians have a direct impact on the demand for many other types of health care personnel.

Technology

Medical and nonmedical technology used in the provision of health care has important implications for the number and skill requirements of the health care workforce. Advances in computerization, information systems, miniaturization, radiologic imaging, and laser technology have the potential to both increase and decrease the demand for various kinds of personnel. Some technologies, such as transluminal coronary angioplasty and positron emission tomography, have led to the elimination of more laborious medical interventions. Others, such as sophisticated patient monitoring systems, have facilitated the shifts to new service settings, such as ambulatory surgical centers. Also, automation of clinical laboratory testing has reduced the need for laboratory personnel. Thus the mix of skills and the numbers of personnel ebb and flow with the discovery and application of new service modalities.

Expansion of Home Care

Health care reforms are likely to continue the shift in health service delivery sites from acute-care hospitals to ambulatory, home care, and long-term care settings. With the emphasis on cost containment and an array of high-technology devices that contribute to more efficient techniques for providing nursing care and occupational, physical, and respiratory therapy in the home, the home care component of the health care industry is expected to expand significantly in the next decade. In addition, there is a growing body of evidence that therapy provided in the home helps patients recover faster and reduces hospital readmissions.

Corporatization of Health Care

It appears that solo practice among the health professions is becoming a practice pattern of the past. The increase in group practices; the development of several forms of provider organizations; the evolution of hospital networks; the assembly of vertically integrated systems that link hospitals, nursing homes, home care, and other services; and the diversification of health providers into various health-related corporate ventures all reflect the corporatization of health care.

It is significant that since the beginning of the U.S. recession, employment in health care continued to rise with gains in ambulatory care, nursing, and residential care. With nationwide employment dropping steadily since the start of the recession, the health care industry added over half a million jobs.[60]

Health Care Workforce Issues

Policymakers at every level of government, insurers, educators, providers, and consumers have a vested interest in the issues that pertain to the health care workforce. The Association of Academic Health Centers clearly defined those issues in a 1994 publication. Those issues are of ongoing concern in 2010[61]:

- The adequacy of supply of various health professionals, such as nurses, allied health professionals, primary care physicians, and geriatrician
- The geographic distribution of health professionals, especially their shortage in rural and underserved urban areas
- The under-representation of minorities in all health professions, in both primary and specialty care, as well as in the health profession's educational programs
- The potential supply and poor distribution of specialty physicians
- The questions about the appropriate scope of practice for various health professionals and concern about legal restrictions on scope of practice for nonphysician practitioners
- The concern about the quality and relevance of the health profession's educational programs; whether educational institutions are producing the health professionals needed for an effective and productive workforce in the 21st century
- The costs associated with educating health professionals and the impact that changes in the health care delivery system may have on the financing of health profession's education
- The competency testing of health care professionals
- The redefinition of health professions as technology and the delivery system change, and various professions reconsider the credentials needed to practice within the profession
- The concern about the supply of faculty to train health professionals

The Health Workforce in a Chaotic System

During the 21st century the aging population, the shifting nature of diseases, health care reforms, new technology, managed care, and economic factors will significantly change the demand for services provided by different types of practitioners. The market for services will expand in some disciplines and contract in others. It will be necessary to modify the roles and scope of practice of many of the health care professions to adapt to changing service patterns. Yet the lack of any single body in the United States being responsible for making data-based demand-and-supply projections and policy decisions leaves these important issues to be addressed piecemeal by a number of interested bodies.

Federal and state governments, educational institutions, professional organizations, insurers, and provider institutions have separate and often conflicting interests in health workforce education and training, regulation, financing, entry-level preparation, and scope of practice. The various levels at which policy decisions are made and the disparate interests that influence those decisions present major obstacles to ensuring a coherent, efficient, and rational health workforce in the United States. Nevertheless, those policies supported the production of an enormous number of health professionals to serve the health care system of the late 20th century.

New health care system reforms and a far more cost-conscious health care market combined with an aging population and technologic advances will likely force health services personnel to adapt to different work settings and service responsibilities. Nevertheless, as it has in the past, the educational and clinical preparation of health care personnel will change in both content and output to meet emerging service needs. Already one of the largest industries in the United States, employment in health care will continue to enjoy significant growth.[62]

References

1. U.S. Department of Labor, Bureau of Labor Statistics. Monthly labor review, Nov. 2007. Available from http://www.bls.gov/opub/mlr/2007/11/art4full. pdf. Accessed July 21, 2009.
2. Collier SN. Report of the State Issues Task Force. *Pew Health Professions Commission State Issues Task Force.* 1991:1–9.
3. Collier SN. Report of the State Issues Task Force. *Pew Health Professions Commission State Issues Task Force.* 1991:7.
4. American Association of Medical Colleges. Total graduates by U.S. medical school and race and ethnicity, 2008. Available from http://www.aamc.org/data/facts/2008/gradschlraceeth08.htm. Accessed July 21, 2009.
5. American Association of Colleges of Osteopathic Medicine. Osteopathic medicine and medical education in brief. Available from http://www.aacom.org/about/osteomed/Pages/default.aspx. Accessed July 23, 2009.

6. Bouldet JR, Morcini JJ, Whelan GP, et al. The international medical graduate pipeline: recent trends in certification and residency training. *Health Affairs*. 2006;25:469–477.

7. U.S. Department of Labor, Bureau of Labor Statistics. Occupational outlook handbook. 2008–2009 edition, physicians and surgeons. Available from http://www.bls.gov/oco/ocos074.htm. Accessed July 24, 2009.

8. Association of American Medical Colleges. Recent studies and reports on physician shortages, April 2009. Washington, DC. Available from http://www.aamc.org/workforce/stateandspecialty/recentworkforcestudies.pdf. Accessed July 24, 2009.

9. O'Brien P. All a woman's life can bring: the domestic roots of nursing in Philadelphia, 1830–1885. *Nursing Res*. 1987;36:12–17.

10. Stevens R. *In Sickness and in Wealth: American Hospitals in the Twentieth Century*. New York: Basic Books; 1989:96–98.

11. Kovner C. Nursing. In: Kovner AR, Ed. *Health Care Delivery in the United States*. New York: Springer; 1995:101–121.

12. U.S. Department of Health and Human Services, Health Resources and Services Administration. The registered nurse population: findings from the 2004 National Survey of Registered Nurses. Accessed July 23, 2009. Available from http://bhpr.hrsa.gov/healthworkforce/rnsurvey04/.

13. Buerhaus PI, Staiger DO, Auerbach DI, et al. Is the current shortage of hospital nurses ending? *Health Affairs*. 2003;22:191–198.

14. U.S. Department of Health and Human Services, Health Resources and Services Administration, Bureau of Health Professions. United States health workforce personnel factbook. Available from http://www.bhpr.hrsa.gov/healthworkforce/reports/factbook02/FB403.htm. Accessed July 23, 2009.

15. U.S. Department of Health and Human Services, Health Resources and Services Administration, Bureau of Health Professions. United States Health workforce personnel factbook. Available from http://bhpr.hrsa.gov/healthworkforce/reports/factbook02/FB401.htm. Accessed July 23, 2009.

16. Hassmiller SB, Cozine M. Addressing the nurse shortage to improve the quality of care. *Health Affairs*. 2006;1:268–274.

17. Robert Wood Johnson Foundation. A new era of nursing: transforming care at the bedside. Available from http://www.rwjf.org/pr/product.jsp?id=18662. Accessed July 23, 2009.

18. U.S. Department of Labor, Bureau of Labor Statistics. Occupational outlook handbook, 2008–2009 edition, licensed practical and licensed vocational nurses. Available from http://www.bls.gov/oco/ocos102.htm. Accessed July 23, 2009.

19. U.S. Department of Labor, Bureau of Labor Statistics. Occupational outlook handbook, 2008–2009 edition, registered nurses. Available from http://www.bls.gov/oco/ocos083.htm#emply. Accessed July 22, 2009.

20. Bullough B, Bullough VI. *Nursing Issues for the Nineties and Beyond*. New York: Springer; 1994:15.

21. Sultz HA, Henry OM, Sullivan JA, et al. *Nurse Practitioners, USA.* Lexington, MA: Lexington Books; 1979:215–229.

22. Dunn I. A literature review of advanced clinical nursing in the United States of America. *J Adv Nursing.* 1997;25:814–819.

23. Krein SL. The employment and use of nurse practitioners and physician assistants by rural hospitals. *Rural Health.* 1997;13:45–58.

24. Hooker RS, McKaig L. Emergency department uses of physician assistants and nurse practitioners: a national survey. *Am J Emerg Med.* 1996;14:245–249.

25. U.S. Department of Labor, Bureau of Labor Statistics. Occupational outlook handbook, 2008–2009 edition. Available from http://www.bls.gov/oco/ocos083.htm#training. Accessed July 23, 2009.

26. U.S. Department of Labor, Bureau of Labor Statistics. Occupational outlook handbook, 2008–2009 edition, registered nurses. Available from http://www.bls.gov/oco/ocos083.htm. Accessed July 24, 2009.

27. American Academy of Nurse Practitioners, P.O. Box 12846, Austin, Texas, 78711. Available at http://www.aanp.org. Accessed December 18, 2009.

28. Ring M. *Dentistry: An Illustrated History.* New York: Harry N. Abrams; 1985:203.

29. Loevy HT, Kowitz AA. Dental development in the midwest of America. *Int Dental J.* 1992;12:157–164.

30. Ring M. *Dentistry: An Illustrated History.* New York: Harry N. Abrams; 1985:283–284.

31. U.S. Department of Labor, Bureau of Labor Statistics. Occupational outlook handbook, 2008–2009 edition, dentists. Available from http://www.bls.gov/oco/ocos072.htm. Accessed July 24, 2009.

32. Sinkford JC, Valachovic RW, Harrison S. Advancement of women in dental education: trends and strategies. *J Dent Ed.* 2003;67:79–83.

33 Mertz E, O'Nell E. The growing challenge of providing oral health care services to all Americans. *Health Affairs.* 2002;21:65–77.

34. Gable FB. *Opportunities in Pharmacy Careers.* Lincolnwood, IL: NTC Publishing Group; 1993:10–14.

35. Higby GJ. American hospital pharmacy from the Colonial Period to the 1930s. *Am J Hosp Pharm.* 1994;51:2817–2823.

36. U.S. Department of Labor, Bureau of Labor Statistics. Occupational outlook handbook, 2008–2009 edition, pharmacists. Available from http://www.bls.gov/oco/ocos079.htm. Accessed July 24, 2009.

37. Board of Pharmaceutical Specialties, Division of the American Pharmacists Association. Current specialties. Available from http://www.bpsweb.org/specialties/specialties.cfm. Accessed August 16, 2009.

38. U.S. Department of Labor, Bureau of Labor Statistics. Occupational outlook handbook, 2008–2009 edition, podiatrists. Available from http://www.bls.gov/oco/ocos075.htm. Accessed July 24, 2009.

39. U.S. Department of Labor, Bureau of Labor Statistics. Occupational outlook handbook, 2008–2009 edition, chiropractors. Available from http://www.bls.gov/oco/ocos071.htm. Accessed July 24, 2009.

40. Shekelle MM, Rachel L. An epidemiologic study of episodes of back pain care. *Spine.* 1995;20:1668–1673.

41. U.S. Department of Labor, Bureau of Labor Statistics. Occupational outlook handbook, 2008–2009 edition, optometrists. Available from http://www.bls.gov/oco/ocos073.htm. Accessed July 24, 2009.

42. U.S. Department of Labor, Bureau of Labor Statistics. Occupational outlook handbook, 2008–2009 edition, medical and health services managers. Available from http://www.bls.gov/oco/ocos014.htm. Accessed July 24, 2009.

43. Explorehealthcareers.org. Field profile: Allied health professions. Available from http://www.explorehealthcareers.org/en/Field.1.aspx. Accessed April 27, 2010.

44. U.S. Department of Labor, Bureau of Labor Statistics. Occupational outlook handbook, 2008–2009 edition, clinical laboratory technologists and technicians. Available from http://www.bls.gov/oco/ocos096.htm. Accessed July 24, 2009.

45. U.S. Department of Labor, Bureau of Labor Statistics. Occupational outlook handbook, 2008–2009 edition, radiologic technologists and technicians. Available from http://www.bls.gov/oco/ocos105.htm. Accessed July 23, 2009.

46. U.S. Department of Labor, Bureau of Labor Statistics. Occupational outlook handbook, 2008–2009 edition, nuclear medicine technologists. Available from http://www.bls.gov/oco/ocos104.htm. Accessed July 24, 2009.

47. U.S. Department of Labor, Bureau of Labor Statistics. Occupational outlook handbook, 2008–2009 edition, physical therapists. Available from http://www.bls.gov/oco/ocos080.htm. Accessed July 24, 2009.

48. U.S. Department of Labor, Bureau of Labor Statistics. Occupational outlook handbook, 2008–2009 edition, occupational therapists. Available from http://www.bls.gov/oco/ocos078.htm. Accessed July 24, 2009.

49. U.S. Department of Labor, Bureau of Labor Statistics. Occupational outlook handbook, 2008–2009 edition, speech-language pathologists. Available from http://www.bls.gov/oco/ocos099.htm. Accessed July 24, 2009.

50. U.S. Department of Labor, Bureau of Labor Statistics. Occupational outlook handbook, 2008–2009 edition, physicians assistants. Available from http://www.bls.gov/oco/ocos081.htm. Accessed July 24, 2009.

51. Sultz HA. *Allied Health Personnel. Consultant Report to the Labor-Health Industry Task Force on Health Personnel.* Albany, NY: New York State Department of Health; 1987.

52. U.S. Department of Labor, Bureau of Labor Statistics. Occupational outlook handbook, 2008–2009 edition, social workers. Available from http://www.bls.gov/oco/ocos060.htm. Accessed July 24, 2009.

53. U.S. Department of Labor, Bureau of Labor Statistics. Occupational outlook handbook, 2008–2009 edition, counselors. Available from http://www.bls.gov/oco/ocos067.htm. Accessed July 24, 2009.

54. U.S. Department of Labor, Bureau of Labor Statistics. Occupational outlook handbook, 2008-2009 edition, medical records and health information technicians. Available from http://www.bls.gov/oco/ocos014.htm. Accessed July 24, 2009.

55. National Center for Complementary and Alternative Medicine, National Institutes of Health. What are complementary and alternative medical practices? Available from http://nccam.nih.gov/health/whatiscam/overview.htm. Accessed July 24, 2009.

56 National Center for Complementary and Alternative Medicine, National Institutes of Health. Press release 2004. More than one-third of U.S. adults use complementary and alternative medicine. Available from http://nccam.nih.gov/news/2004/052704.htm. Accessed July 24, 2009.

57. National Institutes of Health, National Center for Complementary and Alternative Medicine. Draft minutes of the tenth meeting, January 28, 2002. Available from http://nccam.nih.gov/about/naccam/minutes/2002jan.htm. Accessed July 24, 2009.

58. Petersen A. States grant herb doctors new powers. *Washington Post.* August 22, 2002:D1.

59. Rubenstein S. Alternative health plans widen. *Wall Street Journal.* September 22, 2004:D7.

60. U.S. Bureau of Labor Statistics, Division of Labor Force Statistics. Employment statistics summary, September 4, 2009. Available from http://stats.bls.gov/news.release/empsit.nro.htm. Accessed September 25, 2009.

61. McLaughlin CJ. Health work force issues and policy-making roles. In Larson PF, Osterweis M, Rubin ER, Eds. *Health Work Force Issues for the 21st Century.* Washington, DC: Association of Academic Health Centers; 1994: 1–3.

62. U.S. Department of Labor, Bureau of Labor Statistics. Career guide to industries 2008–2009. Health services. Available from http://bls.gov.oco/cg/cgs035.htm. Accessed July 24, 2009.

CHAPTER 7

Financing
Health Care

This chapter reviews the most currently available data on national health care expenditures and sources of payment and provides a historical overview of the developments that played major roles in creating the national health care financing infrastructure. Major factors that affect health care costs are identified and discussed. Significant trends in health care spending are reviewed, along with underlying reasons for evolving changes. The roles of the private sector and government as payers are presented with an overview of continuing efforts to link costs with quality.

Overview

Health care expenditures in the United States are financed through a combination of private and public sources. Most working Americans under the age of 65 have private health insurance coverage provided by their employers.[1] The primary sources of public funding are Medicare, covering health care services for most individuals over 65 years of age and disabled individuals, and Medicaid, which supports services for the low-income population.[1]

Financing of the U.S. health care system continues to evolve from a variety of influences, including provider, employer, purchaser, consumer, and political factors. As pointedly reflected in the national health care reform debates, these influences produce major tensions about the role and responsibility of the government as payer, the financial responsibilities of employers as the primary purchasers of health insurance, consumers, the relationships of costs to quality, and the impact of payment systems on quality. Controlling the rising costs of health care and dealing with the estimated 47 million uninsured or underinsured Americans continue as two of the most challenging issues.

Health Care Expenditures in Perspective

National health expenditures and trends are reported annually by the National Center for Health Statistics of the Centers for Disease Control and Prevention, the Office of the Actuary, National Health Statistics Group, and the U.S. Department of Health and Human Services, Centers for Medicare & Medicaid Services. Expenditures are reported and tracked over time using a standard format that identifies both the private and public sources of funds and the objects of expense. Table 7-1 provides an example of one such report for 2008.[2] National health care expenditures in 2008 totaled $2.33 trillion, 16.2% of the gross domestic product and $7,681 per person[3] (Figure 7-1). Expenditures for personal health care services currently represent 83.6%, or $1.95 billion of the national total.[2] The three top expenses for personal health care in overall national health care expenditures are hospital care at $718.4 billion, physician services at $496.2 billion, and prescription drugs at $234.1 billion[2] (Figure 7-2). Private health insurance is the primary source of payment for health care services, with an outlay of $783.2 billion. Medicare, with expenditures of $469.2 billion, is the next highest source, and Medicaid ranks as third highest at $344.3 billion.[2] Together, all public sources of funding represent 48% of total payments (Figure 7-3).

With the nation in an economic recession in 2008, growth in health care spending slowed to 4.4% over the prior year, the slowest rate of growth in the past 48 years.[3] Historically, the rate of growth in health care expenditures has been an overarching concern of both the private and government sectors as health care expenditure growth outstripped general inflation by significant margins.[4,5] And although insured Americans view the U.S. health care delivery system as superior to that of other developed nations, all of which have some form of universal health care, serious

Table 7-1 National Health Expenditures, 2008, by Type of Expenditure and Source of Payment

Year and Type of Expenditure	Total	Private					Public		
		All Private Funds	Total	Consumer		Other	Total	Federal	State and Local
				Out-of-Pocket Payments	Private Health Insurance				
2008									
National Health Expenditures	2,338.7	1,232.0	1,060.9	277.8	783.2	171.1	1106.7	816.8	289.8
Health Services and Supplies	2181.3	1,138.1	1,060.9	277.8	783.2	77.2	1,043.1	774.0	269.1
Personal Health Care	1,952.3	1,044.5	969.0	277.8	691.2	75.5	907.8	718.0	189.8
Hospital Care	718.4	309.3	282.2	23.2	259.0	27.1	409.0	330.7	78.3
Professional Services	731.2	457.7	425.5	111.1	314.3	42.2	263.5	202.3	61.1
Physician and Clinical Services	496.2	323.9	291.9	50.1	241.8	31.9	172.3	144.6	27.7
Other Professional Services	65.7	43.3	39.8	16.4	23.4	3.5	22.4	17.9	4.5
Dental Services	101.2	93.9	93.8	44.8	49.2	0.1	7.3	4.5	2.8
Other Personal Health Care	68.1	6.6	-	-	-	6.6	61.5	35.3	26.2
Nursing Home and Home Health	203.1	65.8	59.8	43.5	16.1	6.2	137.3	101.9	35.4
Home Health Care	64.7	13.5	12.4	6.6	5.8	1.2	51.1	39.8	11.3
Nursing Home Care	138.4	52.3	47.2	38.9	10.3	5.1	86.2	62.1	24.1
Retail Outlet Sales of Medical Products	299.6	201.7	201.7	100.0	101.7	0.0	97.9	83.0	14.9
Prescription Drugs	234.1	147.0	147.0	48.5	98.5	0.0	87.0	72.5	14.5
Other Medical Products	65.5	54.6	54.6	51.4	3.2	0.0	10.9	10.5	0.4
Durable Medical Equipment	26.6	18.1	18.1	14.9	3.2	0.0	8.4	8.0	0.4
Other Non-Durable Medical Products	39.0	38.5	36.5	36.5	0.0	0.0	2.5	2.5	0.0
Government Administration and Net Cost of Private Health Care	159.6	93.6	92.0	-	92.0	1.7	65.9	45.5	20.4
Government Public Health Activities	69.4	-	-	-	-	-	69.4	10.5	59.0
Investment	157.5	93.9	-	-	-	93.9	63.6	43.0	20.6
Research	43.8	4.7	-	-	-	4.7	38.9	33.5	5.4
Structures and Equipment	113.9	89.2	-	-	-	89.2	24.7	9.5	15.2

Note: Research and development expenditures of drug companies and other manufacturers and providers of medical equipment and supplies are excluded from research expenditures. These research expenditures are implicitly included in the expenditures class in which the product falls, in that they are covered by the payment received for that product. Numbers may not add to totals because of rounding. The figure 0.0 denotes amounts less than $50 million. Dashes (-) indicate "not applicable."

Source: Centers for Medicare & Medicaid, Office of Actuary, National Health Statistics Group.

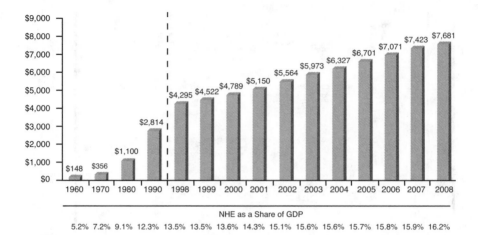

FIGURE 7-1 National Health Expenditures per Capita and Their Share of the Gross Domestic Product, 1960–2008.
Source: Centers for Medicare and Medicaid Services, Office of the Actuary, National Health Statistics Group.

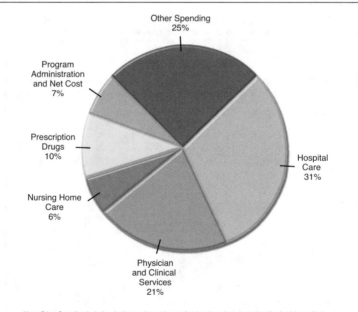

Note: Other Spending includes dentist services, other professional services, home health, durable medical products, over-the-counter medicines and sundries, public health, other personal health care, research, and structures and equipment.

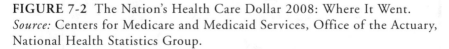

FIGURE 7-2 The Nation's Health Care Dollar 2008: Where It Went.
Source: Centers for Medicare and Medicaid Services, Office of the Actuary, National Health Statistics Group.

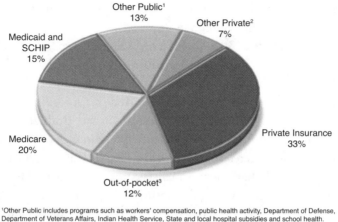

[1]Other Public includes programs such as workers' compensation, public health activity, Department of Defense, Department of Veterans Affairs, Indian Health Service, State and local hospital subsidies and school health.
[2]Other Private includes industrial in-plant, privately funded construction, and non-patient revenues, including philanthropy.
[3]Out of pocket includes co-pays, deductibles, and treatments no covered by Private Health Insurance.
Note: Numbers shown may not add to 100.0 because of rounding.

FIGURE 7-3 The Nation's Health Care Dollar 2008: Where It Came From
Source: Centers for Medicare and Medicaid Services, Office of the Actuary, National Health Statistics Group.

questions have loomed regarding the value returned for U.S. costs that are much higher, while the citizens of those other nations experience better health outcomes.[5] Despite the largest increase in its percentage of gross domestic product devoted to health care among 29 Organization for Economic Cooperation and Development (OECD) countries in the period 1970–2005, the United States had a lower life expectancy than predicted based on per capita income and was just as likely to rank in the bottom half as in the top half on a series of health status indicators.[5] According to these data published by the OECD, the United States spent more than double the median spending per person among OECD countries in 2005, and despite having the third highest level of public source spending for health care, public insurance covered only 26.5% of the U.S. population.[5] The United States also has lower health care utilization rates in terms of factors such as hospital days and physician visits per capita than most other OECD countries and a lower supply of expensive technology. Extensive comparative studies have concluded that the U.S. higher per capita income and much higher U.S. prices for medical care account for much of the spending differences, not superior health care that yields better health outcomes.[6]

Studies indicate that 30% to 40% of U.S. health spending is "waste" in that it provides services of no discernible value and inefficiently produces valuable services; this is another important dimension of U.S. health care spending.[7] One of these studies was reported in a mid-2008 statement by Peter R. Orszag, Director of the Congressional Budget Office at the Health Reform Summit of the Committee on Finance of the U.S. Senate, "Opportunities to Increase Efficiency in Health Care."[8] In his statement Mr. Orszag noted that "future health care spending is the single most important factor determining the nation's long-term fiscal condition" and that changing physician practice norms through the use of evidence-based practices to decrease variability in costs and revised economic incentives are needed to decrease waste.[8]

It is no surprise that a $2-trillion-plus enterprise invites fraud and abuse. The Federal Bureau of Investigation estimates that "fraudulent billings to public and private health care programs are 3-10% of total health spending, or $75-250 billion in fiscal year 2009."[9] There is a decade-long history of collaboration among the U.S. Department of Justice and the Office of the Inspector General of the Department of Health and Human Services to fight health care fraud, which has had impressive results with hundreds of convictions and exclusions of providers from federal health care programs.[9] However, development of complex, sophisticated criminal schemes involving providers, patients, drug dealers, and others continues to evolve.[9] Recognizing that fraud and abuse drain critical and substantial resources from the health care delivery system, in 2009 the U.S. Attorney General and Health and Human Services Secretary announced a multifaceted new approach to curbing fraud and abuse through creation of a Health Care Fraud Prevention and Enforcement Action Team that will use "cutting edge technology to identify and analyze suspected fraud and to build complex health care fraud cases quickly and efficiently."[9]

A well-rounded perspective on health care financing in the United States requires a grasp of much more than just the numbers. It requires an appreciation for the complexity of the human aspects of the multiple players in the health care delivery system, the financing system's historical roots, and the many social, political, and economic characteristics that now interplay in an industry that encompasses one-sixth of the total U.S. economy.

Drivers of Health Care Expenditures

Major drivers of health care expenditures include advancing medical and diagnostic technology, growth in the population of older adults, emphasis on specialty medicine, the uninsured and underinsured, labor intensity, and reimbursement system incentives.

Beginning in the 1950s, health care technology expanded rapidly. Hospitals became high-technology centers, consuming increasing resources in care delivery and capital to expand capacity and add technology. In 1960 national hospital care expenditures totaled $9.2 billion; by 1970 they had increased threefold to $27.6 billion,[2] a growth rate vastly outstripping overall inflation and growth in the gross domestic product. The array of medical interventions and diagnostic modalities continued to increase exponentially in succeeding decades. Examples include the development and several refinements of angioplasty as a routine treatment for blocked coronary blood vessels, and diagnostic modalities such as computed tomography, magnetic resonance imaging, and positron emission tomography, which are continuously upgraded and enhanced through new technology that is significantly expanding applications to an ever-wider variety of clinical situations.

Many other diagnostic, therapeutic, and surgical techniques require changes resulting from the availability of new equipment and computer-aided technologies. Such advances come at a high price.[10] Information technology and computer-aided innovations require expensive software and hardware, new patient care equipment, and highly trained personnel. The large capital investments required drive economic and professional imperatives for their use. Historically, the health care reimbursement system did not require documentation of the necessity for the use of technologic interventions or estimates of their benefit. The tendency to favor broad, rather than discretionary, use has grown with the number of interventions available.

The addition of new pharmacologic agents, increased access to drug coverage through Medicare and managed care, and "direct to consumer" marketing of prescription drugs via television, radio, and print media combined to make the rise in prescription drug spending a focal point of national attention.[11] Recent data indicate that growth in prescription drug spending has slowed due to several factors, including the economic recession, few new product introductions, and safety concerns.[3] However, spending for prescription drugs remains among the top three expenses in total national health care expenditures.[2]

Growth in the number of older adults is another major factor in rising health care expenditures. Current estimates place the population 65 years of age and older at 37.9 million, 12.6% of the population, or about one of every eight Americans. The number of persons aged 65 years or older is expected to grow to 19.3% of the population by 2030, totaling 72.1 million.[12] The population 85 years of age and older is expected to grow from 5.5 million in 2007 to 6.6 million by 2020.[13]

Persons over the age of 65 years are the major consumers of inpatient hospital care. These individuals account for more than one-third of all hospital stays and one-half of all days of care in hospitals.[14,15] In addition, the aging of the baby boomers born between 1946 and 1964 is expected to have a profound effect on health care services consumption beginning with the second decade of the 21st century.[16]

Growth in specialized medicine occurred as medical science and technology advanced. Americans' preference for specialty care resulted in high utilization and rapidly rising costs. Unlike other developed nations, where physician specialists represent half or fewer of physicians in general practice, approximately 60% of practicing physicians in the United States are specialists.[17] Since the 1940s, when employers offset post–World War II wage controls with fully paid health insurance benefits, working Americans were insulated from health care costs. They grew to expect and demand what they perceived as the "best" care, placing a high value on the use of specialists and advanced technology, sometimes resulting in inappropriate use and expense. For most, the costs of treatment were irrelevant, and physicians' recommendations were uninhibited by economic considerations among their well-insured patients. Historically, U.S. health insurance models carried no prohibitions against patient self-referrals to specialty care. Patients freely referred themselves to specialists based on their own interpretations of symptoms. Initially, managed care plans placed strong restrictions on patient self-referrals to specialists. However, consumer backlash in subsequent years significantly loosened restrictions against such self-referrals.

Among all developed countries of the world, the United States has the highest proportion of population without health insurance coverage. In 2009 the U.S. Bureau of the Census estimated that approximately 47 million Americans had no health insurance.[18] Lacking health insurance or having insufficient coverage carries major consequences by affecting the ability of individuals to receive timely preventive, acute, and chronic care. A lack of insurance coverage drives individuals to seek care in hospital emergency departments at costs higher than care provided at the physician's office or other ambulatory settings. Furthermore, uninsured or underinsured individuals tend to be low users of preventive services and are known to delay seeking care, even for acute conditions. These behaviors often result in increased illness severity and more complications, adding to diagnostic and treatment costs. Uninsured Americans are much more likely than insured individuals to enter care in the late stages of disease and require avoidable hospitalizations.[19] Providers absorb increased costs as free care. Insurers pass costs on to the insured in the form of higher premiums, and citizens pay higher taxes to support public hospitals or public insurance programs.[20]

Health care is a labor-intensive industry. It is one of the largest industries in the United States, employing approximately 14.3 million workers, many of whom represent some of the most highly educated, trained, and compensated individuals in the workforce.[21] The U.S. Department of Labor reports that the health care industry will generate approximately 3.2 million new jobs by 2014.[21] Among the most important factors that continue to produce high employment demands are technologic advances and continued growth in the aging population with more intense and diverse health care needs.

Both private and government health care financing mechanisms are recognized as major contributors to rising costs. Until the widespread introduction of prospective payment and managed care in the 1980s, government and private third-party payers reimbursed largely on a piecework, fee-for-service, retrospective basis. This system created economic incentives favoring high utilization among both physicians and hospitals. In combination with other factors fueling increased consumption of health care resources, the economic incentives created by the health care financing system played major roles in the rapid rate of expenditure growth. Later sections of this chapter review the history of attempts to change the health care financing system, providing a foundation for managed care's emergence as the predominant form of health care financing in the United States.

Evolution of Private Health Insurance

As early as the mid-1800s, a movement began to insure workers against lost wages resulting from work-related injuries. Later, insurance to cover lost wages resulting from catastrophic illness was added to accident policies. It was not until the 1930s that health insurance began paying part or all costs of medical treatment to providers. The basic concept of health insurance is antithetical to the central premise by which "insurance" was historically defined. Whereas insurance originally guarded against the low risk of rare occurrences such as premature death and accidents, the health insurance model that evolved provided coverage for predictable and discretionary uses of the health care system as well as unforeseen and unpredictable health events. Known as indemnity insurance because it protected individuals from financial risk associated with the costs of care, the insurance company set allowable charges for services, and providers could bill the patient for any excess.[22] Indemnity coverage prevailed until the advent of managed care in the 1970s.

Development of Blue Cross and Blue Shield and Commercial Health Insurance

In 1930 a group of Baylor University teachers contracted with Baylor Hospital in Dallas, Texas, to provide coverage for hospital expenses.[23] This arrangement created a model for the development of what was to become Blue Cross, a private, not-for-profit insurance empire that grew over the succeeding four decades into the dominant form of health insurance in the United States. The Blue Shield plans providing physician payments began shortly after Blue Cross, and by the early 1940s numerous Blue Shield plans were operating across the country. In 1946 the American Medical Association (AMA) financed the Association Medical Care Plans, which later became the National Association of Blue Shield Plans.

These developments, through which health insurance was transformed from a mechanism to reimburse individuals for lost wages resulting from injury or illness to one that reimbursed providers for the costs of medical care, carried major implications. The basic concept of health insurance is antithetical to the central premise of insurance. Whereas insurance originally guarded against the low risk of a rare occurrence, such as premature death, and unpredictable events such as accidents, the new medical care insurance model provided coverage for predictable, routine uses of the health care system as well as unforeseen and unpredictable illnesses or injuries. Coverage for routine use of health care services added a new dimension to the concept of insurance.

The establishment and subsequent proliferation of the "Blues" signaled a new era in U.S. health care delivery and financing. They played a significant role in establishing hospitals as the centers of medical care proliferation and technology, and by reimbursing for expensive services they put hospital care easily within the reach of middle-class working Americans for the first time. The insulation from costs of care provided by the Blues had a major impact on utilization. By the late 1930s annual hospital admission rates for Blue Cross enrollees were 50% higher on average than for the nation as a whole.[24] In addition to contributing to increased utilization of hospital services by removing financial barriers, the Blue Cross movement had other lasting impacts on national policymaking. Rosemary Stevens noted, "In the United States, the brave new world of medicine was specialized, interventionist, mechanistic and expensive—at least as interpreted, through prepayment, for workers in major organizations" (p. 190).[24] By 1940 the Blue Cross movement represented a major financing alternative, countering forces that had long lobbied politically for a form of national health insurance, a concept opposed vehemently by private medicine. The plans also stimulated the American Hospital Association and local hospitals to consider providing similar forms of reimbursement for low-income populations, modeled after the Blue Cross benefits recognizing private, semiprivate, and ward care. This latter movement, which continued for the next 20 years, focused attention on government as a potential source of insurance that was designed for low-income populations, the unemployed, or sporadic seasonal workers modeled along Blue Cross lines.[24]

Uniform features of all Blue Cross plans included not-for-profit status, supervision by state insurance departments, direct payments through contract arrangements with providers, and the use of community rating, in which all individuals in a defined group pay single premiums without regard to age, gender, occupation, or health status. Community rating helped ensure nondiscrimination against groups with varying risk characteristics to provide coverage at reasonable rates for the community as a whole; however, as commercial insurers entered the health care insurance marketplace, using "experience rating," basing premiums on historically documented patterns of utilization, Blue Cross plans, to remain competitive, began offering a variety of benefit packages. Ultimately, the Blue Cross plans were compelled to switch to experience-rating schemes to avoid attracting a disproportionate share of high-risk individuals for whom commercial insurance was prohibitively expensive.[24] During a period of insurance consolidations and mergers, beginning in the mid-1990s, Blue Cross plans in several states have converted from not-for-profit to for-profit status. The effects of these conversions on costs of coverage and access to care remain under study.[25]

For-profit commercial health insurers entered the market in significant numbers in the decade after start-up of Blue Cross and Blue Shield. Unbounded by the requirement for community-rating by the not-for-profit Blues, they used experience-rating to charge higher premiums to less healthy individuals and successfully competed for the market of healthier individuals by offering lower premiums than the Blues. By the early 1950s commercial insurers had enrolled more subscribers than the Blues.[26]

Managed Care

By the 1960s rapidly increasing Medicare expenditures accompanied by quality concerns captured the attention of health and government policymakers and of industry as the major purchasers of health care benefits, and a proposal was designed by the Nixon administration and Congress that resulted in enactment of the Health Maintenance Organization (HMO) Act of 1973.[22] Although many employer groups had used principles of managed care for prior decades through contracts with health care providers to serve employees on a prepaid basis, provisions of the HMO Act opened participation to the employer-based market, allowing the rapid proliferation of managed care plans.[22]

The HMO Act of 1973 provided loans and grants for the planning, development, and implementation of combined insurance and health care delivery organizations and required that a comprehensive array of preventive and primary care services be included in the HMO arrangement.

The legislation also mandated that employers with 25 or more employees offer an HMO option if one was available in their area and required employers to contribute to employees' HMO premiums in an amount equal to what they contributed to indemnity plan premiums. Initially, this employer mandate helped stimulate the growth of HMO membership in regions where federally funded and qualified plans were first established.

As authorized by the 1973 legislation, HMOs were organizations that combined providers and insurers into one organizational entity. As originally established, members of HMOs usually were required to obtain all their medical care within the organization.

Initially, there were two major types of HMOs. The first was a staff model and was the type most commonly established from the initial HMO legislation. It employed groups of physicians to provide most health care needs of its members. HMOs often provided some specialty services within the organization or contracted for services with community specialists. In the staff model the HMO also operated the facilities in which its physicians practiced, providing on-site ancillary support services, such as radiology, laboratory, and pharmacy services. The HMO usually purchased hospital care and other services for its members through fee-for-service or prepaid contracted arrangements. Staff model HMOs were referred to as "closed panel" because they employed the physicians who provided the majority of their members' care, and those physicians did not provide services outside the HMO membership. Similarly, community-based physicians could not participate in HMO member care without authorization by the HMO.

The second type of HMO stimulated by the 1973 legislation was the individual practice association (IPA). IPAs are physician organizations composed of community-based independent physicians in solo or group practices that provide services to HMO members. An IPA HMO, therefore, did not operate facilities in which members received care but rather provided its members services through private physician office practices. Like the staff model HMO, the IPA HMO purchased hospital care and specialty services not available through IPA-participating physicians from other area providers on a prepaid or fee-for-service basis. Some IPA HMOs allowed physicians to have a nonexclusive relationship that permitted treatment of nonmembers as well as members; however, HMO relationships with an IPA also could be established on an exclusive basis. In this scenario an HMO took the initiative in recruiting and organizing community physicians into an IPA to serve its members. Because the HMO was the organizing force in such an arrangement, it was common for the HMO to require exclusivity by the IPA, limiting its services only to that HMO's membership.[27]

The staff model and IPA-type organizations illustrate two major types of HMOs, but each type spawned several hybrids. Other forms of managed care organizations (MCOs) emerged throughout the 1980s in response to national cost and quality concerns. Peter Kongstvedt identified three additional HMO models as the most common: group practice, network, and direct contract.[27] In a group practice model an HMO contracts with a multispecialty group practice to provide all the physician services required by HMO enrollees. The physicians remained independent—employed by their group rather than the HMO. In the network model the HMO contracts with more than one group practice and maintains contracts with several physician groups representing both primary care and specialty practices. The direct contract model HMOs maintain contractual relationships with individual physicians, in contrast to the physician groups as in the IPA and network models. The direct contract approach gives the HMO the advantages of maintaining a higher level of control over fee arrangements by reducing physicians' negotiating power to an individual basis and avoiding the risk of lost services to its members by contractual termination of a large group of providers.

All forms of managed care entail interdependence between the provision of and payment for health care. Managed care is population, rather than individual, oriented. It is a system through which care-providing groups or networks take responsibility and share financial risk with an insurer for a specified population's medical care and health maintenance. The population basis enables the insurer to determine actuarially, projected use of services related to age, gender, and other factors. Service utilization estimates provide a basis for expected costs over a defined period. Estimates enable the insurer to establish premiums for benefit coverage.

By linking the insurance and delivery of services, managed care reverses the financial incentives of providers in the fee-for-service model. Fee-for-service is essentially a piecework, pay-as-you-go system in which the care provider is financially rewarded for high service utilization. Managed care uses the concept of prepayment, in which providers are paid a preset amount in advance for all services their insured population is projected to need in a given period. Capitation, a method that pays providers for services on a per-member-per-month basis, is a common form of prepayment. The provider receives payment whether or not services are used. If a physician exceeds the predetermined payment level, he or she may suffer a financial penalty. Similarly, if the physician uses fewer resources than predicted, he or she may retain the excess as profit.

Withholds are another form of payment device that seeks to provide financial incentives for efficient resource management. In the withhold scheme a percentage of the monthly capitated fee is withheld from payment to accommodate potential cost overruns for referrals or hospitalizations; all, part, or none of the withholds may be returned to the physician at the end of an annual period, depending on financial performance.[22] The key element of all physician prepayment arrangements is to encourage cost-conscious, efficient, and effective care.

Managed care plans also rely on transferring some measure of financial risk from the insurers to beneficiaries. Transfers of financial risk to beneficiaries most commonly take the form of copayments and deductibles. Copayments require that beneficiaries pay a set fee each time they receive a covered service, such as a copayment for each physician office visit. A deductible requires beneficiaries to meet a predetermined, out-of-pocket expenditure level before the MCO assumes payment responsibility for the balance of charges.

Today, managed care is synonymous with health insurance in the United States, and its principles have been adopted by the Medicare and Medicaid programs. Employers provide the primary source of health insurance, covering approximately 159 million Americans under age 65 years.[28] Sixty percent of employers offered health benefits in 2009, as did almost all firms with at least 50 employees.[28] Most employees in companies offering health care coverage subscribe to one or more managed care plans, with only 1% now enrolled in conventional plans.

As enrollment in managed care accelerated throughout the 1980s and 1990s, concerns emerged about MCO restrictions on consumer choice of providers and services. In response, MCOs spawned point-of-service plans that allow members to use providers outside the MCOs' approved provider networks. To exercise this choice, point-of-service members are charged copayments and deductibles higher than those charged for in-network services. In 2009 point-of-service plans represented 10% of covered employee enrollment.[28] Another form of managed care arrangement, preferred provider organizations (PPOs), were formed by physicians and hospitals to serve the needs of private, third-party payers and self-insured firms. Through these arrangements PPOs guarantee a certain volume of business to hospitals and physicians in return for a negotiated discount in fees. PPOs offer attractive features to both physicians and hospitals. Physicians are not required to share in financial risk as a condition of participation, and PPOs reimburse physicians on a fee-for-service basis. By providing predictable admission volume, PPOs help hospitals to shore up declining occupancy rates and attenuate the competition for admissions with other hospitals. To control costs, PPOs use negotiated discount fees, requirements that members receive care exclusively from contracted providers (or incur financial penalty), requirements for pre-authorization of hospital admission, and second opinions for major procedures. PPOs maintain systems of utilization review to control costs and advocate for more efficient service utilization by hospitals and physicians. Currently, PPOs are the most popular managed care plans, encompassing 60% of employer-covered workers.[28]

The organizational forms of managed care have continued evolving because of changing marketplace conditions, including purchaser preferences, beneficiary demands, and other factors. The emergence of PPOs as the most popular employee choice and the decline of staff model HMOs are notable trends. PPOs represented a means to involve payers and providers in negotiating fees and monitoring utilization while giving beneficiaries more choice. The decline of the staff model HMO resulted from many factors, including beneficiary demands for more choice among providers, large capital outlays associated with facility maintenance and expansion, and increased competition from IPA models. In 1988 staff models constituted about 42% of MCO membership. Currently, they represent less than one-half percent of managed care enrollment.[29] Another trend has been MCOs' increased use of evidence-based clinical practice guidelines contained in programs of disease management for subscribers with potentially medically high-risk and high-cost conditions. The Disease Management Association of America describes disease management as a system of coordinated health care interventions and communications for populations in which patient self care efforts are significant.[22] Candidates for these programs are identified from claims data and enrolled in services through which they are periodically contacted by professional staff of the insurer or a contracted disease management company to ensure compliance with physician orders and monitor condition status between physician visits. The goal is to prevent complications, thereby controlling costs.[22] For very-high-risk conditions such as heart failure, disease management programs may equip subscribers with electronic devices connected to the Internet that allow real-time condition monitoring from the subscribers' homes.[22]

Because physicians are the predominant influence over the use of virtually all patient care resources, managed care emphasizes the primary physician's role as the "gatekeeper" who controls patient entry to all other levels of care. In response to patient demands for easier access to specialty services, some MCOs have relented on specialty referral requirements, but all continue to encourage avoidance of unnecessary use of high-cost services by appropriate and timely treatment at the primary level and, when indicated, participation in disease management programs.

Managed Care Backlash

In what is termed the managed care "backlash" that began in the late 1990s, organized medicine, other health care providers, and consumers railed against MCO policies on choice of providers, referrals, and other practices that were viewed as unduly restrictive.[22] A federal commission was established to review the need for guidelines in the managed care industry.[30] In 1998, President Clinton imposed patient protection requirements on private insurance companies providing health coverage to federal workers.[31] Public dissatisfaction with constraints over the right to receive care deemed necessary and the freedom of physicians to refer patients to specialists received wide publicity. Public concerns driving sentiments toward more government regulation of the managed care industry included the belief that managed care was hurting the quality of patient care and that the managed care industry was not doing as good a job for patients as other sectors of the health care industry. Ultimately, the states took the lead in the patients' rights arena. Beginning in 1998, state legislatures have enacted over 900 laws and regulations addressing both consumer and provider protections.[32]

In another response to the managed care backlash, increasing numbers of employers began allowing employees to make personal decisions about their coverage, dubbed consumer-driven health plans (CDHPs). The ultimate goals of the CDHP are to have employees take more responsibility for health care decisions and exercise more cost consciousness. The typical CDHP consists of either a health reimbursement arrangement or a health savings account (HSA).[33] Eligibility for an HSA requires the employee's enrollment in a high-deductible health insurance plan. Employers and employees may contribute to the HSA up to a qualified amount. CDHPs provide comparative information to employees in web-based and traditional formats to increase knowledge about their health care choices and associated costs. In the HSA high deductible arrangement, the employee draws on the HSA to purchase care until the account is exhausted, when the policy's major medical provision activates. The second type of plan allows employees to design their own provider networks and benefits, based on anticipated needs and costs. The third uses web-based information to enable employees to choose from established groupings of provider networks and benefits to "customize" coverage. In 2009, 8% of those obtaining health benefits from their employers participated in CDHPs.[28] Predictions vary widely regarding the future of such arrangements in the health insurance marketplace.

Trends in Managed Care Costs

Beginning in the 1980s, restrictions imposed on hospital and physician practices through prospective payment and restrictive fee schedules contributed to a decline in health care expenditure growth. Throughout the 1990s market factors that enabled large health insurance purchasers to aggressively negotiate provider arrangements contributed to the impact of expenditure-cutting managed care initiatives.

The surge in managed care enrollment in the 1990s with decreases in premiums significantly contributed to a decline in the average annual growth of national health care expenditures[34]; however, after 4 years of decline health insurance premiums increased 8.2% in 1998, more than double the increase of the 3 previous years.[35] The insurance "underwriting cycle," in which insurers under-price during periods of market development and then increase premiums later to restore profitability, was noted as a major reason for increases.

Since 1999, average premiums for family coverage have increased 131% to a 2009 level of $13,375.[28] On average in 2009, covered workers contributed 17% of premium for single coverage and 27% for family coverage[28] (Figure 7-4). Higher premiums and requirements for larger employee contributions cause workers to drop coverage. This effect increases in severity as the annual earnings of employees decrease, meaning that lower wage workers who can least afford the risk of high health care costs are the most likely to become uninsured. Employers also seek to control costs through "benefit buy-downs." Methods include reducing the scope of benefits, increasing copayments and/or coinsurance, and

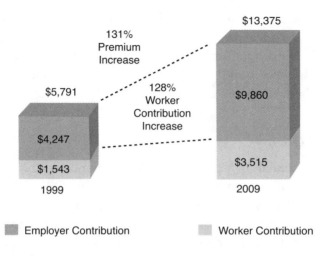

131%
Premium
Increase

$13,375

$5,791

128%
Worker
Contribution
Increase

$9,860

$4,247

$1,543

$3,515

1999

2009

■ Employer Contribution   ■ Worker Contribution

Note: The average worker contribution and the average employer contribution may not add to the average total premium due to rounding.

FIGURE 7-4 Average Annual Health Insurance Premiums and Worker Contributions for Family Coverage, 1999–2009.
Source: Employer Health Benefits 2009 Annual Survey-Summary of Findings (#7937), The Henry J. Kaiser Family Foundation, September, 2009. This information was reprinted with permission from the Henry J. Kaiser Family Foundation. The Kaiser Family Foundation is a non-profit private operating foundation, based in Menlo Park, California, dedicated to producing and communicating the best possible analysis and information on health issues.

increasing copays for prescription drugs.[36] Some experts estimate that every 1% increase in premiums produces a net increase of 164,000 uninsured individuals.[37]

Since the mid-1990s, MCOs have undergone many changes. Company mergers and consolidations have been among the most prominent. Only five publicly traded managed care companies now have enrollment totaling over 103 million members,[38] representing 82% of all managed care subscribers.[39] Changes in managed care company operating policies have responded to provider and consumer demands reflected by state-enacted patient protection legislation, a loosening of early restrictions on patient provider choice and specialty referrals, and patient access to information about operating policies, especially regarding denials of payment.[22] A 5-year literature analysis of MCO performance indicates that MCOs overall did not accomplish their early promises to change clinical practice and improve quality while lowering costs. Findings suggest that a systematic revamping of information systems, coupled with appropriate incentives and revised clinical processes, is required to produce the desired changes in cost and quality performance.[40]

MCOs and Quality

The most influential managed care quality assurance organization is the National Committee on Quality Assurance (NCQA). The NCQA formed in 1979 as two managed care trade organizations, the American Managed Care and Review Association and Group Health Association of America, merged under the title of the American Association of Health Plans. The title was later changed to the NCQA. In 1990, the NCQA became an independent, not-for-profit organization deriving its revenue primarily from fees for accreditation services.[41] The organization also publishes and markets a compendium of quality indicators on 250 health plans serving 50 million Americans.[42]

The NCQA evaluates participating organizations on a voluntary request basis. NCQA programs include accreditation for MCOs, PPOs, managed behavioral health care organizations, new health plans, and disease management programs. The NCQA also provides certification for organizations that verify provider credentials, physician organizations, utilization management organizations, and disease management organizations and programs. It also provides physician recognition programs for performance excellence in several areas of condition management.[43] Accreditation of MCOs entails rigorous reviews of all aspects of the respective organizations, including online surveys and onsite reviews of key clinical and administrative processes. The review focuses on six major areas: management, physician credentials, member rights and responsibilities, preventive health services, utilization, and medical records. Beginning in 1999, the NCQA began including outcomes of care and measures of clinical processes in accreditation reviews, increasing the likelihood that accreditation status accurately reflects the quality of care delivered.[44]

In 1989 a partnership among the NCQA, health plans, and employers developed the Health Plan Employer Data and Information Set (HEDIS).[45] The HEDIS (now the Health Care Effectiveness Data and Information Set) provides a standardized method for MCOs to collect, calculate, and report information about their performance to allow employers, other purchasers, and consumers to compare different plans. The HEDIS has evolved through several stages of development and continuously refines its measurements through a rigorous review and independent audits. The data set contains measures of MCO performance, divided among eight domains[46]:

1. Effectiveness of care
2. Access/availability of care
3. Satisfaction with the experience of care
4. Health plan stability
5. Use of services
6. Cost of care
7. Informed health care choices
8. Health plan descriptive information

The Centers for Medicare & Medicaid Services requires that all Medicare–managed care plans publicly report HEDIS data, and the NCQA requires all accredited plans to allow public reporting of their clinical quality data. A number of states also require plans providing Medicaid-managed care to report HEDIS data.[47]

The NCQA/HEDIS data provide an important avenue of accountability to the employer purchasers and consumers of health care and provide feedback to its providers that is critical in efforts to achieve improvement. The 2009 NCQA report "The State of Health Care Quality" noted an all-time high submission of audited HEDIS data representing 116 million Americans.[48] Benchmarked against the performance of the top 10% of all participating health plans, these data disclose quality disparities and gaps that inform purchasers, plan administrators, and policymakers. Comparisons allow the calculation of numbers of avoidable illnesses and deaths for several of the most common, costly, and life-threatening health conditions.[48]

MCOs also apply several internal techniques to manage quality, many of which directly or indirectly relate to physician performance. They focus attention on the quality of the institutional providers, especially on the hospitals with which they contract for services. Data systems that monitor claims information track the use of services to provide feedback to monitor resource use and quality. Through disease management programs, MCOs are attempting to control costs and improve care quality for individuals with chronic and costly conditions through methods such as the use of evidence-based clinical guidelines, patient self-management education, disease registries, risk stratification, proactive patient outreach, and performance feedback to providers. Programs may also use clinical specialists who provide monitoring and support to patients with disease management issues. Employer purchasers, several states, and the federal government are endorsing disease management programs for their employees and Medicaid and Medicare recipients.[49,50]

Self-Funded Insurance Programs

Since the late 1970s self-funding (full or partial) and self-insurance of employee health benefits have become increasingly common among large employers.[51] Through the self-funded mechanism, the employer (or other group, such as a union or trade association) collects premiums and pools these into a fund or account from which it pays claims against medical benefits instead of using a commercial carrier. Self-funded plans often use the services of an actuarial firm to set premium rates and a third-party administrator to administer benefits, pay claims, and collect data on utilization.[52] Many third-party administrators also provide case management services for potentially extraordinarily expensive cases to help coordinate care and control employer risk of catastrophic expenses.

Self-funded plans offer significant advantages to employers, such as avoiding additional administrative and other charges made by commercial carriers. By self-funding benefits, employers also can avoid premium taxes and accrue interest on the cash reserves held in the benefit account. A major stimulus to the development of self-insurance programs has been their exemption from the Employee Retirement and Income Security Act of 1974 (ERISA), which mandates minimum benefits under state law. This exemption allowed employers much greater flexibility in designing benefit packages and provided one mechanism to control benefit costs.

Major controversies continue to arise from the ERISA exemption of self-insured employer plans. One controversy is based in states' interpretation of their responsibilities for consumer protection through regulation of the types and scope of required coverage in employer-provided plans. ERISA has historically preempted such regulation. Another major area of dispute centers on the states' losses of premium revenue taxes as they struggle with growing financial burdens of uncompensated care and caring for uninsured populations. An additional area of controversy and legal actions surrounding ERISA is its prohibition against employees suing employer-provided health plans over matters involving coverage decisions. Under ERISA, organizations that administer employer-based health benefit plans maintain a degree of legal immunity from litigation and liability for withholding coverage or failing to provide necessary care. In 2004 the U.S. Supreme Court upheld an Appeals Court decision that beneficiaries of employment-related managed care plans cannot hold the plans accountable for damages when injured as a result of coverage denial decisions.[53]

Government as a Source of Payment: A System in Name Only

Federal and state government and, to a lesser extent, local government, finance health care services. Federal funding originally focused on specific population groups, providing health care for those in government service, their dependents, and particular population groups, such as Native Americans. Today, a combination of public programs, chief among them the federal Medicare program and joint federal–state Medicaid program, constitutes almost half of total national care expenditures.[2]

Government payment for health services includes federal support of U.S. Public Health Service hospitals, the Indian Health Service, state and local inpatient psychiatric and other long-term care facilities, services of the Veterans Affairs hospitals and health services, services provided by the Department of Defense to military personnel and their dependents, workers' compensation, public health activities, and other government-sponsored service grants and initiatives.

In the absence of a comprehensive national health and social services policy, government's role in financing health care services can be described as a system only in the loosest interpretation of that term. It may be more accurate to describe government's various roles in health care financing as a mosaic of individual programs of reimbursement, direct payments to vendors, grants, matching funds, and subsidies.

As a source of health care service payments, the system of financing operates primarily in a vendor–purchaser relationship, with government contracting with health care services providers rather than providing services directly. A prime example is the Medicare program in which the federal government purchases hospital, home health, nursing home, physician, and other medical services under contract with suppliers. The Medicaid system operates similarly.

America's history of fierce resistance from the private sector, both organized medicine and, to an extent, the voluntary medicine and hospital systems, has prevented enactment of a comprehensive national health care system. Private sector lobby resistance can be traced from the early 20th century's attempts to provide some form of national health insurance through the current debates of the Obama administration and Congress.

Medicare and Medicaid, comprising the majority of public spending on health, are discussed below. Chapter 10 discusses other government-financed programs.

Medicare

Were it not for the successful opposition of the private sector led by the AMA, the Social Security Act of 1935, the most significant piece of social legislation ever enacted by the federal government, would have included a form of national health insurance. It was not to be for another 30 years, during which time many presidential and congressional acts for national health insurance had been proposed and defeated, that Congress enacted Medicare, "Health Insurance for the Aged," Title XVIII of the Social Security Act, in 1965. Medicare became only the second mandated health insurance program in the United States, after workers' compensation. When Medicare was enacted, approximately one-half of the elderly had any health insurance that usually covered only inpatient hospital costs, and much of health care spending was paid for out-of-pocket.[54] Today, the Medicare program covers 46 million Americans, including most 65 years of age and older, younger individuals who receive Social Security Disability Insurance benefits, and individuals with end-stage kidney disease and Lou Gehrig's disease following their eligibility for Social Security Disability Insurance. Projected 2010 expenditures total $504 billion, approximately 15% of the federal budget.[55]

The enactment of Medicare legislation was an historical benchmark, signaling government's entry into the personal health care financing arena. The Medicare program was established under the aegis of the Social Security Administration, and hospital payment was contracted to local intermediaries chosen by hospitals. Over 90% of hospitals chose their local Blue Cross association as the intermediary. In response to organized medicine's opposition to government certification, the Social Security Administration agreed to accreditation by the private Joint Commission on Accreditation of Hospitals as meeting the certification requirement for Medicare participation. Describing the enactment of Medicare as a "watershed," Rosemary Stevens wrote the following (pp. 281–282)[24]:

> Thus with the stroke of a pen, the elderly acquired hospital benefits, the hospitals acquired cost reimbursement for these benefits, the Blue Cross Association was precipitated into prominence as a major national organization (since the national contract was to be with the association, with subcontracting to local plans), and the Joint Commission was given formal government recognition.

The Medicare amendment stated that there should be "prohibition against any federal interference with the practice of medicine or the way medical services were provided" (pp. 286–287).[24] Ultimately, however, the government's acceptance of responsibility for payment for the care of older adults generated a flood of regulations to address cost and quality control of the services and products for which it was now a major payer.

As originally implemented, the Medicare program consisted of two parts, which differed in sources of funding and benefits. Part A provided benefits for hospital care, limited skilled nursing care, short-term home health care after hospitalization, and hospice care.[55] This portion of coverage was mandatory and was funded by Social Security payroll taxes.[54] Part B, supplementary medical insurance, was structured as a voluntary program covering physician services and services ordered by physicians, such as outpatient diagnostic tests, medical equipment and supplies, and home health services.[55] This portion was funded from beneficiary premium payments, matched by general federal revenues.[54]

The Balanced Budget Act of 1997 added Part C, Medicare + Choice, allowing private health plans to administer Medicare contracts, with beneficiary enrollment on a voluntary basis. In 2003 the Medicare Prescription Drug, Improvement, and Modernization Act changed Part C to "Medicare Advantage," revising the administration of Medicare managed care programs to entice additional participation.[55] Since passage of the Medicare Prescription Drug, Improvement, and Modernization Act beneficiary enrollment in private health plans has increased substantially (Figure 7-5). Today, approximately 10 million beneficiaries participate in private health plans. The Medicare Prescription Drug, Improvement, and Modernization Act also added a new Part D for prescription drug

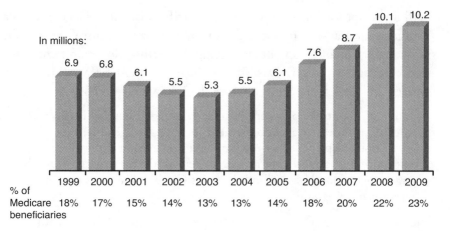

In millions:										
									10.1	10.2
								8.7		
							7.6			
6.9	6.8	6.1	5.5	5.3	5.5	6.1				

	1999	2000	2001	2002	2003	2004	2005	2006	2007	2008	2009
% of Medicare beneficiaries	18%	17%	15%	14%	13%	13%	14%	18%	20%	22%	23%

Note: Includes local HMOs, PSOs, PPOs, regional PPOs, PFFS plans, 1876 Cost Plans, Demonstrations, HCPP and PACE Plans.

FIGURE 7-5 Total Medicare Private Health Plan Enrollment, 1999–2009. *Source:* Medicare Advantage Fact Sheet (#2052-13), The Henry J. Kaiser Family Foundation, November, 2009. This information was reprinted with permission from the Henry J. Kaiser Family Foundation. The Kaiser Family Foundation is a non-profit private operating foundation, based in Menlo Park, California, dedicated to producing and communicating the best possible analysis and information on health issues.

coverage to provide financial relief from these costs, particularly for low-income individuals.

From its inception, Medicare coverage was not fully comprehensive, and that remains true today. Beneficiaries are required to share costs through a system of deductibles and coinsurance, and there is no limit on out-of-pocket expenditures. For Part A, the deductible requires beneficiaries to reach a set amount in personal outlays for hospitalization each 12-month period, and coinsurance requires that patients cover 20% of hospitalization costs. The program also limits total compensated days of hospital care on a lifetime pool of days. For Part B coverage, monthly premiums are deducted from Social Security payments. These limitations gave rise to a variety of private supplemental, or "Medi-gap," policies, designed to assist with cost-sharing requirements and benefit gaps.[55] Also, the prescription drug benefit contains a gap in which beneficiaries are fully exposed to costs between designated levels of expenditures.[56]

Medicare Cost Containment and Quality Initiatives

Within a few years after implementation, Medicare spending was significantly exceeding projections. Although hospital costs for the growing older adult population increased more rapidly than expected, the rise over projected Medicare expenses could not be explained by that phenomenon. A 1976 study by the U.S. Human Resources Administration reviewed the first 10 years of Medicare hospital expenses and attributed less than 10% of increases to utilization by the older adult population. Almost one-fourth of the increase over projected hospital costs was attributed to general inflation and two-thirds to huge growth in hospital payroll and nonpayroll expenses, including profits.[24]

Like Blue Cross, Medicare's hospital reimbursement mechanism was cost based and retrospective on a per-day-of-stay basis. Although facilitating the rapid incorporation of almost 20 million beneficiaries into the new benefit system, cost-based reimbursement also fueled utilization in an era of rapidly advancing medical technology. Paid on a retrospective basis for costs incurred, hospitals had a strong incentive to use services with no incentives for efficiency.

In the decade after Medicare enactment, several amendments to the Social Security Act made significant changes. In general, amendments of the first 5 years increased the types of covered services and expanded the population of eligible persons. During the later period, amendments addressed rising concerns about the costs and quality of the program.

Many initiatives attempted to slow spiraling costs and address quality concerns. They were largely unsuccessful. In 1966 Congress enacted the Comprehensive Health Planning Act to support states in conducting local health planning to ensure adequate facilities and services and avoid duplications.[57] In 1974 the Health Planning Resources and Development Act replaced the Comprehensive Health Planning Act with health systems agencies to develop plans for local health resources based on quantified population needs. The Act also required all states to obtain approval from a state planning agency before starting any major capital project, and several states adopted certificate-of-need legislation for this purpose. Congress repealed the federal mandate in 1987, but most states still maintain some form of certificate-of-need program, focused on development of physician-owned facilities such as ambulatory surgery and diagnostic imaging centers.[58] Health systems agencies were unsuccessful in materially influencing decisions about service or technology expansion, because decisions were dominated by institutional and economic interests. Concurrent with attempts to slow cost increases through a planning approach, a number of other legislative initiatives took shape that were directly related to concerns over Medicare costs and service quality.

Professional standards review organizations, established in 1972, signaled the first federal attempt to review care provided under Medicare, Medicaid, and certain other federally funded health care programs.[59] Each local professional standards review organization was a not-for-profit organization composed of a group of local physicians who performed record reviews and made payment recommendations to the local Medicare intermediary. Plagued by questionable effectiveness and high administrative costs, professional standards review organizations were replaced by peer review organizations in 1982. Peer review organizations were given more specific and measurable cost and quality standards than their predecessor professional standards review organizations.[60] In 2001 peer review organizations were renamed "quality improvement organizations" as part of broad, quality improvement initiatives of the Centers for Medicare & Medicaid Services.

Both not-for-profit and investor-owned for-profit hospitals saw the opportunity for expansion offered by Medicare's guarantee of full-cost reimbursement. Between 1970 and 1980 there was over a 200% increase in the number of hospitals involved in multihospital systems of both types.[61]

The federal budgets of 1980 and 1981 again amended the Medicare legislation with a strong focus on reducing the number and length of hospitalizations. Amendments advocated home health services as a hospital alternative by eliminating the limit on annual number of home health care visits, a 3-day hospitalization requirement for home health visit coverage eligibility, and occupational therapy as a requirement for initial entitlement to home health care services. Budget provisions also lifted exclusion from Medicare participation of for-profit home health care agencies in states that did not require agency licensure.

The unsuccessful efforts at Medicare cost containment and quality control of the 1970s and 1980s culminated in Medicare's 1983 enactment of a case payment system that radically changed hospital reimbursement. The new payment system shifted hospital reimbursement from the retrospective to prospective mode. Using diagnosis-related groups (DRGs) developed for the Health Care Financing Administration, the new system provided a patient classification method to relate the type of patients a hospital treated (i.e., age, sex, gender, diagnoses) to costs.[62] The DRG payment system based hospital payments on established fees for services required to treat specific diagnoses rather than on discreet units of services. The DRGs group 10,000+ International Classification of Disease codes into approximately 500 patient categories. Patients within each category are grouped for similar clinical conditions and expected resource use.[63] DRGs form a manageable, clinically coherent set of patient classes that relate a hospital's case mix to the resource demands and associated costs experienced by the hospital. The payment an individual hospital receives under this system is ultimately calculated using input from a variety of other data known to impact costs, such as hospital teaching status and wage data for its geographic location.

The DRG system provided incentives for the hospital to spend only what was needed to achieve optimal patient outcomes. If outcomes could be achieved at a cost lower than the preset payment, the hospital received an excess payment for those cases. If the hospital spent more to treat cases than allowed, it absorbed the excess costs. The DRG system also financially provided for cases classified as "outliers" due to complications. The DRG system did not build in allowances to the payment rate for direct medical education expenses for teaching hospitals, hospital outpatient expenses, or capital expenditures. These continued to be reimbursed on a cost basis.

The principle of case-based prospective payment soon was adopted in varying forms by numerous states and private third-party payers as their reimbursement basis. The prospective payment system raised many concerns among hospitals, health care providers, and consumers about its possible effects, including fears about premature hospital discharges, hospitals' questionable ability to streamline services to conform to preset payments, and the home health care industry's capacity to accommodate an increased caseload.

"Quicker and sicker" was the slogan popularized by the media during the first years of the prospective payment system to characterize the drive for shorter hospital stays. The media also popularized the term "patient dumping," referring to documented hospitals' transfer of patients at high risk of expensive and potentially unprofitable service needs to other hospitals.

Subsequent research on the impact of the prospective payment system demonstrated that many early concerns were unfounded and that DRGs did have a measurable impact on the overall growth of Medicare spending.[64] Extensive research also compared quality indicators before and after DRG implementation. The federal Prospective Payment Assessment Commission was established to monitor the effects of the prospective system. Studies revealed few effects on Medicare patient readmission rates attributable to the DRG system.[65] The RAND Corporation also conducted several studies of another indicator of patient care quality, in-hospital mortality rates. The studies reviewed almost 17,000 records of Medicare patients admitted to hospitals for five common diagnoses. Findings included a drop of 24% in the average length of hospital stay for these conditions and an overall improvement in mortality rates among the diagnoses studied.[65]

Concerns about patient dumping were formally addressed in the 1985 federal budget by the Emergency Medical Treatment and Labor Act of 1986, which required hospitals to treat everyone who presented in their emergency departments, regardless of ability to pay. Stiff financial penalties, as well as risk of Medicare certification loss by hospitals inappropriately transferring patients, accompanied the Emergency Medical Treatment and Labor Act provisions.[66]

Evidence indicates that the prospective payment system slowed hospital cost growth during the early years after implementation through reductions in lengths of stay, hospital personnel, and new medical technologies; however, total Medicare cost growth later reaccelerated, in part because of increased volume in outpatient spending and other factors whose impacts have not been clearly determined.[65] Concerns about the capacity of the home health care industry to meet anticipated increases in demand dissipated quickly. Both the not-for-profit and proprietary sectors of the industry responded by creating new or expanding existing home health care services as components of vertically integrated systems. In the early years of the prospective payment system, hospitals did not experience the predicted negative financial impact, and they actually posted substantial profits.[65] In fact, the federal government partially justified subsequent reductions in prospective payment on the basis that early payments were too high relative to costs.[66] It has even been suggested that the large surpluses generated by not-for-profit hospitals in the early years of prospective payment fueled hospital costs by making new surpluses available for investment.[65]

From the outset, the prospective payment system's cost-containment effectiveness was limited by its application to only inpatient hospital care for Medicare recipients. Aggressive shifting of Medicare-covered services to the outpatient setting and shifting hospital costs onto private pay patients were two major reactions that dampened the prospective payment system's cost-containment results.

Medicare Physician Reimbursement

Medicare Part B physician reimbursement was established as fee-for-service, based on prevailing fees within geographic areas. The Medicare physician payment rate increase averaged 18% annually between 1975 and 1987 and provoked legislative action.[67] Medicare first enacted a temporary price freeze for physician services.[67] Assessments of the price freeze suggested that physicians offset the lower fees by increasing the volume of services.[67] This raised the issue of whether physicians respond to fee pressures by using more services to compensate for lower reimbursement. Concerns over absolute cost increases and overuse of costly specialty care prompted additional congressional cost-containment action.

The 1989 Federal budget established a new method of Medicare physician reimbursement that became effective in 1992, using a resource-based relative value scale to replace the fee-for-service reimbursement system.[68] The resource-based relative value scale intended to control cost growth by instituting the same payments for the same services, whether performed by a generalist or specialist physician, reducing the numbers of expensive procedures and lowering the incentive for physicians to specialize. Relative value units were adjusted for geographic area variations in costs. The resource-based relative value scale continues to be used with a committee of the AMA and national medical specialty societies recommending annual updates.[68]

Balanced Budget Act of 1997

Medicare reforms enacted by the DRG prospective payment system, managed care influences, market competition, technology advances, and consumerism produced unprecedented changes in hospital and physician reimbursement, hospitals' affinity for technology, and consumer expectations of hospital care. The Medicare prospective payment system had succeeded in demonstrating that "more is not necessarily better," as lengths of stay and service intensity declined to accommodate the DRG framework, with no demonstrable negative impact on the quality of patient care. Then, in the early 1990s, the nation witnessed vigorous debates regarding the Clinton administration's National Health Security Act. Although the Act never reached a congressional vote, many months of debate thrust national concerns about Medicare spending, lack of access to services, beneficiary costs, and provider choice into the public spotlight. Popular and political sensitivities rose against the backdrop of escalating national predictions about potential insolvency of the Hospital Insurance Trust Fund.[69]

Several trends supported the need for major changes in the Medicare system. First, Congressional Budget Office projections indicated that Medicare cost growth could not be sustained without cuts in other government programs, major increases in taxes, or larger budget deficits.[70]

Second, Medicare's fee-for-service indemnity structure was becoming rapidly outmoded, as employer-sponsored plans, Medicaid, and private insurance were rapidly embracing managed care principles.

Third, Medicare coverage left significant gaps requiring copays and coinsurance that many beneficiaries were unable to fill with supplemental "Medi-gap" insurance policies. Although some Medicare beneficiaries were eligible for Medicaid subsidies of these expenses, subsidies created additional financial burdens for the states.

Acknowledging the president's and Congress's discord on a national health reform program, in 1995 Congress focused on slowing Medicare cost growth and achieving broader choices for Medicare beneficiaries through managed care plans as models of cost-containment and consumer satisfaction.[70]

The presidential and congressional campaigns of 1996 focused heavily on the health care issues brought to light during debate on the National Health Security Act and consumer concerns about managed care. This political environment supported the rapid formulation and passage of the bipartisan Health Insurance Portability and Accountability Act of 1996, or HIPAA, also called the Kassenbaum-Kennedy Bill. Among its important health insurance features, HIPAA included prohibiting insurance companies from denying coverage due to preexisting medical conditions or denying sale of personal insurance policies to individuals who were previously covered in group plans. It also established a pilot program to enable workers to save tax-free dollars for future medical expenses through medical savings accounts.[71] Though the act accomplished important beneficial outcomes, it fell far short of addressing the pervasive problems of the overall health care system in general or the Medicare and Medicaid programs in particular.

The 1998 federal budget process reflected pressures to produce a balanced budget and to respond meaningfully to national health issues from both the consumer and cost-containment perspectives. The resulting Balanced Budget Act (BBA) created major new policy directions for Medicare and Medicaid and took important incremental steps toward universal coverage through an initiative to insure uninsured children through a $16 billion allocation for a new State Children's Health Insurance Program (SCHIP).[72]

The Act was characterized as containing "some of the most sweeping and significant changes to Medicare and Medicaid since their inception in 1965."[72] Overall, the BBA proposed to reduce growth in Medicare and Medicaid spending by $125.2 billion in 5 years through regulatory changes and payment changes to hospitals, physicians, post–acute-care services, and health plans. It also increased premiums for Medicare Part B and required new prospective payment systems for hospital outpatient services, skilled nursing facilities, home health agencies, and rehabilitation hospitals. It also reduced allowances for medical education expenses of teaching hospitals and funded incentives to hospitals for voluntarily reducing the numbers of medical residents. As the largest Medicare spender, the BBA targeted hospitals for more than one-third of total anticipated savings. Decreased Medicare spending growth in the period 1998–2002 demonstrated the immediate impact of the BBA. After growing at an average annual rate of 11.1% for the 15 years before 1997, the average annual rate of spending growth between 1998 and 2000 dropped to 1.7%, resulting in approximately $68 billion in savings.[73]

Among the most significant policy shifts of the BBA was opening the Medicare program to private insurers through the Medicare + Choice Program, for the first time allowing financial risk sharing for the Medicare program with the private sector. The participation of private insurers was intended to increase both the impact of competitive market forces on the program and consumer awareness of alternatives to the fee-for-service system.

The BBA constituted federal commissions to carry out monitoring and recommendation functions during implementation, including the Medicare Payment Advisory Commission and an independent National Bipartisan Commission on the Future of Medicare whose functions entailed the analyzing numerous dimensions of Medicare's financial condition and benefits design over time.[74]

Implementation of the Medicare BBA provisions experienced widespread challenges and delays. Significant changes to the Medicare and Medicaid program structure, payment methods, and amounts all drew fire from industry advocacy groups, professional organizations, and consumers. Just before several of the BBA's provisions took effect, President Clinton signed the Balanced Budget Refinement Act of 1999, providing $17.5 billion to restore cuts to industry sectors negatively impacted by the BBA and outlining later implementation schedules for many of the BBA's original mandates.[75]

The Medicare managed care enrollment initiative experienced serious challenges. Because of reduced Medicare reimbursement, costs of working with federal bureaucracy, and market shifts reducing profitability, MCOs lost their early enthusiasm for participation in the program. Plan withdrawals resulted in a decline from 6.3 million beneficiaries in 2000 to 4.6 million in 2003.[76] In response, in 2000 Congress enacted the Benefits Protection and Improvement Act that increased participating health plans' and provider payments.[77]

In 2001 the Centers for Medicare & Medicaid Services inaugurated the "Quality Initiative," encompassing every dimension of the health care delivery system. The Quality Initiative includes nursing homes, hospitals, home health care agencies, physicians, and other facilities.[78] The program collects and analyzes data to monitor conformance with standards of care and performance. In addition to the Quality Initiative, the Medicare Quality Monitoring System "processes, analyzes, interprets and disseminates health-related data to monitor the quality of care delivered to Medicare fee-for-service beneficiaries."[79] The Medicare administration also is experimenting with hospital pay-for-performance plans designed to improve quality and avoid unnecessary costs.[80] With the goal of providing public, valid, and user-friendly information about hospital quality, in 2005 Medicare launched the website "Hospital Compare," in a collaboration with the Hospital Quality Alliance, a public–private partnership organization. Hospital Compare encompasses common conditions and criteria that assess individual hospitals' performance consistency with evidence-based practice; reporting is required for hospitals to qualify for Medicare rate updates.[81] Data from the "Hospital Consumer Assessment of Healthcare Providers and Systems" surveys has been added to the

Hospital Compare information, providing patient perspectives on their hospital experience.[82] In 2007 the Medicare administration announced that beginning in 2008 it would no longer pay for procedures resulting from hospital-acquired infections, an aggressive step in using quality standards as a basis for public reporting and payment.[83] In consultation with the Hospital Quality Forum and many other expert organizations, Medicare also identified categories of untoward hospital events, dubbed "never happen events," for which it is investigating hospital payment reductions for resulting treatment.[84]

Medicaid and the SCHIP

In 1965 Medicaid legislation was enacted as Title XIX of the Social Security Act. Medicaid is administered by the Centers for Medicare & Medicaid Services and is a mandatory joint federal–state program in which federal and state support is shared based on the state's per capita income. Before Medicaid's implementation, health care services for the economically needed were provided through a patchwork of programs sponsored by state and local governments, charitable organizations, and community hospitals.

Today, Medicaid supports health care and long-term care services for 47.1 million low-income Americans.[85] The program represents a major source of health care system funding, accounting for over 16% of $1.9 trillion in personal health services spending and 41% of spending for nursing home care in 2008.[2] The Medicaid program is the third largest source of health insurance in America after employer-based programs and Medicare.

The federal government establishes broad program guidelines, but program requirements are the prerogative of state governments. Medicaid requires states to cover certain types of individuals or groups under their plans, and states may include others at their discretion. The program provides three types of coverage:

1. Health insurance for low-income families with children
2. Long-term care for older Americans and individuals with disabilities
3. Supplemental coverage for low-income Medicare beneficiaries for services not covered by Medicare, including Medicare premiums, deductibles, and coinsurance[86]

Until the enactment of Medicare Part D, the third type of coverage also pays for prescription drugs.

Medicaid federal guidelines established a mandated core of basic medical services for state programs. Included were inpatient and outpatient hospital services, physician services, diagnostic services, and nursing home care for adults. Later Medicaid amendments expanded mandated benefits to include home health care, preventive health screening services, family planning services, and assistance to recipients of Supplemental Security Income. State Medicaid programs currently must extend benefits to all pregnant women who meet federal income level guidelines and children whose family incomes fall below specified federal income guidelines. Individual states have broad discretion to include additional services in their Medicaid programs, and many have elected extended benefits beyond the core of mandated benefits.

Medicaid funding sources are distinct from those for Medicare. Medicare, funded from contributions of payroll taxes matched by employers, is an entitlement because individuals have contributed to their cost of coverage. Medicaid, which is funded by personal income and corporate and excise taxes, is a transfer payment representing funds transferred from more economically affluent individuals to those in need.[87]

Unlike Medicare, which reimburses providers through intermediaries such as Blue Cross, Medicaid directly reimburses service providers. Rate-setting formulas, procedures, and policies vary widely among states. Because of the variations in benefits and reimbursement policies, Medicaid has been described as "50 different programs."[87]

Throughout the 1980s as costs grew rapidly, states tested various prepaid, managed care approaches, and some implemented prospective payment systems modeled on DRG reimbursement. Several states experimented with voluntary Medicaid managed care enrollment, contracting with HMOs to provide some or all of their Medicaid benefits under federally approved demonstration projects. Through a provision of the BBA, the federal government allowed states to mandate managed care enrollment for their Medicaid beneficiaries, and today all 50 states offer some type of Medicaid managed care plans.

In 2008, over 70% of Medicaid beneficiaries were enrolled in managed care plans.[85] The number and proportion of Medicaid enrollees in managed care plans continue to increase as states seek ways to control costs and ensure access. All states are struggling with the burden of rising

Medicaid costs. The 2008 economic recession accelerated Medicaid enrollment, spending, and growth that are expected to continue through 2010[88] (Figure 7-6).

Children's Health Insurance Program

The BBA contained a child health initiative to build on the Medicaid program by targeting uninsured children whose family income was too high to qualify for Medicaid and too low to afford private health insurance through SCHIP. SCHIP targeted enrollment of 5 million children through federal matching funds for states over the period 1998 to 2007.[89] In 1999 all 50 states were receiving federal support from BBA allocations under the SCHIP. By 2008 over 7 million children had been enrolled in the program since its inception (Figure 7-7). Renamed the "Children's Health Insurance Program," the program was reauthorized in 2008 and

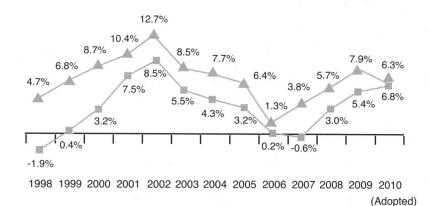

Note: Enrollment percentage changes from June to June of each year; spending growth percentage changes in state fiscal year.

FIGURE 7-6 Percent Change in Total Medicaid Spending and Enrollment, 1998–2008.
Source: The Crunch Continues: Medicaid Spending, Coverage and Policy in the Midst of a Recession (#7985), The Henry J. Kaiser Family Foundation, September 2009. This information was reprinted with permission from the Henry J. Kaiser Family Foundation. The Kaiser Family Foundation is a non-profit private operating foundation, based in Menlo Park, California, dedicated to producing and communicating the best possible analysis and information on health issues.

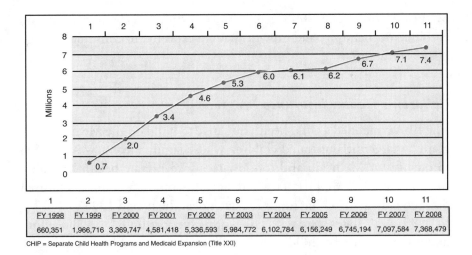

	FY 1998	FY 1999	FY 2000	FY 2001	FY 2002	FY 2003	FY 2004	FY 2005	FY 2006	FY 2007	FY 2008
	660,351	1,966,716	3,369,747	4,581,418	5,336,593	5,984,772	6,102,784	6,156,249	6,745,194	7,097,584	7,368,479

CHIP = Separate Child Health Programs and Medicaid Expansion (Title XXI)

FIGURE 7-7 Number of Children Ever Enrolled in the Children's Health Insurance Program.
Source: Children's Health Insurance Statistical Enrollment Data System (SEDS) 1/29/09

again in 2009 with significant enhancements for the period through 2013.[89] However, in 2008, 8.1 million or approximately 10.3% of all children remained uninsured.[90]

Medicaid Quality Initiatives

The Centers for Medicare & Medicaid Services and State Operations has the principle responsibility for developing and carrying out Medicaid and SCHIP quality initiatives through working partnerships with the respective state's programs. The Centers for Medicare & Medicaid Services and State Operations articulates a quality strategy encompassing five key elements[91]:

1. Evidence-based care and quality measurement
2. Payment aligned with quality
3. Health information technology
4. Partnerships
5. Information dissemination, technical assistance, and sharing of best practices

A Division of Quality, Evaluation, and Health Outcomes focuses on providing technical assistance to states in their quality improvement initiatives.[92]

Future Prospects

A 2007 Henry J. Kaiser Family Foundation's health tracking poll on 2008 presidential election issues indicated that health care was the top domestic issue, behind only the Iraq war in voter priority for candidates' attention.[93]

The 2007 candidate, and now President Obama, campaigned with strong promises of swift, major health reform legislation to address the continuing issues of costs, quality, and access. Almost one year to the date of his inauguration as President, and after many months of acrimonious dialogue as the Senate and House constructed reform bills, in January 2010 *Modern Health Care* headlined, "Requiem for Reform," following the election of a Republican Massachusetts senator to replace the late Democrat, Edward Kennedy.[94] Democrats lost their filibuster-proof Senate majority and, with it, the likelihood of passing a hoped-for comprehensive bill. Incremental alternatives remained possible, but strong partisanship suggested that outcomes would fall far short of a major overhaul of health care financing and the service delivery system.

Passage of the Patient Protection and Affordable Care Act of 2010 recognized that America's health care investment is more of a moral than economic issue as U.S health status indicators lag behind other developed countries that spend much less and provide universal health care coverage.

Against the current federal backdrop, several states have continued to experiment with health care reform. Maine, Massachusetts, and Vermont are notable examples.[95] In 2003 Maine committed to making affordable health care coverage available to every citizen, to decrease health care cost growth and enhance care quality with a subsidized insurance product and expansions of Medicaid eligibility.[95] In 2006, Massachusetts enacted a model very close to universal coverage, using a mandate of personal responsibility to purchase health insurance combined with government subsidies to ensure affordability.[96] Since the plan's implementation, estimates are that two-thirds of previously uninsured individuals have obtained coverage.[96] Also in 2006, Vermont enacted a plan with over 35 special initiatives targeted to increase access, contain costs, and improve quality.[97] The Vermont plan includes a new health insurance product for the uninsured that provides employer-sponsored premium assistance through employer contributions and a statewide plan for preventing and managing chronic conditions.[97]

The new health care reform legislation will confront policymakers with a daunting array of issues demanding creativity and courage to enact meaningful changes. Paying for required changes may be considerably easier than breaking loose from old philosophies, value systems, and politics that have brought the U.S. health care enterprise to its present paradoxical state of superior technology embedded in an antiquated delivery system.

References

1. Congressional Budget Office. Long-term look for health care spending: overview of the U.S. health care system. Available from http://www.cbo.gov/ftpdocs/87xx/doc8758/MainText.3.1.shtml. Accessed January 17, 2010.
2. U.S. Department of Health and Human Services, Centers for Medicare & Medicaid Services. National health expenditures tables, 2008. Available from http://www.cms.hhs.gov/nationalhealthexpenddata/downloads/tables.pdf. Accessed January 15, 2010.
3. Hartman M, Martin A, Nuccio O, et al. Health spending growth at a historic low. *Health Affairs.* 2010;29:147–152.
4. Altman S, Tompkins C, Eliat E, et al. Escalating health care spending: is it desirable or inevitable? *Health Affairs.* 2003:W1–W14. Available from http://content.healthaffairs.org/cgi/reprint/hlthaff.w3.1v1?maxtoshow=&HITS=10&hits=10&RESULTFORMAT=&fulltext=Altman+S%2C+Tompkins+C+&andorexactfulltext=and&searchid=1&FIRSTINDEX=0&resourcetype=HWCIT. Accessed January 14, 2010.
5. Anderson GF, Frogner BK. Health spending in OECD countries: obtaining value per dollar. *Health Affairs.* 2008;27:1718–1727.
6. Anderson GF, Reinhardt UE, Hussey PS, et al. It's the prices, stupid: why the United States is so different from other countries. *Health Affairs.* 2003;22:89–105.
7. Milstein A, Gilbertson E. American medical home runs. *Health Affairs.* 2009;28:1317–1318.
8. Orszag PR. Opportunities to increase efficiency in health care, June 2008. Congressional Budget Office. Available from http://www.cbo.gov/ftpdocs/93xx/doc9384/06-16-healthsummit.pdf. Accessed January 14, 2010.
9. Morris L. Combating fraud in health care: an essential component of any cost containment strategy. *Health Affairs.* 2009;28:1351–1356.
10. Chernew ME, Jacobson PD, Hofer TP, et al. Barriers to constraining health care cost growth. *Health Affairs.* 2004;23:122–128.
11. Levit K, Smith C, Cowan C, et al. Inflation spurs health spending in 2000. *Health Affairs.* 2002;21:179.

12. U.S. Department of Health and Human Services, Administration on Aging. Profile of older Americans: 2008. Available from http://www.aoa.gov/AoAroot/Aging_Statistics/Profile/2008/index.aspx. Accessed December 14, 2009.

13. U.S. Department of Health and Human Services, Administration on Aging. Population 65 and over by age: 1900–2050. Available from http://www.aoa.gov/AoARoot/Aging_Statistics/future_growth/docs/By_Age_65_and_over.xls. Accessed December 14, 2009.

14. Coile RC Jr, Trusko BE. Healthcare 2020: challenges of the millennium. *Health Care Manage Technol.* 1999;20:37.

15. DeFrances CJ, Lucas CA, Buie VC, et al. 2006 National hospital discharge survey, July 2008. Available from http://www.cdc.gov/nchs/data/nhsr/nhsr005.pdf. Accessed December 21, 2009.

16. Smith S, Heffler S, Freeland M, et al. The next decade of health care spending: a new outlook. *Health Affairs.* 1999;18:89–90.

17. U.S. Department of Labor, Bureau of Labor Statistics. Occupational outlook handbook, 2010–2011 edition, physicians and surgeons. Available from http://www.bls.gov/oco/ocos074.htm. Accessed December 12, 2009.

18. DeNavas-Walt C, Proctor BD, Smith JC. U.S. Census current population reports, P60-236, income, poverty, and health insurance coverage in the United States: 2008. Washington, DC: U.S. Government Printing Office; 2009. Available from http://www.census.gov/prod/2009pubs/p60-236.pdf. Accessed January 12, 2010.

19. The Henry J. Kaiser Family Foundation. The uninsured: A primer: Key facts about Americans without health insurance. Available from http://www.kff.org/uninsured/upload/7451.pdf. Accessed January 12, 2010.

20. American College of Physicians and American Society of Internal Medicine. No health insurance: it's enough to make you sick. Available from http://www/acponline.org/pressroom/applauds.htm. Accessed January 16, 2010.

21. U.S. Department of Labor, Bureau of Labor Statistics. Career guide to industries, 2010–2011, Healthcare. Available from http://www.bls.gov/oco/cg/cgs035.htm. Accessed January 12, 2010.

22. Kongstvedt PR. *Essentials of Managed Health Care,* 5th ed. Sudbury, MA: Jones and Bartlett; 2007.

23. Wilson F, Neuhauser D. *Health services in the United States,* 2nd ed. Cambridge, MA: Ballinger; 1982.

24. Stevens R. *In Sickness and in Wealth: American Hospitals in the Twentieth Century.* New York: Basic Books; 1989.

25. Conover CJ, Hall MA, Ostermann J. The impact of Blue Cross conversions on health spending and the uninsured. *Health Affairs.* 2005;24:473–482.

26. Thomasson, M. Health insurance in the United States. Available from http://eh.net/encyclopedia/article/thomasson.insurance.health.us. Accessed January 15, 2010.

27. Kongstvedt PR. *The Managed Health Care Handbook.* Gaithersburg, MD: Aspen; 1989.

28. The Henry J. Kaiser Family Foundation and Health Research and Educational Trust. Employer health benefits 2009, summary of findings. Available from http:/ehbs.kff.org/pdf/2009/7937.pdf. Accessed December 19, 2009.

29. Trespacz KL. Staff-model HMOs: don't blink or you'll miss them. *Managed Care Magazine*. Available from http://www.managedcaremag.com/archives/9907/9907.staffmodel.html. Accessed January 12, 2010.

30. Blendon RJ, Brodie M, Benson J, et al. Understanding the managed care backlash. *Health Affairs*. 1998;17:80.

31. White House Backgrounder. President Clinton releases report documenting actions federal government is taking to implement a patients' bill of rights. Available from http://www.hhs.gov/news/press/1998pres/981102.html. Accessed January 16, 2010.

32. National Conference of State Legislatures. Managed care state laws and regulations including consumer and provider protections. Available from http://www.ncsl.org/IssuesResearch/Health/ManagedCareStateLaws/tabid/14320/Default.aspx. Accessed January 16, 2010.

33. Gabel JR, Pickreign JD, Witmore HH, et al. Behind the slow growth of employer-based consumer-driven health plans. Available from http://www.hschange.com/CONTENT/900/?topic=topic01#ib1. Accessed January 15, 2010.

34. Congressional Budget Office. Projections of national health expenditures: 1997–2008, the economic and budget outlook: fiscal years 1999–2008. Available from http://www.cbo.gov/doc.cfm?index=316. Accessed January 15, 2010.

35. Levit K, Cowan C, Lazenby H, et al. Health spending in 1998: signals of change. *Health Affairs*. 2000;19:131.

36. Centers for Medicare & Medicaid Services. Health care industry market update, managed care. Available from http://www3.cms.hhs.gov/CapMarket Updates/Downloads/hcimu11122002.pdf . Accessed January 17, 2010.

37. Chernew M, Cutler D, Keenan P, et al. University of Michigan, Economic Research Institute on the Uninsured. Increasing health insurance costs and the decline in insurance coverage. Available from http://eriu.sph.umich.edu/pdf/wp8.pdf. Accessed January 18, 2010.

38. Atlantic Information Services. Health plans, company intelligence. *Health Plan Week*. Available from http://www.aishealth.com/ManagedCare/CompanyIntel/TenLargest.html. Accessed January 21, 2010.

39. Managed Care On-line. Managed care national statistics. National managed care enrollment, 2009. Available from http://www.mcareol.com/factshts/factnati.htm. Accessed January 21, 2010.

40. Miller RH, Luft HS. HMO plan performance update: analysis of the literature, 1997–2001. *Health Affairs*. 2002;21:81.

41. Iglehart JK. The National Committee for Quality Assurance. *N Engl J Med*. 1996;335:995.

42. National Committee for Quality Assurance. Report cards. Available from http://www.ncqa.org/tabid/60/Default.aspx. Accessed January 21, 2010.

43. National Committee for Quality Assurance. Programs. Available from http://www.ncqa.org/tabid/74/Default.aspx. Accessed January 21, 2010.

44. Pawlson L, O'Kane M. Professionalism, regulation, and the market: impact on accountability for quality of care. *Health Affairs*. 2002;21:202.

45. Epstein M. The role of quality measurement in a competitive marketplace. In: Altman SH, Reinhardt UE, Eds. *Strategic Choices for a Changing Health Care System*. Chicago: Health Administration Press; 1996:217.

46. National Committee for Quality Assurance. HEDIS compliance audit program, 2010. Available from http://www.ncqa.org/tabid/205/Default.aspx. Accessed January 21, 2010.

47. National Committee for Quality Assurance. Medicare advantage deeming program, 2009. Available from http://www.ncqa.org/tabid/102/Default. aspx. Accessed January 21, 2010.

48. National Committee for Quality Assurance. The state of health care quality 2009. Available from http://www.ncqa.org/Portals/0/Newsroom/SOHC/ SOHC_2009.pdf. Accessed January 21, 2010.

49. Fireman B, Bartlett, J, Selby J, et al. Can disease management reduce health care costs by improving quality? *Health Affairs*. 2004;23:63–64.

50. Mays GP, Au M, Claxton G. Convergence and dissonance: evolution in private sector approaches to disease management and care coordination. *Health Affairs*. 2007;20:1683–1691.

51. Moran DM. Whence and whither health insurance? A revisionist history. *Health Affairs*. 2005;24:1415–1425.

52. Health Insurance On-line. Self-funded plans. Available from http://www. online-health-insurance.com/health-insurance-resources/part2/page94.php. Accessed January 22, 2010.

53. Butler PA. ERISA update: the Supreme Court Texas decision and other recent developments. National Academy for State Health Policy. 2004;5. Available from http://www.statecoverage.org/node/180. Accessed January 21, 2010.

54. U.S. Congressional Budget Office. The long-term outlook for health care spending: medicare and medicaid: an overview. Available from http:// www.cbo.gov/ftpdocs/87xx/doc8758/AppendixA.4.1.shtml. Accessed January 19, 2010.

55. The Henry J. Kaiser Family Foundation. Medicare at a glance. Available from http://www.kff.org/medicare/upload/1066-12.pdf. Accessed January 17, 2010.

56. The Henry J. Kaiser Family Foundation. The Medicare prescription drug benefit. Available from http://www.kff.org/medicare/7044-10.pdf. Accessed January 19, 2010.

57. American Society of Planning Officials. Reviews of government reports and public documents. *Soc Serv Rev*. 1970;44:491–492. Available from http:// www.jstor.org/pss/30021773. Accessed January 24, 2010.

58. National Conference of State Legislatures. Certificate of need: state health laws and programs. Available from http://www.ncsl.org/IssuesResearch/Health/CONCertificateofNeedStateLaws/tabid/14373/Default.aspx. Accessed January 23, 2010.

59. Congressional Budget Office. Testimony on the professional standards review organizations program. Available from http://www.cbo.gov/ftpdoc.cfm?index=5226&type=0. Accessed January 23, 2010.

60. Compilation of the Social Security laws: Social Security online. Available from http://www.ssa.gov/OP_Home/ssact/title11/1154.htm. Accessed January 24, 2010.

61. Sloan FA, Vraciu RA. Investor-owned and not-for-profit hospitals: addressing some issues. *Health Affairs.* 1983;2:26. Available from http://content.healthaffairs.org/cgi/reprint/2/2/25.pdf. Accessed January 23, 2010.

62. Economic Expert.com. Diagnosis-related group. Available from http://www.economicexpert.com/a/Diagnosis:related:group.htm. Accessed January 23, 2010.

63. Mistichelli J. National Reference Center for Bioethics Literature. Diagnosis-related groups and the prospective payment system: forecasting social implications. Available from http://bioethics.georgetown.edu/publications/scopenotes/sn4.pdf. Accessed January 23, 2010.

64. Russell LB, Manning CL. The effect of prospective payment on medicare expenditures. *N Engl J Med.* 1989;320:439. Available from http://content.nejm.org/cgi/content/abstract/320/7/439. Accessed January 23, 2010.

65. Thorpe KE. Health care cost containment: results and lessons from the past 20 years. In: Shortell SM, Reinhardt UE, Eds. *Improving Health Policy and Management.* Ann Arbor, MI: Health Administration Press; 1992:246.

66. Centers for Medicare & Medicaid Services. EMTALA overview. Available from http://www.cms.hhs.gov/EMTALA. Accessed January 23, 2010.

67. Kovner A. *Jonas' Health Care Delivery in the United States,* 5th ed. New York: Springer; 1995.

68. American Medical Association. The resource-based relative value scale: overview of the RBRVS. Available from http://www.ama-assn.org/ama/pub/physician-resources/solutions-managing-your-practice/coding-billing-insurance/medicare/the-resource-based-relative-value-scale/overview-of-rbrvs.shtml. Accessed January 21, 2010.

69. Board of Trustees, Federal Hospital Insurance Trust Fund. 1995 Annual report of the Board of Trustees of the Hospital Insurance Trust Fund. Washington, DC: U.S. Government Printing Office; 1995.

70. Reischauer RD. Medicare: beyond 2002, preparing for the baby-boomers. *Brookings Rev.* 1997;15:24.

71. U.S. Department of Labor. Health plans—portability of health coverage. Available from http://www.dol.gov/ebsa/newsroom/fshipaa.html. Accessed January 22, 2010.

72. The Balanced Budget Act of 1997, Public Law 105-33, Medicare and Medicaid Changes. Washington, DC: Deloitte & Touche LLP and Deloitte & Touche Consulting Group LLC; 1997:1.

73. Medicare Payment Advisory Commission. Report to the Congress: Medicare payment policy (March 2003), chapter 1, context for Medicare spending. Available from http://www.medpac.gov/publications/congressional_reports/Mar03_Ch1.pdf. Accessed January 23, 2010.

74. National Bipartisan Commission on the Future of Medicare Task Forces. Available from http://medicare.commission.gov/medicare/task.html. Accessed January 23, 2010.

75. U.S. Department of Health and Human Services. Balanced Budget Refinement Act of 1999: highlights, November 18, 1999. Available from http://www.hhs.gov/news/pres/1999pres/1999pres/19991118b.html. Accessed January 23, 2010.

76. The Henry J. Kaiser Family Foundation. Fact sheet: Medicare, Medicare + Choice, April 2003. Available from http://www.kff.org/medicare/upload/Medicare-Choice-Fact-Sheet-Fact-Sheet.pdf. Accessed January 23, 2010.

77. Ross MN. Paying Medicare + Choice plans: the view from MedPac. *Health Affairs.* Available from http://content.healthaffairs.org/cgi/reprint/hlthaff.w1.90v1.pdf. Accessed January 23, 2010.

78. Centers for Medicare & Medicaid Services. Quality initiatives—general information. Available from http://www.cms.hhs.gov/QualityInitiatives GenInfo/01_overview.asp. Accessed January 23, 2010.

79. Centers for Medicare & Medicaid Services. About MQMS. Available from http://www.cms.hhs.gov/QualityInitiativesGenInfo/15_MQMS.asp. Accessed January 23, 2010.

80. U.S. Department of Health and Human Services, Centers for Medicare & Medicaid Services. Developing the Medicare hospital pay-for-performance plan. Available from http://www.cms.hhs.gov/MLNGenInfo/downloads/Hospital_Pay-for-Performance_plan.pdf. Accessed January 23, 2010.

81. U.S. Department of Health and Human Services, Centers for Medicare & Medicaid Services. Hospital quality compare. Available from http://www.hospitalcompare.hhs.gov/Hospital/Home2.asp?version=alternate&browser=IE%7C6%7CWinXP&language=English&defaultstatus=0&pagelist=Home. Accessed January 24, 2010.

82. HCAHPS on line. Hospital Consumer Assessment of Healthcare Providers and Systems. HCAHPS fact sheet. Available from http://www.hcahpsonline.org/facts.aspx. Accessed January 24, 2010.

83. Pear R. Medicare won't cover hospital errors. *New York Times.* Available from http://www.nytimes.com/2007/08/19/washington/19hospital.html. Accessed January 24, 2010.

84. U.S. Department of Health and Human Services, Centers for Medicare & Medicaid Services. CMS proposes to expand quality program for hospital

inpatient services in FY 2009. Available from http://www.cms.hhs.gov/
apps/media/press/release.asp?Counter=3041. Accessed January 24, 2010.

85. U.S. Department of Health and Human Services, Centers for Medicare &
Medicaid Services. Medicaid managed care enrollment as of June 30, 2008.
Available from http://www.cms.hhs.gov/MedicaidDataSourcesGenInfo/
downloads/08June30508.pdf. Accessed January 25, 2010.

86. Almanac of Policy Issues. Medicaid: an overview. Available from http://
www.policyalmanac.org/health/archive/hhs_medicaid.shtml. Accessed January
25, 2010.

87. Koch AL. Financing health care services. In: Williams SJ, Torrens PK, Eds.
Introduction to Health Care Services, 4th ed. Albany, NY: Delmar; 1993:309.

88. The Henry J. Kaiser Family Foundation. The crunch continues: Medicaid
spending, coverage and policy in the midst of a recession, results from a 50-state
Medicaid budget survey for state fiscal years 2009 and 2010. Available from
http://www.kff.org/medicaid/upload/7985_ES.pdf. Accessed January 24, 2010.

89. U.S. Department of Health and Human Services, Centers for Medicare &
Medicaid Services. Low cost health insurance for families and children.
Available from http://www.cms.hhs.gov/lowcostHealthInsFamChild/. Ac-
cessed January 26, 2010.

90. The Henry J. Kaiser Family Foundation. The uninsured: a primer, October
2009. Available from http://www.kff.org/uninsured/upload/7451-05.pdf.
Accessed January 25, 2010.

91. U.S. Department of Health and Human Services, Centers for Medicare &
Medicaid Services. Medicaid and CHIP quality practices overview. Available
from http://www.cms.hhs.gov/MedicaidCHIPQualPrac/. Accessed January
26, 2010.

92. U.S. Department of Health and Human Services, Centers for Medicare &
Medicaid Services. State quality strategy tool kit for state Medicaid agencies.
Available from http://www.cms.gov/MedicaidCHIPQualPrac/Downloads/
qtkitwtablec.pdf. Accessed January 27, 2010.

93. The Henry J. Kaiser Family Foundation. Health08.org. Available from
http://www.kff.org/kaiserpolls/h08_pomr083007pkg.cfm. Accessed January
27, 2010.

94. Lubell J, DoBias M. Looking for a pulse. *Modern Health Care.* 2010;40:6–7, 16.

95. Lipson D, Verdier J, Quincy L, et al. Mathematica Policy Research, Inc.
Leading the way? Maine's initial experience in expanding coverage through
Dirigo health reforms. Available from http://www.mathematica-mpr.com/
publications/pdfs/Dirigofinalrpt.pdf. Accessed January 27, 2010.

96. The Henry J. Kaiser Family Foundation, Kaiser Commission on Medicaid
and the Uninsured. Massachusetts health care reform: three years later.
Available from http://www.kff.org/uninsured/upload/7777-02.pdf. Accessed
January 27, 2010.

97. State of Vermont, Agency of Administration. Vermont's health care reform of
2006. Available from http://hcr.vermont.gov. Accessed January 27, 2010.

Long-Term Care

Long-term care needs are not confined only to older Americans, but the fastest growing proportion of the U.S. population is older Americans who are the major consumers of long-term care services. Advances in medical care have made a longer life span possible, with accompanying challenges presented by chronic disease and physical limitations. This chapter provides an overview of the major components of the diverse array of long-term care services presently available in institutional, community, and home-based settings to individuals in all age groups who require long-term care.

Each individual life span, from birth to death, can be seen as a connected flow of events—a continuum. The unrelenting progression of time is the one constant that expresses the diverse range of life's possibilities. An infant may be born with a birth defect, a young adult may suffer a head injury from an automobile accident, or an older adult may have a stroke. Such unanticipated events as these have a profound long-term impact on an individual's capacity to develop or to maintain abilities for self-care and independence. These individuals may require very different kinds and intensities of personal care assistance, health care services, and/or psychosocial and housing services over an extended segment of their life span.

The age, diagnosis, and ability to perform personal self-care and the sites of care delivery vary widely for recipients of long-term care. Thus, long-term care requires diversified, yet coordinated, services and flexibility within the service system to respond to recipients' changing needs over time.

The ideal health care delivery system provides participants with comprehensive personal, social, and medical care services. This ideal delivery system requires mechanisms that continually guide and track individual clients over time through the array of services at all levels and intensity of care that they require.[1] Because it generates a continuous flow of high costs over an extended period, long-term care has a particular need to use what the American Hospital Association calls a seamless continuum of care[2] that promotes the highest quality of life but still responds to growing public concerns about cost effectiveness.[3] The particular package of services provided to each person should be tailored to meet his or her needs. Service needs vary from assistance with personal care and basic needs for food and safe shelter to rehabilitation when possible and socialization opportunities. Additionally, the type and extent of physical disability and the intensity of services required determine the location of long-term care. For example, an older individual with paralysis after a stroke may be able to remain at home with services that dovetail with family caregivers in the home. Another with a similar disability may require nursing home placement because that environment best meets the particular requirements of the situation.

Configuring a package of services that promotes independence and maintains lifestyle quality as far as is possible within personal, community, and national resources makes the variety of long-term care services complex and sometimes confusing. Concern about cost effectiveness and the desire to accommodate personal and family desires, finances, and reimbursement eligibility result in the need for both the availability of an array of services and coordination of those services to meet individual needs in the most effective way.

Within the last 50 years, extensive changes in demographics and the types and availability of health care services have occurred in the United States. The economic ramifications of a rapidly increasing population of older Americans, advances in medicine that have made many heretofore unknown life-sustaining measures available to health care professionals, and an emphasis on preventive care and healthy lifestyle all have had an impact on the continued growth of the population who presently require or potentially will require long-term care services. Older adults represent the largest population group requiring long-term care services. Current estimates place the population 65 years of age and older at 37.9 million, 12.6% of the population, or about one of every eight Americans. The number of persons aged 65 years or older is expected to grow to 19.3% of the population by 2030, totaling 72.1 million.[4] The population 85 years of age and older is expected to grow from 5.5 million in 2007 to 6.6 million by 2020 (Figures 8-1 and 8-2).[4,5] Many will grow old alone because of smaller family size, single parenting, and divorce. The increasing economic need for family members to delay retirement and work outside the home also reduces the availability of family caregivers to participate in the informal family caregiving system.

Development of Long-Term Care Services

The colonists who emigrated from Europe to the New World brought with them many of the social values and institutional models of their native countries. One of these, the almshouse, was a place where people who were sick or disabled or older adults who lacked adequate family or financial support could be cared for in a communal setting. Charitable community members purchased private homes and converted them to almshouses that operated as communal residences. Municipal and county

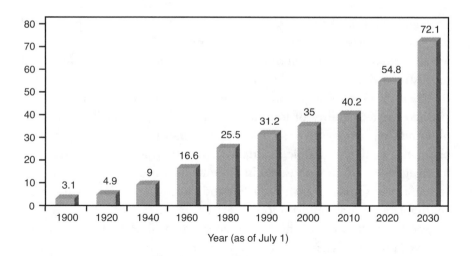

FIGURE 8-1 Projected Number of Persons 65 Years of Age or Older by 2030. *Source:* U.S. Bureau of the Census.

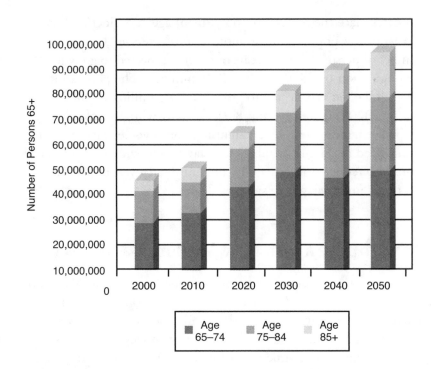

FIGURE 8-2 Projected Population, Age 65 Years and Older, 2000–2050.
Source: U.S. Bureau of the Census.

governments also created homes and "infirmaries" to care for impoverished older adults. These early models were the basis for "homes for the elderly," which existed until the economic upheavals of the Great Depression and the restructuring of the social welfare system after World War II.

The economic devastation experienced during the Great Depression affected the availability of long-term care services, especially homes for older adults, in several ways. Operating small private nursing homes became attractive to people in financial danger of losing their homes to mortgage foreclosure because taking in outsiders and providing care generated a new source of income. After the Great Depression, many local charitable agencies could no longer afford to provide care based on the almshouse tradition, and the federal government became more involved in developing, overseeing, and paying for long-term care services as part of the social welfare reforms, such as the 1935 Social Security Act.[6] The Social Security Act provided financial assistance for particular categories of older Americans and people with disabilities. Additionally, the Social

Security Act established a form of old age and survivors insurance that allowed workers and their employers to contribute to a fund that could supplement retirement income. This form of income security reduced the extent of indigence frequently found in the older population and increased the amount of secure income that older Americans could spend on services and care in later years. Government lending programs available to not-for-profit organizations beginning in the 1950s spurred the development of nursing homes in this sector; major growth in the proprietary sector did not occur until after the passage of Medicare and Medicaid in 1965. Today, 61.5% of nursing homes operate on a for-profit basis, 30.8% operate as not-for-profit organizations, and 7.7% operate under government auspices (Figure 8-3).[7]

Public and private homes for older adults often varied in the adequacy of care and the kinds of services provided. Nursing homes often were thought of as homes where minimal custodial care required to meet the basic needs of food, clothing, and shelter was provided, sometimes in very unhygienic and inhumane environments. Nursing homes often were places where older and frail adults, some of society's most vulnerable members, were taken to die and were not seen as residence options where they could receive needed care to prolong or enhance the quality of their lives. Physical care often was substandard, and emotional, spiritual, and social needs were ignored. Because many frail, older people suffer from perceptual and cognitive disabilities in addition to physical disabilities, their behavior in a group setting was often considered by nursing home

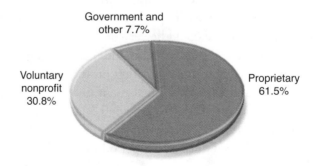

FIGURE 8-3 Percent Distribution of Nursing Homes, According to Type of Ownership: United States, 2004.
Source: CDC/NCHS, National Nursing Home Survey, 2004.

staff to be a problem, and sometimes it led to the overuse of physical and chemical restraints such as sedatives and mood-altering drugs.

The provision of home nursing care also has a long tradition in the United States as an alternative to institutional care provided in hospitals and nursing homes. Family members traditionally have provided home care to their own relatives. An interest in providing formal professional home care services began in the late 19th century as a social response to the unhealthy living conditions of immigrants residing in urban tenements. Such crowded and unsanitary conditions became a public health concern because they were frequently implicated in the spread of contagious diseases, such as tuberculosis, typhoid, and smallpox. Agencies such as the Visiting Nurses Association were established to provide trained nurses to tend to the sick in their homes. Their role quickly expanded to include preventive education regarding hygiene, nutrition, and coordination of social welfare intervention, especially in caring for society's most vulnerable populations of people with illnesses, low incomes, or disabilities.[8]

The passage of Medicare and Medicaid legislation in 1965 provided more stable sources of reimbursement than were previously available through private pay and charitable funding and promoted expansion of the long-term care industry. Medicare and Medicaid affected the long-term care industry in several overt ways. They established minimal standards of care and services required for recipients to qualify for reimbursement, as well as funding sources for older Americans, people with disabilities, and those lacking the means to pay. This funding simultaneously attracted both the scrupulous and the unscrupulous into the long-term care industry, as it quickly became apparent that being a provider of long-term care could be very profitable.

The long-term care industry came under increasing scrutiny in the early 1970s during congressional hearings on the nursing home industry, after several hundred exposés published in newspapers and additional publications such as the Nader Report and Mary Adelaide Mendelson's book, *Tender Loving Greed*. The litany of nursing home corruption and abuses that were exposed during that period included[9,10]

- Care that did not recognize the right to human dignity
- A lack of activities for residents
- Untrained and inadequate staff, including untrained administrators
- Unsanitary conditions

- Theft of residents' belongings
- Inadequate safety precautions (especially fire protection)
- Unauthorized and unnecessary use of restraints
- Both overmedication and undermedication of patients
- Failure to act in a timely manner on complaints and reprisals against those who complained
- Discrimination against patients who were members of minority groups
- A lack of dental and psychiatric care
- Negligence leading to injury and death
- Ineffective inspections and nonenforcement of laws that were meant to regulate the nursing home industry
- Reimbursement fraud

These congressional hearings and simultaneous public outcry resulted in more strict enforcement of Medicare and Medicaid guidelines and credentialing, increased establishment and enforcement of nursing home and home care licensure, more active accreditation procedures by the Joint Commission, laws related to elder abuse reporting, federal guidelines regulating the use of physical restraints, and establishment of ombudsman programs. All these measures have led to a much more regulated and responsive long-term care industry. More vocal and astute consumers also have provided economic and social mandates for high-quality standards of care—which had previously not been adhered to in any meaningful, organized quality assurance process—to be maintained in the long-term care industry overall. The Omnibus Budget Reconciliation Act of 1987 legislated new guidelines and restrictions on the use of physical and chemical restraints, established a nursing home resident bill of rights, mandated quality assurance standards, established a standard survey process, and mandated training and educational requirements.[11]

Modes of Long-Term Care Service Delivery

The site of care delivery categorizes long-term care programs. Institution-based services are those long-term care services provided within an institution such as a nursing home, hospital with inpatient extended care or rehabilitation facility, or inpatient hospice. Community-based services coordinate, manage, and deliver long-term care services such as adult day-care programs or care in the recipient's home.

Skilled Nursing Care

A skilled nursing facility (SNF) that is Medicare and Medicaid certified is defined as "a facility, or distinct part of one, primarily engaged in providing skilled nursing care and related services for people requiring medical or nursing care, or rehabilitation services."[12] Skilled nursing care is provided by or under the direct supervision of licensed nursing personnel, such as registered nurses and licensed practical nurses, and emphasis is on the provision of 24-hour nursing care and the availability of other types of services.

Current estimates are that 1.5 million Americans reside in 16,100 SNFs.[7] At $219 per day, the national average annual rate in 2009 was $79,935 for a private room and $72,270 for a semiprivate room.[13] Annual national expenditures for nursing home care in 2008 totaled $138.4 billion. Medicare, Medicaid, and other public funds pay the largest portion (62%), and 38% is funded by out-of-pocket, private insurance, and other private funds (Table 8-1).[14] The nursing home industry remains the dominant sector of the long-term care industry, with expenditures greater than double those for home care.[14]

Despite the burgeoning numbers of older Americans, national nursing home bed occupancy rates are declining.[15] Many factors are believed to be contributing to the decline. Today's older adults are healthier, delaying the need for skilled nursing services. The vastly increased availability of assisted-living facilities and the availability of other community-based assistance through day care and home care are also playing roles in delaying the need for skilled, institutional care.

Nursing home residents can be of any age, although most are adults in their later years. The typical nursing home resident is an older woman

Table 8-1 Sources of Payment for Nursing Home Care, 2008

Source of Payment	Amount in Billions*	Percent
Total	138.4	100
Medicare	25.7	18.6
Medicaid	56.3	40.7
Other Public	4.2	3.0
Private (out-of-pocket, other private funds)	42.0	30.3
Private Insurance	10.3	7.4

*Numbers may not add to totals due to rounding

Source: Centers for Medicare and Medicaid Services.

with cognitive impairment who was living alone on a limited income before nursing home placement. The decreased ability to function independently and a lack of family caregivers are additional factors associated with an increased risk of nursing home admission.

Typical staffing in SNFs includes a physician medical director, a nursing home administrator, a director of nursing, at least one registered nurse on the day and evening shifts, and either a registered nurse or a licensed practical nurse on the night shift. Certified nursing assistants provide direct custodial care under the supervision of licensed nursing personnel and represent the majority of all nursing staff employed by SNFs.[7] SNFs use services of an array of ancillary professionals who may be employed by the SNFs or contracted. These services include physical therapy, occupational therapy, pharmacy, nutrition, recreational therapy, podiatry, dentistry, laboratory, and hospice.[7] Support staff, including dietary, laundry, housekeeping, and maintenance workers, complete the employee complement. The licensed nursing home administrator, along with the owner/operator, is responsible for carrying out the regulatory mandates regarding the mix and ratio of licensed and unlicensed personnel and the availability of licensed nursing personnel on an around-the-clock basis to provide skilled care and supervision.

Nursing homes are highly regulated by both state licensure and federal certification. The 1987 Omnibus Budget Reconciliation Act increased government involvement in nursing home industry regulation by[11]

- Mandating regularly scheduled comprehensive assessments of the functional capacity of residents in nursing homes
- Establishing training standards for nursing home aides
- Placing restrictions on the use of physical restraints and psychoactive drugs
- Establishing a nursing home resident bill of rights
- Setting guidelines for the role of the medical director, including continuing education, involvement, and responsibility

States license nursing home administrators. Individual states set criteria for licensure in relationship to minimum age, educational requirements, passing examination scores, and continuing education requirements. In 2006 the National Association of Boards of Examiners of Long-Term Care Administrators announced endorsement of a uniform set of "principles of interstate licensure" that allows reciprocity between and among states' licensing requirements. This new interstate licensure endorsement intends to assist mobility of administrators across states while ensuring maintenance of the highest entry-level standards in the profession.[16] A lack of nursing home compliance with state and federal mandates can lead to penalties such as direct fines, exclusion from Medicare and Medicaid certification, and withdrawal of nursing home licensure. Accreditation through the Joint Commission provides an additional quality check. Although highly desirable, Joint Commission accreditation remains voluntary.

Assisted-Living Facilities

Assisted-living facilities are appropriate for long-term care for individuals who do not require skilled nursing services and whose needs lie more in the custodial and supportive realm. The American Association of Homes and Services for the Aging defines assisted living as a "program that provides and/or arranges for daily meals, personal and other supportive services, health care and 24-hour oversight to persons residing in a group residential facility who need assistance with the activities of daily living."[17]

Current estimates place the number of assisted-living facilities at 20,000, housing over 1 million people.[18] The assisted-living population is expected to grow to over 2 million individuals by 2025 (Figure 8-4).

Assisted-living facilities vary significantly in size, ranging from just a few residents to several hundred. They may take the form of small to large homes with just a few residents or large multiunit apartment complexes

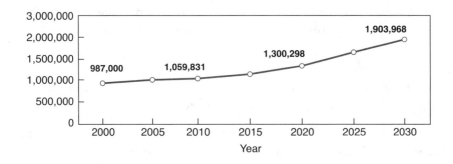

FIGURE 8-4 Projected Growth of Assisted Living Beds Based on Population Growth for Those 75 Years and Older.
Source: National Center for Assisted Living, reprinted with permission.

with several hundred residents. Available services also vary, but generally include, in addition to housing, congregate meals, 24-hour monitoring for emergencies, medication supervision, and assistance with one or more activities of daily living such as bathing, dressing, and personal grooming. Assisted-living facilities also typically provide scheduled activities, including communal recreation and group transportation for medical appointments and for social and cultural events. Many assisted-living facilities contract with home health agencies to provide skilled nursing care and with hospice service providers.

States carry out oversight and regulation of assisted-living facilities at varying levels. These variations in laws and regulations create a diverse operating environment as well as a wide range of terminology and available services for consumers.[18] The quality of facilities, care, and services therefore may be an exclusive function of the policies of the owner organization or a combination of owner and organization policies coupled with state regulatory oversight.

Costs of assisted living are borne largely from private resources, although in certain circumstances Supplemental Social Security Income, private health insurance, long-term care insurance (LTCI), or special government rent subsidies for low-income older adults may apply. Estimates place the average monthly cost at $3,131, but costs can range across a broad continuum, depending on the level of amenities desired in a facility and the types of services required. Residents fund accommodations from personal resources or from LTCI policies.[13,18]

Residential institutions such as adult homes, board and care homes, and centers for people with mental or developmental disabilities also represent assisted-living arrangements. Care provided in adult homes has been available only to people who are for the most part healthy but limited in their ability to do their own housekeeping, household maintenance, and cooking. Residents must be able, for the most part, to meet their own personal care needs for dressing, eating, bathing, toileting, and ambulation, unassisted. Oversight of residents may include services such as supervision of medications to the extent of reminding residents to take their medication or providing some assistance with bathing, grooming, transportation, laundry, and simple housekeeping. If provided at all, direct nursing care can be provided only in the case of minor illness of a temporary nature. Staffing levels in adult homes are state defined, with the ratio determined by the number of beds.

Home Care

Home care is community-based care provided to individuals in their own residences. Home care may be either a long-term provision of supportive care and services to chronically ill clients to avoid institutionalization, or short-term intermittent care of clients after an episode of illness or hospitalization. Home care may be provided through the formal system of agency-employed professional home care providers, such as registered nurses, licensed practical nurses, home health aides, physical therapists, occupational therapists, speech-language pathologists, social workers, personal care aides, and homemakers who make home visits. A considerably smaller number of home care staff may be self-employed individuals who contract privately with clients. An informal system also provides home care through caregivers consisting of family, neighbors, and friends of people in need of health care support services. Very often, a combination of both formal and informal systems delivers home care.

Professional home care services originated in social welfare initiatives in the early 20th century in public response to the horrific living conditions of immigrants in U.S. industrialized cities. Public health concerns also gained impetus at that time as the germ theory of disease became accepted, and the control of contagious disease using preventive measures of hygiene and sanitation became a public health concern and mandate of local, state, and national health departments and agencies.

After Medicare's enactment of reimbursement for home care services in 1965, between 1967 and 1985 the number of Medicare-certified home health agencies grew more than threefold to 5,983, with public health agencies dominating the home care industry.[19] In the late 1980s significant additional growth in the number of agencies ceased due to Medicare reimbursement issues.[19] However, with Medicare reimbursement changes since the 1990s, the number of Medicare-certified, hospital-based, and freestanding for-profit home health agencies grew rapidly.[19] The home care industry expanded its scope of services in response to demographic, economic, and legislative changes that include

- An increase in the number of older persons and their expressed desire to remain in their own homes for care whenever possible
- Decreased numbers of informal caregivers that are available to provide in-home care to their relatives

- Increased innovations in high-technology home care that have re-defined and expanded the categories of diseases and chronic conditions that can be cared for effectively in the home
- Medicare and Medicaid reimbursement that supported expanded coverage
- The 1999 Olmstead decision of the Supreme Court upholding the right of citizens to receive care in the community

Now, over 9,000 agencies serve over 3 million individuals.[20] For-profit home health agencies comprise 65.2% of all Medicare-certified agencies.[21] Medicare remains the largest payer for home health care services, accounting for approximately 41% of total annual home care expenditures (Table 8-2).[14]

Eligibility for Medicare reimbursement of home care services includes four criteria:

1. Home care must include the provision of skilled nursing care; physical, occupational, and speech therapies; and medical social services as warranted by the patient's condition.
2. The person must be confined to the home.
3. A physician must order that home care services are required.
4. The home care agency must meet the minimum quality standards as outlined by Medicare and be Medicare certified.

In 2006 the Centers for Medicare & Medicaid Services recommended a "post-acute care reform plan" that emphasized a consumer-centered approach giving more choice and control of post-hospitalization services to patients and caregivers, providing a seamless continuum of care

Table 8-2 Sources of Payment for Home Care, 2008

Source of Payment	Amount in Billions*	Percent
Total	64.7	100
Medicare	26.6	41.1
Medicaid	22.4	34.6
Other Public	2.1	3.2
Private (out-of-pocket, other private funds)	7.8	12.0
Private Insurance	5.8	9.0

*Numbers may not add to totals due to rounding
Source: Centers for Medicare and Medicaid Services.

through better service coordination, and ensuring quality services in the most appropriate setting. The reform plan sets demonstration projects in motion that will be carried out over the next several years.[22]

Research published between 1999 and 2004 in the *Journal of the American Medical Association*, the *New England Journal of Medicine*, the *Journal of the American Geriatrics Society*, and other sources notes the significantly higher cost effectiveness of home care when compared with institutional care for a variety of treatments such as long-term oxygen therapy, intravenous antibiotic therapy, and treatment of congestive heart failure.[23] In 2008, home health care represented only 6% of combined total of Medicare and Medicaid expenditures.[14]

State licensing is required for Medicare certification.[24] Most states issue a license for 1 year and require resubmission of an application and an annual state reinspection performed by a survey team. The state licensing agency has the right to investigate complaints and to conduct periodic reviews of all licensure requirements. Those few agencies that treat only private pay or private insurance patients may not require a license; however, most home health care agencies want to participate in Medicare and Medicaid so they maintain certification standards. Participation in voluntary accreditation indicates that home care agencies have a commitment to continuous quality improvement. Organizations that are actively engaged in the accreditation process for home health care agencies include the Community Health Accreditation Program, an independent, consumer-based subsidiary of the National League for Nursing; The Joint Commission; and the National Association for Home Care and Hospice.

Until the proliferation of social programs in the 1960s and 1970s, individuals requiring long-term health care were almost always cared for by family members and/or friends in the family home. This informal care system provided a valuable social service at little or no public cost. This arrangement is still the most used system of long-term care—family members care for about 80% of older adults needing some level of assistance. The informal care system offers a significant savings to the public; however, the potential for caregivers to suffer physical and emotional burnout and the growing inability of family caregivers to fully manage care without outside assistance have begun to diminish these savings.

Recent estimates place the number of family caregivers at over 65 million, of whom 66% are women.[25] Because women are an integral part of the workforce, the available pool of caregivers for family members needing care at home is much smaller than in the past. Now, family caregivers are frequently required to make major compromises in their finances, lifestyles, and personal freedom to care for another. The costs can be high. Stresses experienced by the caregiver can lead to exhaustion, illness, and depression.[26] In addition, with increased longevity, middle-aged individuals often find themselves caring for children and aged parents simultaneously. Dubbed the "sandwich generation," these caregivers suffer even more stress from this dual role.

Employers also experience losses because of the demands of caregiving on their employees. One study estimates the annual costs of lost productivity for U.S. businesses due to caregiving at $34 billion.[27] Employer costs are associated with worker replacement, absenteeism, workday interruptions, elder care crises, and supervisory time.[26,27] Some larger employers are responding with flexible scheduling and other considerations to help accommodate their employees' caregiving responsibilities.[27]

Estimates place the market value of long-term care delivered by unpaid family members and friends at $354 billion per year, more than double the annual national health care expenditures for nursing home and home care combined.[28] Both the economic and personal contributions of the informal caregiving system form the bedrock of the nation's chronic care system and require more policy-level attention and support. The federal government took an important first step to assist family caregivers through the Family Medical Leave Act (FMLA) of 1993. The FMLA provides up to 12 months unpaid leave per year for the birth of a child or adoption of a child, or for employees to care for themselves or a sick family member while ensuring continuation of health benefits and job security. The FMLA has serious shortcomings, however. It provides only for unpaid leave, a condition that makes its use financially unfeasible for many individuals. Also, the FMLA does not cover workers in companies of 50 or fewer employees, effectively excluding approximately half of America's workers.[29]

States have responded with programs to assist caregivers by expanding paid leave provisions. California was a leader in this regard when it enacted The Paid Family Leave Law in 2002, allowing workers up to 6 weeks of partially paid leave to bond with a new biological, adopted, or foster child or to care for a seriously ill family member.[29] Fifteen additional states have enacted paid leave legislation or regulations for private sector employees, and several additional states have such legislation under consideration. Similar provisions now exist for public employees in at least 40 states.[29]

Historically, home health care services have been vulnerable to breaches in operational integrity. In the 1990s the Clinton administration and Congress responded to dramatic increases in Medicare and Medicaid home care spending and concerns about service quality and fiscal integrity.[30] One major response was authorization of an antifraud and abuse pilot project, Operation Restore Trust, which investigated home health agencies, nursing homes, hospice organizations, and medical product suppliers in five states with the highest rates of use. Subsequently, Operation Restore Trust was expanded to selected home health care agencies in 12 states and included training for agency surveyors in identifying care improperly billed to Medicare.[30]

The Balanced Budget Act of 1997 also contained several provisions to enable the Health Care Financing Administration to control costs and address service quality issues more effectively in Medicare-certified home health care agencies. Provisions targeted reducing unnecessary and inappropriate services, including dividing Medicare home health services funding into separate streams for posthospital and chronic health problems to enhance accountability. Other provisions of the Balanced Budget Act changed Medicare reimbursement from a retrospective to prospective basis, and several measures were introduced to thwart fraudulent practices by home health clients and agencies.[31] The Clinton administration also proposed revisions in the federal standards that home health care agencies must meet to continue participation in the Medicare program. Revisions included criteria such as requiring criminal background checks of home health aides as a condition of employment, requiring agencies to discuss expected treatment outcomes with patients, and requiring coordination of care when patients are being served by multiple providers.[31]

Also in 1997, the Department of Health and Human Services promulgated new regulations requiring home health agencies to implement a standardized reporting system, the Outcomes and Assessment Information Set, to monitor patients' conditions and satisfaction with services.[32]

Home health care services are an integral component of the health care delivery system's continuum, which can provide an effective, safe, and humane alternative to institutional care for the medical treatment and personal care of individuals of all ages. Ideally, lessons learned from

Operation Restore Trust and industry responses will help ensure that home health care is a beneficiary-centered service that safeguards both payers and recipients from fraud and abuse while ensuring adherence to appropriate standards of quality care.

Hospice Care

Hospice is a philosophy supporting a coordinated program of care for the terminally ill. The most common criterion for admission into hospice is that the applicant has a diagnosis of a terminal illness with a limited life expectancy of 6 months or less. Aggressive medical treatment of the patient's disease may no longer be medically feasible or personally desirable. The disease may have progressed despite available medical treatments, making continuance of curative treatment futile or intolerable, or the patient may elect to discontinue such treatment for a variety of personal reasons, such as continued deterioration of quality of life related to treatment side effects.

The term "palliative care" often is used synonymously with hospice care. Palliative care is care or treatment given to relieve the symptoms of a disease rather than attempting to cure the disease. Pain, nausea, malaise, and emotional distress caused by feelings of fear and isolation are only some of the difficulties that patients encounter during the stages of a terminal illness. Hospice treatment is directed toward maintaining the comfort of the patient and enhancing the patient's quality of life and sense of independence for however long is possible.

Hospice has its historical roots in medieval Europe. Hospices were originally way stations where travelers on religious pilgrimages received food and rest. Over time, the concept evolved into sanctuaries where impoverished people or those who were sick or dying received care.

English physician Dame Cicely Saunders established St. Christopher's, a hospice located in a London suburb, in 1967, and it became a model for the modern hospice. Here, terminally ill patients received intensive symptom management, modern techniques of pain control, and psychological and emotional support. She brought the founding concepts of modern hospice to the United States in a lecture tour in the late 1960s, during which she emphasized that dying patients were also on a kind of pilgrimage and needed a more responsive environment than could be provided in high-technology, impersonal, cure-oriented hospitals.

The U.S. hospice movement began as a consumer-based grassroots movement supported by volunteer and professional members of the community. Today, almost one-half of hospice organizations continue operating as not-for-profit entities (Figure 8-5).[33] The U.S. founders shared the belief that the hospice concept was a more humane alternative to the technology-driven, curative emphasis in hospitals. Because the medical system can view choosing to discontinue aggressive medical treatment as a failure, terminally ill patients can feel depersonalized and isolated inside a traditional hospital setting. Ideally, the physician, the patient, and the patient's family jointly recognize the need to refer the patient to hospice when deciding to stop curative treatment.

The first U.S. hospice was established in New Haven, Connecticut, in 1974. The number of hospices has increased steadily every year, with over 4,800 hospices now serving over 1.4 million individuals annually (Figures 8-6 and 8-7).[33] Major growth in the availability of hospice care followed the enactment of 1982 legislation that extended Medicare coverage to hospice services, allowing the movement to escape its prior dependency on grant support and philanthropy. A 73-fold increase in the number of hospice providers occurred between 1984 and 1998. In 2008, approximately 38.5% of all U.S. deaths occurred in hospice care.[33]

Consistent with the hospice philosophy, a multidisciplinary team of nurses, social workers, counselors, physicians, and therapists provides services. Hospices also provide drug therapies and medical appliances and

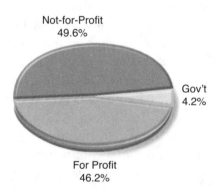

Not-for-Profit
49.6%

Gov't
4.2%

For Profit
46.2%

FIGURE 8-5 Tax Status of Hospice Agencies.
Source: The National Hospice and Palliative Care Organization, reprinted with permission.

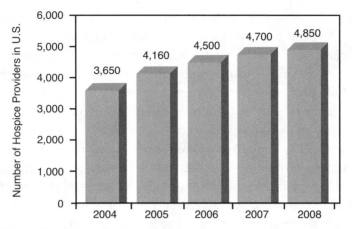

FIGURE 8-6 Total Hospice Providers by Year.
Source: National Hospice and Palliative Care Organization, reprinted with permission.

supplies. Bereavement services for surviving family members continue for a year or longer after the patient's death. Most hospice organizations also provide bereavement services for the larger community.[33]

A variety of different settings accommodates hospice care, including the home, hospitals, SNFs, assisted-living facilities, or hospice inpatient

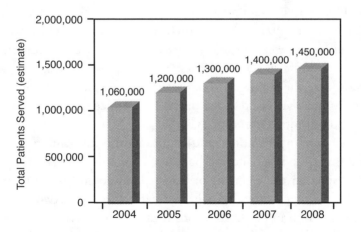

FIGURE 8-7 Total Hospice Patients Served by Year.
Source: National Hospice and Palliative Care Organization, reprinted with permission.

facilities. The most important unifying concept about hospice is that no matter where the care is delivered, a specialized multidisciplinary team of health care professionals works together to manage the patient's care. A physician directs the team, coordinated by a nurse. The team members can include physicians, nurses, respiratory and physical therapists, pharmacists, pastoral care providers, social workers, psychologists, home health aides, and homemakers. Each team member contributes his or her particular skills and expertise to assist in managing pain, alleviating emotional distress, promoting comfort, and maintaining the independence of the hospice patient. Hospice care strongly encompasses the patient's family and routinely includes counseling (including bereavement counseling), spiritual support, and respite care for family members.

The hospice philosophy emphasizes volunteerism, and it is the only health care provider whose Medicare certification requires that at least 5% of total patient care hours are contributed by volunteers. In 2008, The National Hospice and Palliative Care Organization estimated that 550,000 volunteers assisted hospice organizations with over 25 million contributed hours of service.[33,34] Volunteers from the community are actively encouraged to participate in a wide range of hospice activities, including direct services to patients and families, clerical, and other support services and assistance with fundraising.

Hospice care has demonstrated its cost savings in care for the terminally ill. The unique blend of care provided by a specialized team, use of volunteers, and frequent use of family members as primary caregivers in the home all decrease expenses. The focus on palliative care rather than on cure-oriented care also decreases the cost. A number of research studies have examined the savings from the use of hospice care. Similar to Medicare, annual Medicaid expenditures for hospice care represent only a small fraction of total expenditures.[33]

Managed care organizations and traditional health insurers recognize both the human and economic benefits of hospice care and typically include hospice in their benefit packages. Insurers may have their own team of hospice-type providers within their respective networks or may contract with community hospice organizations to provide hospice care. Medicare-eligible subscribers of Medicare-participating health plans are automatically eligible for hospice care, and services must be provided through a Medicare-certified hospice organization. The patient is not required to obtain a referral from their health plan or to discontinue their managed care contract to receive hospice care.

A basic tenet of the hospice philosophy is that hospice care should be available regardless of ability to pay. When the patient does not have health insurance and does not qualify for Medicare or Medicaid, hospice services may still be available. A hospice may offer a sliding payment scale to the patient, with the hospice drawing on internal funds garnered through its fundraising activities to supplement available patient payments.

Ongoing quality assurance to monitor care quality is an inherent concept in hospice care. Three standards used most frequently are licensure, certification, and accreditation. Licensure is based on state-imposed statutes as part of the consumer protection code of a state. Not all states have such licensing statutes. States that have licensing statutes require that all hospices within their jurisdiction meet the standards set forth in the law. Certification means that hospices have been examined on the federal level and have been found to at least minimally meet mandated requirements for Medicare and Medicaid reimbursement. A hospice program that is not certified may still operate legally but is ineligible to bill Medicare or Medicaid for its services.

Respite Care

Family caregivers continue to be a key factor in keeping many long-term care recipients in their communities rather than using institutions. Providing care up to 24 hours a day can place enormous physical and emotional stress on family caregivers.

Respite care is temporary surrogate care given to a patient when that patient's primary caregiver must be absent. In the 1970s formal respite-care programs originated to meet the increasing need for assistance after the rapid deinstitutionalization of individuals who had developmental disabilities or mental illness. Since then, the respite-care model has expanded to include any family-managed care program that helps to avoid or forestall the placement of a patient in a full-time institutionalized environment by providing planned, intermittent caregiver relief. Respite care offers an organized, reliable system in which both patient and primary caregiver are the beneficiaries.

Respite care may be offered in a variety of settings: the home, a daycare situation, or at institutions with overnight care, such as hospitals or nursing homes. Respite-care auspices may include private, public, and voluntary not-for-profit agencies. The length of respite care varies, but it is intended to be short term and intermittent.

Respite-care services are highly differentiated. Some are very structured and self-contained; others are highly flexible and exist in a more casual support capacity. A number of services are oriented to treating only patients with a particular ailment, but, for many, the only criterion the patient must meet for admission is that he or she requires supervised medical treatment and nursing care, provided by family or friends as principal caregivers. Respite models include

- Alzheimer's disease care on an inpatient basis with admissions lasting for several weeks
- Community-based, adult daycare centers that offer nursing, therapeutic, and social services
- In-home aides, where visiting aides supply services
- Temporary patient furloughs to a hospital or nursing home at regular intervals

Respite-care program staffing varies widely, deploying both professionals and/or nonprofessionals. For example, respite care could be as informal as having a member from the caregiver's church come into the home for a few hours while the caregiver goes out or as professional as a specialized dementia daycare program where nurses, aides, and recreational and physical therapists are specifically educated to care for dementia patients in a structured, caregiving environment. When respite care entails overnight care in an institutional setting, such as a nursing home or hospital, the staff providing care is the same staff employed by the institution to provide care to their regular patients in the institution.

Formal respite programs in the United States that are financially accessible to all in need have remained sparse. One of the greatest barriers limiting the expanded use of respite care is cost. Family caregivers operating on a limited budget may have difficulty finding funds to compensate a respite provider. Although some respite providers offer care on a sliding scale, almost any fee may exceed the financial means of the family. In these situations, not-for-profit organizations may assist by providing respite assistance at a tolerable cost for patients who meet certain financial or medical parameters.

Historically, there have been few provisions in the Medicare and Medicaid programs to support formal respite care. Medicare contains no allowances for respite, unless services are provided by a certified hospice organization. Medicaid has stringent requirements regarding the specific type and length of care provided as well as financial eligibility for services. Some states do allow family members to receive a wage subsidy for respite services for persons over age 60 with very low incomes, but eligibility, types of care, and funding vary on a state-by state basis.[35] Available respite programs offered by voluntary agencies as the result of federal grants often provide service for only specific medical conditions, such as Alzheimer's disease. Both proprietary and not-for-profit organizations are developing specialized dementia and connected respite-care programs in response to recent federal legislation. Many specialized dementia respite-care programs currently are developed and marketed to private pay customers, but such programs often are beyond the financial capability of many families.

One of the major barriers to responsive changes in reimbursement for respite care has been that funding mechanisms have viewed respite care as meeting a social need but not an acute medical care need. In addition, community systems of respite care can be difficult to organize because the level of need is intermittent and unpredictable. Family caregivers often are viewed as the most direct beneficiaries of respite care, rather than the patients who actually receive the health care. With the indisputable conclusion that respite-care programs offer society value and cost savings through postponement or avoidance of costly institutionalization, bipartisan federal legislation was developed in 2003 to address respite-care issues. Entitled The Lifespan Respite Care Act, over 200 national, state, and local organizations advocated its passage, culminating in its signing into law in 2006.[36] The law authorized $289 million over 5 years for state grants to develop respite programs. The Act defines respite programs as "coordinated systems of accessible, community-based respite care services for family caregivers of children and adults with special needs."[36] Passage of this legislation was a landmark, because it provided a nationwide acknowledgment of the inherent economic value of the informal family-provided care system. In addition, as a major thrust of federal initiatives, the U.S. Administration on Aging continues to pilot several different types of demonstration programs targeted at determining the cost effectiveness and consumer acceptability of various combinations of community-based services that support older persons' ability to continue living independently. In its adoption of the 2010 Administration on Aging budget, Congress authorized a $7 million increase for home and community-based services for older Americans, emphasizing the federal government's role in assisting older Americans to remain independent members of their communities.[37]

Adult Day Care

An adult daycare center may provide a supervised program of social activities and custodial care (social model), medical and rehabilitative care through skilled nursing (medical model), or specialized services for patients with Alzheimer's disease or other forms of dementia. An adult daycare center operates during the day in a protective group setting outside the home. The primary intent of adult day care is to prevent the premature and inappropriate institutionalization of older adults by providing socialization, health care, or both. Older adults maintain their mental and physical well-being longer and at a higher level when they continue to reside in their homes and communities. Furthermore, for those who depend on the services of a regular family caregiver, an adult daycare center can provide respite for the caregiver and therapeutic social contacts for the care recipient.[38]

The concept of adult day care grew out of social concern for the quality of life and care of older adults based on the work of Lionel Cousins, who in the 1960s established the first adult daycare center in the United States to "prepare patients for discharge by teaching and promoting independent living skills."[39] Originally, development and growth in such programs were slow because there was no national policy to support the idea and no permanent funding base, as the prototype Medicare and Medicaid programs supported and encouraged institutionalization; however, as the cost of institutionalization, the inhumanity of many nursing homes, and the burden placed on family caregivers were recognized, the focus of long-term care has been redirected toward support of community-based care as a preferred alternative to institutionalization whenever possible. Since then, growth in the number of adult daycare programs has been rapid. In 1978 only 300 adult daycare centers existed nationwide; today, according to the National

Adult Day Services Association, approximately 4,000 are in operation.[40] Not-for-profit organizations operate 80% of adult daycare centers.[40]

The services that adult daycare centers offer are similar, but the emphasis varies with the model they follow. Most adult daycare centers offer a variety of medical, psychiatric, and nursing assessments; counseling; physical exercises; social services; crafts; and rehabilitation in activities of daily living skills. Special-purpose adult daycare centers serve particular populations of clients, such as veterans, older persons with mental health problems, the blind, people with Alzheimer's disease, or people with cerebral palsy.

Staffing patterns of adult daycare programs vary from program to program and are directly related to the type of program and specific services offered. The mix of unskilled to skilled employees also depends on the kinds of services being offered. For example, programs based on the medical model are more likely to employ more registered nurses, occupational therapists, and physical therapists to provide skilled assessment, direct care, and rehabilitative therapies than in a social model, where aides may perform most of the custodial care and a recreational therapist may be employed to plan and deliver recreational and socialization activities. The number of clients enrolled in a daycare program varies according to the staffing pattern and facility size. The cost of care may vary widely depending on the range and scope of services provided. Medicare generally does not provide reimbursement for daycare services. Medicaid may provide reimbursement for services in a medical model daycare program, but this practice varies from state to state. Often, services are paid for through private fees or through programs supported by grant funds or by charitable or religious organizations.

Most centers are licensed by the states in which they operate.[40] Most also are certified by the particular community agency that is funding the daycare center. Licensure and credentialing ensure that the daycare center meets minimum standards and guidelines set by the overseeing funding agency for the community agency to meet criteria for obtaining underlying federal government grants. In 1999 the Commission on Accreditation of Rehabilitation Facilities, along with the National Adult Day Services Association, published adult daycare standards, which include organizational measurement and quality and information systems and outcomes quality. The new standards provided an enhanced level of quality guidance to adult daycare management, as well as more recognition of the value of adult daycare services in the overall continuum of long-term care.[41]

Innovations in Long-Term Care

Innovative long-term care services that meet the diverse medical needs, personal desires, and lifestyle choices of older Americans have made important strides. The continuum of care model recognizes the complex configuration of individual needs and encourages the implementation of programs and services of adequate variety, intensity, and scope to provide the best configuration of care to any individual. Concepts such as aging in place, life care communities, naturally occurring retirement communities, and high-technology home care are some of the changes that offer enriched alternatives to long-term care recipients.

Aging in Place

Moving to a nursing home or dependent care facility is seen by many as a change in lifestyle to be steadfastly avoided for as long as possible. Most people prefer to remain actively engaged in their own support and care, in their own residence, and within the context of their own family. Research indicates enhanced quality of life and longevity when older adults are able to remain in their own residences. The term "aging in place," in the context of older and frail persons, refers to at least partial fulfillment of this desire. An aging-in-place health care system allows older adults to maintain their health while living as independently as possible in their own homes, without a costly, and in many cases traumatic, move to an institutional setting. At the federal, state, and local governmental levels, as evidenced by legislation, and at the grassroots level, an increasingly favorable light is shining on the well-documented cost effectiveness of health care programs that encourage the aging-in-place concept and the concurrent maintenance of independent living.

Aging-in-place programs bring together a variety of health and other supportive services to enable participants to live independently in their own residences as long as safely possible. Services that participants receive most frequently include

- Nursing services provided by registered and licensed nurses
- Home care aide assistance
- Homemaker services to assist with meals and housekeeping
- 24-hour emergency response system
- Home-delivered groceries
- Transportation to health care appointments

In 1972 a model of aging-in-place service delivery, called On Lok Senior Health Services, was established as a demonstration project to provide health services to a selected population of frail older people in San Francisco. The term "On Lok" derives from the Chinese language, meaning "peaceful and happy abode."[42] Participants in the On Lok program live in their own residences with an interdisciplinary team of health care professionals managing their health care. When institutional care is required (either in a nursing home or hospital) or ancillary diagnostic or specialty physician services are needed, they are provided through contractual arrangements with outside providers. The prototype program was so successful that Congress mandated replication of this model by establishment of demonstration programs, called the Program for All-Inclusive Care for the Elderly, or PACE, in other parts of the country. The early success of PACE was evidenced by the fact that although its clients were certified eligible for nursing home placement, only 6% were placed in nursing homes; the rest were able to remain in their homes.[43] Also impressive was the low hospitalization rate of participants when compared with typical Medicare beneficiaries with similar health status. Through provisions of the Balanced Budget Act, PACE earned permanent status as a Medicare-approved benefit.[43]

Continuing Care Retirement and Life Care Communities

Continuing care retirement communities (CCRCs) are available for those Americans who do not wish to stay in their own homes as they get older yet are essentially well enough to avoid institutionalization. Current estimates place the number of licensed CCRCs at over 2,200, accommodating approximately 725,000 older Americans.[44,45] Over 80% of CCRCs are operated by not-for-profit organizations and nearly 50% are faith-based.[44] CCRCs provide residences on a retirement campus, typically in apartment complexes designed for functional older adults. Unlike ordinary retirement communities that offer only specialized housing, CCRCs offer a comprehensive program of social services, meals, and access to contractual medical services in addition to housing.

A continuing life care community (CLCC) is a type of CCRC but health care services are prepaid and can be guaranteed for life. A CLCC typically provides services ranging from independent living accommodations to skilled nursing care. Cost varies widely, and such programs are expensive; however, as advocates for this lifestyle point out, many Americans approaching their retirement years have sufficient equity in their homes and investment income to pay the required entrance and monthly maintenance fees.

CLCCs achieve financial viability by using an insurance-based model and as such are regulated by state insurance departments as well as other regulatory agencies to which their services may be subject in their respective states. The program administrators establish eligibility criteria for participants using actuarial data from the insurance industry. The future lifetime medical costs of participants are anticipated, and rates and charges are set accordingly. Prospective CLCC residents are provided a contract outlining what the CLCC provides in terms of home accommodations, social activities, services and amenities, and access to onsite levels of health care. Most CLCCs require a one-time entrance fee and a monthly fee. There are many variations to the types of contracts offered.[46] In general, services may include

- Meals
- Scheduled transportation
- Housekeeping services
- Housing unit maintenance
- Linen and personal laundry
- Health monitoring
- Wellness programs
- Some utilities
- Social activities
- Home health care
- Skilled nursing care

A life care community offers more comprehensive benefits and support systems for the older persons than any other option available today in the United States. Less than 1% of older citizens have taken advantage of this option, in great part because of the expense and requirement of an extended commitment.

Naturally Occurring Retirement Communities

A "naturally occurring retirement community" (NORC) is a term coined by Professor Michael Hunt of the University of Wisconsin–Madison in the 1980s to describe apartment buildings where most residents were 60 years of age or older.[47] Now, the NORC acronym is widely used to describe apartment complexes, neighborhoods, or sections of communities where residents have opted to remain in their homes as they age. Today, numerous communities throughout the United States formally recognize NORCs.

The U.S. Administration on Aging recognized NORCs through the development of a competitive grant awards program for demonstration projects designed to test and evaluate methods to assist older Americans in their desire to age in place. Community centers and other not-for-profit organizations could compete for grant funding, and demonstration projects were enacted in several states.[47] NORC programs use a combination of services such as case management, nursing, social and recreational activities, health education, transportation, nutrition, and referral linkages to enhance quality of life and safety for older adults who wish to remain in their homes during their aging process. NORCs appear to hold much potential as a positive alternative to institutionalization and possible cost savings for individuals and government.[47]

High-Technology Home Care: Hospitals Without Walls

Traditionally, home health care focused on providing supportive care to persons with long-term disability and chronic disease. Changes in reimbursement mechanisms to a prospective payment system based on diagnosis-related groups have led to the more rapid discharge of all patients from hospitals after episodes of hospitalization for acute illness, exacerbation of chronic disease, progression of disability, or surgery. Patients frequently are discharged home while they still require advanced intensive therapeutic treatments and rely on complex, high-technology services such as ventilators, kidney dialysis, intravenous antibiotic therapy, parenteral nutrition, and cancer chemotherapy.

The delivery of high-technology home care is not only more cost effective than hospitalization or institutionalization in a nursing home, but it also allows the client to move from the more dependent patient role to the more autonomous role as a client in their own residence. Home health care agencies have accommodated this trend toward provision of advanced high-technology therapy in the home setting through innovations in the type and organization of the specialty services they provide. Improvements and innovations have taken place in the portability, mobility, reliability, and cost of medical devices such as intravenous therapy pumps, long-term venous access devices, continuous ambulatory peritoneal dialysis equipment, and ventilators. Innovative teams of skilled practitioners in specialized areas such as intravenous therapy and kidney dialysis and the concurrent development of innovative support teams of pharmacists and specialty technicians who prepare and deliver necessary intravenous, parenteral nutrition, and dialysis solutions and medications have made the home setting an appropriate environment for the delivery of high-technology therapies.

Long-Term Care Insurance

LTCI is a financing option for the various components of long-term care. The earliest long-term care policies were first offered in the 1970s and covered only care in nursing homes.[48] In 2007 the American Association for Long-Term Care Insurance estimated that 8.25 million Americans owned LTCI policies.[49] Individuals purchase the majority of policies, but an increasing number of employers are now offering coverage through group purchase plans. The federal government encourages the purchase of long-term care policies by offering tax deductions to employers, and many states now offer incentives for individuals who purchase tax-qualified long-term care policies.[50]

The benefits of LTCI policies vary across a broad spectrum. The most desirable policies cover services across the continuum of potential long-term care needs, with maximum subscriber flexibility. Specialists counsel buyers to be wary of limitations relative to inflationary factors in the costs of coverage, renewal clauses, limits on payments for various modes of long-term care, requirements for prior hospitalization for eligibility for home care, cancellation features of policies, and lifetime benefit limits. As with life insurance, the premium cost reflects age at purchase of the policy. LTCI companies also use underwriting criteria and may reject applicants or increase premiums for individuals with preexisting conditions that render them at high risk for future long-term care services.

Insurance industry advocates and other analysts contend that individuals and society will benefit in the future from the proliferation of LTCI. In this view, public dependency, especially on Medicaid, to fund long-term care needs would decrease, and individuals would have the ability to access the highest quality long-term care services without risk of impoverishment.[51]

The decision to invest in an LTCI product is very personal and depends on many factors, primarily on the level of assets the individual has or expects to have at risk if long-term care is required. Other alternatives to LTCI, such as transferring assets to children to become financially eligible for Medicaid, using the equity in a home, selecting special living arrangements, and using personal savings, are not universally applicable. All these options must be carefully assessed against the cost of LTCI to make viable and appropriate future plans.

Future of Long-Term Care

The United States will need more and diverse long-term care programs in the future to serve increasing needs, especially of older adults. Some of the causes underlying the intensifying need for diverse long-term care service options are

- Changes in the demographics of the U.S. population
- Social and economic changes in families
- Increasingly sophisticated medical technology
- Greater consumer sophistication and demands
- Increasing scrutiny of federal and state government financial involvement in support of long-term health care

The future configuration of the long-term care service delivery system is difficult to predict, although an analysis of current trends suggests certain directions.

Long-term care services have become increasingly diversified and specialized, which allows programs and providers to focus on becoming experts in meeting specific needs of specialized populations such as people with Alzheimer's disease or AIDS. To be avoided is one danger in allowing specialization to lead to fragmentation, duplication of services, and pressure to categorize participants into narrow service niches. Services such as subacute care and the provision of transitional health care after hospitalization for medically complex long-term care patients are responding as the drive to discharge patients from hospitals quickly results in a greater need for more intense supportive care environments beyond hospital walls. Service delivery systems that function within the managed care environment are becoming increasingly common, and the bundling of post-hospitalization care with hospitalization into one episode of care provided through one integrated service provider is occurring more frequently. Whether such trends contribute to a seamless continuity of care will remain under study.

Demonstrated cost effectiveness and expressed client preferences for community-based care continue to increase the demand for home health services. Federal and state administrations are increasingly recognizing consumer preferences, exemplified by legislation emphasizing community-based care over institutional care.

Long-term caregivers traditionally have been paid less and given less status than workers in the acute-care health services. The long-term care industry is enduring an employment crisis with an inadequate number and quality of applicants to fill vacancies in the direct caregiver positions across all industry sectors. Factors contributing to the long-term care employment crisis include[52]

- The growing need for services
- Competition among employers
- Workload and working conditions
- Employee turnover
- Wages and benefits constrained by reimbursement policies
- A lack of social supports for workers, including child care and transportation
- A lack of opportunities for education and career mobility

Staffing shortages seriously affect the quality of long-term care services. The industry's ability to develop innovative approaches to attracting and retaining staff will have important implications as service demands swell with aging of the baby-boom generation. Supported by government, not-for-profit organizations, and major philanthropies, identifying solutions to the staffing crises in long-term care is the subject of ongoing research at academic and policy development institutions throughout the country.[52]

Until recently, the needs of the informal caregiver system were virtually ignored. Significant legislative action at the federal and state levels only recently began to recognize these needs in terms of employer allowances and other programmatic and economic considerations at the federal and state levels.

An undercurrent of concern runs beneath all aspects of long-term health care delivery, especially with regard to the development of responsive, patient-centered, quality-driven, accessible, affordable, and cost-effective health care services for all citizens—including society's most vulnerable: people with chronic disabilities and frail older adults. Many concerns related to future long-term care will remain open ended, and the part that long-term care services will play within any restructuring of the U.S. health care system is undetermined, although it undoubtedly will be of major concern to the increasingly large portion of older adults in U.S. society. Insurance industry experts suggest the need for a national long-term care strategy that incorporates four primary components of education and awareness, caregiving, healthy aging, and long-term care financing (Figure 8-8). Given the industry's current unmet needs and rising demands, future years will be a period of experimentation, innovation, and change in the long-term health care system.

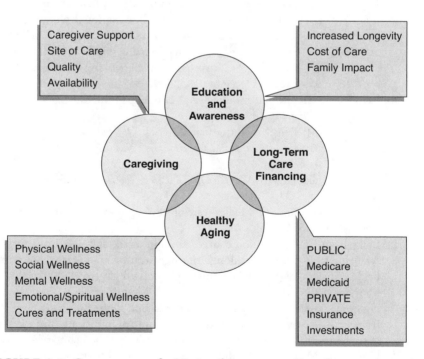

FIGURE 8-8 Components of a National Long-term Care Strategy.
Source: Genworth Financial, reprinted with permission.

References

1. Evashwick CJ. Strategic management of a continuum of care. *J Long-Term Care Admin.* 1993;21:13–24.

2. Shortell SM. *Transforming Health Care Delivery: Seamless Continuum of Care.* Chicago: American Hospital Publishing; 1994:1–7.

3. Jack CM, Paone DL. *Toward Creating a Seamless Continuum of Care: Addressing Chronic Care Needs.* Chicago: Section for Aging and Long-Term Care Services of the American Hospital Association; 1994:3–5.

4. U.S. Department of Health and Human Services, Administration on Aging. Profile of older Americans: 2008. Available from http://www.aoa.gov/ AoAroot/Aging_Statistics/Profile/2008/index.aspx. Accessed December 14, 2009.

5. U.S. Department of Health and Human Services, Administration on Aging. Population 65 and over by Age: 1900-2050. Available from http://www.aoa. gov/AoARoot/Aging_Statistics/future_growth/docs/By_Age_65_and_over.xls. Accessed December 14, 2009.

6. Shore HH. History of long-term care. In: Goldsmith SB, Ed. *Essentials of Long-Term Care Administration.* Gaithersburg, MD: Aspen; 1994:5–6.

7. Jones AL, Dwyer LL, Bercovitz AR, et al. The National Nursing Home Survey: 2004 overview. National Center for Health Statistics. *Vital Health Stat.* 2009:13(167). Percent distribution of nursing homes, according to type of ownership. Available from http://www.cdc.gov/nchs/data/series/sr_13/ sr13_167.pdf. Accessed December 18, 2009.

8. Pavri JM. Overview: one hundred years of public health nursing: visions of a better world. *Imprint.* 1994;4:43–48.

9. Glasscote RM, Beigel A, Butterfield A, et al. *Old Folks at Homes: A Field Study of Nursing and Board and Care Homes.* Washington, DC: American Psychiatric Association; 1976.

10. Moss FE, Halamandaris VJ. *Too Old, Too Sick, Too Bad.* Gaithersburg, MD: Aspen; 1977:15–37.

11. Evans JM, Fleming KC. Medical care of nursing home residents. *Mayo Clin Proc.* 1995;70:694.

12. Long Term Care Education.com. Definition of the skilled nursing facility. Available from http://www.longtermcareeducation.com/learn_about_the_ field/definition_of_the_skilled_nurs.asp. Accessed January 4, 2009.

13. MetLife Mature Market Institute. The 2009 MetLife market survey of nursing home, assisted living, adult day services, and home care costs. Available from http://www.metlife.com/assets/cao/mmi/publications/studies/mmi-market-survey-nursing-home-assisted-living.pdf. Accessed January 4, 2010.

14. Centers for Medicare & Medicaid Services. National health expenditures by source of funds and type of expenditure: calendar years 2003–2008 (Table 4). Expenditures for health services and supplies under public programs by type

of expenditure and program: calendar year 2008 (Table 11). Available from http://www.cms.hhs.gov/NationalHealthExpendData/downloads/tables.pdf. Accessed January 5, 2010.

15. Health United States, 2008, Table 120. Nursing homes, beds, occupancy, and residents by geographic division and state: United States, selected years 1995–2007. Available from http://www.cdc.gov/nchs/data/hus/hus08.pdf. Accessed December 18, 2009.

16. Association of Boards of Examiners of Long Term Care Administrators. NAB urges states to approve nationwide standards for nursing home administrator licensing. Available from http://www.nabweb.org/nabweb/common/newsRoom.aspx?id=80. Accessed December 18, 2009.

17. Long-term Care Education.com. Definition of assisted living. Available from http://www.longtermcareeducation.com/learn_about_the_field/definition_of_assisted_living.asp. Accessed December 18, 2009.

18. Assisted Living Federation of America. Cost of assisted living. Available from http://www.alfa.org/alfa/Assessing_Cost.asp?SnID=383408770. Accessed January 4, 2010.

19. National Association for Home Care and Hospice. Basic statistics about home care: updated 2008. Available from http://nahc.org/facts/08HC_stats.pdf. Accessed December 18, 2009.

20. Centers for Medicare & Medicaid Services. Home health quality initiatives. Available from http://www.cms.hhs.gov./HomeHealthQualityInits/. Accessed December 19, 2009.

21. Centers for Medicare & Medicaid Services. 2007 CMS Statistics, Table 20. Available from http://www.cms.hhs.gov/capmarketupdates/downloads/2007cmsstat.pdf. Accessed December 19, 2009.

22. Centers for Medicare & Medicaid Services. Post acute care reform policy council document. Available from http://www.cms.hhs.gov/SNFPPS/11_post_acute_care_reform_plan.asp. Accessed January 7, 2010.

23. Medical News Today. Medical literature shows homecare is cost-effective in Medicare, Medicaid-USA (August 21, 2005). Available from http://www.medicalnewstoday.com/printerfriendlynews.php?newsid=29446. Accessed January 7, 2010.

24. Centers for Medicare & Medicaid Services. Home health agencies, certification and compliance, home health providers. Available from http://www.cms.hhs.gov/CertificationandComplianc/06_HHAs.asp. Accessed January 7, 2010.

25. National Alliance for Caregiving. Caregiving in the U.S.: a focused look at those caring for the 50+. Available from http://www.caregiving.org/data/2009CaregivingAARP_Full_Report.pdf. Accessed December 19, 2009.

26. Family Caregiver Alliance. Caregiving. Available from http://www.caregiver.org/caregiver/jsp/content_node.jsp?nodeid=2313. Accessed December 19, 2009.

27. MetLife Mature Market Institute and National Alliance for Caregiving. The MetLife caregiving cost study: productivity losses to U.S. businesses. Available from http://www.caregiving.org/data/Caregiver%20Cost%20Study.pdf. Accessed January 7, 2010.

28. Gibson MJ, Houser A. Valuing the invaluable: a new look at the economic value of family caregiving. AARP Public Policy Institute Issue Brief 2007. Available from http://assets.aarp.org/rgcenter/il/ib82_caregiving.pdf. Accessed December 19, 2009.

29. Family Caregiver Alliance, National Center on Caregiving. Support for working family caregivers: paid leave policies in California and beyond, issue brief, June 2006. Available from http://www.caregiver.org/caregiver/jsp/content/pdfs/op_2006_paid_leave2.pdf. Accessed January 8, 2010.

30. Centers for Medicare & Medicaid Services. Operation restore trust accomplishments. Fact sheet. Available from http://www.hhs.gov/news/press/1997pres/970520d.html. Accessed December 19, 2009.

31. U.S. Department of Health and Human Services, Assistant Secretary for Legislation. Testimony on the Balanced Budget Act Home Health Provisions by Administrator, Health Care Financing Administration. Available from http://www.hhs.gov/asl/testify/t980331a.html. Accessed January 8, 2010.

32. Centers for Medicare & Medicaid. OASIS and outcome-based quality improvement in home health care: research and demonstration findings, policy implications, and considerations for future change. Available from http://www.cms.hhs.gov/homehealthqualityinits/downloads/HHQIOASIS ReportSummary.pdf. Accessed December 19, 2009.

33. National Hospice and Palliative Care Organization. NHPCO facts and figures: hospice care in America, 2009. Available from http://www.ecommunity.com/homehealth/uploads/files/NHPCO_facts_and_figures.pdf. Accessed January 8, 2010.

34. Hospice Foundation of America. Volunteering and hospice. Available from http://www.hospicefoundation.org/pages/page.asp?page_id=53134. Accessed January 8, 2010.

35. Helpguide.org. Respite Care. Available from http://www.helpguide.org/elder/respite_care.htm. Accessed January 9, 2010.

36. National Family Caregivers Association. President signs critical respite bill for family caregivers. Available from http://www.nfcacares.org/press_room/detail.cfm?num=93. Accessed January 8, 2010.

37. U.S. Administration on Aging. AoA FY 2010 budget signed into law. Available from http://www.aoa.gov/AoARoot/Press_Room/News/2009/12_18_09.aspx. Accessed December 19, 2009.

38. Cefalu CA, Heuser M. Adult day care for the demented elderly. *Am Fam Phys.* 1993;47:723–724.

39. Lamden RS, Tynan CM, Warnke J, et al. Adult day care. In: Goldsmith SB, ed. *Long-Term Care Administration Handbook*. Sudbury, MA: Jones and Bartlett; 1993:395–396.

40. National Respite Network and Resource Center. Adult day care: one form of respite for older adults. Available from http://www.archrespite.org/archfs54.pdf. Accessed December 19, 2009.

41. MacDonnell C. CARF accredits adult day care. *Nursing Homes*. 1999;48:53.

42. Miller JA. *Community-Based Long-Term Care*. New York: Sage; 1991.

43. Deloitte & Touche, LLP, and Deloitte & Touche Consulting Group, LLC. The Balanced Budget Act of 1997, Public Law 105-33 Medicare and Medicaid Changes. Washington, DC: Deloitte & Touche, LLP, 1997.

44. National Commission for Quality Long-Term Care. Long-term care in America, an introduction. Available from http://www.qualitylongtermcarecommission.org/pdf/ltc_america_introduction.pdf. Accessed January 9, 2010.

45. American Association of Homes and Services for the Aging. Continuing care retirement communities (CCRC) fact sheet. Available from http://www.aahsa.org/uploadedFiles/providers/CCRC/CCRCFactSheet2009.pdf. Accessed January 9, 2010.

46. Senior Resource for Continuing Care Retirement Communities. Continuing care retirement communities (CCRCs) and life care. Available from http://www.seniorresource.com/hccrc.htm. Accessed January 9, 2010.

47. U.S. Department of Health and Human Services Assistant Secretary for Planning and Evaluation, Office of Disability, Aging and Long Term Care Policy. Supportive services programs in naturally occurring retirement communities. Available from http://aspe.hhs.gov/daltcp/reports/Norcssp.pdf. Accessed December 19, 2009.

48. Long-Term Care Insurance America. What is long term care insurance? Available from http://www.ltciamerica.com/individualtci.html. Accessed January 9, 2010.

49. American Association for Long-Term Care Insurance. Learn about long-term care insurance. Available from http://www.aaltci.org/. Accessed January 9, 2010.

50. American Association for Long-Term Care Insurance. Long-term care insurance tax deductibility rules. Available from http://www.aaltci.org/long-term-care-insurance/learning-center/tax-for-business.php/. Accessed January 9, 2010.

51. Merlis M. *Financing Long Term Care in the Twenty-first Century: The Public and Private Roles*. Institute for Health Policy Solutions. New York: The Commonwealth Fund; September 1999:20.

52. Institute for the Future of Aging Services. The long-term care workforce: can the crisis be fixed? Available from http://www.aahsa.org/uploadedFiles/IFAS/Publications_amp;_Products/LTCCommissionReport2007.pdf. Accessed December 19, 2009.

CHAPTER 9

Mental Health Services

Susan V. McLeer, MD, MS

This chapter provides an overview of mental health services in the United States and describes the clinical characteristics of people who receive mental health services. It examines historical trends and the forces affecting the distribution and kinds of mental health services, compared with epidemiologic data on the prevalence of psychiatric disorders to hypothesize whether national needs for mental health care are being met. States' fiscal burdens for mental health services are highlighted. Evolution in the science and technology available for the treatment of psychiatric disorders is briefly reviewed. Opportunities for improvement and evidence of the impact of health insurance and service financing on effective mental health service delivery are examined.

Historical Overview

In the early years of our nation, the mentally ill were confined at home, in jails, or in almshouses, where they suffered severely. It was not until the early 19th century that sensitivity to the special needs of the mentally ill emerged through the Quaker emphasis on mental illness as being treatable. This approach, established earlier in Europe and known as "moral treatment," was tried in a few mental hospitals where patients received kind, but firm, treatment while participating in work, educational activities, and recreation.[1] Effective biologic treatments were nonexistent, and most patients did not have access to moral treatment; rather, they were confined under the most adverse circumstances. Hospitals became over-crowded custodial facilities, not only for the mentally ill but also for criminals, alcoholics, and low-income, homeless people.

Awareness of the needs of the mentally ill became more focused after World War I with the return of thousands of men with disabilities and suffering from "war neurosis," also known as "shell shock," a condition synonymous with current criteria for posttraumatic stress disorder. In the 1930s, the first effective biologic treatments emerged in the forms of insulin coma, drug-induced convulsions, and electroconvulsive therapy. Psychosurgery emerged briefly as an area of potential benefit to psychiatric patients. With the advent of World War II, the federal government became active in the mental health field, passing the National Mental Health Act in 1946, which resulted in the establishment of the National Institute of Mental Health (NIMH). Federal, state, and county dollars were allocated for training, research, and service in mental health. The Department of Veterans Affairs recognized the need for increased mental health services and established psychiatric hospitals and ambulatory clinics.

Psychiatric care still remained focused on inpatient services, with the number of people placed in inpatient facilities expanding to a new maximum by the mid-1950s, when over half a million patients were hospitalized in state or county mental hospitals. Fortuitously, this corresponded with the development of the first psychoactive medications specifically targeted for treating psychiatric disorders. These agents included chlorpromazine (Thorazine) and reserpine, used for the treatment of schizophrenia and other psychotic disorders. These advances profoundly changed patterns of care, reducing the need for convulsive therapies and psychosurgery and providing patients with effective interventions that allowed them to live outside of a mental hospital. Ambulatory services were intensified with the addition of partial hospitalization programs, intensive after-care programs, and the development of nonhospital transitional residential facilities, or halfway houses, for the mentally ill.

By 1955 Congress established the Joint Commission on Mental Illness and Health. The commission attacked the quality of care and patient access to care in the large state and county mental hospitals. This was the first time a federal body had considered the allocation of resources for the mentally ill. The commission's report began a substantial shift in sites for the provision of mental health services from the inpatient state and county mental hospitals to outpatient facilities.

The commission's recommendations fell on fertile ground and were reiterated by President Kennedy in his first message to Congress.

By the early 1960s, the winds of change had been whipped up not only by the commission, but also by the development of new, effective psychotropic medications and psychosocial treatments that could provide positive intervention for many disorders outside the hospital. Congress passed the Mental Retardation Facilities and Community Mental Health Centers Construction Act, resulting in considerable federal support for community-based services. Large entitlement programs became accessible to the mentally ill, mainly Medicaid, Medicare, Supplemental Security Income, Social Security and Disability Insurance, and housing subsidies, among others.

Throughout the 1960s and 1970s, the federal government became more involved in financing mental health care. Community mental health centers developed and expanded, and more health professionals entered the mental health field. Federal and state money, originally targeted for severely mentally ill patients, was shunted through the community mental health systems to provide services for those with less severe illness.[2,3] This shift in service was based on two untested assumptions that provided the underpinnings for changes in program planning in community mental health centers: (1) mental disorders lie on a quantitative continuum, with severe mental illness not differing qualitatively from lesser forms of mental distress, and (2) early intervention can prevent the development of major psychiatric disorders. Neither assumption has been demonstrated to be valid. Nonetheless, based on these assumptions, much money was invested and services provided to people with mild to moderate dysfunction and "problems in living," with the hope that the incidence of severe mental illness would be reduced through primary prevention.[4]

Treatment of less severe problems was handled through psychosocial interventions without proven efficacy and without systematic and standardized evaluations of outcome. In addition, payment for mental health services with public dollars was allocated on the basis of units of service provided; therefore there was no incentive for limiting the duration of treatment, and patients were provided nonspecific, psychosocial interventions for years. From 1955 to 1980, the number of patient care episodes provided in organized mental health settings increased fourfold, from 1.7 million to 7 million.[5] Few of these patients were severely mentally ill.[6]

Simultaneously with the institution of these programmatic changes in community mental health centers, many severely mentally ill patients who formerly had been warehoused in large state or county mental hospitals were discharged to community boarding houses and nursing homes. The deinstitutionalization movement was presented as being important to the rehabilitation of those with severe mental illness. Emphasis was placed on the necessity of providing services in community settings. In actuality, the states, through Medicaid, were receiving major financial incentives to move patients from inpatient mental hospitals to nursing homes. This transfer, coupled with the changes in the staffing and programs at community mental health centers, resulted in many severely mentally ill patients finding limited access to care. Treatments provided at the mental health centers no longer targeted the vulnerable group of people with severe disabilities. Advocacy groups such as the National Alliance for the Mentally Ill (NAMI) emerged, directing their efforts to have public dollars reallocated to include the funding of biomedical research that targeted severe and persistent psychiatric disorders. Advocates maintained that the pivotal issue was the treatment of psychiatric illness, not the maintenance of mental health. Through their efforts, those of NIMH, and clinical researchers across the United States, the assumptions fueling the staffing and programming of mental health centers during the 1970s and early 1980s were proved erroneous. Psychiatric disorders are not on a quantitative continuum but are discontinuous in development. They are biologically based illnesses, frequently precipitated and exacerbated by psychosocial stressors. These disorders and their symptoms require specific, targeted treatments.

By the late 1970s, health care costs had soared, and the federal government became concerned with identifying mechanisms for restraining health-related spending. President Carter, recognizing that new research findings presented opportunities for improving care to the mentally ill, appointed a Presidential Commission on Mental Health. Because of fiscal constraints and political infighting both in Washington and in the field of psychiatry itself, the majority of the commission's findings and recommendations were not put into operation; however, the commission's work quietly filtered down to the Department of Health and Human Services, resulting in substantial changes of great importance to those with severe mental illness. Psychosocial rehabilitation programs were expanded under Medicaid. Medicaid payment for outpatient mental health care was expanded; copayment requirements for case management services were reduced. Patients with severe and persistent mental illness became eligible for Supplemental Security Income funding. These changes meant a substantial shift in quality-of-life issues for this population; however, by the mid-1980s programs became sharply curtailed again, with cutbacks in housing subsidies, social services, and increased exclusion of people with mental illness from Supplemental Security Income benefits.

By 1990, although controversy still raged over which services should be delivered to whom, the locus of mental health care in the United States had shifted from inpatient to outpatient settings. Of the 1.7 million episodes of mental health services delivered in 1955, 77% were in inpatient settings and 23% in outpatient programs. By 1990, 67% of the 8.6 million episodes of mental health services delivered were provided in outpatient programs, 7% in partial hospitalization settings (not 24-hour facilities), and 21% in inpatient services.[7]

Over the past two decades, because of constant and rigorous pressure placed on Congress and legislative bodies by advocacy groups such as the NAMI, the American Psychiatric Association, and psychiatric researchers, the focus on severe mental illness has returned. Through block grants, state departments of mental health have refocused their energies and reallocated resources to ensure the provision of services to the most vulnerable population—those afflicted with severe and persistent mental illness. Federal money has been reallocated for research and training, with efforts focused on treatment, not prevention. Since the late 1990s, enactment of the Medicare Prescription Drug, Improvement and Modernization Act expanded drug coverage for older Americans; the State Child Health Insurance Program expansion increased the number of covered children, and the Wellstone-Domenici Parity Act of 2008 advanced the cause of insurance parity for mental health services.[8] The 2010 federal budget reflects this continuing trend. The budget increases the Substance Abuse and Mental Health Services Administration budget by $45 million for initiatives, including state homelessness grants for the severely mentally ill, Children's Mental Health Services, community mental health centers, and the Substance Abuse and Treatment Block Grant. The 2010 federal budget also includes $4.6 billion for veterans' mental health care including posttraumatic stress disorder, a $300 million increase over the 2009 allocation.[9] With these structural changes in funding of psychiatric benefits, the chances of people with severe mental illness receiving significant benefit through effective treatments have never been better. Nonetheless, those in need of psychiatric services still encounter major barriers in accessing treatment. These barriers are discussed later in the chapter.

Recipients of Mental Health Services

The recipients of mental health services in the United States constitute a small subpopulation of those individuals afflicted with a mental illness. Access to mental health services is and has been controlled by a variety of factors, including, but not limited to, persistent myths regarding the nature and treatability of mental illness, nonparity in insurance coverage for mental illness, and political decisions regarding the distribution of resources in our communities. Although the Wellstone-Domenici Parity Act of 2008 was passed by the Congress, the federal regulations for implementation still had not been released by the beginning of January 2010; their release is expected in late January. It is too early to predict how this legislation will be implemented and how it will impact benefits that enhance people's ability to access and utilize mental health services. The Act has much room for interpretation, and considerable debate is expected over which psychiatric services should be considered "comparable services" with those authorized for nonpsychiatric illness. Specific provisions of the Act are discussed later in this chapter.

Mental illness is enormously painful and debilitating, both for those directly afflicted and for their families. Well-designed epidemiologic studies, conducted by the Epidemiologic Catchment Area Program and the National Co-Morbidity Survey and the National Co-Morbidity Survey Replication, estimate that 26.2% of Americans, ages 18 and older, approximately one in four adults, suffers from a diagnosable mental disorder in a given year, approximately 57.7 million people.[10,11] However, many of these disorders are temporary and have minimal effects on personal functioning. Less than 7% of adults in the United States have mental disorders that persist for 1 year or more,[12] and approximately 9% of the population have reported significant disability associated with a mental disorder.[13] A total of about 15% of the adult U.S. population uses mental health services in any given year (Table 9-1).[14] However, over the course of a year less than one-third of adults with diagnosable mental disorders receives treatment.[15] Factors recognized as contributing to barriers to care access

Table 9-1 Proportion of Adult Population Using Mental/Addictive Disorder Services in One Year

Type of Service	Percentage of Population
Total health sector services	11*
Specialty mental health	6
General medical	6
Human services professionals	5
Voluntary support network	3
Any of above services	15

*Subtotals do not add to total due to overlap.

Source: Reprinted from U.S. Department of Health and Human Services Publication No. SMA-96-3098.

include financial limitations, social stigmatization, misunderstandings about the treatability of conditions, personal and provider attitudes, cultural issues, and an insensitive delivery system organization.[16]

In contrast to widely held assumptions, mental disorders can now be diagnosed and treated as effectively as physical disorders. They are classified according to criteria that provide predictability regarding the natural history of the illness and its responsiveness to specific, disorder-targeted treatments. Seventeen diagnostic categories are described in the American Psychiatric Association's *Diagnostic and Statistical Manual of Mental Disorders*, and within these categories the specific diagnostic criteria for over 450 conditions are delineated.[17] Criteria for specific diagnoses in each of these categories have been subjected to extensive field testing for diagnostic reliability and validity.

Although these diagnostic categories are useful for obtaining precise diagnoses and prescribing specific treatment plans for mentally ill patients, they have not been used extensively by those who set policy and distribute resources nationally. Rather, the concept of "severe mental illness" has evolved, and those with mental disorders that fall into this broad category have been targeted to receive services. This group represents approximately 6% the U.S. population, or 1 in 17 Americans.[10,11]

According to the National Advisory Mental Health Council,[18] severe mental illness encompasses a group of discrete mental disorders that differ in cause, course, and treatment. This population encompasses people afflicted with schizophrenia, schizoaffective disorders, autism, affective disorders (bipolar, formerly called manic-depressive disorder and severe depression), other psychotic disorders, as well as some of the anxiety disorders (severe panic disorders and obsessive-compulsive disorders).

In addition to carrying a primary psychiatric diagnosis, people with severe mental illness are highly likely to have additional problems with substance abuse as well as developmental disorders that are neurologically based (e.g., mental retardation or specific learning disabilities). These conditions further compromise patients' abilities to function.

The coexistence of two diagnoses is called "comorbidity." According to the NIMH, nearly half of those with any mental disorder meet criteria for two or more disorders, with severity strongly related to comorbidity.[19] Epidemiologic Catchment Area studies in both clinical and nonclinical settings have determined that the prevalence of substance abuse comorbidity ranges between 23% and 80% depending on the specific mental illness diagnosis.[20] In addition, studies of clinical populations of people with mental retardation revealed that 30% to 60% have comorbid psychiatric disorders.[21] In extensive research conducted by the Agency for Healthcare Research and Quality published between 2007 and 2009, mental disorders led the list of the five most costly conditions, exceeding costs of heart conditions, cancer, trauma-related disorders, and asthma in 2006.[22] Between 1996 and 2006 the number of people accounting for mental health treatment expenses nearly doubled from 19.3 million to 36.2 million.[22] The importance of these studies cannot be overemphasized; research on service provision to subpopulations with substantial comorbidity demonstrates that comorbidity adds significantly to the complexity of providing adequate and effective treatments. The implications to resource allocation are considerable.

Only a little over half of the people who are most vulnerable and have severe mental illness use mental health services; however, the use of services does not imply adequate access or use of effective services. Although some of these individuals have severe disabilities, are treatment resistant, and hence require lifelong supervision of living arrangements, the vast majority are people who, with accurate diagnosis and access to effective treatment and rehabilitative services, can lead productive and fulfilling lives in the community. Yet many of these individuals go undiagnosed or untreated.

Children and Adolescents

Data on service use by children and adolescents with diagnoses of mental disorder and at least minimal impairment first became available from a NIMH survey of children and adolescents between 9 and 17 years of age, published in the 1999 U.S. Surgeon General's Report on Mental Health. Approximately 9% of the child/adolescent sample (less than one-half of those affected) received some mental health services in the general medical and specialty mental health delivery sectors; the largest provider of services to this population group was the school system.[23] In a study using multiple data sources and reported in 2009, children ages 4 to 17 years diagnosed with a mental health problem increased more than 40% between the mid-1990s and 2006 to approximately 7% of the population; the rate at which a mental health diagnosis was rendered at a primary care visit doubled in the same period.[24]

Clinical research targeted toward determining effective treatments for children and adolescents suffering from mental illness has lagged considerably behind that for adults. Although diagnostic techniques have been highly refined through standardized diagnostic interviews and symptom rating scales that facilitate the accurate identification of those in need of service, research funding for treatment of mental illness in childhood and adolescence has not kept pace. The effects of a mental disorder on the developmental process of children are only beginning to be appreciated, but they clearly interfere with emotional, social, and cognitive growth and development. The need for early intervention that provides treatment and rehabilitation is urgent. Nevertheless, few practitioners have access to research findings regarding treatment efficacy, and few well-trained child and adolescent psychiatrists are available to the population at risk. Although some progress has been made, much more research is urgently needed. The results of newer research on effective treatments of specific disorders need widespread dissemination, with improved training and skills of those providing services for children and adolescents.

Older Adults

Although many advances have been made in the treatment of mental disorders, a crisis looms in providing mental health services to the older population. By 2030 there will be about 71.5 million older Americans, more than twice their number in 2000. People aged 65 and over represented 12.4% of the population in the year 2000 but are expected to grow to be 20% of the population by 2030.[25] In addition to sheer volume, epidemiologic studies have indicated that baby-boomer cohorts have high prevalence rates for depression, suicide, anxiety, and alcohol and drug abuse.[26,27] Studies have indicated that one in four older Americans have a significant psychiatric disorder with depression and that anxiety disorders are the most common. The prevalence of psychiatric disorders in this population is expected to more than double over the next 25 years with numbers increasing from 7 to 15 million people. In addition, there looms yet another problem regarding the abuse of alcohol and substances, particularly the abuse and misuse of prescription medication. In 2000–2001 estimates were that 1.7 million older adults abused substances and alcohol and that the prevalence is expected to increase to 4.4 million by 2020.[28] The implications of these findings on future resource allocation decisions are enormous.

Older adults suffer from many of the same mental disorders suffered by their younger counterparts; however, assessment and diagnosis may be more difficult and complicated because of accompanying medical conditions that mimic or mask mental disorders and patients' reluctance to accurately report symptoms. Patients tend to emphasize physical complaints and minimize complaints about their mental status. In addition, stereotypes about aging, leading older adults to believe that mental changes are to be expected, can make assessment and diagnosis particularly challenging.[29]

Primary care providers carry much of the burden of diagnosing mental disorders in older adults, and the rates at which they recognize and properly identify disorders are low. In addition, primary care providers may be reluctant to communicate a diagnosis of mental disorder to their patients and have strikingly low confidence rates in diagnosing and prescribing treatments for these disorders.

Researchers estimate that up to 63% of older adults with mental disorders may not be receiving treatment.[30] The lack of parity in Medicare coverage for psychiatric and substance abuse diagnostic and treatment services has been a major barrier in accessing care. Whether or not new parity legislation will rectify this problem is yet to be determined.

Accessible programs designed for detection, early intervention, and implementation of evidence-based treatments of psychiatric disorders and substance use disorders in older adults are needed. Coordination of health care with monitoring of medications and their interactions is critical because older patients are frequently on several prescribed drugs that affect behavior, mood, and cognition. The treatment of psychiatric disorders in older adults differs from that for other age groups because it must take into account age-related changes in metabolism and physiologic function that affect the impact of drugs. Progressive social isolation and financial losses also clearly affect symptom formation and may have substantial effects on treatment responsiveness and outcome.

Organization and Financing of Mental Health Services

Mental health problems and disorders are treated by a group of providers representing several disciplines working in a diverse array of public and private settings. The loose coordination of facilities and services has resulted in the mental health delivery system being referred to as "de-facto mental health service system."[12] The system is usually described as having four major components.[30]

The first component is the specialty mental health sector with mental health professionals such as psychiatrists, psychologists, psychiatric nurses, and psychiatric social workers providing the majority of care in outpatient settings, in private office practices, or in private or public clinics. Most acute hospital care is provided in psychiatric units of general hospitals or beds located throughout the hospitals. Intensive treatment for adults and children is provided in private psychiatric hospitals or residential treatment centers for children and adolescents. Public sector facilities include state and county mental hospitals and multiservice facilities that provide or coordinate a wide range of outpatient, intensive case management, partial hospitalization, or inpatient services.

The second component is the general medical/primary care sector consisting of health care professionals such as internists, pediatricians, and nurse practitioners in private office-based practices, clinics, hospitals, and nursing homes. This sector often is the initial point of contact and may be the only source of mental health services for a large proportion of mental health patients. The rates of mental health diagnosis in the primary care setting have increased materially in the past decade. The rates have doubled for children and increased by almost 30% for adults.

The third component is the human services sector, composed of social service agencies, school-based counseling services, residential rehabilitation services, vocational rehabilitation services, criminal justice/prison-based services, and religious professional counselors.

The fourth component is the voluntary support network sector consisting of self-help groups. This sector continues to be an important component of the mental health system.

Mental health services are funded in many ways, including private health insurance, Medicaid, Medicare, state and local services provided directly or through contracts with local agencies, Veterans Affairs hospitals and clinics, and other programs for specialized populations. Because many U.S. citizens lack basic health insurance coverage for the treatment of mental disorders, people with severe mental illness often depend on the welfare system for services and supports for basic living.[31–33]

In their review of the establishment of mental health priorities, Mechanic and Rochefort write that

> mental health policy has evolved in a disjointed and nonlinear fashion, reflecting the multiplicity of decision points, prevailing ideologies, emerging technologies, and financial, and other incentives as they interact with the local political, economic, and organizational frameworks of care.[34]

Mental disorders impose an enormous personal and financial burden on ill individuals, their families, and society as a whole. Their national toll is taken in reduced and lost productivity and the use of medical and other resources for diagnosis, treatment, and rehabilitation. Estimated total U.S mental health treatment spending is $100 billion, representing 6.2% of all health care spending and an 82% increase since 1993.[35] Between 1993 and 2003 a decline in hospital services provided by specialty providers accounted for a marked decrease in payments to specialty mental health providers (specialty units of general hospitals, specialty hospitals, psychiatrists, other mental health professionals, and multiservice mental health organizations).[35] In the same period mental health spending for retail prescription drugs increased almost fourfold due to the availability of safer and more efficacious drugs from primary physicians whose services engendered less stigma and greater accessibility to more patients.[36] Lost earnings by the seriously mentally ill are estimated at $193 billion per year; the estimated annual costs of disability benefits add another $24 billion.[37] These annual costs for treatment, lost earnings, and disability benefits total $317 billion and do not account for the costs of comorbid conditions such as substance abuse, criminal incarceration, institutionalization, homelessness, or the economic burdens on family members or other caretakers.[37]

Federal state and local governments account for almost 60% of mental health expenditures with private insurance, out-of-pocket, and other private sources accounting for the balance[38] (Figure 9-1). The reliance on federal and state budgets for the vast majority of funding of psychiatric services has resulted in new funding problems with the onset of the 2008–2009 economic recession. State budgets have been substantially affected by the near collapse of the financial markets, collapse of the housing market, and the increase in unemployment.

A 50-state study[39] conducted by the Kaiser Family Foundation Commission on Medicaid and the Uninsured reported that despite Federal assistance through the American Recovery and Reinvestment Act, state budgets are being challenged as Medicaid enrollment increases sharply. The numbers of people on Medicaid and state spending on the program have increased significantly due to the recession, resulting in the need to decrease costs despite increased financial help from the federal government.

Kaiser's 50-state study[39] also reports that these trends are expected to continue well into the 2010 fiscal year, with the slumping economy contributing to further loss of jobs, private health care coverage, and state tax revenue at a time when more people are seeking help from public programs.

Across the country, states estimate Medicaid enrollment grew by an average of 5.4% in state fiscal 2009, the highest rate in 6 years, surpassing

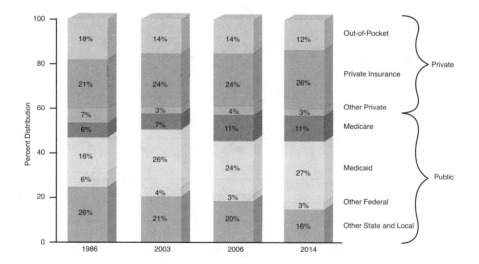

FIGURE 9-1 Distribution of Mental Health Expenditures Among Payers: 1986, 2003, 2006, 2014.
Source: U.S. Department of Health and Human Services, Substance Abuse and Mental Health Services Administration.

the projected 3.6% increase at the start of the year. Similarly, total Medicaid spending growth averaged 7.9% in 2009, the highest rate in 5 years, well above the 5.8% projected growth. For the year 2010, states estimate Medicaid enrollment will grow by 6.6% over 2009 levels.[39]

In a separate study, conducted by The Nelson A. Rockefeller Institute of Government, an even bleaker picture emerged regarding state budgets.[40] It was noted that the 2008 federal stimulus package would provide fiscal relief to state governments exceeding $150 billion between 2008 and 2011. Such aid is massive, but temporary, and hopes were that with economic recovery, state tax revenues would rise sharply. But in studying the course of past recessions, it became clear that states lag considerably behind in recovery. The Institute developed models based on past recessions using a "low gap" scenario and a "high gap" scenario for determining budgets when the American Recovery and Reinvestment Act monies cease in 2011–2012. Assuming a low prestimulus gap, states could face a 4% fiscal gap in general expenditures, which would approximate $70 billion (Figure 9-2). If a higher gap scenario is assumed with

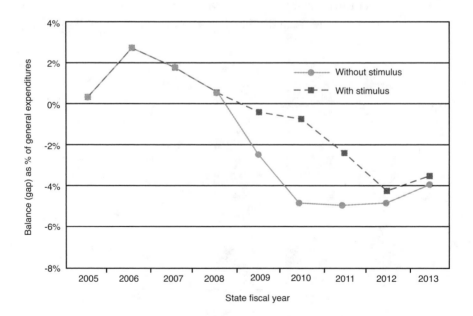

FIGURE 9-2 After Stimulus Wanes, Gaps Could Approximate 4% of Spending or $70 Billion, Even Under the Low Gap Scenario.
Source: D. J. Boyd, The Nelson A. Rockefeller Institute of Government, reprinted with permission.

prestimulus approximating $370 billion, then states would face a 2011–2012 fiscal gap of more than 6% of general expenditures, accounting for more than $100 billion (Figure 9-3). It is clear from these analyses that states will face substantial budget dilemmas when stimulus monies end, and they cannot assume "recovery" of the economy will prevent the need for restructuring and cutting expenditures and increasing tax revenues (Figure 9-4).[40]

In response to their current budget shortfalls and not yet planning for future budget gaps, states have sharply reduced their funding of psychiatric and behavioral health services, and costs have been shifted "downstream" to county and community levels, which also suffer from inadequate budgets secondary to the recession and its impact on the local tax base. Many psychiatric hospitals and community-based programs have been closed. Some states have declared their mental health programs to be in shambles. People with severe and persistent mental illness appear to be disproportionately affected. Whether or not the 2008 Parity Act can be used to prevent mental health services from being affected more than other medical

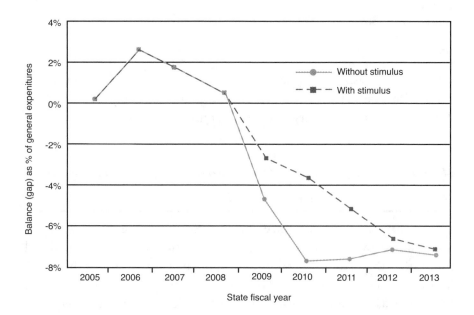

FIGURE 9-3 After Stimulus Wanes, Gaps Could Approximate 7% of Spending or $120 Billion, Under the High Gap Scenario.
Source: D. J. Boyd, The Nelson A. Rockefeller Institute of Government, reprinted with permission.

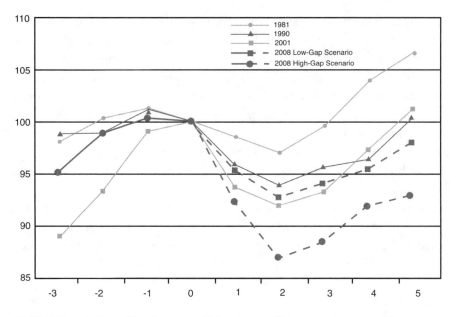

FIGURE 9-4 State Tax Revenue Takes Several Years to Recover After a Recession.
Source: D. J. Boyd, The Nelson A. Rockefeller Institute of Government, reprinted with permission.

services is in question. It is clear, however, that monies are inadequate and that health care services at state levels will be affected adversely for at least 2 to 4 more years secondary to the recession.

Health Insurance Coverage and Managed Behavioral Health Care

The history of health insurance coverage for mental health services has been sullied by some private treatment providers' drive for financial gain rather than clinical need, resulting in an exaggeration of the severity of clinical diagnoses to maximize payments. Additionally, because coverage was so limited for ambulatory services, hospitalization often was overprescribed.[41] Mary Jane England, president of the American Psychiatric Association from 1995 to 1996, stated that costs had been increased "through sophisticated marketing campaigns targeting adolescents and substance abusers, resulting in many unjustified and even harmful hospitalizations as well as sharply increased costs."[42] On the other end of the continuum, those with severe and persistent psychiatric disorders—those who truly needed intensive services—found that inpatient benefits were used up before stabilization was gained. Less costly forms of intensive treatment, such as partial hospitalization and day hospitalization programs, frequently were not covered by insurance plans, resulting in ill patients being transferred from the private into the public sector the moment insurance coverage was depleted. This transfer resulted in interrupted treatment, changes in providers, loss of continuity, substantial financial hardship, and impoverishment.

In the public sector, insurance programs, including those of federal, state, and local government, provided payment for services based on units of service delivered. Limits were placed on the duration of inpatient treatment, particularly through Medicare, but not substantially on the duration of day treatment, partial hospitalization, or outpatient treatments. Financial incentives were solidly in place for providing increased units of service. As long as need could be documented, there were few checks and balances on the use of ambulatory services or on evaluation of treatment efficacy, as long as payment would be forthcoming.[43] Mental health professionals, particularly in ambulatory settings, were frequently psychodynamically trained and provided patients with generic outpatient care, not targeted treatments of proven efficacy for specific psychiatric disorders.

Bringing new research findings to clinicians in the trenches and retraining and reengineering service delivery are costly. Consequently, for as long as financial incentives for change were lacking, minimal effort went into ensuring that clinicians were providing state-of-the-art interventions. Incentives ensured that practitioners overused ambulatory services. Also, the private sector increased its use of inpatient services, and both sectors escalated their indicators of diagnostic severity. This not only resulted in an increase in the costs of caring for people with mental illness, but also provided support for assumptions held by third-party payers that[44]

- Costs of psychiatric treatment are uncontrollable and unpredictable.
- Mental health care costs are unstable because insurance coverage encourages unnecessary and excessive use.
- Mental health care is not cost effective.
- Psychiatric treatment is not accountable to insurance carriers due to inadequate utilization review.

In fact, it appears that inadequate health insurance coverage for mental health services has paradoxically provided financial incentives for some private practitioners to abuse the system, resulting in increased use and costs without ensuring access to quality and efficacious care. Saul Feldman, chairman of the board at U.S. Behavioral Health and former director of the staff college at the NIMH, summarized the financial incentives of the 1980s and 1990s by stating that without a structure for ensuring utilization review, the problem becomes one of "people getting too much of the wrong care, in the wrong place."[45]

In the mid-1990s expenditures for health care hit new highs in the United States. Dramatic cost increases for mental health care paralleled those of the rest of medicine. Between 1986 and 1990 employer spending for meeting the mental health component of health care costs increased by 50%.[46] Feldman noted the following in his analysis of the role of the market in shaping new directions for mental health care:

> But the greatest contributors to the development of managed mental health, a development they now bemoan, have been the service providers themselves, practitioners and facilities. By not paying sufficient attention to or not caring about costs and length of treatments, they killed or at least seriously wounded the goose that laid the golden egg, a goose that for them is not likely ever to be as prolific. It is ironic that those who are most unhappy about the advent of managed mental health have done the most to bring it about.[45]

As a consequence of escalating costs, mechanisms for financing mental health services were radically restructured. Managed care was designed to control costs through financial incentives that rewarded outcomes of care, not service utilization. Managed care systems for people with mental illness tightly control utilization and closely monitor heavy users of mental health services. Managed care firms often did not incorporate coverage for mental illness in their basic contracts due to concerns about the costs of chronic care.[47] If coverage was provided, it was "carved out" and outsourced to a subcontractor who would assume the risk as well as the benefits of managing budgets and authorization for access to mental health services.

Today, over 176 million Americans, 58.5% of the adult population, receive their health coverage through their employer.[48] Employer surveys indicate that 99% of all workers covered by employer benefits are enrolled in some type of managed care plan.[49] Managed care contracts have limited mental health benefits to a greater extent than general health care benefits. Mental health benefits now typically cover 30 inpatient days and 50 outpatient visits per year.[50] Although covered treatment limits undercut accessibility for those with the most severe and persistent mental illness, service utilization data indicate that few patients actually exhaust their inpatient day and outpatient visit limitations.[50]

Insurers additionally protected themselves from "catastrophic" costs by setting annual or lifetime limits on benefit amounts paid for mental illnesses. With these exaggerated concerns regarding costs, the growth of managed care spawned an enormous managed behavioral health care industry to which managed care companies delegated both psychiatric service utilization and financial risk management.[51] Concerns that the "worried well" would consume a disproportionate amount of service resulted in insurers and health maintenance organizations instituting strict criteria for accessing reimbursement for mental health services. Utilization review mechanisms were developed to require preapproval before referral for service.[52] Concerns regarding the potential costs of caring for those with severe and persistent mental illness resulted in most insurers and health maintenance organizations seeking mechanisms for offsetting financial risk through contracting with external vendors rather than providing or overseeing the provision of psychiatric care themselves.[53] Such patterns of delegation of both responsibility and financial risk to external vendors are referred to as "carve-outs."

Managed behavioral health care vendors provide oversight by a qualified person, usually remote from the site of service, who monitors rendered or proposed care using predetermined, protocol-driven criteria. Communication between the reviewer and provider is usually by telephone. Both positive and negative effects can be realized by such oversight. Positively, clinicians who have the skill to treat patients with concentrated brief but efficient treatments that limit hospitalization are rewarded. Standardization of care through the use of protocols with demonstrated efficacy is encouraged, thus potentially reducing much of the individual provider variations from medical care. Unmonitored provision of services with dubious levels of efficacy can be reduced, as can the excessive use of hospitalization. On the other hand, service authorization by remote utilization managers, who are working from protocols that may not fit individual patients and who may not know the providers' credentials, expertise, and competence, may not be in the best interest of quality patient care.

Public sector initiatives paralleled private sector efforts to control mental health services costs. Throughout the 1990s state governments experiencing dramatic increases in Medicaid spending sought ways to control costs of mental health services for public beneficiaries. Massachusetts and Iowa began contracting with managed behavioral health care corporations in the anticipation that they would experience savings similar to private sector employers who were seeing reductions in psychiatric hospitalizations and lengths of stay.[54] For the most part these programs provide payment for mental health services on a per capita basis. Such an approach builds on the cost-savings incentives of managed care firms, relying heavily on closely monitored use of costly services and increased reliance on measuring outcome versus the number of units of service provided. In such systems, less is better, assuming an acceptable outcome level.

Early data assessing the cost effectiveness and outcome with managed care approaches in this publicly supported population with special needs suggested that there were no significant differences in outcome and that cost savings were considerable.[55–58] States continue to turn to the managed behavioral health care industry to serve Medicaid and other populations receiving publicly financed mental health benefits. Recent research indicates that managed behavioral health care corporations and public programs are facilitating access to those in greatest need as more people with serious mental illness are now more likely to receive mental health specialty services than in the past.[50,59]

Advocacy to achieve parity in mental health insurance benefits as compared with general health insurance benefits has been a continuing issue dating back to the 1950s.[60] "Parity" refers to requirements that insurers cover mental health care at the same level as medical care. The 1990s saw much legislative activity on parity at both the state and federal levels as discrepancies between mental health and medical care coverage grew with claims that private employers and managed behavioral health care corporations cut both care and costs too drastically.[61] Medical plans typically do not limit the number of covered outpatient visits or inpatient days of care; historically, however, a typical employer-sponsored mental health plan often carried several limits, including outpatient-visit or hospital-day limits in addition to annual or lifetime dollar limits in coverage. Discrepancies between medical and mental health coverage also occurred in deductibles, copayments, and coinsurance rates.[60] The impact of parity legislation in terms of both costs and quality of care is controversial. Some argue that the costs of such mandates cause employers to reduce contributions to employee benefits; however, empirical studies have demonstrated that employers switching to managed care see dramatic drops in mental health costs even when benefits are expanded.[60]

The Mental Health Parity Act of 1996 was introduced into Congress and was passed after receiving overwhelming bipartisan support. Enacted in 1998, this legislation equated aggregated lifetime limits and annual limits for mental health services with aggregate lifetime and annual limits for medical care; however, the law did allow many cost-shifting mechanisms, such as adjusting limits on mental illness inpatient days, prescription drugs, and outpatient visits; raising coinsurance and deductibles; and modifying the definition of medical necessity.[62] The Act did not require employers to offer mental health coverage, nor did it impose any limits on coinsurance, deductibles, days, or visits. Furthermore, coverage was not required for people suffering from substance use and abuse disorders, a problem of substantial public health significance.

In 2001 the Mental Health Equitable Treatment Act, which would have expanded coverage to an additional 15 million Americans, was introduced into Congress; however, by the close of 2002 Congress had abandoned the proposed legislation.[63]

In 2008, contained within the Emergency Economic Stabilization Act, Senators Paul Wellstone (D-Minnesota) and Pete Domenici (R-New Mexico) proposed the Mental Health Parity and Addiction Equity Act to build upon the Mental Health Parity Act of 1996. Enacted in 2008 with bipartisan support, the law took effect in October 2009, intending to end health insurance benefit inequity between mental health/substance abuse disorders and medical/surgical benefits for group health plans with more than 50 employees. However, the federal regulations to implement this legislation had not yet been released as of January 2010, delaying its projected effective date. It remains unclear when this new law will be fully implemented. The law is projected to provide parity protection for 113 million Americans, including 82 million individuals enrolled in self-funded insurance plans, which are not regulated by state parity laws. It ensures that financial requirements and treatment limitations applicable to mental health/substance abuse disorder benefits are no more restrictive than the predominant requirements and limitations placed on substantially all medical/surgical benefits. Significant features of the legislation include the following:

- Equity coverage applicable to all deductibles, copayments, coinsurance, and out-of-pocket expenses and to all treatment limitations, including frequency of treatment, numbers of visits, days of coverage, or other similar limits.
- Parity coverage for annual and lifetime dollar limits with medical coverage.
- Broad definition of mental health and substance abuse benefits.
- If a plan offers two or more benefit packages, the parity requirements apply to each package.
- Mental health/substance abuse benefit coverage is not mandated, but if a plan offers such coverage, it must be provided at parity with other medical/health benefits coverage.
- A group health plan or coverage that provides out-of-network coverage for medical/surgical benefits must also provide out-of-network coverage, at parity, for mental health/substance use disorder benefits.
- Preserves existing state parity laws and would only preempt a state law that "prevents the application" of the federal act. Therefore state parity laws applicable to health insurance coverage continue in effect unless the state laws conflicts with the Act's ban on inequitable financial requirements and treatment limitations.[64]

In addition to congressional actions directed toward insuring parity of coverage for mental illness, when the Mental Health Equitable Treatment Act was defeated in 2002 the states took up the cause of parity. By 2009, 48 states had enacted some form of parity legislation (Alaska and Wyoming are exceptions), although the comprehensiveness of state laws varies on a broad spectrum from minimal to comprehensive assurance of comparability with medical coverage.[65] Although parity legislation focuses on achieving equity for mental health services coverage with that of medical services, the removal of caps on benefits and other restraints do not attenuate other significant financial barriers to accessing services experienced by people with severe and persistent mental illness. Both employers and insurers have a broad range of alternatives in responding to state and federal parity laws, including totally dropping mental health benefits.[60]

In addition, in light of the 2009 enactment of new federal parity legislation, health plans must confront revamping benefit plans with their respective state insurance departments to remove inpatient day and out-patient visit limitations, clarify new administrative requirements, and reevaluate the cost–benefits of "carve outs," delegated to managed behavioral health care companies.[50]

It is clear that people with severe and persistent mental illness should receive the services and support necessary for them to recover from their acute illness and live relatively stable and high-quality lives within their communities. Nonetheless, this population has been subjected to episodic rather than continuous care, and focus has not been as much on personal life goals and recovery as on a monofocal model of treating the illness with medication while not attending to that person's life apart from his or her illness. Evidence-based protocols for treatment coupled with treatment planning for recovery require the involvement of the person with mental illness in treatment planning to address any long-term impairments and disabilities that require the coordination of resources that may cross funding streams and agency interests. These issues must be addressed if individuals suffering from mental illness are to live lives not characterized by chaos, poverty, homelessness, and social ostracism.[66]

Barriers to Accessing Services

If so many people require mental health services but do not seek them out or receive them, what is preventing them from gaining access to necessary services?

The mentally ill still suffer from stigmatization. A person is much more likely in casual conversation to mention that they are going to an appointment with the family doctor or gynecologist than mention an appointment with a psychiatrist. A poignant reminder of the stigmatization of the mentally ill is exemplified by mental health services formerly bureaucratically placed in the State Department of Corrections in one of the New England states, an action that might be interpreted as mental illness being perceived as a criminal problem. In spite of enormous advances in delineating the neurobiologic basis and treatment of many psychiatric disorders, many people still believe that having a psychiatric disorder is shameful and in some way reflective of personal failure.[67]

Consumer and advocacy groups working with professional societies have done much to dispel the myths fueling these societal misunderstandings. Nonetheless, they continue to exist and provide both direct and indirect barriers to service. Directly, an undetermined number of people may not seek needed care because of personal and familial shame and embarrassment. The indirect consequences are even more significant. Those determining public policy and establishing guidelines for health insurance and systems of care traditionally have viewed mental illness as being poorly defined, with diagnostic uncertainty and ineffective treatments. A major consequence of this misinformation has been that health insurance coverage for psychiatric disorders was designed to be less than that provided for other medical conditions.[68–71] The Mental Health Parity and Addiction Equity Act of 2008 provides hope that at least that inequity might be reversed.

Priorities for Mental Health Services

In 2005, the Substance Abuse and Mental Health Services Administration posted a plan for "Transforming Mental Health Care in America."[72] The transformation targeted the reengineering of the mental health systems so that care would be evidence based, recovery focused, and consumer and family driven. The transformation was additionally designed to help Americans understand that mental illnesses are treatable and that recovery should be the expectation. Overarching goals were as follows:

- Close the 15- to 20-year gap it takes for new research findings to become part of day-to-day services for people with mental illnesses.
- Harness the power of health information technology to improve the quality of care for people with mental illnesses, to improve access to services, and to promote sound decision-making by consumers, families, providers, administrators, and policymakers.
- Identify better ways to work together at the federal, state, and local levels to leverage human and economic resources and put them to their best use for children, adults, and older adults living with—or at risk for-mental disorders.
- Expand access to quality mental health care that serves the needs of racial and ethnic minorities and people in rural areas.
- Promote quality employment opportunities for people with mental illnesses.

These goals are laudable, but until there is a fiscal base and an evidence-based plan for service delivery and access, the likelihood of success in achieving these goals is low. It is crucial to ensure that parity is implemented rigorously in a manner that truly improves financial coverage for people with mental illness. Likewise, the fall-out from the 2008–2009 recession is expected to be felt at a state level for at least 2 years after there is evidence of national economic recovery. This means that Medicaid funding for treatment of mental illness and state support of mental health systems will continue to be significantly threatened. Expanded services and programs are unlikely to develop, and there is substantial concern that the gains made over the past decade may be lost because of inadequate funds at a state and local level. Federal intervention may be needed in a more substantial way than currently planned if those with severe and persistent mental illness are to truly expect not only that treatment is accessible but that recovery is achievable.

Payment systems dependent on outcome criteria have done much to hasten the application of recent scientific advances to the care of people with mental illness. Managed care systems have supplied an incentive for emphasizing quality over quantity in mental health care. However, people must be partners in their treatment planning, and their unique needs and aspirations must be recognized if services are to be sensitively and realistically accessed.

Need for Further Research

Over the past two decades, health systems research has increased markedly.[73–75] However, a strong need remains for well-designed studies that examine the effects of patterns and modalities of care on both mental and physical outcome.

There is no single "mental health system" but a variety of systems that provide services. These systems differ widely in what services are provided, for whom, by whom, and in what setting. Decisions regarding resource allocation rarely are made on the basis of documented need and the distribution of psychiatric illness in U.S. communities. Instead, they are made in our nation's capital or in state legislatures. Choices of specific services are based on beliefs held by generations of psychiatrists, other mental health professionals, and politicians rather than on demonstrated efficacy. The gap between research and practice continues to be considerable. There is a pressing need to examine pharmacologic studies and data to ensure that those who designed the studies and collected the data were not caught up in multiple conflicts of interest. Medications recommended as evidence based must be chosen on the basis of demonstrated efficacy rather than through the effects of pharmaceutical marketing strategies.

At a more basic level, highly sophisticated laboratory methods as well as neuroimaging technologies, such as functional magnetic resonance imaging and positron emission tomography, have advanced the neuropsychiatry research agenda. However, a continued challenge remains to facilitate the translation of basic science findings regarding molecular aspects of brain function into the design of more effective approaches to treatment. There also awaits the challenge of transferring new, evidence-based treatments into diverse service delivery settings.

When managed care models of care were first introduced, there were many accusations and statements of moral outrage suggesting that financial incentives were driving the market and that medical decisions were being based on economic considerations, not patient need. This is a simplistic analysis of a complicated issue. The delivery of mental health care has been driven for years in part by financial incentives that differ from those present under managed care. More research is needed to identify the impact of changing reimbursement systems on the access, quality, and cost-to-benefit ratio for various types of service arrangements to inform policymakers, payers, clinicians, and advocates more accurately.

Finally, over the next 10 years there will be a need for improved communication between primary care providers and mental health providers to ensure that patients receive integrated health care and that adverse drug interactions are minimized. The advent of electronic medical records shows much promise in this regard, but early reports suggest a fine line between integration of service and information overload. Confidentiality issues over the sharing of information in psychiatric settings pose a challenge as well, a challenge that is intimately related to stigma associated with mental illness. More research is needed on the advantages and risks of information transfer between medical providers.

The concept that people can not only be treated but can "recover" from mental illness is now at the center of efforts to restructure mental health care. However, it actually was introduced by the Freedom Commission on Mental Health, established by the executive order of President George W. Bush in 2002. The Commission's mission was to conduct a comprehensive review of the mental health service delivery system and "to recommend improvements in the U.S. mental health service system for adults with serious mental illness and for children with serious emotional disturbances."[76] The President requested a review of both public and private sectors to identify policies that could be implemented by federal, state, and local governments to maximize the utility of existing resources, to improve coordination of treatments and services, and to promote successful community integration.[76] Within 6 months of its establishment the Commission issued an interim progress report stating that, "America's mental health service delivery system is in shambles." Further describing the system as severely fragmented, the report cited needless suffering, frustrated caregivers, and millions of dollars in wasted resources.[77] The Commission's final report, issued in 2003, concluded that "traditional reform measures are not enough to meet the expectations of consumers and families."[76] The report further noted that successfully transforming the mental health service delivery system must facilitate "recovery and build patient resilience, not only treat symptoms." The Commission summarized its findings and recommendations in six goals[76]:

1. Americans understand that mental health is essential to overall health.
2. Mental health care is consumer and family driven.
3. Disparities in mental health services are eliminated.
4. Early mental health screening, assessment, and referral to services are common practice.
5. Excellent mental health care is delivered, and research is accelerated.
6. Technology is used to access mental health care and information.

Keeping these goals high on the political agenda and incorporating them into research, bureaucratic, consumer, and policymaking decisions would have posed numerous, provocative challenges in the foreseeable future and, if implemented, might well have changed the course of service delivery for those suffering from mental illness. Such was not the case, however. In the several years since the report was published, little if any progress has been noted. The reasons lie with the Commission's impractical and unrealistic advisories that had little or no chance for achievement.

Two of the many recommendations are illustrative of the unrealistic nature of the commission report. One recommendation called for "eliminating the disparities in mental health services between urban centers and rural and geographically remote areas."[76] Another recommendation called for "addressing mental health with the same urgency as physical health."[77] Those familiar with both the political climate and the apparent trend toward progressive decreases in Medicare, Medicaid, and private, third-party benefits for people with psychiatric illnesses quickly recognized that the Commission's goals were not likely to be achieved. Thus the work of the Commission, like that of so many other commissions, was essentially ignored.

A detailed national survey of state mental health services by the NAMI further underscored the absence of mental health system improvement since the 2003 report of the Freedom Commission on Mental Health. In 2006 the NAMI first published "Grading the States: A Report on America's Mental Health Care System for Adults With Serious Mental Illness" to provide a baseline for measuring progress toward the transformation envisioned by the New Freedom Commission. In 2006 the national average was a grade of "D," based on 39 specific criteria, with 4 subcategory grades of infrastructure, information access, available services, and recovery supports.[78] Three years later the NAMI report "Grading the States 2009, A Report on America's Health Care System for Adults With Serious Mental Illness" used 65 specific criteria in the subcategories applied in 2006. A rating of "D" again resulted, indicating a "stagnant" national average.[78]

Michael J. Fitzpatrick, Executive Director of the NAMI, summarized the continuing need for system improvement in the following words, "For (the) NAMI, change means mental health care systems that are accessible, flexible, and promote continuity of care, while paying for only those services that work."[79] Perhaps as the details of initiatives such as national health reform and insurance parity are advanced, there will be another opportunity for positive change; however, the political process at the federal and state level does not always move in a deliberate, linear manner. At the time this chapter goes to press, negotiations continue, and the details of the proposed new systems of health care reform have yet to be clearly delineated.

References

1. Bockoven JS. *Moral Treatment in Community Mental Health*. New York: Springer; 1972.
2. Morrissey JP, Goldman HH. Cycles of reform in the care of the chronically mentally ill. *Hosp Commun Psychiatry*. 1984;35:785–789.

3. Gronfein W. Incentives and intentions in mental health policy: a comparison of the Medicaid and community mental health programs. *J Health Social Behav.* 1985;26:192–206.

4. Mechanic D. *Mental Health and Social Policy,* 3rd ed. Englewood Cliffs, NJ: Prentice Hall; 1989:27–46.

5. Klerman GL. The psychiatric revolution of the past 25 years. In: Gove WR, Ed. *Deviance and Mental Illness.* Newbury Park, CA: Sage; 1982:180.

6. Mechanic D. Establishing mental health priorities. *Milbank Q.* 1994; 72:501–514.

7. Redick RW, Witkin MJ, Atay JE, et al. The evolution and expansion of mental health care in the United States between 1955 and 1990. In: *Mental Health Statistical Note 210.* Washington, DC: U.S. Department of Health and Human Services; 1994.

8. Glied SA, Frank RG. Better but not best: recent trends in the well-being of the mentally ill. *Health Affairs.* 2009;28:637–638.

9. National Alliance on Mental Illness. Policy news and alerts December 2009: Congress agrees on FY 2010 spending bills for mental illness research. Available from http://www.nami.org/Template.cfm?Section= Policy_Newsand_Alerts&template=/contentManagement/ContentDisplay. cfm&ContentID=90614. Accessed December 20, 2009.

10. Kessler, RC, Chiu WT, Demler O, et al. Prevalence, severity, and comorbidity of twelve-month DSM-IV disorders in the National Comorbidity Survey Replication (NCS-R). *Arch Gen Psychiatry.* 2005;62:617–627.

11. National Institute of Mental Health. The numbers count: mental disorders in America 2008. Available from http://www.nihm.nih.gov/health/ publications/the-numbers-count-mental-disorders-in-america/index.shtml. Accessed December 22, 2009.

12. Regier DA, Narrow WE, Rae DS, et al. The de facto U.S. mental and addictive disorders service system: epidemiological catchment area prospective 1-year prevalence rate of disorders and services. *Arch Gen Psychiatry.* 1995; 50:85–94.

13. Regier DA, Burke JR, Manderscheid RW, et al. The chronically mentally ill in primary care. *Psychol Med.* 1995;15:265–273.

14. Kessler RC, Berglund PA, Zhao S, et al. The 12-month prevalence and correlates of serious mental illness (SMI). In: Manderscheid RW, Sonnenschein MA, Eds. *Center for Mental Health Services, Mental Health United States, 1996* (DHHS Publication No. SMA 96-3098). Washington, DC: Superintendent of Documents, U.S. Government Printing Office; 1998:59–70.

15. U.S. Department of Health and Human Services. *Mental Health: A Report of the Surgeon General*—Chapter 6. Rockville, MD: U.S. Department of Health and Human Services, Substance and Mental Health Services Administration, Center for Mental Health Services, National Institutes of Health, National Institute of Mental Health; 1999:408.

16. U.S. Department of Health and Human Services. *Mental Health: A Report of the Surgeon General*—Chapter 6. Rockville, MD: U.S. Department of Health

and Human Services, Substance and Mental Health Services Administration, Center for Mental Health Services, National Institutes of Health, National Institute of Mental Health; 1999:72–73.

17. American Psychiatric Association. *Diagnostic and Statistical Manual of Mental Disorders,* 4th ed. Washington, DC: American Psychiatric Press; 1994.

18. National Advisory Mental Health Council. Health care reform for Americans with severe mental illnesses: report of the National Advisory Mental Health Council. *Am J Psychiatry.* 1993;150:1447–1465.

19. National Institute of Mental Health. Statistics. Available from http://www.nimh.nih.gov/health/topics/statistics/index.shtml. Accessed December 21, 2009.

20. Regier DA, Farmer ME, Rae DS, et al. Comorbidity of mental disorders with alcohol and other drug abuse: results from the Epidemiological Catchment Area (ECA) Study. *JAMA.* 1991;264:2511–2518.

21. Campbell M, Malone RP. Mental retardation and psychiatric disorders. *Hosp Commun Psychiatry.* 1991;42:374–379.

22. Agency for Healthcare Research and Quality. Mental health research findings: program brief. Publication no. 09-P011, September 2009. Available from http://www.ahrq.gov/research/mentalhth.htm. Accessed December 4, 2009.

23. U.S. Department of Health and Human Services. *Mental Health: A Report of the Surgeon General*—Chapter 3. Rockville, MD: U.S. Department of Health and Human Services, Substance and Mental Health Services Administration, Center for Mental Health Services, National Institutes of Health, National Institute of Mental Health; 1999:409.

24. Glied SA, Frank RG. Better but not best: recent trends in the well-being of the mentally ill. *Health Affairs.* 2009;28:639–640.

25. U.S. Department of Health and Human Services Administration on Aging. Aging Statistics 2009. Available from http://www.aoa.gov/AoARoot/Agining_Statistics/index.aspx. Accessed December 2, 2009.

26. Regier DA, Boyd JH, Burke JD Jr, et al. One month prevalence of mental disorders in the United States: based on five epidemiological catchment area sites. *Arch Gen Psychiatry.* 1988;45:977–986.

27. Klerman GL, Weissman MM. Increasing rates of depression. *JAMA.* 1989;261:2229–2235.

28. Bartels SJ, Blow FC, Brockmann LM, et al. Substance abuse & mental health among older Americans: the state of the knowledge and future directions. 2005. Older American Substance Abuse and Mental Health Technical Assistance Center, Substance Abuse and Mental Health Services Administration. Available from www.samhsa.gov/.../SA_MH_%20AmongOlderAdultsfinal 102105.pdf. Accessed January 10, 2009.

29. U.S. Department of Health and Human Services. *Mental Health: A Report of the Surgeon General*—Chapter 6. Rockville, MD: U.S. Department of Health and Human Services, Substance and Mental Health Services Administration,

Center for Mental Health Services, National Institutes of Health, National Institute of Mental Health; 1999:340–341.

30. U.S. Department of Health and Human Services. *Mental Health: A Report of the Surgeon General*—Chapter 6. Rockville, MD: U.S. Department of Health and Human Services, Substance and Mental Health Services Administration, Center for Mental Health Services, National Institutes of Health, National Institute of Mental Health; 1999:406–407.

31. Rowland D, Garfield R, Elias R. Accomplishments and challenges in Medicaid mental health. *Health Affairs.* 2003;22:73–76.

32. Goldman H, Grob G. Defining "mental illness" in mental health policy. *Health Affairs.* 2006;25:738–739.

33. Frank RG, Glied S. Changes in mental health financing since 1971: implications for policymakers and patients. *Health Affairs.* 2006;25:604–607.

34. Mechanic D, Rochefort D. Deinstitutionalization: an appraisal of reform. *Ann Rev Sociol.* 1990;16:301–327.

35. Mark TL, Levit KR, Coffey RM, et al. National expenditures for mental health services and substance abuse treatment, 1993–2003 SAMHSA Publication no. SMA 07-4227. Available from http://www.SAMHSA.gov. Accessed December 19, 2009.

36. Insel TR. Assessing the economic costs of serious mental illness. *Am J Psychiatry.* 2008;165:663–664. Available from www.ncqa.org/Portals/0/Newsroom/SOHC/SOHC_2009.pdf. Accessed December 20, 2009.

37. Levit KR, Kassed CA, Coffey, RM, et al. Future funding for mental health substance abuse: increasing burdens for the public sector. *Health Affairs.* 2008;27:w518.

38. U.S. Department of Health and Human Services, Substance Abuse and Mental Health Services Administration. Projections of national expenditures for mental health services and substance abuse treatment 2004–2014. Available from http://www.samhsa.gov/financing/file.axd?file=2009%2f6%2fprojections+of+national+expenditures+for+mental+health+services+and+substance+abuse+treatment%2c+2004-2014.pdf. Accessed January 16, 2010.

39. The Henry J. Kaiser Family Foundation, Kaiser Commission on Medicaid and the Uninsured. The crunch continues: Medicaid spending, coverage and policy in the midst of a recession: results from a 50-state Medicaid budget survey for state fiscal years 2009–2010. Executive summary. Available from http://www.kff.org/medicaid/upload/7985.pdf. Accessed January 10, 2010.

40. Boyd DJ. What will happen to state budgets when the money runs out? The Nelson A. Rockefeller Institute of Government. Available from http://www.rockinst.org/pdf/government_finance?2009-02-19-What_Will_Happen_to.pdf. Accessed January 11, 2010.

41. Strumwassen I, Paranjpe NV, Udow M, et al. Appropriateness of psychiatric and substance abuse hospitalizations. *Med Care.* 1991;29:AS77–AS89.

42. England MJ, Goff VV. Health reform and organized systems of care. In: England MJ, Goff VV, Eds. *New Directions for Mental Health Services.* San Francisco: Jossey-Bass; 1993:5–12.

43. Frank PG, Lave J. Economics of managed mental health. In: Feldman S, Ed. *Managed Mental Health Services.* Springfield, IL: Charles C Thomas; 1992:83–99.

44. Sharfstein SS, Magnas HL, Taube CA, et al. Mental health services. In: Kovner A, Ed. *Health Care Delivery in the United States,* 5th ed. New York: Springer; 1995:253–255.

45. Feldman S. *Managed Mental Health Services.* Springfield, IL: Charles C Thomas; 1992:xiv.

46. Gabel J. Job-based health benefits in 2002: some important trends. *Health Affairs.* 2002;21:143.

47. Iglehart JK. Health policy report: managed care and mental health. *N Engl J Med.* 1996;334:131–135.

48. U.S Department of Commerce, Economics and Statistics Administration, U.S. Census Bureau. Income, poverty and health insurance coverage in the United States: 2008. Available from http://www.census.gov/prod/2009pubs/p60-236.pdf. Accessed December 22, 2009.

49. Kaiser Family Foundation and Health Research and Educational Trust. 2009 Survey of employer-sponsored health benefits, exhibit 5.1. Available from http://ehbs.kff.org/pdf/2009/7936.pdf. Accessed December 21, 2009.

50. Dixon K. Implementing mental health parity: the challenge for health plans. *Health Affairs.* 2009;28:663–665.

51. Findlay S. Managed behavioral health care in 1999: an industry at a cross-roads. *Health Affairs.* 1999;5:117.

52. Boyle PJ, Callahan D. Managed care in mental health: the ethical issues. *Health Affairs.* 1995;14(suppl 3):7–22.

53. Hodgkin D, Horgan CM, Garnick CW. Make or buy: HMOs' contracting arrangements for mental health care. *Admin Policy Mental Health.* 1997; 24:359–376.

54. Bailit MH, Burgess LL. Competing interests: public-sector managed behavioral health care. *Health Affairs.* 1999;18:112–113.

55. Davidson H, Schlesinger M, Dowart RA, et al. State purchase of mental health care: models and motivations for monitoring accountability. *Int J Law Psychiatry.* 1991;14:387–403.

56. Brotman A. Privatization of mental health services: the Massachusetts experiment. *J Health Politics Policy Law.* 1992;17:541–551.

57. Johnson RE, McFarland BH. Treated prevalence rate of severe mental illness among HMO members. *Hosp Commun Psychiatry.* 1994;45:919–924.

58. Lurie N, Finch M, Christianson J. Does capitation affect the health of the chronically mentally ill? Results from a randomized trial. *JAMA.* 1992;267:3300–3304.

59. Mechanic D, Bilder S. Treatment of people with mental illness: a decade-long perspective. *Health Affairs.* 2004;23:93.

60. Sturm R, Liccardo Pacula R. State mental health parity laws: cause or consequence of differences in use? *Health Affairs.* 1999;18:182–183.

61. Findlay S. Managed behavioral health care in 1999: an industry at a crossroads. *Health Affairs.* 1999;18:118.

62. National Alliance on Mental Illness. The Mental Health Parity Act of 1996. Available from http://www.nami.org/Content/ContentGroups/E-News/1996/The_Mental_Health_Parity_Act_of_1996.htm. Accessed December 6, 2009.

63. National Alliance on Mental Illness. The Mental Health Equitable Treatment Act. Available from http://www.nami.org/Content/ContentGroups/E-News/2003/February_2003/Paul_Wellstone_Mental_Health_Equitable_Treatment_Act_of_2003_Introduced.htm. Accessed December 6, 2009.

64. Mental Health America. Fact sheet: Paul Wellstone and Pete Domenici Mental Health Parity and Addiction Equity Act of 2008. Available from http://takeaction.mentalhealthamerica.net/site/PageServer?pagename=Equity_Campaign_detailed_summary. Accessed December 16, 2009.

65. National Alliance on Mental Illness. State mental health parity laws. Available from http://www.nami.org/Template.cfm?Section=Parity1&Template=/ContentManagement/ContentDisplay.cfm&ContentID=45313. Accessed December 6, 2009.

66. Bridges K, Huxley P, Oliver J. Psychiatric rehabilitation: redefined for the 1990s. *Int J Social Psychiatry.* 1994;40:1–16.

67. National Institutes of Health. *Basic Behavioral Science Research for Mental Health: A National Investment: A Report of the National Advisory Mental Health Council.* Washington, DC: National Institutes of Health; 1995.

68. Morton JD, Aleman P. Trends in employer-provided mental health and substance abuse benefits. *Monthly Labor Rev.* 2005;128:25–35. Available from http://www.bls.gov/opub/mlr/2005/04/art3full.pdf. Accessed December 23, 2009.

69. McLaughlin CG. Delays in treatment for mental disorders and health insurance coverage. *Health Serv Res.* 2004;39:221–223. Available from http://www.ncbi.nlm.nih.gov/pmc/articles/pmc1361004/pdf/hesr_00224.pdf. Accessed December 22, 2009.

70. Sethi R, Jee J, Mauery DR, et al. Designing employer-sponsored mental health benefits. (2006) DHHS Pub. No. SMA-06-4177. Rockville, MD: Center for Mental Health Services, Substance Abuse and Mental Health Services Administration. Available from http://download.ncadi.samhsa.gov/ken/pdf/SMA06-4177/SMA06-4177.pdf. Accessed December 22, 2009.

71. Mark TL, Coffey RM, Vandivort-Warren R, et al. U.S. spending for mental health and substance abuse treatment, 1991–2001. Health Affairs Web Exclusive March 29, 2005. Available from http://content.healthaffairs.org/cgi/reprint/hlthaff.w5.133v1.pdf. Accessed December 14, 2009.

72. U.S. Department of Health and Human Services. Substance Abuse and Mental Health Services Administration. Transforming mental health care in America: the federal action agenda, 2005. Available from http://www.samhsa.gov/federalactionagenda/NFC_execsum.aspx. Accessed January 15, 2010.

73. National Institute of Mental Health. *The Future of Mental Health Services Research*. Washington, DC: U.S. Department of Health and Human Services; 1989.

74. Newman FL, Howard KI. Introduction to the special section on seeking new methods in mental health services research. *J Consult Clin Psychol*. 1994; 61:667–669.

75. Stein II, Hollingsworth EJ. *Maturing Mental Health Systems: New Challenges and Opportunities*. San Francisco: Jossey-Bass; 1995.

76. President's New Freedom Commission on Mental Health. Achieving the promise: transforming mental health care in America, Executive Summary, 3–4. Available from http://www.mentalhealthcommission.gov/reports/FinalReport/FullReport.htm. Accessed. December 9, 2009.

77. U.S. Department of Health and Human Services, Substance Abuse and Mental Health Services Administration. Interim report of the President's New Freedom Commission on Mental Health. Available from http://www.mentalhealth.org/publications/allpubs/NMH02-0144/default.asp. Accessed December 9, 2009.

78. National Alliance for the Mentally Ill. Grading the states 2009, a report on America's health care system for adults with serious mental illness. Executive Summary. Available from http://www.nami.org/gtsTemplate09.cfm?Section=Overview1&Template=/ContentManagement/ContentDisplay.cfm&ContentID=75090. Accessed December 23, 2009.

79. National Alliance for the Mentally Ill. Grading the states 2009, a report on America's health care system for adults with serious mental illness. Letter from NAMI Executive Director. Available from http://www.nami.org/gtsTemplate09.cfm?Section=Overview1&Template=/ContentManagement/ContentDisplay.cfm&ContentID=75089. Accessed December 23, 2009.

CHAPTER 10

Public Health and the Role of Government in Health Care

This chapter presents the history of governmental efforts to prevent or control the problems of health and disease. Efforts to protect the public's health, begun in early European history and transferred to Colonial America, are traced, with emphasis on their purpose, motivation, and success. The rise and decline of America's once elaborate federal, state, and local partnerships in the delivery of public health services are described, as well as the efforts of private and voluntary agencies. Also discussed are the barriers to effective preventive services that result from the lack of a population perspective in the U.S health care system. The chapter concludes with a discussion of public health challenges and goals, emerging issues, and the changing role of government.

The term "public health" is usually defined broadly as the efforts made by communities to cope with the health problems that arise when people live in groups. Community life creates the need to control the transmission of communicable diseases, maintain a sanitary environment, provide safe water and food, and sustain disabled and low-income populations.[1]

The world history of public health is a fascinating study of civilized society's attempts to deal with the biologic, social, and environmental forces that have contributed to the pervasive problems of morbidity and mortality and with the unfortunate citizens who have been handicapped by illness, disability, and poverty. The following observations are presented primarily to set the stage for understanding the development of government's role in the evolution of public health in the United States.

Throughout history public health activities have reflected the state of knowledge at the time regarding the nature and cause of the diseases that afflict humankind, the practices used for their control or treatment, and the dominant social ideologies of political jurisdictions. From the concepts of spiritual cleanliness and community responsibility codified by the ancient Hebrews for religious reasons to the systems of personal hygiene practiced by the Greeks in an effort to achieve a perfect balance between body and mind, ancient civilizations learned patterns of individual behavior they believed promoted health and reduced the risk of disease. It remained for the Romans, however, to develop public health as a governmental matter beyond individual practice.

The feats of engineering and administrative accomplishments that provided the Romans with clean water and effective sewage and swamp drainage systems were the forerunners of politically sanctioned environmental protections of the public's health. In addition, the Roman Empire is given credit for establishing a network of infirmaries to treat illness among the disadvantaged populations. These infirmaries are considered to be the first public hospitals.

The medieval period that followed the fall of Rome was characterized by the disintegration of the cities and the return of anarchy. The overpopulated walled towns built to withstand enemy attacks crowded families together in the unhealthiest circumstances. The pest-ridden, unsanitary living conditions and the narrow, dark streets that overflowed with human waste and refuse provided fertile environments for disease epidemics that decimated large segments of those populations. Superstitious, demonic, and theologic theories of epidemic disease displaced ancient concerns for personal hygiene and the quality of the environment.

The Renaissance, however, was characterized by a great revival of learning. Along with advances in art, literature, and philosophy and the rise of industry and commerce, there was a renewed interest in science and medicine. From the 16th to the 18th centuries public health was shaped by two countervailing trends.[2] Although the administration of rudimentary medical and nursing services continued to be the responsibility of towns and other local units, the concept of the modern state was beginning to emerge.

Because only a political jurisdiction that protected and cared for its citizens could reap the continuing economic benefits of production and world trade, healthy laborers and soldiers became valuable commodities. Thus in the centralized national governments of Europe during the 16th and 17th centuries, maintaining the health of laborers and soldiers became important economic, political, and public health concerns.

Public Health in England

Poverty, illness, and disability were common problems in the towns and parishes of England during the 16th and 17th centuries, and most communities responded with some form of publicly supported medical care provided in private homes or at public infirmaries. The Elizabethan Poor Laws of 1601 addressed the issue of the "lame, impotent, old, blind, and such other among them being poor and not able to work" without dealing directly with health matters.[2] The law was expanded subsequently to include the provision of nursing and medical care.

It was also in England that the collection and analysis of national statistics regarding industrial production and demographics began in the 17th century. The work of the father of political arithmetic, William Petty (1623–1687), and the statistical analyses of his friend John Graunt (1620–1674), established the importance of vital statistics and led to such epidemiologic tools as population-specific and disease-specific morbidity and mortality rates, life tables, and the calculus of probability. Study of the vital statistics contained in the Bills of Mortality published weekly in London led to a better understanding of the social phenomena that were factors in the promotion of health and the occurrence of disease.

Of interest, in light of subsequent debates about the merits of national health services, was the proposal of John Bellers, a London merchant and philanthropist (1654–1725). At the turn of the century he proposed dealing with public health problems on a national scale. In *An Essay Toward Improvement of Physick*, Bellers suggested that the people's health was too important to the community to be left to the uncertainty of individual initiative. He argued that the health of the people was the responsibility of the state, whose task it was to establish and maintain hospitals and laboratories, erect a national health institute, and provide medical care for the sick.

The Elizabethan Poor Laws obligated each parish in England to maintain its own disadvantaged citizens. Despite a variety of schemes to deal with the health problems of the low-income populations, including the widespread development of workhouses to teach the unemployed to support themselves, the fundamental economic and social problems that led to pervasive poverty remained unsolved. By the 19th century, the industrialization of England had made poverty and social distress more prevalent than ever. It was in that climate that the drastic Poor Law Amendment Act of 1834 was passed. The dual intent was to reduce the rates of dependency and free the labor market to spur industrialization. The law required that able-bodied people and their families be given aid only in well-regulated workhouses.

The circumstances of the new industrial society, factories, and the congested dwellings of urban environments produced new health problems. As people crowded into burgeoning towns and cities, diseases flourished and spread. It was the Poor Law Commission of 1834 under the leadership of Edwin Chadwick that developed the means to address public health problems. Motivated by the belief that it would be good economy to prevent disease, Chadwick advocated the use of carefully collected data to link population characteristics, environmental conditions, and the incidence of diseases.

After many investigations, political debates, and subsequent political compromises, England's Public Health Act became law in 1848, and a General Board of Health was created. Although the subsequent history of public health in England is a chronicle of social change, epidemics, and political machinations, it is evident that the growth of their sanitary reform movement and the creation of the General Board of Health in 1848 established the British as the world leaders in public health philosophy and practice. Public health in early America was heavily influenced by the medical and administrative experience of the British.[2]

Public Health and Government-Supported Services

The history of public health in the United States from the early colonial period to the end of the 19th century followed the same development pattern as that of England. Yellow fever and cholera epidemics stimulated sanitary reforms, and the early cities and towns began to assume responsibility for the collective health of their citizens. Public medical care in the United States, however, bore the stigma of its "Poor Law" legacy. The New York Poor Law of 1788 provided that any town or city could establish an almshouse, and within a few years most towns and cities had done so. Although there was a series of shocking exposés of terrible conditions in many of these facilities, the concept of the almshouse and town-employed physicians remained the mainstay of sick people among the low-income population until the depression of the 1930s.

Lemuel Shattuck, a Massachusetts statistician, conducted U.S. sanitary surveys similar to those of Chadwick in England. In his Report of the Sanitary Commission, published in 1850, he documented differences in morbidity and mortality rates in different locations and related them to various environmental conditions. Consequently, he argued, the city or state had to take responsibility for the environment. Although largely ignored at the time of its release, the report has come to be considered one of the most influential documents in the evolution of public health in the United States.[3]

In 1865, emulating the Shattuck survey in Massachusetts, the New York City Council of Hygiene and Public Health published a shocking exposé of unsanitary conditions in the city. Within a year a public health law was passed that created a city board of health. Creating an appropriate administrative structure for local public health efforts became a turning point for public health in the United States.

As in England and other countries, early federal public health initiatives were motivated more by economic and commercial concerns than humanitarian values. For instance, the Public Health Service came into being in 1798 as the Marine Hospital Service when President John Adams signed into law an act providing for the care and relief of seamen who were sick or disabled. Because healthy sailors were a valuable commercial commodity and because the seaport towns took responsibility for only their own citizens, it was left to the federal government to provide health services to the seamen and passengers of the important shipping industry. Additionally, it was of serious concern to the citizens of seaports that the personnel of foreign ships not transmit to them diseases contracted elsewhere.

Soon thereafter the first Marine Hospital was set up in Boston Harbor, and seamen received care in port cities along the East Coast. In 1870, the Marine Hospital Service was reorganized as a national hospital system with a central headquarters in Washington, DC. The medical officer in charge, known at first as the supervising surgeon, was later given the title of surgeon general. It is significant in light of the commercial motivation for its creation that the Marine Hospital Service was established as a component of the Treasury Department.

In 1889 Congress established the Public Health Service Commissioned Corps. Envisioned as a mobile force of physicians to assist the nation in fighting disease and protecting health, the Corps was set up along military lines, with titles and pay corresponding to Army and Navy grades and physicians subject to duty wherever assigned.[4] In 1891, the bacteriologic laboratory of Dr. Joseph J. Kinyuon in the Staten Island Marine Hospital was moved to Washington, DC, where it was expanded to include pathology, chemistry, and pharmacology. It was the forerunner of the National Institutes of Health, which today provides two-thirds of all federal support for biomedical research in this country.

Eleven years later, in 1902, a new law changed the Marine Hospital Service's name to the Public Health and Marine Hospital Service. In 1912, the name would be changed again to its present designation: the U.S. Public Health Service. From this modest start, the Public Health Service underwent a series of reorganizations and expansions until it became a major agency of the U.S. Department of Health and Human Services (HHS) and responsible for the largest public health program in the world.[5]

In 1933 it became apparent that state and local governments with limited tax revenues required help from the federal government to provide welfare assistance, and the Federal Emergency Relief Act was passed. It provided federal aid to the states and authorized general medical care for acute and chronic illness, obstetric services, emergency dental extractions, bedside nursing, drugs, and medical supplies. Because participation by the states was optional, the act was not implemented in many parts of the country.[6]

The passage of the Social Security Act of 1935 ended the era of makeshift federal and state programs to meet the health needs of the sick people among the low-income population. Title VI of the landmark Social Security Act of 1935 was instrumental in the expansion of the Public Health Service. The Act delegated to the Public Health Service the authority to assist states, counties, health districts, and other political subdivisions to establish and maintain public health services. Title VI provided the impetus for all political jurisdictions to create public health agencies and services. After 141 years, the Public Health Service was removed from the Treasury Department to become a component of a new Federal Security Agency, created in 1939 to bring together most of the health, welfare, and educational services scattered throughout the federal government.

During World War II the Public Health Service carried out emergency health and sanitation efforts that contributed substantially to the country's defense efforts. Immediately thereafter, a critical shortage of medical facilities prompted the passage of the National Hospital Survey and Construction Act, called Hill-Burton after its congressional sponsors. The Act stimulated the growth of the health care industry by providing federal aid to the states for hospital and health center construction. Since 1946, the Public Health Service has provided national leadership in hospital planning, research, and operation. In 1946, the Federal Security Agency also was expanded to include the Children's Bureau and the Food and Drug Administration.

In 1953, the Public Health Service, with the other components of the Federal Security Agency, became part of the newly created Department of Health, Education and Welfare (HEW). During the next decade the health care industry faced the multiple challenges of coping with a rapidly expanding U.S. population, rising public expectations for health services, and a host of technologic advances in health care with an inadequate supply of health professionals.

HEW responded in 1963 with the Health Professions Educational Assistance Act, which provided grants to build health professional schools, and in 1964 with the Nurse Training Act, which authorized federal aid for construction and rehabilitation of nursing schools and provided loans to nursing students.

The National Institute for Occupational Health and Safety, the National Institute on Alcohol Abuse and Alcoholism, the National Health Service Corps, and major initiatives in addressing cancer and heart, lung, and blood diseases were initiated in the early 1970s. In 1979, the education component of HEW was transferred to a new Department of Education, and HEW was renamed the Department of Health and Human Services.[4]

Now, with a proposed 2010 budget of $879 billion, the HHS is the federal government's principal agency concerned with health protection and promotion and provision of health and other human services to vulnerable populations. In addition to administering the Medicare and Medicaid programs, HHS includes over 300 separate programs[7] that encompass activities such as

- Medical and social science research
- Infectious disease prevention and control
- Assurance of food and drug safety
- Child support enforcement
- Improvement of maternal and child health
- Management of preschool education services (e.g., Head Start)
- Prevention of child abuse and domestic violence
- Substance abuse prevention and treatment
- Provision of services for older Americans

HHS carries out these activities through the following Public Health Service Operating Divisions[8]:

1. *National Institutes of Health (NIH)*: Established first as a laboratory in 1887, the NIH is the world's premier medical research organization and includes 18 separate health institutes, the National Center for Complementary and Alternative Medicine, and the National Library of Medicine. The NIH supports over 30,000 research projects on a variety of medical conditions and has a proposed budget for 2010 of almost $31 billion.

2. *Food and Drug Administration (FDA)*: This agency is responsible for ensuring the safety of foods and cosmetics and the safety and efficacy of pharmaceuticals, biologic products, and medical devices. Its 2010 proposed budget is $2.10 billion.

3. *Centers for Disease Control and Prevention (CDC)*: Established in 1946, the CDC is the primary federal agency responsible for protecting the American public's health through monitoring disease trends, investigations of outbreaks and health and injury risks, and implementation of illness and injury control and prevention measures. The proposed 2010 budget is over $10 billion.

4. The *Indian Health Service (IHS)*: The IHS operates 38 hospitals, 56 health centers, 4 school health centers, and 44 health stations. Through transfers of IHS services operating authority, tribes also administer an additional 13 hospitals, 160 health centers, 3 school health centers, 76 health stations, and 160 Alaska village clinics.

Services are provided to nearly 1.5 million Native Americans and Alaska Natives of 557 federally recognized tribes in Alaska and the 48 contiguous states. The agency has a proposed 2010 budget of almost $5 billion.

6. *Health Resources and Service Administration (HRSA)*: Established in 1982 to provide a coordinated agency for multiple programs serving low-income, uninsured, and medically underserved populations, the HRSA provides funds for comprehensive primary and preventive services through community-based health centers at more than 3,000 sites nationwide. The HRSA also supports maternal and child health programs, programs to increase diversity and numbers of health care professionals in underserved communities, and supportive services for HIV/AIDS victims through the Ryan White Care Act. It has a proposed 2010 budget of over $7 billion.

7. *Substance Abuse and Mental Health Services Administration (SAMHSA)*: The agency works to improve the quality and availability of substance abuse prevention, addiction treatment, and mental health services through federal block grants. It provides a variety of grants to states and local communities to address emerging substance abuse trends, mental health service needs, and HIV/AIDS. The agency's proposed 2010 budget is over $3.5 billion.

8. *Agency for Healthcare Research and Quality (AHRQ)*: Established in 1989, AHRQ is the lead agency for supporting research to improve the quality of health care, reduce its cost, improve patient safety, address medical errors, and broaden access to essential services. Major activities include sponsoring and conducting research to provide evidence-based information on health care outcomes with respect to quality, costs, uses, and access. The agency's proposed budget for 2010 is $372 million.

9. *Centers for Medicare & Medical Services (CMS), formerly the Health Care Financing Administration*: This agency administers the Medicare and Medicaid programs. Medicare insures over 40 million Americans, and Medicaid, a joint federal–state program, provides coverage for over 34 million low-income persons, including 18 million children, and nursing home coverage for low-income older adults. It administers the Children's Health Insurance Program, which covers several million children. The agency has a proposed 2010 budget of $759 billion.

10. *Administration for Children and Families (ACF)*: The ACF administers over 60 programs to promote the economic and social well-being of families, children, individuals, and communities. It administers the state/federal welfare program, Temporary Assistance to Needy Families, national child support enforcement, and the Head Start program. It provides funds to assist low-income families with childcare expenses, supports state programs in adoption assistance and foster care, and funds child abuse and domestic violence prevention programs. The agency has a proposed 2010 budget of almost $16 billion.

11. *Administration on Aging (AoA)*: The federal focal point and advocate agency for older persons, the AoA administers federal programs under the Older Americans Act. Programs assist older persons to remain in their own homes by supporting services such as Meals on Wheels. The AoA collaborates with its nationwide network of regional offices and state and area agencies to plan, coordinate, and develop community-level systems of services that meet needs of older individuals and their caregivers. The agency has a proposed 2010 budget of almost $1.5 billion.

HHS has been the federal government's largest grant-making agency under the aegis of its various operating divisions. In recent years, however, there has been a sharp reduction in research grants with most research and demonstration activities funded through solicited contracts. Unsolicited research proposals are unlikely to be funded.[9]

Veterans Health Administration System

Initiated to provide care for Civil War veterans who were disabled or indigent, or both, the Veterans Health Administration (VHA) system has grown to become one of the world's largest health care delivery systems. It currently operates 153 medical centers, 909 ambulatory care and community outpatient clinics, 135 nursing homes, 47 residential rehabilitation treatment programs, 232 Veterans Centers, and comprehensive home care programs.

The VHA maintains major affiliations with 105 medical schools throughout the United States. VHA medical centers also affiliate with 54 dental schools and 1,140 other schools throughout the United States. Each year approximately 90,000 health professionals receive training at VHA medical centers. The VHA also conducts a broad array of world-class clinical and health services research projects.[10]

Because the VHA system usually has a lifelong relationship with its patients, it has instant access to each patient's complete medical record, an advantage over private medicine that reduces both costs and medical errors. The long-term relationship also allows more preventive care, higher quality services, and greater patient satisfaction along with monetary savings.[7]

Through the Department of Defense Military Health Service program, the federal government provides both direct health care services and support for health care services for U.S. military personnel and their dependents, military retirees and their families, and others entitled to Department of Defense benefits.[11] The Military Health Service operates 98 hospitals and 480 clinics worldwide, primarily servicing active-duty members of the armed forces. Most civilian care is purchased through managed care support contracts implemented under a program entitled TRICARE. Since the "war on terror," the Department of Defense has not revealed the actual costs of providing medical care to military personnel.

The states also play an important role in funding health care and health-related services. Each year, state and local governments contribute about 14% of total health care expenditures, including hospital, nursing home, or home health care services.[12] Many states also operate and fund state mental institutions, support medical schools, maintain health departments that provide direct preventive and primary care services, and support maternal and child health improvement, infectious disease monitoring and control, and other community health initiatives.

City and county government jurisdictions support and deliver general and specialty health care services through their health departments and over 100 hospitals and health systems that together comprise the infrastructure of many of America's metropolitan health systems. The outpatient and inpatient services of government-supported public hospitals provide a community's "safety net" for individuals who are uninsured or underinsured and cannot access care elsewhere. Public hospitals also are often the sites of major teaching programs for an area's medical school. Frequently, they provide services that are financially unattractive to other community hospitals, such as burn care, psychiatric medicine, trauma care, and crisis response units for both natural and human-made disasters.[13] In addition, city and county health departments may provide direct patient care services in clinics or health centers, referrals for care, and other services to meet community needs of their high-risk, medically underserved populations.

Decline in Influence of the Public Health Service

Over the years, public health agencies' many accomplishments have contributed to significant improvements in both the health and life expectancy of Americans. Using population-based strategies for disease and injury prevention, public health has contributed to substantial declines in morbidity and mortality and dramatically changed the profiles of disease, injury, and death in the United States. Yet, despite the centrality of public health in providing the basis for the health of Americans, its funding has always competed with other more highly valued demands in the health sector.[14]

The several reorganizations of federal public health agencies occurred in response to continuing criticism of their failure to improve access to at least minimally adequate medical care to underserved populations. Pressures emanated from public health professionals, medical care organizations, political leaders, and the popular media. Criticism of the Public Health Service rose in the 1960s when its efforts to provide incentives to state and local agencies for more innovative approaches to meeting these demands through categorical and project grants were judged ineffective. Thus when several new and important programs for improving access to medical care were passed, agencies other than the Public Health Service were assigned to administer them. Medicare was assigned to the Social Security Administration, Medicaid to the Social and Rehabilitation Services, Head Start and Neighborhood Health Centers to the Office of Economic Opportunity, and the Model Cities Program to Housing and Urban Development.

The end of President Johnson's term of office in 1968 marked the end of an era in federal health policy. The Nixon administration took issue with the three-tiered system of the federal Public Health Service, state health agencies, and local public health departments that was expected to combine local initiative with policy input and national standards for advancing access to adequate health services. In its place, a new policy, dubbed the "New Federalism," was initiated. It involved the progressive removal of federal responsibilities for a uniform, cooperative national public health system and the transfer of those responsibilities to the states. It was the beginning, at the federal level, of the Republican strategy of converting federal program support to block grants, reducing the available funds and sending them to the states for administration. Though the effort was relatively unsuccessful during the Nixon–Ford administrations, it was revived in a new and more extreme form when Ronald Reagan was elected in 1980, and public health became the primary target. The decline of the government's organized system of public health services accelerated thereafter.[14]

Responsibilities of the Public Health Sector

In 1990, the HHS published *Public Health Service: Healthy People 2000: National Health Promotion and Disease Prevention Objectives*.[15] Objective 8.14 of that document calls for 90% of the population to be served by local health departments that would effectively carry out the three core functions of public health: assessment, policy development, and quality assurance. These core health department functions are intended to put into operation, within the resource and other constraints extant in each jurisdiction, the following generally accepted health department performance responsibilities[16]:

- Focus on primary prevention: prevention that occurs before the onset of disease. Identify environmental and behavioral factors that are associated with conditions, such as lung cancer or heart disease, and educate the community or protect it from the risk.
- Protect communities from infectious and toxic agents through monitoring or surveillance. Gather information to control and, where possible, prevent health problems resulting from these agents.
- Respond to unanticipated natural and human-generated disasters. Assess health risks posed by contaminated food, water, or air and inform the public and the medical care system of sources of danger and strategies for appropriate response.

- Promote the well-being of the public through programs to notify and educate people about risks and protective measures that can be applied at the community level.
- Target hard-to-reach populations with clinical services. Create outreach programs to link high-risk populations to medical services to address individual health care need, as well as to interrupt the spread of disease in the community.
- Maintain diagnostic laboratory services to support diverse monitoring and prevention programs. These facilities permit identification of emerging threats from infectious agents and environmental toxins. Set and enforce standards for new and existing laboratory tests conducted in medical settings.
- Collect information on health outcomes to ensure the quality of services provided through hospitals, nursing homes, and other medical care delivery institutions. Develop referral systems for high-risk perinatal care, and plan regionalization of trauma and cardiac care. Provide aggregate information on health outcomes to inform consumers and medical care professionals about the quality of care being delivered at the community level.

It is through the fulfillment of these public health responsibilities that public health departments protect the public against preventable communicable diseases and exposure to toxic environmental pollutants, harmful products, and poor quality health care. These public health practices promote healthy personal behaviors and risk factor reduction communitywide by identifying and modifying patterns of chronic disease and injury, informing and educating consumers and health care providers about appropriate use of medical services, developing and maintaining comprehensive health programs in schools and child daycare facilities, providing occupational safety and health programs, and ensuring that HIV and sexually transmitted disease prevention programs are implemented. These public health practices are the bedrock foundations of modern population-focused health care.

However, in 1993, a team of investigators from the School of Public Health at the University of Illinois at Chicago, working with representatives of the CDC, surveyed 208 health departments responding from a random national sample stratified by jurisdiction and population base. The findings suggested that less than 40% of the U.S. population was served by a health department that effectively addressed the core functions of public health.[17]

Clearly, with resource support for public health continuing to decline, it was not surprising that the United States had failed to meet 85% of the challenging goals of *Healthy People 2000*. In the 10-year plan *Healthy People 2010* released by the HHS in January 2000,[18] the government admitted that the nation had met only 15% of the 319 targets established in 1990. In some areas, particularly obesity, marijuana use, exercise, asthma, and diabetes, the health of Americans either stayed the same or worsened.

Nevertheless, *Healthy People 2010*, the third set of 10-year targets for health improvement in the United States, set two broad goals, supported by 467 objectives that are grouped into 28 focus areas: to increase the years and quality of health life and to eliminate health disparities.[19]

These goals and their supporting objectives were developed for the new decade by Healthy People Consortium, a group of 650 national, professional, and voluntary organizations; the business community; and state and local public health agencies. Meetings began in 1996 and the first completed draft of 7,704 pages was posted on the Internet for public comment in September 1998. More than 11,000 comments were received electronically. The recommendations from a series of public hearings and other web-based communications were processed before publication of the final report.

Given the dismal failure to meet the multitudinous objectives of the two previous Healthy People reports, one might question whether the extraordinary effort expended in these highly labor-intensive, expensive, and time-consuming exercises might be better spent in more pragmatic and potentially productive efforts.

In 1985 the Institute of Medicine, concerned about the need to protect the nation's health through an effective, organized public health sector, convened a special committee to study the status of public health in the United States. The committee reported its findings and recommendations in 1988. The report concluded, "Public health is a vital function that is in trouble."[3] In an analysis of the contributing factors, it noted the following:

> We have observed disorganization, weak and unstable leadership, a lessening of professional and expert competence in leadership positions, hostility to public health concepts and approaches, outdated statutes, inadequate

financial support for public health activities and public health education, gaps in the data gathering and analysis that are essential to public health functions of assessment and surveillance, and lack of effective links between the public and private sectors for the accomplishment of public health objectives.[3]

The report linked the poor public image of public health and the public's lack of knowledge and appreciation for the mission and content of public health to those deficiencies and to a number of other problems. Particular emphasis was placed on the failure of sound policy development in public health as evidenced by ambiguous responses to the AIDS epidemic, the "politicalization" of public health agencies, and the lack of clear delineation of the responsibilities between levels of government.

In 1988, the committee made organizational, educational, financial, and political recommendations for addressing these complex and interrelated problems. Unfortunately, its strategies depended on continuing strong financial support for existing public health agencies and stronger, more sharply focused leadership that could build increasingly productive links with the private and voluntary health care sectors. In the ensuing years the required leadership has not been evident, financial support for public health continued to decline, and public and political support for government public health agencies has further diminished.

Although the goals and objectives of the Healthy People reports are commendable and their definition gives the agencies involved a sense of accomplishment, it should be obvious that the lack of an effective, well-organized public health sector makes the effort an exercise in futility. Clearly, one of the weaknesses of public health is the propensity of its advocates to set arbitrary and usually unobtainable goals rather than face the more difficult challenge of developing the leadership, expertise, and political strength to achieve them.

The September 11 terrorist attacks and the subsequent anthrax incidents revealed public health as ill prepared to provide an effective health defense system. A report of the CDC called for a system of "public health armaments," including a "skilled professional workforce, robust information and data systems and strong health departments and laboratories."[20]

There are serious concerns that the inadequate numbers of skilled public health professionals, such as public health nurses, epidemiologists, laboratory workers, and others, result from public-sector budget restraints and competition with other sectors of the economy. As a result, many public health employees are inadequately prepared through education and training for the jobs they perform.[21]

Relationships of Public Health and Private Medicine

Public health and clinical medicine have complementary roles in caring for the health of the American people. Although they often address the same health problems, their attention is directed at different stages of disease or injury. Clinical medicine devotes its most intensive resources to restoring health or palliating disease in relatively small numbers of individuals. Rather than targeting individuals, public health uses strategies that promote health or prevent disease in large populations.[16]

Unfortunately, the implementation of these roles has been hindered by the often contentious relationship that has existed for decades between public health leadership and the private medical practitioners and their advocacy organization, the American Medical Association. Although the need for curative medicine administered to individuals and the need for preventive measures for the protection of populations have coexisted in all societies since ancient civilizations, and physicians who specialize in public health or preventive medicine have received the same basic medical education as those who pursue the diagnostic and therapeutic specialties, the ideologic differences between them have produced vigorous debate. J. G. Freymann suggests that the reasons for the persistent discord include the identification of public health by practicing physicians with governmental bureaucracy, the linking of the care of low-income populations with welfare, the focus of physicians toward individuals, and the custom of being paid only for active therapy.[22]

Historically, the different emphasis of the two types of practitioners, that is, the population-based orientation of public health professionals and the individual-centered focus of private health providers, has often divided rather than enhanced public and private health services. The scientific advances in medicine since World War II only served to emphasize the value differences between practitioners with a population perspective and those focused on individual patients. Physicians educated and socialized to a biologic model of medicine that emphasized sophisticated technologies and practice specialization have shown little appreciation for the simpler organizational measures that reach out to the underserved and provide access to basic health monitoring, preventive care, and primary medical care.

Understandably, individual physicians with the daily responsibility and heavy workloads of caring for waiting rooms full of patients consider that their personal professional efforts fully meet their community or societal obligations. For the most part, they are more than willing to delegate to the public health professionals concerns for the overall health of society and for those who do not have access to their offices.

Opposition to Public Health Services

The history of public health is marked by struggles over the limits of its mandate. Just as the opponents of the several attempts to initiate programs of national health insurance described public health prejudicially as "socialized medicine," special interest groups are threatened by the perception that public health programs represent subversive social change that constitutes an unjustified intrusion of government into the lives of private individuals.

The medical profession had both philosophical and economic reasons for voicing their concerns. P. Starr observed: "Doctors fought against public treatment of the sick, requirements for reporting cases of tuberculosis and venereal disease, and attempts by public health authorities to establish health centers to coordinate preventive and curative medicine."[23] Extending the boundaries of public health was regarded as the opening wedge for usurping the physicians' role. Physicians opposed disease screening and primary care services, even though they were targeted at the populations with the lowest incomes, because physicians feared that public health agencies were expanding into activities they believed were rightfully their own.

There are, of course, many examples of the synergistic effects of private and public medicine. The immunization of children and adults against a variety of preventable diseases is a good example of how public health and private medical practitioners have worked together effectively. A number of screening programs, such as those for tuberculosis, lung cancer, breast cancer, and hypertension, have linked the personal services of private medicine and the population-oriented practice of public health in productive liaisons.

Resource Priorities Favor Curative Medicine

The allocation of U.S. health resources provides persuasive evidence of the public's and the professionals' fascination with dramatic high-technology diagnostic and therapeutic medicine. Despite the centrality of public health in providing basic health programs and the effectiveness and economic advantages inherent in prevention as compared with cure, there is little funding for research or practice for public health promotion or disease prevention. This is in contrast to the large sums that finance the research in and practice of remedial medical care. Less than 1% of the almost $1 trillion spent annually for health care was allocated to government public health activities. In fact, between 1981 and 1993 there were public health imperatives on the emergence of AIDS, the reemergence of tuberculosis and measles, and the escalating problems of substance abuse, violence, and teenage pregnancy. Total U.S. health expenditures increased by more than 210%, whereas funding of public health services as a proportion of the health care budget declined by 25%.[16]

In 2006, the July/August issue of the prestigious journal *Health Affairs* was devoted to the "State of Public Health." In a prologue to one of its published articles, the editors wrote the following:

> Public health has always been the neglected stepchild of the U.S. health care system. It subsisted on whatever funding was left over after flashier parts of the system took their cut, and it took on tasks, such as being the provider of last resort for the uninsured and indigent, that no one else was willing to perform. In Washington, D.C., legions of lobbyists in expensive suits frequented congressional hearings on Medicare policies toward physicians or pharmaceutical manufacturers, while public health hearings attracted much smaller crowds and less sartorial splendor. After September 11, 2001, and the anthrax attacks around the country, some $5 billion made its way from Washington to state public health and emergency preparedness systems. Many thought that between this and the reemergence of infectious disease threats, public health's neglect was a thing of the past. .... the new money, rather than sparking a long-needed new vision for public health, reinforced the status quo. It flowed according to existing geographic lines, reflecting political, not functional boundaries. States that sought to use the grants in imaginative ways were, ironically, criticized by their local public health agencies.[24]

Clearly, public health has neither public nor political recognition as an essential and all-encompassing effort to prevent illness and promote health. Rather, it has a continuing identity problem when people persist in thinking of public health as publicly funded medical care for the poor. And, in the decades since it lost its positive image and financial support, it has failed to develop the leadership to change that image.[25]

One might expect with the many schools of public health in the United States that offer masters and doctorate degrees in public health there would be a continuing source of future public health officials, leaders with skills in leadership, management, and negotiation. Unfortunately, most such graduates gravitate toward academia, forsaking public health administration for teaching and research. Thus a substantial portion of politically appointed public health officials continue to lack formal public health training.[25]

Absence of Preventive Care

The current medical care system fails to provide effective preventive services even when they are demonstrated to be the most cost-effective procedures available. In contrast, new treatment technologies are implemented despite serious reservations about their efficacy and cost effectiveness. Thus, with all its groundbreaking research, talented workforce, and technologic know-how, the United States has the distinction of having the world's most costly and inefficient health care system.[26]

The major investment in hospital neonatal intensive care units during the last two decades is a dramatic example of the lack of balance in the health care system. Though numerous studies have demonstrated that funds expended for prenatal care of high-risk mothers reduce the number of premature births requiring exceedingly expensive and often futile efforts to save those infants, public subsidies for prenatal care have declined, while more and more costly technology has been introduced to increase the ability to salvage increasingly small and premature infants. For example, the federal Special Supplemental Food Program for Women, Infants, and Children (WIC), which provides supplemental food, nutrition, and health education to low-income pregnant and postpartum women, infants, and children, is estimated, after careful studies, to reduce low-birth-weight rates by 25% and very-low-birth-weight rates by 45%, with Medicaid savings of $4.21 for every WIC dollar spent on pregnant women. In contrast, neonatal intensive care, although effective in reducing neonatal mortality, is the least cost-effective strategy.[27]

Challenge of an Aging America

These questionable funding priorities will be of critical importance in determining the effectiveness of health care in the future. Just as the preference for support of costly neonatal intensive care units rather than public health programs of prenatal care contributes to the unacceptably high rates of infant mortality in the United States, the focus on remedial medicine for America's growing older population denies the reality of the changing distribution of illness and disability. The major causes of disease and disability among the increasing numbers of older adults are chronic conditions that result from multiple causes that are not usually amenable to technologic remedies.

Thus, the traditional medical model of clinical practice poorly serves many older individuals. Normal function and the absence of disease characterize the medical definition of health. Health is assumed by the absence of symptoms and signs that the human body is in some state of biologic equilibrium. The accepted medical focus on the biomedical aspects of care with an emphasis on specific diseases and organ systems assumes that nonphysiologic malfunction, such as the inability, common to advancing age, to carry out the roles and tasks of one's usual social milieu, is not part of health.

Most older patients need a multidisciplinary approach that focuses on overall needs. Attention needs to be paid to managing chronic conditions—helping patients adjust to their limitations and maintain daily functioning within the context of their living arrangement and family and social support.

Unfortunately, the medical and public health systems that evolved from the remarkable scientific achievements since World War I placed their emphases on tests, drugs, surgeries, vaccines, and environmental controls. Personal behaviors were considered either outside the scope of medical care system or immutable to change. Medical insurance companies that rarely reimbursed providers for preventive services in general, and behavioral counseling in particular, reinforced these assumptions.

Hospital-Sponsored Public Health Activities

The market forces that have changed the structure and character of hospitals during the last two decades have stimulated them to initiate or expand a variety of outpatient public health–type services, including community-based and worksite health promotion. This integration of outpatient medical and public health services is a direct response to the pressure placed on hospitals by third-party payers to reduce inpatient admissions and lengths of stay. In many cases acute-care hospitals have added services such as community education on healthy behaviors and risk factor reduction, comprehensive school health programs, preventive health programs in child daycare facilities, community education on chronic disease prevention and management, and occupational safety and health programs. These services have both helped their service populations and provided new sources of much-needed revenue.

Public Health Services of Voluntary Agencies

The role of volunteerism, voluntary agencies, and institutions as adjunct resources and services to those provided by governments and for-profit practices and corporations is a major theme in the evolution of health care in the United States. Private, not-for-profit institutions have been the prevailing mechanism through which health care services in the United States, and with the government, share the responsibilities for meeting the needs of communities and special populations.[28]

In addition to this country's not-for-profit hospitals, there are a host of voluntary agencies providing nursing home care, hospice care, home care, medical and vocational rehabilitation, and other personal health care services. A variety of voluntary agencies serves the special needs of persons with specific medical conditions such as AIDS, asthma, diabetes, cerebral palsy, hemophilia, and muscular dystrophy. Similar organizations support research on conditions such as cancer, heart disease, and respiratory disorders. Others, such as the American Red Cross, Planned Parenthood, and Meals on Wheels, focus on providing specific services. Of significant importance is the fact that voluntary agencies provide many valued and effective services that are not prominent in the private medical care sector. Programs directed at health education, disease prevention, disease detection, health maintenance, rehabilitation, and terminal care have been the province of voluntary not-for-profit agencies.

The influence of large nonprofit foundations, such as the Robert Wood Johnson Foundation and the Pew Charitable Trusts, on the advancement of health care from a population perspective has been considerable. By providing funds on a competitive basis to stimulate research and innovative program demonstrations, these and other foundations have caused hospitals and other agencies, in collaboration with universities and colleges, to engage in progressive health service delivery improvements that may otherwise have been years in development. Particularly commendable is the selection of health care objectives to which those funds are dedicated.

The synergistic effect of government, private, and voluntary efforts has been both a bane and a blessing in the provision of health care in the United States. Our system's disorderly evolution as a combination of the charitable efforts of voluntary and religious organizations, multilevel government responses to community needs, and traditional U.S. free enterprise ensured the development of a complex network that is both inordinately successful in a technologic sense and plagued by costly inefficiencies, duplications, and inequities in access and quality. Nevertheless, this pluralistic approach, rather than the types of national health care systems common to other industrial societies, appears, at least for the near future, to be the only health care system strategy acceptable to the U.S. people.

Changing Roles of Government in Public Health

For decades, all three levels of government in the United States—federal, state, and local—have played significant roles in financing and regulating public health services and in maintaining agencies and systems that directly or indirectly deliver health care. The federal government surveys the population's health status and health needs, sets policies and standards, passes laws and regulations, supports biomedical and health services research, provides technical assistance and resources to state and local health agencies, helps finance health care through support of programs (such as Medicare and Medicaid), and delivers personal health care services through networks of facilities (such as those maintained by the

Department of Defense, the Department of Veterans Affairs, and the Administration on Native Americans).[3]

Public health services in the states are financed, regulated, and delivered through a variety of organizational structures. In some states, public health activities are divided among several entities, including health departments, social service, welfare, aging, and Medicaid. Many states now combine health and social service agencies to create large human service operations that join health and social services for children and youth, for people with developmental disabilities and other special populations, and for special problems such as alcoholism and drug abuse. Most states contribute heavily to the financing of Medicaid, medical education, and public health programs, and to mental health through both community mental health programs and state-operated psychiatric hospitals. States also are involved in regulation through health codes, licensing of facilities and personnel, and supervision of the insurance industry.

Considerable variation exists in the organizational structure of agencies engaged in public health activities in local governmental jurisdictions. Counties, districts, and other local governments may have health, social service, environmental, and mental health departments. They can be independent or divisions of state agencies. Many cities and counties support and operate local health departments, public hospitals, clinics, and various other services. They also establish and enforce local health codes.

Rather than supporting and acknowledging the many benefits of this multilevel configuration of public health agencies that ensure safe food and water, control of epidemic diseases, and programs of care for infants, children, and adults with special needs and, in general, improve the length and quality of life in the United States, the nation has moved toward increased privatization, withdrawn support from public health activities, and allowed the system to fall into disarray. Before the terrorist attacks of September 11, the United States appeared to have lost sight of both the goals and benefits of public health.[3]

Public Health in an Era of Privatization and Managed Care

The market forces affecting hospitals, nursing homes, voluntary agencies, and other institutions of the U.S. health care system are also significantly changing the financial base and functions of public health departments. The declines in public health funding and the trend toward privatization of those public health services that could be delivered more efficiently outside of local bureaucracies have left many local health departments with minimal staff focused on only the most essential public health services.

Outsourcing to private providers who often had more comprehensive clinical capacity was one of several organizational strategies to contain or reduce costs while maintaining or improving the quality and efficiency of necessary public health services. Survey findings indicate that those health departments merely became smaller while cost savings were rare.[29]

With few exceptions, most health departments have maintained their responsibilities for assessing and ensuring the delivery of necessary public health services even though privatized. As might be expected, however, the reduction of health department–delivered services has made it difficult for many departments to maintain a strong community presence. In addition, negotiating with private service entities for the delivery and monitoring of public health services requires staff not customarily employed by public health departments. Health departments now find it necessary to replace service personnel with management staff knowledgeable in contracting and other business-related skills.

Future Role of Government in Promoting the Public's Health

Because the provision of medical treatment and related services accounts for approximately 99% of aggregate national health expenditures, national debate and efforts to reform the U.S. health care system have focused on financing, insurance, and cost containment of treatment. Various estimates suggest that only about 10% of all early deaths can be prevented by medical treatment. In contrast, population-wide public health approaches have the potential to help prevent some 70% of early deaths in the United States through measures targeted to the social, environmental, and behavioral factors that contribute to those deaths.[30] Clearly, the value placed on high-technology clinical medicine by individuals, societies, and governments within the United States overwhelms consideration of the more cost-effective, but less dramatic, prevention strategies of public health. Unlike pictures of heart transplant recipients, for example, images of the hundreds of thousands of children who have *not* been crippled and have *not* died due to poliomyelitis since successful immunization programs have been instituted cannot be shown by the media.

State and local governments struggling with large deficits have considered it necessary to sacrifice the personnel and services of their public health agencies. The shortsightedness of those decisions, however, is becoming increasingly evident. Although there is continued general unhappiness with tax-supported programs and institutions, pressures for improving state and local public health services are developing outside the community of public health advocates. Leaders in business and industry connect a healthy and educated public to economic growth and development. They, and others concerned about the demise of such programs as school health, maternal and child health, water quality, community nutrition, environmental control, and disease control, are rethinking the wisdom of some of these governmental cost-cutting priorities. Private foundations and voluntary agencies are not able to fill the gaps left by the withdrawal of governmental support.

The people and political leaders of the United States are going through an unprecedented reassessment of guiding principles, core values, and funding priorities. Experience with the democratic process suggests that the voting public will respond to legislative and policy errors only after the untoward effects of faulty decisions touch on them personally and significantly.

After the terrorist assaults of September 11, 2001, lawmakers, prodded by the public, recognized that a broader public health infrastructure is required to protect Americans against chemical or biologic attacks. A number of public health defense programs have been proposed that include stockpiling vaccines against anthrax, plague, and smallpox. Of particular importance is the need to prepare health care professionals, hospitals, and other agencies to respond quickly and effectively to threats or actual disasters.[31]

To that end, the largest reorganization of the federal government since World War II took place in April 2003 with the establishment of the Department of Homeland Security (DHS). Twenty-two new and existing governmental agencies that include 180,000 employees were assembled under the leadership of a newly appointed Secretary of Homeland Security. The DHS has the broad mission of strengthening this country's borders, improving intelligence analyses, infrastructure protection, and comprehensive response and recovery operations should there be a terrorist attack with chemical or biologic weapons.

To help fulfill its mandate, the new department has a host of interlocking governmental relationships with other federal and state units. Among those are liaisons with the NIH, the CDC, the U.S. Public Health Service, the FDA, and other units of the HHS. Most importantly, state and local health departments are expected to play principal roles in prevention of spread or in response and recovery operations should any attacks occur.[32]

That federal strategy, or lack thereof, has resulted in a series of completely disjointed public health activities and practices across 3,000 local agencies operating under 50 state health departments. Without nationally consistent plans and systems, public health responses will, as occurred during the New Orleans experience, find it difficult to coordinate with other responders such as law enforcement and transportation during disasters that cross political jurisdictions. Clearly, there is no forethought of how national health protection activities should be organized and delivered. The objective of protecting the nation against catastrophic events may have been gravely weakened by leaving local and state health departments to make up their own goals and priorities. After 6 years of preparedness funding, states and localities still lack the guidance and capabilities to develop effective preparedness capabilities.[33]

Health Care Reform and the Public Health–Medicine Relationship

Important factors in the current effort to reform the U.S. health care system give promise of a more functional future partnership between public health and private practice medicine. The drive by those paying for health care (employers, organized consumers, and governments) for improved measures of health status and system performance and the emphasis on integrated health systems that focus on health improvement for defined populations are creating pressures within the system for more cost-effective, community-driven strategies for combining the resources of public health and networks of personal care services.

Table 10-1 reveals the magnitude of preventable mortality. In total, these causes of death account for 40% of all deaths occurring each year. Tobacco, diet, and sedentary lifestyles are major contributors to early mortality, yet effective medical interventions are not integrated into the practice standards that drive the delivery of medical services.

Table 10-1 Deaths from Preventable Causes, USA, Year 2000

Cause	Number	Percent of Total U.S. Deaths
Smoking	435,000	18.1
Poor diet/physical inactivity	400,000	16.6
Alcohol consumption	85,000	3.5
Motor vehicle crashes	43,000	1.8
Firearms	29,000	1.2
Sexual behaviors	20,000	.08
Illicit use of drugs	17,000	.07
Total preventable deaths	1,029,000	41.35

Source: Author-created from data presented by A. H. Mokdad et al. in "Actual Causes of Death in the United States, 2000," *Journal of the American Medical Association* 291, no. 10, March 2004.

Both public health leaders and clinicians would need sufficient motivation to improve preventive service rates. Strong external incentives or requirements as well as perceptive internal vision are required to change organizational commitment. A new emphasis on prevention would have to be seen as important for organizational promotion or financial viability before providers would be galvanized to action. The history of public and preventive health services in the United States illustrates, time and again, that the prestige priorities—and profits—in its remedial medicine system lie with diagnosing and treating already existing disease.

Although complementary, if not integrated, systems of public health and medical care services seem like ideal models with which to address the nation's health care problems of the 21st century, the long-standing differences in philosophy, values, and assumptions between public health and organized medicine are likely to make cooperative ventures difficult. Nevertheless, in the current era of previously inconceivable health system changes, a new and functional relationship driven by mutual needs could develop between these two sectors.

Nevertheless, the fear of bioterrorism and concern for addressing potential epidemics such as evidenced by the response to the potential of a "swine flu" outbreak may provide persuasive motivation to create a system of highly effective public health departments after years of neglect. With proper systems development, operational practices, and personnel who meet high standards of professional preparation and performance, public health departments could achieve high levels of both health promotion and health protection. The next few years will be crucial to the future of public health. If governments at every level do not seize the moment to create vibrant and effective systems of public health practice, the opportunity will be lost.

References

1. Shindell S, Salloway JL, Oberembt CM, et al. *A Coursebook in Health Care Delivery*. New York: Appleton & Lange; 1976:304–308.
2. Rosen G. *A History of Public Health*. New York: MD Publications; 1957.
3. Committee for the Study of the Future of Public Health, Division of Health Care Services, Institute of Medicine. *The Future of Public Health*. Washington, DC: National Academy Press; 1988.
4. U.S. Department of Health and Human Services. *The Public Health Service: Some Historical Notes*. Washington, DC: Public Health Service; 1988.
5. Raffel MW, Raffel NK. *The U.S. Health System: Origins and Functions*, 4th ed. Albany, NY: Delmar Publishers; 1994.
6. Yerby AS. Public medical care for the needy in the United States. In: DeGroot LJ, Ed. *Medical Care, Social and Organizational Aspects*. Springfield, IL: Charles C. Thomas; 1966:382–401.
7. Asch SM, McGlynn EA, Hogan MM, et al. Comparison of quality of care for patients in the Veterans Health Administration and patients in a national sample. *Ann Intern Med*. 2004;141:938–945.
8. U.S. Department of Health and Human Services. Available from http://www.hhs.gov/asrt/ob/docbudget/2010budgetInBrief.pdf. Accessed September 16, 2009.
9. National Institutes of Health. Available from http://www.grants.nih.gov. Accessed September 16, 2009.
10. Department of Veterans Affairs. Veterans Health Administration. Available from http://www.va.gov/About_va. Accessed September 16, 2009.
11. Office of the Assistant Secretary of Defense (Health Affairs) and the TRICARE Management Activity. Available from http://www.tricare.mil. Accessed September 16, 2009.
12. Monaco, RM, Phelps, JH. Effects of health spending on the U.S. economy. Available from www.cms.hhs.gov/statistics. Accessed December 12, 2009.
13. National Association of Public Hospitals and Health Systems. America's essential community providers. Available from http://www.naph.org/welcome.html. Accessed September 18, 2009.
14. Shonick W. *Government and Health Services: Government's Role in the Development of U.S. Health Services, 1930–1980*. New York: Oxford University Press; 1995.
15. U.S. Department of Health and Human Services. Healthy people 2000 educational and community-based programs progress review. Available from http://odphp.osophs.dhhs.gov/pubs/HP2000/PROGRVW/Education/Educational.htm. Accessed April 3, 2010.

16. U.S. Department of Health and Human Services. *Public Health Service, for a Healthy Nation: Returns on Investment in Public Health.* Washington, DC: U.S. Government Printing Office; 1994.

17. Tornock BJ, Handler A, Hall W, et al. Local health department effectiveness in addressing the core functions of public health. *Public Health Rep.* 1994;109:653–658.

18. Healthy People 2010, National Health Promotion and Disease Prevention Objectives, U.S. Department of Health and Human Services, Office of Disease Prevention and Health Promotion. Available from http://www.healthypeople.gov. Accessed April 3, 2010.

19. O'Hara, JL. AHRQ reports outline quality shortfalls, healthcare disparities. AAIM Alliance for Academic Internal Medicine, March 8, 2009. Available from http://www.im.org. Accessed December 2, 2009.

20. America's health priorities revisited after September 11. Health Affairs Web Exclusives. Posting Date: November 12, 2001. Available from http://www.healthaffairs.org/cgi/reprint/hlthaff.w1.96r1. Accessed May 20, 2010.

21. Gebbie KM, Turnock BJ. The public health workforce, 2006: new challenges. *Health Affairs.* 2006;25:923–933.

22. Freymann JG. Medicine's great schism: prevention vs. cure: an historical interpretation. *Med Care.* 1975;13:525–536.

23. Starr P. Transformation in defeat: the changing objectives of national health insurance. *Am J Public Health.* 1982;72:78–88.

24. Public Health Partnerships and Reform. Editorial. *Health Affairs.* 2006;25:016.

25. Robert Wood Johnson Foundation Institute for the Future. Public health services: a challenging future. In: *Health and Health Care 2010. The Forecast, The Challenge.* San Francisco, CA: Jossey-Bass; 2003:156–157.

26. Vogt TM, Hollis JF, Lichtenstein E, et al. The medical care system: the need for a new paradigm. *HMO Pract.* 1999;12:5–12.

27. Avruch S, Cackley AP. Savings achieved by giving WIC benefits to women prenatally. *Public Health Rep.* 1995;110:27–34.

28. Seay JD, Vladeck BC. *Mission Matters: A Report on the Future of Voluntary Health Care Institutions.* New York: United Hospital Fund of New York; 1988.

29. Research and Writing Supported by the Annie E. Casey Foundation. *Privatization and Public Health: A Study of Initiatives and Early Lessons Learned.* Washington, DC: Public Health Foundation; 1997.

30. Nolte E, Mckee CM. Measuring the health of nations: updating an earlier analysis. *Health Affairs.* 2008;27:58–71.

31. McGinley, L. Suddenly, Public Health Administration Is Seen as Top Priority. *Wall Street Journal.* September 28, 2002:A16.

32. U.S. Department of Homeland Security. Brief documentary history of the department of homeland security. Available from http://www.dhs.gov/xlibrary/assets/brief_documentary_history_of_dhs_2001_2008.pdf. Accessed March 24, 2010.

33. Salinsky E, Gursky EA. The case for transforming governmental public health. *Health Affairs.* 2006;25:1017–1028.

CHAPTER 11

Research: How Health Care Advances

This chapter explains the focus of different types of research and how each type contributes to the overall advances in health and medicine. Health services research, a newer field that addresses the workings of the health care system rather than specific problems of disease or disability, is described. The offices and goals of its major funding source, the federal Agency for Healthcare Research and Quality, are listed. Finally, research into the quality of medical care, the problems being addressed, and the research challenges of the future are discussed.

The last half of the 20th century saw a remarkable growth of scientifically rigorous research in medicine, dentistry, nursing, and the other health professions. The change from depending on the clinical impressions of individual physicians and other health care practitioners to relying on the statistical probability of accurate findings from carefully controlled studies is one of the most important advances in scientific medicine. No longer is the literature of the health professions filled with subjective anecdotal reports of the progress of treatment in one or more individual cases. Now readers of peer-reviewed professional journals can monitor the progress of basic science or clinical or technologic discoveries with confidence, knowing that published findings are, with few exceptions, based on research studies that have been rigorously designed and conducted to yield statistically credible results.

In contrast, the ever-growing volumes of reports of medical developments that appear in the popular media are often premature and, depending on the source, may be cause for skepticism. The imprudent publication of inadequately or unproven therapies, the sensationalizing of minor scientific advances, and the promotion of fraudulent devices and treatments create unrealistic expectations that often result in disappointments, mistreatment, and costly deceptions.

From both professional and public perspectives, the continuing research yield of new technologies and clinical advances creates ongoing challenges of evaluation, interpretation, and potential applications.

Focus of Different Types of Research

Figure 11-1 illustrates the focus of the different types of health care research. There are clear distinctions among researchers in terms of methods and the nature of their subsequent findings. Although the kinds of information derived from each type of research may be different, each knowledge gain is an essential step in the never-ending quest to create a more efficient and effective health care system.[1]

Types of Research

Research studies conducted by those in the professional disciplines fall into several categories. Basic science research is the work of biochemists, physiologists, biologists, pharmacologists, and others concerned with sciences that are fundamental to understanding the growth, development, structure, and

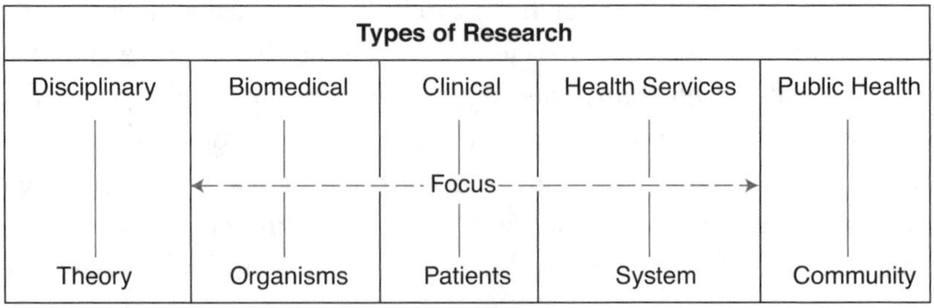

Types of Research				
Disciplinary	Biomedical	Clinical	Health Services	Public Health
		←————— Focus —————→		
Theory	Organisms	Patients	System	Community

FIGURE 11-1 Variations in Research Focus.
Source: Aday et al.: *Evaluating the Healthcare System: Effectiveness, Efficiency and Equity,* 3rd edition (2004). Reprinted with permission.

function of the human body and its responses to external stimuli. Much of basic science research is at the cellular level and takes place in highly sophisticated laboratories. Other basic research may involve animal or human studies. Whatever its nature, however, basic science research is the essential antecedent of advances in clinical medicine.

Clinical research focuses primarily on the various steps in the process of medical care—the early detection, diagnosis, and treatment of disease or injury; the maintenance of optimal physical, mental, and social functioning; the limitation and rehabilitation of disability; and the palliative care of those who are irreversibly ill. Individuals in all the clinical specialties of medicine, nursing, allied health, and related health professions conduct clinical research, often in collaboration with those in the basic sciences. Much of clinical research is experimental, involving carefully controlled clinical trials of diagnostic or therapeutic procedures, new drugs, or technologic developments.

Clinical trials test a new treatment or drug against a prevailing standard of care. If no standard drug exists or if it is too easily identified, a control group receives a placebo or mock drug to minimize subject bias. To reduce bias further, random selection is used to decide which volunteer patients are in the experimental and control groups. In a double-blind study neither the researchers nor the patients know who is receiving the test drug or treatment until the study is completed and an identifying code revealed.

Research studies have a number of safeguards to protect the safety and rights of volunteer subjects. Studies funded by governmental agencies or foundations are subject to scrutiny by a peer-review committee that judges the scientific merit of the research design and the potential value of the findings. Then a hospital-based or institutional review board checks for ethical considerations and patient protections. Finally, volunteer subjects must receive and sign an informed consent form that spells out in clear detail the potential risks or side effects and the expected benefits of their participation. Volunteers must weigh any potential risks against the likelihood that, by participating in research, they will receive state-of-the-art care and close health monitoring and will contribute to the advancement of science.

Epidemiology

Epidemiology, or population research, is concerned with the distribution and determinants of health, diseases, and injuries in human populations.

Much of that research is observational; it is the collection of information about natural phenomena, the characteristics and behaviors of people, aspects of their location or environment, and their exposure to certain circumstances or events.

Observational studies may be descriptive or analytical. Descriptive studies use patient records, interview surveys, various databases, and other information sources to identify those factors and conditions that determine the distribution of health and disease among specific populations. They provide the details or characteristics of diseases or biologic phenomena and the prevalence or magnitude of their occurrence. Descriptive studies are relatively fast and inexpensive and often raise questions or suggest hypotheses to be tested. They usually are followed by analytic studies, which try to explain biologic phenomena by seeking statistical associations between factors that may contribute to a subsequent occurrence and the occurrence itself.

Some analytic studies attempt, under naturally occurring circumstances, to observe the differences between two or more populations with different characteristics or behaviors. For instance, data about smokers and nonsmokers may be collected to determine the relative risk of a related outcome such as lung cancer, or a cohort study may follow a population over time, as in the case of a Framingham, Massachusetts, study. For years, epidemiologists have been studying a cooperating population of Framingham to determine associations between such variables as diet, weight, exercise, and other behaviors and characteristics related to heart disease and other outcomes. These observational studies are valuable in explaining patterns of disease or disease processes and providing information about the association of specific activities or agents with health or disease effects.

Experimental Epidemiology

Observational studies are usually followed by experimental studies. In experimental studies, the investigator actively intervenes by manipulating one variable to see what happens with the other. Although they are the best test of cause and effect, such studies are technically difficult to carry out and often raise ethical issues. Control populations are used to ensure that other nonexperimental variables are not affecting the outcome. Like clinical trials, such studies may raise ethical issues when experiments involve the use of a clinical procedure that may expose the subjects to significant or unknown risk. Ethical questions also are raised when experimental studies require the withholding of some potentially beneficial drug or procedure from individuals in the control group to prove decisively the effectiveness of the drug or procedure.

Other Applications of Epidemiologic Methods

Because the population perspective of epidemiology usually requires the study and analysis of data obtained from or about large-scale population samples, the discipline has developed principles and methods that can be applied to the study of a wide range of problems in several fields. Thus, the concepts and quantitative methods of epidemiology have been used not only to add to the understanding of the etiology of health and disease but also to plan, administer, and evaluate health services; to forecast the health needs of population groups; to assess the adequacy of the supply of health personnel; and, most recently, to determine the outcomes of specific treatment modalities in a variety of clinical settings.

Advances in statistical theory and the epidemiology of medical care make it possible to analyze and interpret performance data obtained from the large Medicare and other insurance databases. Many of the findings of inexplicable geographic variations in the amount and cost of hospital treatments and in the use of a variety of health care services resulted from analysis of Medicare claims data and other large health insurance databases.

Health Services Research

Until the last two decades most research addressed the need to broaden understanding of health and disease, to find new and more effective means of diagnosis and treatment, and, in effect, to improve the quality and length of life. For the two decades after World War II, supply-side subsidy programs dominated federal health care policy. Like other subsidy programs, Medicare and Medicaid were politically crafted solutions rather than research-based strategies. Nevertheless, those major health care subsidy programs were the driving forces behind the rise of health services research. The continuous collection of cost and utilization data from these programs revealed serious deficiencies in the capability of the health care system to deliver efficiently and effectively the knowledge and skills already at hand. In addition, evidence was growing that the large variations in the kinds and amounts of care delivered for the same conditions represented unacceptable volumes of inappropriate or questionable care and too much indecision or confusion among clinicians about the best courses of treatment. Health services research was born of the need to improve the efficiency and effectiveness of the health care system and to determine which of the health care treatment options for each condition produces the best outcomes.

Agency for Healthcare Research and Quality

Ever since John Wennberg documented large differences in the use of medical and surgical procedures among physicians in small geographic areas in the late 1980s, a number of similar studies brought the value of increasingly more costly health care into serious question. Wennberg noted that the rate of surgeries correlated with the numbers of surgeons and the number of hospital beds, rather than with differences among patients.

He found that per-capita expenditures for hospitalization in Boston were consistently double those in nearby New Haven.[2–4] Widely varying physician practice patterns provided little direction as to the most appropriate use of even the most common clinical procedures. In addition, adequate outcome measures for specific intervention modalities generally were lacking.

The problem did not escape the attention of the 101st Congress. The development of new knowledge through research has long been held as an appropriate and essential role of the federal government, as evidenced by the establishment and proactive role of the National Institutes of Health. When it became clear that the indecision about the most appropriate and effective ways to diagnose and treat specific medical, dental, and other conditions was contributing to unacceptably large variations in the cost, quality, and outcomes of health care, federal legislation was passed to support the development of clinical guidelines. The Agency for Health Care Policy and Research (AHCPR) was established in 1989 as the successor to the National Center for Health Services Research and Health Care Technology. It was one of eight agencies of the Public Health Service within the Department of Health and Human Services.

AHCPR was responsible for updating and promoting the development and review of clinically relevant guidelines to assist health care practitioners in the prevention, diagnosis, treatment, and management of clinical conditions. The authorizing legislation directed that panels of qualified experts be convened by AHCPR or by public and not-for-profit private organizations. These panels were to review the literature that contained the findings of numerous studies of clinical conditions and, after considering the scientific evidence, to recommend clinical guidelines to assist practitioner and patient decisions about appropriate care for specific clinical conditions.[5]

The agency's priority activities included funding two types of research projects: patient outcome research teams and literature synthesis projects or meta-analyses. Both the patient outcome research teams and the smaller literature synthesis projects identified and analyzed patient outcomes associated with alternative practice patterns and recommended changes where appropriate. During its decade-long existence, AHCPR supported studies that resulted in a prodigious array of publications focused on patient care and clinical decision making, technology assessment, the quality and costs of care, and treatment outcomes. Although no longer directly involved in producing clinical practice guidelines, the agency assists private-sector groups by supplying them with the scientific evidence they need to develop their own guidelines.

Some changes occurred in the mandate of AHCPR since its 1989 inception. The agency narrowly escaped the loss of funding and possible elimination in 1996 after incurring the wrath of national organizations of surgeons. In keeping with its original mission, AHCPR issued clinical guidelines. One such guideline discouraged surgery as a treatment for back pain on the grounds that it provided no better outcomes than more conservative treatments. Organizations of angry surgeons led a lobbying effort that convinced key members of Congress that the agency was exceeding its authority and establishing standards of clinical practice without considering the expertise and opinions of the medical specialists involved.[6]

The dispute was resolved when AHCPR agreed to function as a "science partner" with public and private organizations by simply assisting in developing knowledge that could be used to improve clinical practice. The agency would no longer produce clinical guidelines but would focus instead on funding research on medical interventions and analyzing the data that would underlie the development of clinical guidelines. The guidelines themselves would be generated by medical specialty and other organizations.

Subsequently, a Healthcare Research and Quality Act of 1999 was passed, which retitled the AHCPR to the Agency for Healthcare Research and Quality (AHRQ) and changed the title of the administrator to director. The mission of AHRQ is to (1) improve the outcomes and quality of health care services, (2) reduce its costs, (3) address patient safety, and (4) broaden effective services through establishment of a broad base of scientific research that promotes improvements in clinical and health systems practices, including prevention of disease.[7]

A top priority of AHRQ is getting its sponsored research results and new health information into the hands of consumers. In addition to a number of consumer-oriented publications, the agency provides information to the public via the Internet. Its website, www.ahrq.gov, offers a great deal of health care information.

Health Services Research and Health Policy

Health services research combines the perspectives and methods of epidemiology, sociology, economics, and clinical medicine. Although the basic concepts of epidemiology and biostatistics apply, process and outcome measures that reflect the behavioral and economic variables associated with questions of therapeutic effectiveness and cost benefit are also used. The ability of health services research to address issues of therapeutic effectiveness and cost benefit during this period of fiscal exigency contributed to the field's substantial growth and current value.

The contributions of health services research to health policy within recent years are impressive. Major examples include the Wennberg studies of small area variation in medical utilization, the prospective payment system based on diagnosis-related groups,[8,9] research on inappropriate medical procedures,[10] resource-based relative value scale research,[11–13] and the background research that supported the concepts of health maintenance organizations and managed care.

The RAND Health Insurance Experiment,[14,15] one of the largest and longest running health services research projects ever undertaken, began in 1971 and contributed vast amounts of information on the effects of cost sharing on the provision and outcomes of health services. Participating families were assigned to one of four different fee-for-service plans or to a prepaid group practice. As might have been expected, individuals in the various plans differed significantly in their rate of use, with little measurable effect on health outcomes. The Health Insurance Experiment was followed by two large research studies: the Health Services Utilization Study and the Medical Outcomes Study. The findings of both gave impetus to the federal support of outcomes research.[16] Determining the outcomes and effectiveness of different health care interventions aids clinical decision making, reduces costs, and benefits patients.

Quality Improvement

Until the last few years, health care's impressive accomplishments made it difficult for health care researchers, policymakers, and organizational leaders to acknowledge publicly that poor quality health care is a major problem within the dynamic and productive biomedical enterprise in the United States. In 1990, after 2 years of study, hearings, and site visits, the Institute of Medicine issued a report that cited widespread overuse of expensive invasive technology, underuse of inexpensive "caring" services, and implementation of error-prone procedures that harmed patients and wasted money.[17,18]

Although these conclusions from so prestigious a body were devastating in their significance to health care reformers, they were hardly news to health service researchers. For decades, practitioners assumed that quality, like beauty, was in the eye of the beholder and therefore was unmeasurable except in cases of obvious violation of generally accepted standards. The medical and other health care professions had promoted the image of health care as a blend of almost impenetrable, science-based disciplines, leaving the providers of care as the only ones capable of understanding the processes taking place. Thus only physicians could judge the work of other physicians. Such peer review–based assessment has always been difficult for reviewers and limited in effectiveness. Peer review recognizes that only part of medical care is based on factual knowledge. A substantial component of medical decision making is based on clinical judgment. Clinical judgment means combining consideration of the potential risks and benefits of each physician's internal list of alternatives in making diagnostic and treatment decisions with his or her medical intuition regarding the likelihood of success based on the condition of each patient. Under these complex and often inexplicable circumstances, physicians are repelled by the notion of either judging or being judged by their colleagues.

That is why, until recently, quality assurance, whether in hospitals or by regulatory agencies, was focused on identifying only exceptionally poor care. This practice, popularly known as the bad apple theory, was based on the presumption that the best way to ensure quality was to identify the bad apples and remove or rehabilitate them. Thus, during the 1970s and 1980s, quality assurance interventions only followed detection of undesirable occurrences. For example, flagrant violations of professional standards had to be in evidence before professional review organizations required physicians to begin quality improvement plans. Of course, physicians were guaranteed due process to dispute the evidence.

Focusing on isolated violations required a great deal of review time to uncover a single case that called for remedial action. In addition, it was an unpleasant duty for reviewers to assign blame to a colleague who might soon be on a committee reviewing their records. Most importantly, such an inspection of quality represented a method that implicitly defined quality as the absence of mishap. Clinician dislike of quality assurance activities during the 1970s and 1980s was well founded. The processes were offensive and had little constructive impact.

Specifying and striving for excellent care are very recent quality assurance phenomena in the health care arena. Just as the automobile and other industries were late giving up supervision as a control mechanism and introducing "quality circles" or teamwork, so too were hospitals and other health care organizations that had long focused on peer-review committees, incident reports, and other negative quality monitoring activities.

Health services researchers had known for decades that health care quality was measurable and that excellent, as well as poor, care could be identified and quantified. In 1966, Avedis Donabedian[19] characterized the concept of health care as divided into the components of structure, process, and outcomes and the research paradigm of their assumed linkages, all of which have guided quality of care investigators to this day.

Donabedian suggested that the number, kinds, and skills of the providers, as well as the adequacy of their physical resources and the manner in which they perform appropriate procedures, should, in the aggregate, influence the quality of the subsequent outcomes. Although today the construct may seem like a simple statement of the obvious, at the time attention to structural criteria was the major, if not the only, quality assurance activity in favor. It was generally assumed that properly trained professionals, given adequate resources in properly equipped facilities, performed at acceptable standards of quality. For example, for many years the then Joint Commission on Accreditation of Hospitals made judgments about the quality of hospitals on the basis of structural standards, such as physical facilities and equipment, ratios of professional staff to patients, and the qualifications of various personnel. Later, it added process components to its structural standards. Aspects of process are the diagnostic, treatment, and patient management decisions and their appropriateness in relationship to current knowledge and practice. These quality assessments were directed to process components and did not attempt to determine what happened to the patients as the result of the medical decisions and interventions. Only recently did The Joint Commission include outcomes in its accreditation assessments.

Early landmark quality-of-care studies used implicit and explicit normative or judgmental standards. Implicit standards rely on the internalized judgments of the expert individuals involved in the quality assessment. Explicit standards are those developed and agreed on in advance of the assessment. Explicit standards minimize the variation and bias that invariably result when judgments are internalized. More current studies judge the appropriateness of hospital admissions and various procedures and, in general, associate specific structural characteristics of the health care system with practice or process variations.

There is another method for assessing the quality of health care practices that is based on empirical standards. Derived from distributions, averages, ranges, and other measures of data variability, information collected from a number of similar health service providers is compared to identify practices that deviate from the norms. A current popular use of empirical standards is in the patient severity-adjusted hospital performance data collected by health departments and community-based employer and insurer groups to measure and compare both process activities and outcomes. These performance "report cards" are becoming increasingly valuable to the purchasers of care who need an objective method to guide their choices among managed care organizations, health care systems, and group practices. The empirical measures of quality include such variables as

- Timeliness of ambulation
- Compliance with basic nursing care standards
- Average length of stay
- Number of home care referrals
- Number of rehabilitation referrals
- Timeliness of consultation completion
- Timeliness of orders and results

- Patient wait times by department or area
- Infection rates
- Decubitus rates
- Medication errors
- Patient complaints
- Readmissions within 30 days
- Neonatal and maternal mortalities
- Perioperative mortalities

Normative and empirical standards are both used in studying the quality of health care in the United States. For example, empirical analyses are performed to test or modify normative recommendations. Empirical or actual experience data are collected to confirm performance and outcome improvements after the imposition of clinical guidelines derived from studies using normative standards.

Medical Errors

In November 1999 the Institute of Medicine again issued a report on the quality of medical care.[20] Focused on medical errors, the report described mistakes occurring during the course of hospital care as one of the nation's leading causes of death and disability. Citing two major studies estimating that medical errors kill some 44,000 to 98,000 people in U.S. hospitals each year, the Institute of Medicine report was a stunning indictment of the current systems of hospital care. The report contained a series of recommendations for improving patient safety in the admittedly high-risk environments of modern hospitals. Among the recommendations was a proposal for establishing a center for patient safety within the AHRQ. The proposed center would establish national safety goals, track progress in improving safety, and invest in research to learn more about preventing mistakes.[20] Congress responded by designating part of the increase in the budget for the AHRQ for that purpose.

Evidence-Based Medicine

Evidence-based medicine is defined as "the systematic application of the best available evidence to the evaluation of options and decisions in clinical practice, management and policy-making."[21] Although that statement may appear to be a description of the way physicians and other health care providers have practiced since the inception of scientific medicine, it reflects a spreading concern that quite the opposite is true. The wide range of variability in clinical practice, the complexity of diagnostic testing and medical decision making, and the difficulty that physicians have in keeping up with the overwhelming volumes of scientific literature suggest that a significant percentage of clinical management decisions are not supported by reliable evidence of effectiveness.

Although it is generally assumed that physicians are reasonably confident that the treatments they give are beneficial, the reality is that medical practice is fraught with uncertainty. In addition, the ethical basis for clinical decision making allows physicians to exercise their preferences for certain medical theories or practices that may or may not have been evaluated to link treatment to benefits.[22]

Proponents of evidence-based medicine propose that if all health services are intended to improve the health status and quality of life of the recipients, then the acid test is whether services, programs, and policies improve health beyond what could be achieved with the same resources by different means or by doing nothing at all. Evidence is the key to accountability. The decisions made by health care providers, administrators, policymakers, patients, and the public need to be based on appropriate, balanced, and high-quality evidence.[22]

The evidence-based approach to assessing the acceptability of research findings considers the evidence from randomized clinical trials involving large numbers of participants to be the most valid. Evidence-based medicine advocates dismiss outcomes research that uses large data files created from claim records, hospital discharges, Medicare, or other sources because the subjects are not randomized. "Outcomes research using claims data is an excellent way of finding out what doctors are doing, but it's a terrible way to find out what doctors should be doing," stated Thomas C. Chalmers, MD, of Harvard School of Public Health, Boston.[23]

In general, most of the investigations reported in the peer-reviewed medical literature have been preliminary tests of innovations and served science rather than providing guidance to practitioners in clinical practice. Only a small portion of those efforts survive testing well enough to justify routine clinical application.[24]

The situation is changing rapidly, however. Articles on evidence-based medicine are appearing with increasing frequency in the medical literature.[24] Cost-control pressures that encourage efforts to ensure that therapies have documented patient benefit, growing interest in the quality of patient care, and increasing sophistication on the part of patients concerning the care that they receive have stimulated acceptance of the concepts of evidence-based medical practice.[24]

Outcomes Research

Given the huge investment in U.S. health care and the inequitable distribution of its services, do the end effects on the health and well-being of patients and populations justify the costs? Insurance companies, state and federal governments, employers, and consumers are looking to outcomes research for information that will help them make better decisions about what kinds of health care should be reimbursed, for whom, and when.

Because outcomes research evaluates results of health care processes in the real world of physicians' offices, hospitals, clinics, and homes, it contrasts with traditional randomized controlled studies that test the effects of treatments in controlled environments. In addition, the research in usual service settings, or "effectiveness research," differs from controlled clinical trials, or "efficacy research," in the nature of the outcomes measured. Traditionally, studies measured health status, or outcomes, with physiologic measurements—laboratory tests, complication rates, recovery, or survival. To capture health status more adequately, outcomes research measures a patient's functional status and well-being. Satisfaction with care also must complement traditional measures.

Functional status includes three components that assess patients' abilities to function in their own environment:

1. Physical functioning
2. Role functioning—the extent to which health interferes with usual daily activities, such as work or school
3. Social functioning—whether health affects normal social activities, such as visiting friends or participating in group activities

Personal well-being measures describe patients' sense of physical and mental well-being—their mental health or general mood, their personal view of their general health, and their general sense about the quality of their lives. Patient satisfaction measures the patients' views about the services received, including access, convenience, communication, financial coverage, and technical quality.

Outcomes research also uses meta-analyses, a technique to summarize comparable findings from multiple studies. More importantly, however, outcomes research goes beyond determining what works in ideal circumstances to assessing which treatments for specific clinical problems work best in different circumstances. Appropriateness studies are conducted to determine circumstances in which a procedure should and should not be performed. Even though a procedure is proven effective, it is not appropriate for every patient in all circumstances. The frequency of inappropriate clinical interventions is one of the major quality-of-care problems in the system. Research is also underway to develop the tools to identify patient preferences when treatment options are available. Although most discussions about appropriateness stress the cost savings that could be achieved by reducing unnecessary care and overuse of services, it is important to remember that outcomes research may be just as likely to uncover underuse of appropriate services.

It is important to recognize that the ultimate value of outcomes research can be measured only by its ability to incorporate the results of its efforts into the health care process. To be effective, the findings of outcomes research must first reach and then change the behaviors of providers, patients, health care institutions, and payers. The endpoint of outcomes research, the clinical practice guidelines intended to assist practitioners and patients in choosing appropriate health care for specific conditions, must be disseminated in acceptable and motivational ways. With the health care industry in a state of rapid and generally unpredictable change, the need to make appropriate investments in outcomes research has become increasingly apparent. The conclusion is now inescapable that the United States cannot continue to spend over $2 trillion each year on health care without learning much more than is now known about what that investment is buying.[25,26]

Patient Satisfaction

Patient satisfaction has become an important component of the quality of care. Although the subjective ratings of health care received by patients may be based on markedly different criteria from those considered important by care providers, they capture aspects of care and personal preferences that contribute significantly to perceived quality. It has become increasingly important in the competitive market climate of health care that the providers' characteristics, organization, and system attributes important to the consumers be identified and monitored. In addition to caregivers' technical and interpersonal skills, such patient concerns as waiting times for appointments, emergency responses, helpfulness and communication of staff, and the facility's appearance contribute to patient evaluations of health services delivery programs and subsequent satisfaction with the quality of care received.

A number of instruments have been devised to measure patient satisfaction with health care, and most managed care plans, hospitals, and other health service facilities and agencies have adopted one or more to assess patient satisfaction regularly. Some, such as the Patient Satisfaction Questionnaire developed at Southern Illinois University School of Medicine, are short, self-administered survey forms. Others, such as the popular patient satisfaction instruments of the Picker Institute of Boston, Massachusetts, may be used as self-administered questionnaires mailed to patients after a health care experience or completed by interviewers during telephone surveys.[27] Whether by mail, direct contact, or telephone interview, questioning patients after a recent health care experience is an effective way to both identify outstanding service personnel and uncover fundamental problems in the quality of care as defined by patients. It not only serves the purpose of providing humane and effective care, but it is also good marketing to do everything possible to increase patient satisfaction, maintain patient loyalty, and enhance patient referrals.

Research Ethics

In the six decades since World War II, the federal government has invested heavily in biomedical research. The ensuing public–private partnership in health has produced some of the finest medical research in the world. The growth of medical knowledge is unparalleled, and the United States can take well-deserved pride in its research accomplishments.

However, many, if not most, of the sophisticated new technologies address the need to ameliorate the problems of the patients who already have the condition or disease under treatment. Both the priorities and the profits intrinsic to the U.S. health care system focus on remedial rather than preventive strategies. Only in the case of frightening epidemics, such as that of polio in the 1940s, AIDS in the 1990s, and H1N1 influenza in 2009, have there been the requisite moral imperatives to fund adequately abundant research efforts that address public health problems. Clearly, much of the recent funding for medical research has failed to fulfill the generally held belief that the products of taxpayer-supported research should benefit not only the practice of medicine, but also the community at large.

Conflicts of Interest in Research

The increasing amount of research funding emanating from pharmaceutical and medical device companies is of serious concern. Pharmaceutical companies that pay researchers to design and interpret drug trials have been accused of misrepresenting the results or suppressing unfavorable findings. The conflicts that arise in the testing of new drugs and instruments and publishing the results deepen as increasing numbers of studies are shifted from academic institutions to commercial research firms.[28]

For example, in May 2009 the Attorney General of New Jersey issued subpoenas to five major medical device makers for failing to disclose financial conflicts of interest among physicians researching their products. It was learned that physicians who were testing and recommending the use of certain medical devices were being compensated with stock in the companies making those devices.[29]

To compound the problem further, the funding of the U.S. Food and Drug Administration (FDA), which regulates about a fourth of the U.S. economy, has been shifted from the government to the same pharmaceutical companies it is supposed to monitor with damaging effect. Political and pharmaceutical pressures have caused the FDA to stray from its science-based public health mandate. For example, the FDA has been sharply criticized for its alleged failure to monitor adequately the risks of widely advertised and commonly used drugs for the treatment of arthritis.[30] The FDA's handling of clinical trial data collected by pharmaceutical manufacturers to establish the efficacy and safety of their products is a major problem. Although the information collected is necessary for FDA approval of a product, once the product is approved, the FDA does not provide the public with a full report of the drug's safety and efficacy. The withheld information falls into the definition of "trade secrets," and the

FDA has taken the position that research data are entitled to protection as proprietary information. That explains the number of recent examples of FDA-approved drugs later discovered to have major safety risks.[31] Clearly, the FDA has to reconsider its position that clinical trial data fall into the classification of "trade secrets."

The most egregious violation of professional ethics is found in the growing body of evidence that physicians at some of the most prestigious of U.S. medical schools have been attaching their names and reputations to scientific publications ghostwritten by employees of pharmaceutical companies. The publications are intended, of course, to boost sales of the pharmaceutical product.[32]

The National Institutes of Health, which funds much of the nation's medical research, suggests that the universities involved, rather than the government, should address the problem. Because the universities find it difficult to censure prestigious medical faculty, the problem remains unaddressed.[32]

Future Challenges

Most U.S. health care research has been directed toward improving the health care system's ability to diagnose and treat injury, disease, and disability among those who seek care. Now, largely because of the influences of managed care, research studies are increasingly focused on identifying and improving the health status of populations. Research priorities are shifting from an individual patient perspective to a population orientation and toward continuous scrutiny of the efficiency and effectiveness of the care delivered.

Basic science research will continue to contribute to the diagnostic and therapeutic efficacy of health care by adding to the knowledge about the human body and its functions. In small but critically important increments, basic science research will unlock many of the secrets of aging, cell growth regulation, mental degradation, and other mysteries of immunology, genetics, microbiology, and neuroendocrinology. The propensity of medicine to use newly obtained knowledge to alter certain physiologic processes, as in the several forms of gene manipulation, will produce new ethical, legal, and clinical issues that then will require further research and adjudication.

Massive databases of gene and protein sequences and structure/function information have made possible a new worldwide research effort called bioinformatics. Bioinformatics research probes those large computer databases to learn more about life's processes in health and disease and to find new or better drugs. It is considered the future of biotechnology.

Of particular interest is research in genomics, the study of genetic material in the chromosomes of specific organisms. The sequencing of the human genome will reshape biology and medicine and lead to significant improvements in the diagnosis of disease and individual responses to drugs.[33]

Similarly, certain advances in clinical medicine and the other health disciplines will result in new and particularly disturbing moral dilemmas. Medical achievements, such as those that permit the maintenance of life in otherwise terminal and unresponsive individuals or the transplantation of organs in short supply that require choosing among recipient candidates when those denied will surely die, generate extremely complex ethical, economic, religious, personal, and professional issues. Thus, much of the basic and clinical research that solves yesterday's problems relating to individual patient care will create new problems to be addressed in the never-ending cycle of discovery, application, and evaluation.

Medical researchers and clinicians are becoming increasingly concerned that health care in the United States is entering a "postantibiotic" era in which bacterial infections will be unaffected by even the most powerful of available antibiotics. Evidence is accumulating that a growing number of microbes, including strains of staphylococcus and streptococcus bacteria, are becoming resistant to common antimicrobials.[34] Staphylococcus bacteria are a major cause of hospital infections. According to the Centers for Disease Control and Prevention, these infections are responsible for about 13% of the 2 million infections that occur in U.S. hospitals each year. Overall, infections result in the deaths of up to 99,000 hospital patients each year.[35]

Although infectious disease epidemiologists and clinical specialists warned for decades that misuse and overuse of antibiotics would result in a host of deadly drug-resistant pathogens, neither physicians nor patients took the warnings seriously, with a widespread belief that the development of new antimicrobial drugs would keep medicine a step ahead of bacterial resistance. Limited development of new antibiotic drugs has failed to keep step with antibiotic resistance; however, scientists now see promising alternatives in bacterial genetics to address antibiotic resistance.[35]

While researchers address the problems of treating lethal infections, hospitals strive to prevent them. Because bacteria can be transmitted on blankets, clothing, walls, medical equipment, and by hand, hospitals are implementing rigorous infection control and surveillance policies and new education programs for both providers and patients.

Health services research, on the other hand, will continue to focus on the performance of the health care system as the basis for proposing or evaluating health policy alternatives. It is interdisciplinary, value-laden research concerned with the effectiveness or benefits of care, the efficiency or resource cost of care, and the equity or fairness of the distribution of care. Documenting the influence of financial incentives that affect both patient and provider, understanding the important relationships of socioeconomic status to health and health care, determining the effects of the training and experience of the health care team and the ability of the members to work together, and understanding how these many influences interact are basic to improving the quality of care. Reducing the monumental quandaries in medicine and health care about what works well in what situations is the challenge of health services research and the key to a more effective, efficient, and equitable health care system.

Public health research is a related research arena that deserves to receive higher priority and significantly increased political support. If health care is ever to develop a true population perspective rather than an individual patient perspective and reap the health and economic benefits of preventive rather than curative medicine, then epidemiology and public health research must be charged with finding ways to better understand and resolve the huge differences in health, health behaviors, health care, and health system effectiveness among communities and the population groups within them. Epidemiology, the core discipline of public health research, can assess the health problems and the provision of health care for the total population rather than just those who are in contact with health services. Surveillance and monitoring of health conditions and assessing the effect of health care measures on the entire population are important factors in formulating health policy, organizing health services, and allocating limited resources.[36] The strategy for identifying and dealing with real or suspected biologic attacks on citizens of the United States will depend heavily on the ability of epidemiologists to identify the common source of such outbreaks, the patterns of transmission, and the outcomes of preventive and remedial efforts.

As health care adds to its traditional focus on theories, disease, and individual patient care, the performance of the health care system and the health status of populations, public health, and health services research assume increasing relevance and importance. No matter how well the health care system performs for some of the people, it cannot be fully satisfactory until it can provide a basic level of care for all.

References

1. Aday LA, Lairson DR, Balkrishnan R, et al. *Evaluating the Medical Care System: Effectiveness, Efficiency, and Equity.* Ann Arbor, MI: Health Administration Press; 1993.
2. Wennberg JE, Freeman JL, Culp WJ, et al. Are hospital services rationed in New Haven or over-utilized in Boston? *Lancet.* 1987;1:1185–1189.
3. Wennberg JE. Which rate is right? *N Engl J Med.* 1986;314:310–311.
4. Wennberg JE, Freeman JL, Shelton RM, et al. Hospital use and mortality among Medicare beneficiaries in Boston and New Haven. *N Engl J Med.* 1989;321:1168–1173.
5. Agency for Health Care Policy and Research, U.S. Department of Health and Human Services. *AHCPR Program Note.* Rockville, MD: Public Health Service; 1990.
6. Stephenson J. Revitalized AHCPR pursues research on quality. *JAMA.* 1997;278:1557.
7. U.S. Department of Health and Human Services, Rockville, MD. Agency for Healthcare Research and Quality: Reauthorization Fact Sheet. Available from http://www.ahrq.gov/About/ahrqfact.htm. Accessed April 16, 2010.
8. Mills R, Fetter RB, Riedel DC, et al. AUTOGRP: an interactive computer system for the analysis of health care data. *Med Care.* 1976;14:603–615.
9. Berki SE. DRGs, incentives, hospitals and physicians. *Health Affairs.* 1985;4:70–76.
10. Chassin MR, Kosecoff J, Park RE, et al. Does inappropriate use explain geographic variations in the use of health care services? A study of three procedures. *JAMA.* 1987;258:2533–2537.
11. Hsiao WC, Stason WB. Toward developing a relative value scale for medical and surgical services. *Health Care Finan Rev.* 1979;1:23–28.
12. Hsiao WC, Braun P, Yntema D, et al. Results and policy implications of the resource-based relative value study. *N Engl J Med.* 1988;319:881–888.
13. Hsiao WC, Braun P, Yntema D, et al. *A National Study of Resource-Based Relative Value Scale for Physician Services: Final Report to the Health Care Financing Administration.* Boston, MA: Harvard School of Public Health; 1988.

14. Newhouse JP. A design for a health insurance experiment. *Inquiry.* 1974; 11:5–27.
15. Newhouse JP, Keeler EB, Phelps CE, et al. The findings of the RAND health insurance experiment—a response to Welch et al. *Med Care.* 1987;25: 157–179.
16. Newhouse JP. Controlled experimentation as research policy. In: Ginzberg E, Ed. *Health Services Research: Key to Health Policy.* Cambridge, MA: Harvard University Press; 1991:162–194.
17. Lohr KN. *The Institute of Medicine. Medicare: A Strategy for Quality Assurance,* Vol. 1. Washington, DC: National Academy Press; 1990.
18. Surver JD. Striving for quality in health care: an inquiry into policy and practice. *Health Care Management Review.* 1992:17(4);95–96.
19. Donabedian A. Evaluating the quality of medical care. *Milbank Mem Fund Q.* 1966;44:166–206.
20. Kohn LT, Corrigan JM, Donaldson MS, et al. *To Err Is Human: Building a Safer Health System.* Washington, DC: Institute of Medicine; 1999.
21. Watanabe M. A call for action from the National Forum on Health. *Can Med Assoc J.* 1997;156:999–1000. Available from http://www.cmaj.ca/cgi/reprint/156/7/999. Accessed September 13, 2009.
22. Marwick C. Federal agency focuses on outcomes research. *JAMA.* 1993; 270:164–165.
23. Castiel LD. The urge for evidence based knowledge. *J Epidemiol Commun Health.* 2003;57:482.
24. Hooker RC. The rise and rise of evidence-based medicine. *Lancet.* 1997; 349:1329–1330.
25. Reinhardt UE, Hussey PS, Anderson GF, et al. U.S. health care spending in an international context. *Health Affairs.* 2004;23:10–25.
26. Kerr D, Scott M. British lessons on health care reform. *N Engl J Med.* Available from www.nejm.org. Accessed September 12, 2009.
27. Gerteis M, Edgman-Levitan S, Daley J. *Through the Patient's Eyes: Understanding and Promoting Patient-Centered Care.* San Francisco: Jossey-Bass; 1993.
28. Walker EP. HHS report slams FDA's conflict of interest oversight. Available from http://www.medpagetoday.com/PublicHealthPolicy/ClinicalTrials/12407. Accessed September 13, 2009.
29. New Jersey Office of the Attorney General. Landmark settlement reached with medical device maker synthes. Available from http://www.nj.gov/oag/newsreleases09/pr20090505a.html. Accessed September 13, 2009.
30. FDA hearing to determine arthritis drugs' safety. Available from http://today.uchc.edu/headlines/2005/feb05/arthritisdrug.html. Accessed September 12, 2009.
31. Bodenheimer T. Uneasy alliance-clinical investigators and the pharmaceutical industry. *N Engl J Med.* 2000;342:1516–1544.

32. Singer N. Ghosts in the journals. *New York Times.* August 18, 2009:B1–B2. Available from http://www.nytimes.com/2009/08/19/health/research/19ethics. html?_r=1&scp=1&sq=Ghosts%20in%20the%20Journals&st=cse. Accessed September 12, 2009.

33. Human Genome Project information: medicine and the new genetics. Available from http://www.ornl.gov/sci/techresources/Human_Genome/ medicine/medicine.shtml. Accessed September 13, 2009.

34. Bren L. Battle of the bugs: fighting antibiotic resistance. Available from http://www.rxlist.com/script/main/art.asp?articlekey=85705. Accessed September 13, 2009.

35. Klevens MR, Edwards JR, Richards C, et al. Estimating health-care associated infections and deaths in U.S. hospitals, 2002. Available from http://www. cdc.gov/ncidod/dhqp/pdf/hicpac/infections_deaths.pdf. Accessed September 13, 2009.

36. Ibrahim MA. *Epidemiology and Health Policy.* Gaithersburg, MD: Aspen; 1985.

12

Future of
Health Care

This concluding chapter provides some forecasts about the future of various components of the U.S. health care system. It outlines the changes that have occurred and projects those trends into the future. The chapter also sketches the corporate growth in health care and the impact of technologic advances, managed care, and the forthcoming health care reform initiatives and draws conclusions about the future of America's health care system.

In the previous chapters we presented a mix of facts, expert opinions, findings of published studies, and historical background. Although the selection of content and the interpretations of historical events undoubtedly reflect our own public health or population perspective, we tried to provide a balanced view of the health care system and its evolution, strengths, and weaknesses. When discussing the future, however, we are entering uncharted territory, progressing from the current structure and conduct of health care to conjecture about its reformation. Looking ahead is far more hazardous than looking back, and we acknowledge that the predictions that follow represent only our personal educated guesses about the directions our health care system will take in the coming years. Even the most thoughtful forecasts, founded on carefully studied trends and data-based projections by reputable authorities, will be affected by unforeseeable and rapid changes in the health care environment.

According to chaos theory, "A small change in input can quickly translate into overwhelming differences in output,"[1] and as has been demonstrated already, the health care system is particularly sensitive to input changes. In the past, every tinkering effort to address one of the three basic problems of the health care system—cost, quality, and access—has resulted in significant changes in one or both of the others. Improving access to health care for low-income populations and older adults through Medicaid and Medicare had a significant inflationary effect on costs. Containing costs through managed care now raises questions about quality and access. Similarly, seemingly small changes within a health care institution, such as a leadership response to an outside financial, technologic, or market development, may result in unanticipated pressures on the operations within the organization. Thus, many of the recent organizational machinations of the institutions and agencies struggling to cope with health care reforms may, in the long run, turn out to be counterproductive.

Paradox of U.S. Health Care

It is unfortunate that the extraordinary successes of the U.S. health care system and the technologic accomplishments that brought worldwide acclaim to U.S. scientists are offset by the system's persistent and increasingly evident deficiencies. The policy decisions of health care leadership after World War II are duly credited with medicine's impressive advances, its prestige, and its wealth. Those health care policies led the National Institutes of Health and the National Science Foundation to invest heavily in the potential of our nation's universities and medical schools to develop basic and applied research and to dedicate federal and state funds to the expansion of academic medical centers. The burgeoning health care industry prompted the initiation of federal programs that significantly expanded the number and size of U.S. hospitals and led to an exponential increase in the size of the health care workforce. Those health care policies that produced the financial incentives in the health care reimbursement system encouraged specialization among physicians and other health care practitioners.

Those policies also contributed to the long-standing problems of inequitable access, variable quality, and runaway costs. The success of the health care industry, the growth of its workforce, its astounding physical and technologic infrastructure, its impressive outcomes, and its unfettered revenues must be weighed against its failure to recognize a social mission broader than addressing the individual needs of those who accessed its services. Until recently, the technology-oriented, can-do culture that pervades health care, and medicine in particular, appeared to have mesmerized the consuming public and health care providers into thinking that more dramatic medical marvels would solve the ills of the system. For many years, the public that supported the rising costs of health care had equally ascending expectations for what medicine could accomplish.

Now, however, there is growing discontent with a system that cannot deliver even a basic level of health care to significant portions of the public, that cannot control costs that have increased at twice the rate of other commodities, and that provides some services of doubtful necessity and therapeutic benefit. Nothing has shaken the public's previously durable faith in medicine as much as the growing awareness that many of the new technologies that yield economic benefits to providers may be of only marginal value in the diagnosis and treatment of patients.

Major Challenges Facing Health Care

The competitive managed care systems that followed the demise of President Clinton's national health care reform effort were somewhat effective in containing health care costs. That influence was short-lived, however, and rising costs and several other very serious problems continued to plague the system. Those problems, described over a decade ago as "major forces reshaping the health care system industry," remain unaddressed and are as relevant today as they were then. Both the consumers and the providers of health care are increasingly concerned that the negative consequences of social, technical, and economic forces impacting the health system are resulting in a more disordered and less trustworthy health care system.

The U.S. health care system is beset by several major forces.[2] First, the sluggish economy, receding governmental budgets, and rising health care costs have dissuaded an increasing number of middle- and upper-income people to forgo health insurance. In addition, employers, deterred by double-digit inflation in health insurance premiums, are finding ways to break away from paying for employee health insurance.[3] Comprehensive health care coverage is simply too expensive for most small businesses and low- to moderate-income individuals. If health care costs continue to rise at unacceptable rates, more and more people will find health insurance unaffordable. The concept of medical savings accounts in which people simply set aside money, tax free, to cover medical expenses and each year roll over unspent funds may become more attractive.

Demand for Greater Accountability, Fiscal and Clinical

The health care system, apart from the advances in clinical practice, has a built-in resistance to change. Entrenched interests; the many professions; employers; employees; and service, financial, and educational institutions have repeatedly demonstrated the capability of exercising the power necessary to maintain the status quo. As a consequence, the long and escalating problems of health care costs and unconscionable rates of unacceptable clinical quality have remained unabated for decades. Because there are no single solutions to these complex problems and little likelihood that all or most of the vested interests would support a set of simultaneously applied solutions, the problems continue. Anything more than tinkering with the system would have a negative effect on at least one of the major players capable of nullifying the proposed changes.

The failed attempts to address the issue of the variable quality of clinical care illustrate one facet of the problem. Concerns about the quality of health care, both anecdotally and empirically, have been expressed for decades. Because there were always small numbers of patients involved in medical errors in any individual hospital, physicians and hospital executives tended to overlook the problems. Finally, in 1999, the credible, widely publicized assessment of the problem by the Institute of Medicine, entitled *To Err Is Human: Building a Safer Health System*,[4] produced a brief flurry of discussion in Congress and then moved far down on the list of U.S. concerns. When 3,000 people died on September 11, 2001, the United States went to war. When over 3,000 people die every 2 weeks as a result of medical errors, the silence is incomprehensible and discouraging.

The lack of immediate response by physicians and policymakers reflects the generally held assumption that the medical profession effectively polices itself. The esteemed position of physicians in society and the confidentiality of the interactions between doctors and their patients have long shielded medicine from the sweeping reforms that corrected abuses in other industries. Nevertheless, the truth is that the medical profession has only recently begun to exercise the leadership necessary to correct the long-standing medical care system deficiencies that the Institute of Medicine report identified.

Michael L. Millenson, author of the 1997 book *Demanding Medical Excellence: Doctors and Accountability in the Information Age,* published by the University of Chicago Press, described that shortcoming in the journal *Health Affairs*[5]:

> The blunt answer is that professionalism alone has consistently failed to protect patients. Rather, it has been professionalism pushed into action by pressure from the press, public, politicians, and the pocketbook. For example, anesthesiologists finally acted to improve patient safety only after a television exposé of anesthesia accidents. Rising malpractice premiums—an economic incentive—provided an extra sense of urgency. Similarly, the "sign your site" protocol came in reaction to a nationally publicized incident in which a Florida surgeon amputated the wrong foot of a diabetic man in 1995. The People's Medical Society, a consumer group, had suggested a "sign your site" initiative a decade before, only to be met by indignation and ridicule on the part of surgeons. In mid-2002, the provider-dominated Joint Commission on Accreditation of Healthcare Organizations (JCAHO) finally proposed rules requiring hospitals to reduce wrong site surgery—seven years after the scandal and seventeen years after the consumer group had suggested such a move. Even with this delay and even with the utter simplicity of the act of signing one's name, 20–40 percent of surgeons continue to resist efforts to get them to sign voluntarily, a past president of the orthopedic academy admitted to the Washington Post.

In fairness, physicians and other providers are beset by so many individual problems that they willingly leave the more global problems of clinical practice to their organizational leadership. They are caught between patient demands, their own uncertainties as to the best course of treatment, and the need to constrain costs. In addition, the steady production of new drugs, devices, and procedures makes current knowledge quickly obsolete. The time and effort required to remain current with clinical developments place a heavy burden on busy practitioners. They readily admit that they find it impossible to keep up with their voluminous literature and attend even the most relevant continuing professional education courses. That many practitioners become outmoded, despite their best efforts, contributes to the quality chasm.

Although achieving system-wide improvements in health care quality depends on resolving complex, multidimensional issues, there are some hopeful signs on the horizon. Continuously rising health care costs encourage purchasers of health care coverage, individuals, employers, and state and federal governments to become more involved in assessing and improving the quality of care. Nothing is more expensive or wasteful than the cost of inappropriate or error-prone care and its outcomes.

The federal Agency for Healthcare Research and Quality is helping to pierce the culture of silence that seems to surround medical errors by establishing the first peer-reviewed, web-based medical journal, www.webmm.ahrq.gov, to stimulate discussion of medical errors in a blame-free environment.[6] Physicians and other health professionals submit medical errors cases to the site for interactive discussion and analysis. Contributors may remain anonymous if they prefer.

In addition, the Department of Health and Human Services is participating in the Hospital Quality Information Initiative, a joint effort with the leadership of the nation's hospitals to provide the public with information on the quality of care. A similar effort was launched in 2002 that involved providing quality measures of nursing home care. These concepts are different from the contentious issue of a proposed national mandatory, or even voluntary, error reporting system. The federal government's strategy is clearly moving away from assigning blame and toward educating both providers and consumers to function as full partners.

As previously described, the successful "100,000 Lives Campaign" of the Institute for Healthcare Improvement and its subsequent "5 Million Lives Campaign," sponsored principally by the Blue Cross and Blue Shield health plans, have the potential to make huge gains in patient safety by inducing hospitals to institute critically important and long-ignored safety interventions.[7]

With the capability of the Internet to dispense knowledge that used to be available only to the few "insiders," previously thwarted consumers, purchasers, legislators, and other interested parties are driving the demand for information. When purchasers of health care services have the information and performance measures that allow them to identify high-quality, safe medical care based on scientific evidence of effectiveness, poor-performing providers and institutions will be forced to shape up or lose their market to higher quality competitors. Clinical practice guidelines, evidence-based medicine, and other mechanisms for improving the practice of medicine will find greater acceptance among service facilities and practitioners.

Health Care Costs

Like the long-standing "quality of care" problem, the comparable dilemma of escalating health care costs has received only infrequent and generally ineffective attention. The sweeping takeover of health care in the United States by managed care organizations had only a temporary impact on the rate of national health care spending. There has been a rapid acceleration of health spending since 1998 and no promising measures in sight to curb spending growth.[8]

In fact, no initiatives in the last 30 years, either regulatory or voluntary, have had other than a temporary impact on this nation's health care costs. However, the current war on terrorism and its ripple effects on federal and state budgets and the economy, in general, make runaway health care costs a far more critical problem. On one side, new and costly drugs and procedures continue to proliferate and add to medicine's already impressive capability. On the other, the aging population and others with persistent medical care needs are increasingly finding the high cost of drugs and other medical services beyond their means. The problem intensifies as the economy weakens and governmental support and personal budgets decline.

The increasing use of the Internet to obtain health information by the public reflects the will and ability of Americans to understand complex issues and make informed decisions about their health care. It is increasingly evident that judgments about the consumption of medical services, formerly the province of providers with compliant patients, will be made in the future by more knowledgeable consumers who are concerned about the economic consequences of those decisions. If and when assertive users of health care services take charge of their medical care, market forces will begin to function on the basis of cost and quality as they do in other service areas.

The alternative to reducing excessive costs is a single-payer system that eliminates the substantial amount of health care dollars that are wasted on the administration of multiple insurance plans and the huge burden of their required paperwork. While the forthcoming health care reform effort, lacking a public insurance option, may dampen the largess of big corporate insurers, their continued presence in the system will persist in adding to the nation's health care costs.

Growth of Home, Outpatient, and Ambulatory Care

The changes occurring in hospital care and the demographics of aging have produced rapid growth of home care in recent years. In fact, home health care has been the fastest growing segment of the health care industry in the last 20 years. Spending for home health services increased many times the rate of increase of the whole health care industry. Lacking any major change in Medicare (which still reimburses home health care on a retrospective basis), growth within the home care industry is expected to continue rapidly over the next few years.[9]

A number of factors are responsible for the extraordinary growth in the number of medical and surgical procedures performed in outpatient and ambulatory settings. Advances in diagnostic technology, anesthesiology, and surgery have combined to make same-day surgery possible for procedures that formerly required hospital inpatient admissions. Third-party payers were quick to recognize the considerable cost savings of ambulatory surgery and began producing an ever-lengthening list of diagnostic and surgical procedures that would no longer be reimbursed if patients were admitted to hospitals as inpatients unless there were extenuating medical circumstances.

With federal and state incentives to encourage the development of more outpatient and ambulatory facilities and broad consumer acceptance, every service possible is now being provided in outpatient or ambulatory settings. These include cancer treatment, kidney dialysis, diagnostic imaging, rehabilitation services, urgent care, wellness and preventive medicine activities, and sports medicine, in addition to surgery. With the care comparable with, if not better than, that received in hospitals and provided at far lower cost, it is clear that ambulatory care reduces the mission of hospitals to serving only those patients in need of intensive nursing and medical interventions.

Technology

A revealing example of the coercive power of glamorous and expensive technologic developments over thoughtful considerations of cost benefit to patients is the medical popularity of magnetic resonance imaging (MRI). More than 7,000 of these very profitable, high-technology imaging devices have been installed in hospitals and outpatient facilities across the country. At an average cost of about $2 million or more each, the national investment in them is nearly $14 billion. Each machine is paid for by charging patients $900 to $1,200 per MR image, generating billions more in health care costs. How has this huge investment in admittedly superior diagnostic capability paid off in terms of medical care improvements? An extensive literature search published in the American College of Physicians' *Annals of Internal Medicine* in 1994 could not find a single study that documented a change in patient outcomes. Although the diagnostic information the MR image provided was considered clearer and a truer demonstration of the disease or the anatomy, neither controlled comparisons of diagnostic accuracy nor changes in therapeutic choices documented patient benefits.[10] It is particularly discouraging that in many communities the number of MR scanners installed near each other exceeds any reasonable estimate of population need or service requirement. They are only adding to the costs of health care as redundant entrepreneurial ventures.

Similarly, the technology that permits physicians to save the lives of extremely low-birth-weight babies (1 to 2 pounds), only to have them suffer from lifelong neurosensory impairments, behavior problems, and learning disorders, raises serious questions about the role of technology in modern medicine. With all of America's impressive neonatal technology, infant mortality is worse than that of at least 24 other countries.[11] Because most infant deaths occur among very-low-birth-weight infants, the problem relates to the lack of prenatal instruction and care. Clearly, the health care value system does not give high priority to such a low-tech, relatively low-cost solution. As a result, an infant born in Cuba has a statistically better chance of surviving than an infant born in the United States.

It is becoming increasingly clear that technologic progress in health care has been a mixed blessing. The impersonal, if not inhumane, imposition of high-technology medicine between patients and practitioners has changed both the image and the mission of the health care enterprise. The complex social problems that affect access to health care; the geographic, economic, and other demographic inequities in the value and availability of care; and the serious discrepancies in the quality of care are issues that cannot be remedied by technologic means.

Changing Population Composition

The U.S. population is not only growing older and increasing in size relative to younger groups, but a growing number of older adults will survive to very advanced ages. In addition, the number of large, intact families capable of housing and caring for aged relatives has diminished rapidly. Families raise fewer children, and those children often migrate to other locations when they attain maturity. Consequently, the health care needs of the larger population of the more frail older adults are expected to place increasing demands on the health care system. Those demands will focus particularly on the chronic care component of the U.S. system, a sector that has not been particularly attractive to health care providers. In addition, much of the long-term care capability in the United States is in the hands of the private, for-profit sector, which has an uneven record for the quality of its services.

The health care needs of this growing adult population will also be influenced by its changing racial and ethnic diversity. The major changes occurring in the total U.S. population will be reflected in the older population. Minority groups and Hispanics in particular will become larger proportions of the older population. These changes have important implications for medical care. There are significant differences in mortality rates, chronic conditions, service preferences and use, and attitudes toward medical care across racial/ethnic groups. For instance, Hispanics have lower rates of diseases such as hypertension and arthritis than whites and higher rates of conditions such as diabetes. Blacks are more likely to require treatment for hypertension, cerebrovascular disease, diabetes, and obesity than whites and have persistently higher mortality rates.[12]

The increased demands on the health care system posed by population changes coupled with the problems of health care workforce supply portend serious staffing problems ahead. The growth in demand for nurses, nursing aides, various types of therapists, and aides in the acute-care sector and the relative unattractiveness of long-term facilities as employment sites for those service personnel have left many chronic-care facilities dangerously understaffed. At the moment, there are neither the funds available in the long-term care system to attract those difficult-to-recruit service personnel nor alternative plans for meeting the residential needs of the Medicaid-dependent older population.

The chronically ill who do not require placement in the long-term care facility also have problems with a health care system that retains its historical focus on acute illness or injury and those conditions that are amenable to remediation. The current system does not deal well with the aged chronically ill who present persistent symptoms, increasing disability, psychosocial sequelae, and difficult lifestyle adjustments. Although small gains have been made by managed care organizations addressing specific chronic conditions, effective chronic illness care would require a major change in health service priorities. Simply adding new geriatric services to a system focused on acute care does not solve the basic problem.[13]

In addition to the need to change organizational designs and services, obstacles to improving the care of the chronically ill also include changing the personal values and clinical behaviors of physicians, nurses, and other health professionals. Educated for and trained in acute-care facilities, it requires a major shift in mindset and practice behaviors for clinicians to accept the less dramatic, multidisciplinary nature of geriatric practice. As a result, improvements in the services for the chronically ill aged will be slow and will not keep pace with the more dramatic advances in other areas of clinical practice.

Changing Professional Labor Supply

Health care workers, other than physicians, have generally been ignored in the debates over health care policy and reforms. Nevertheless, the economic and other forces reducing the size and services of the hospital industry, shifting inpatient procedures to outpatient settings, and producing other organizational changes are likely to result in significant disruptions in the established employment practices of many classes of health care workers. Although the health care industry always will employ a significant portion of the U.S. workforce, the number and kinds of employees and the sites of their employment will be in transition during the next several years as the health care system adjusts itself.

Health economist Uwe E. Reinhardt lists several reasons that predicting the size or composition of the future health workforce is ill advised.[14] He points out that health care providers are exercising considerable flexibility in assigning tasks to the various health professions. He expects that staffing patterns of health institutions will be sensitive to the relative cost of different types of providers. In the quest for efficiency, Reinhardt expects a great deal of experimentation and variation in staffing patterns across health care systems and regions in the United States. In addition, scientific advances constantly provide new opportunities to substitute technology for human labor. Other technologic advances create needs for new types of health personnel. Under all these disparate and evolving circumstances, it would be imprudent, indeed, to predict a future surplus or shortage for any type of health professional. It is likely, however, that whatever health care staffing patterns eventually result, the impact of health care reforms on the health care workforce will be considerable.

Physicians

Nothing has been more dramatic during the last decade than the reduction in power, prestige, and independence of physician specialists. In the 1990s managed care limitations on the number of specialists that could join their systems and on the frequency and circumstances of their use temporarily altered their positions in the health care hierarchy. In contrast, the demand for primary care practitioners increased as more people enrolled in managed care plans. There was a critical need for physicians who could provide primary care, serve as gatekeepers to limit access to more expensive specialists, and emphasize preventive medicine and health promotion. As the supply of primary care physicians increased and managed care organizations relaxed their more stringent restrictions on specialist care, however, the ratio of specialists to generalists began returning to its former levels.

It appears that no matter how many physicians practice in the United States, a shortage of physicians will exist in various regions of the country. In addition, less desirable practice locations such as inner city and rural areas continue to suffer from an undersupply of both primary care and specialty physicians. It is now apparent that those who believed that physician distribution problems would be solved by producing more physicians did not reckon with the ability of newly trained physicians to start up busy practices and earn satisfactory incomes in areas already well served.

In the absence of medical workforce policies or government intervention, market forces will continue to reconfigure the system on the basis of economic concerns, with little or no regard for considerations of quality or access. Quality and access are public and professional concerns, not market concerns, and are the issues that governments and health organizations should be addressing. Even in geographic areas where physicians are in adequate supply, too many individuals remain without access to medical care, and too many hospitals depend on graduates of foreign medical schools to provide essential inpatient services.

Major gaps in the availability of primary care physicians have been filled by substitution of nurse practitioners and physician assistants. In addition, the increasing popularity of chiropractors, acupuncturists, and other alternative practitioners reflects public dissatisfaction with the complexity and impersonal nature of today's medical care. The increasing number of substitutes for traditional medical practitioners presents a formidable problem for health policy planners that could have severe economic, public, and professional consequences. If nothing is done, the profession of medicine is likely to find itself competing with an ever-increasing array of nonphysician practitioners.[15]

New Physician Roles

Two relatively new roles have emerged for physicians in the changing health care system. The first is the hospitalist, who provides all care to hospital inpatients of office-based physicians. Because these physicians are constantly in hospitals and are more familiar with their inner workings, they are considered to be more efficient and more capable of continually monitoring and managing inpatient care than are office-based physicians. More and more hospitals are employing hospitalists to gain the benefits of shorter lengths of stay, decreased complications, and increased patient satisfaction.

The second promising role for physicians is that of medical manager or administrator. Physicians, many with additional management or administration training, are entering the medical management area through employment in pharmaceutical companies, managed care organizations, hospitals, or large group practices. The demand for physicians with advanced training in management or administration is expected to increase as the corporatization of health care continues. At the same time, physicians, frustrated by the changes wrought in private practice, see health care administration as a highly regarded alternative to patient care.

Nurses

In many ways, nurses are the most qualified to respond to the changes that have occurred in the health system. Nurses' training focuses more on the behavioral and preventive aspects of health care than does physician education. Their skills are as relevant to outpatient care as they are to inpatient care. Nurses are important members of health care teams and have experience in managing lesser-trained caregivers. Nevertheless, the radical changes occurring in both the organization and delivery of health care are particularly disconcerting to the nursing profession. The financial pressures on acute-care hospitals and the major movements to managed care and integrated health care systems profoundly affected the over 2.6 million registered nurses who constitute the largest component of the health professions. Throughout the last decade two-thirds of all nurses were employed in hospitals.[16] Increased case-mix severity, decreased nurse–patient ratios, and delegation of traditional nursing duties to lesser-trained personnel have given hospital nurses reason to be concerned over the quality of patient care that has long been their responsibility. That this large proportion of the health care workforce is singularly vulnerable to the staff reductions that must accompany the declining admission and occupancy rates of acute-care hospitals is of major concern to nursing leaders and educators.

With mounting evidence that pervasive understaffing of hospital nurses is resulting in preventable complications and patient deaths, provider, public, and governmental pressures to improve the hospital nursing environment and give inpatient nurses reason to once again take pride and pleasure in their work are increasing. The number of entrants to schools of nursing is growing. More men are entering the field, and an influx of foreign-trained nurses is relieving some of the pressures.

Much will have to change, however, to improve the circumstances of hospital nursing. Excessive paperwork, inefficient communication systems, managerial responsibilities, and supervision of lesser-trained aides require an inordinate amount of time spent in functions other than providing direct patient care. Combined with long work hours and other difficulties, they contribute to low job satisfaction and frustrating work environments.

Nurse Practitioners and Physician Assistants

Nurse practitioners (NPs) and physician assistants (PAs), described in detail in Chapter 6, are in great demand and will be increasingly important in the provision of primary health care. Public satisfaction with the services provided by NPs and PAs is high, and demand for their services will continue as they fill niches where physician services are in short supply. Estimates suggest that there could be as many as 110,000 clinically active NPs and PAs in the next several years, representing one-sixth of the total U.S. medical providers.[17] It is realistic to expect that NPs and PAs, supported by effective practice guidelines and computerized treatment protocols, could become the patient's first point of entry into the health care system.[18]

Future of America's Health Insurance Systems

For over 50 years, employer-sponsored health insurance protected most Americans from overwhelming medical expenses. Although weakened by employer reluctance to absorb the increasing costs of health insurance premiums, the insurers themselves are enjoying a period of strong financial growth. Although there are increasing calls for expanding publicly sponsored programs, such expansions are more likely to benefit rather than harm commercial insurers. Most recently, the health insurance industry gained by diversifying into Medicare and Medicaid. State and federal programs are increasingly outsourcing to commercial insurers the difficult tasks of managing care and dealing with taxpaying beneficiaries.[19] Clearly, whether it is employment-based or governmentally sponsored health insurance, the commercial insurers have managed to maintain their primary profit-making roles. Although they add significantly to the costs of America's annual health care bill, it would be unwise to predict that anything less than conversion to a single-payer health care system will diminish the costly role of commercial health insurers.

Although physicians have always been vehemently opposed to what they call "universal health care," no one would be happier to see the demise of managed care insurers than physicians. Angered by ever more stringent cost-containment tactics that reduced their incomes and autonomy and subjected them to continuing disputes over service decisions, physicians have built public and legislative pressure to correct perceived abuses. In addition, many physicians have changed practice patterns in response to loss of income. They formed coalitions that increased their clout when contracting with managed care organizations and reduced the number of alternative sources of care with which managed care organizations could contract. "Any-willing-provider" laws, which require managed care organizations to open their networks to any physician who wants to join, also increased physician power.[20]

Patients, too, are gaining more control in their relationships with physicians, hospitals, and insurers because of widespread dissemination of health information about alternative treatments and sources of care in the media and on the Internet. The result has been a more equitable balance of power among managed care organizations, physicians, and patients.

Changing Composition of the Delivery System

Hospitals, although still critically important to medical care, are no longer the hub of the health care system. Although occupancy rates for many facilities are improving, they have not returned to the levels of more than a decade ago, and occupancy rebound is not likely to occur. The growing development of privately owned ambulatory surgery centers, diagnostic facilities, and now specialty hospitals has the potential to cause traditional acute-care hospitals to become a combination of high-level intensive care units and full-service facilities for those with more serious conditions, the uninsured, and the indigent. Regardless of excess hospital capacity, a variety of business, political, and social reasons makes hospital closings very difficult.[21] More importantly, almost all hospitals are now part of for-profit or not-for-profit corporate networks. Where many separate and competing hospitals once served a particular geographic area, now a somewhat smaller number of institutions divided among a few health care networks are meeting regional needs.

Information Management

The growing numbers of new and efficient technologies for managing and transferring volumes of data allow providers and health plans to replace voluminous and often disorganized medical records with standardized, reliable, and clinically relevant information. Opportunities for transcription mistakes, misinterpretation of handwriting or medication orders, and other common errors of information transfer are minimized.

Although the technology for management of data, once collected, is at a high level of sophistication, there are serious obstacles to obtaining and assembling complete health information about individual patients. Because most patients obtain health care services from a number of providers and facilities, the information about their care is divided among the various settings and sites. The still unmet information management challenge is dealing with fragmentation of patient information, as those patients move through a disorganized treatment system.[22]

Originators of seamless health information systems that allow sharing of patient diagnostic, treatment, and outcome information face other problems as well. Incredibly complex confidentiality, compatibility, and transferability issues have challenged system designers for years. Nevertheless, the critical role of advanced information and communications technologies in evidenced-based assessments of clinical practice, physician report cards, clinical guidelines, patient education, and a large number of other uses is recognized by everyone concerned with the future of health care. As with other obstacles to health service advances, the growing need to solve those intrinsic system problems will drive information experts to develop acceptable solutions.

In the meantime, the importance of those health information technologies has alerted the business community to the promise of an emerging health information infrastructure. Although much of the current information system development has been the result of the academic medical researchers and developers, a number of private health information technology industries are already engaged in the building of the technical components of that hardware and software infrastructure. Other private companies are working on paperless solutions to recording and monitoring clinical procedures. It appears that the free-enterprise system is augmenting, if not supplanting, the years of information systems development by in-house designers employed by hospitals and academic institutions.

Whether harmonious or competitive, it appears that the common interests of the clinical communities and the profit-motivated commercial sector will eventually result in a new era of health care information technology. It will be a giant step forward in advancing the efficacy, efficiency, and safety of medical care.[23]

Government's New Role in Public Health

The terrorist attack of September 11 was the stimulus for a national examination of the numerous, inconsistent, and outdated public health laws in the United States. Suddenly, the protection of the public's health in case of any one of a number of possible attacks became an immediate priority. Out of the crisis came the political and legislative will to ensure coordinated responses among federal, state, and local agencies in case of a public health emergency. The long overdue effort resulted in the drafting of the Model State Emergency Health Powers Act. The Act assists states in reviewing their emergency health powers and provides governors with the authority to declare a public health emergency and implement an adequate response. That response may involve the allocation of health resources and the implementation of actions to safeguard public health such as isolation and quarantine.[24]

In addition to addressing the basic public health functions of preparedness, disease surveillance, management of property, communication, and individual protection, the Model State Emergency Health Powers Act seeks to reconcile various antiquated and inconsistent public health statutes. Many were written before modern disease-prevention methods existed.[25]

The evident lack of public health preparedness at the time of the September 11 attack made it apparent that clear and effective communication with the public in crisis situations is an essential component of public health practice. The U.S. Department of Health and Human Services, Centers for Disease Control and Prevention responded by addressing the crisis preparedness education of health professionals and developing a more comprehensive information dissemination system for the public.[26]

It is a reflection of this country's health care priorities that it took a devastating terrorist attack to draw attention to the fact that the U.S. public health system is poorly funded, fragmented, and ill-prepared to provide an effective health defense system—even when the routine public health functions of offering credible health information, safeguarding air quality, protecting and educating workers, and ensuring food safety were basic elements of the called-for response. If anything positive results from the ill-fated September 11 experience, it will be that the public of the future will have public health safeguards appropriate to the latest high-technology health care expertise.

The long accepted, but often unfulfilled, core functions of regional and local public health agencies now must be enhanced with a broad array of protections and services. Achievement of those new responsibilities, however, requires a major restructuring of local and regional resources, procedures, staffing, and communication systems. New and more forceful leadership, effective planning, communication, working relationships among different levels of government, and adequate resource allocations are basic to meeting threats to the public's health in times of crisis.

Whether the system reforms itself to create a vibrant public health structure capable of meeting new demands while serving traditional needs is still an open question. The importance of the outcome, however, in case of potential disasters should not be underestimated.[27]

Conclusion

The social and economic changes affecting society during the last decade altered public perceptions of health care and prepared many Americans for sweeping reforms in both the organization and delivery of health care services. Although tensions exist between the advocates of immediate system revisions and those who prefer more limited, incremental changes, all agree that the health care industry is in a period of unprecedented instability and transition. In addition, there are strong pressures on providers to analyze and document the outcomes and effectiveness of their health care interventions.[28]

The continuing presence of over 46 million uninsured Americans reflected the nation's reluctance to decide whether the federal government should ensure health coverage for all its citizens or only fill the gaps for those without the means to obtain their own. Other nations have long considered health care a right of citizenship and provide the subsidies necessary to give everyone reasonable access to basic care.

Repeatedly in the history of health care in the United States, however, the public has been persuaded to instruct its representatives that health care is a "good" that should be supplied privately with as few exceptions as possible. That the system costs more and has large gaps, illogical redundancies, and inexplicable variations in quality and access is countered by the prevailing belief that its scientific and technologic superiority makes up for its deficiencies.

The need for industry restructuring to remedy the deficiencies in the health care system, however, is the overriding concern of those who believed the United States should develop a more socially responsible system of health care and end its embarrassing distinction as the only Western democracy that permits a sizable percentage of its population to live without health insurance coverage. Given that health care in the United States evolved out of the professional and economic objectives of providers rather than consumer needs and has been financed by a convoluted system of private insurance augmented by inadequately managed and inflationary public sector programs, it is not surprising that the resulting system is characterized by escalating costs and glaring gaps in coverage. Clearly, the problems could not be solved satisfactorily without major structural revisions.[29]

The idealized solutions to the problems of huge variations in costs, treatments, and outcomes; fragmented services; episodic treatment of illness; and badly distributed overcapacity all have general support as concepts but engender opposing views on how to resolve them. Among the most frequently voiced suggestions are these:

- Alter the health care focus from diagnosing and treating illness to maintaining wellness and preventing illness.
- Expand the health care system's accountability from the health status of individual patients to that of defined populations.
- Change the health services' emphasis from acute episodic care to continuous comprehensive care and chronic disease management.
- Eliminate the financial incentives to provide more services and fill hospital beds, and substitute incentives to provide appropriate care at an appropriate level.
- Assume universal access to health care.
- Change from merely coordinating the delivery of services to actively managing the quality of processes and outcomes.
- Add a serious commitment to the resolution of community and public health issues.

Current trends suggest that the future of health care in the United States will include more reforms at the state level. As individual state experiments show positive results, other states will adopt the changes. For instance, other states have looked at the experience of Massachusetts, Vermont, and Maine, where health care reforms were initiated during the last 3 years.[30]

Health care reforms can make the systems of care different, but they cannot make the care better. Only the providers working in concert with supportive systems can improve health care outcomes. Freed from many of the disincentives of fee-for-service medicine, providers may emphasize wellness and prevention and reduce unnecessary interventions. They may become as effective in improving the health status of entire populations as they have for patients they formerly treated on an individual basis.

It is anticipated that the public and purchasers will be aided in choosing from among competing providers and managed care plans by having access to a great deal of timely performance information. Unlike the selective secrecy that has characterized health care in the past, it is expected that future health care organizations will be required to provide annual quality performance "report cards" for public and purchaser scrutiny. Some institutions and managed care organizations already produce these.

Hospitals face a harsh short-term future. Unrelenting economic pressures in the face of reduced occupancy rates will undoubtedly result in a significant number of closings, and those that survive will be different institutions from those that presently exist. Hospitals are likely to be just one component of a vertically integrated system of care that includes long-term as well as ambulatory care and a variety of community-based services. Because many of the acute-care services will be provided in ambulatory settings, the major role of hospitals probably will be in the provision of intensive patient care and, perhaps, the diagnosis and management of the chronically ill.

The relationship of hospitals to physicians will take on increasing importance as the old assumptions about medical care and surgery continue to undergo profound change. The future of hospitals depends on the future of medicine. The future of medicine is grounded in the scientists and clinicians developing the cutting-edge advances in medicine and surgery. Thus, it behooves hospitals to convene and respond to those whose combined expertise and judgment can formulate solutions to deficits in quality and patient satisfaction and can anticipate the service modalities of the future.

In addition, hospitals, which have long benefited from their tax-exempt status based on public and governmental assumptions that they provide substantial amounts of charity care, will, for the first time, be required to list, on public records, the exact amount they spend on subsidies for needy patients and other related activities. Congress and the Internal Revenue Service with the power to withdraw tax-exempt status will then judge those reports.[31] The trials and tribulations of hospitals never end.

The changing demographics in the United States will compel a major expansion of long-term care facilities and services. Long-term care will become an increasingly complex array of services integrated into vertical systems. Of all the problems facing the future health care system, the aging of the population, with its attendant burden of chronic disease and disability, presents the most formidable organizational and economic challenge. Needless to say, those facilities and services striving mightily to survive the more immediate challenges have yet to develop longer range plans to cope with that future inevitability.

The growing demand for support of chronic care is likely to force a major change in the structure and financing of health care in the United States. Unlike the acute-care system, chronic care is unplanned and often insensitive to desperate situations. For example, regardless of type, the insurance coverage for the extraordinary care provided in a hospital to save a life often abruptly ceases when the patient is brought home. Although essential patient services such as feeding, bathing, transferring from bed to wheelchair, and preventing bedsores are considered "medically necessary" when provided by skilled nurses in institutions, those same services are dismissed as "custodial care" when delivered at home.

As more and more middle-aged Americans find themselves faced with the care of aged and functionally limited relatives, the demand for expanded support of chronic care services will increase. Public awareness of the deficiencies of the current system will grow and bring considerable pressure for change in public and private financing mechanisms.

People with chronic conditions already consume almost 70% of the nation's expenditures on personal care, mostly for physician and hospital services, a reflection of the system's focus on acute incidents.[31] Clearly, there is a monumental challenge in this era of severe economic constraint to create and finance a chronic care system that meets social as well as medical needs. Until that can be accomplished, the aged and chronically ill and their caregivers will be required to meet their home care, transportation, social support, and other needs however they can.

Although the health care system itself is in turmoil, the sciences within health care are making extraordinary progress. Medical technology is a major driver of the health care system, and the system quickly absorbs new devices and pharmaceuticals. Just as clinicians and researchers embraced the use of new imaging techniques, so too will they adopt new devices for minimally invasive surgery, gene mapping and therapy, new vaccines, artificial blood, and other advances that will transform the practice of medicine.

These dramatic advances, however, will be accompanied by new and vexing problems of cost, accessibility, inadequate training, and professional ethics. Practicing physicians are already overwhelmed with the profusion of new knowledge. Currently, there are 10 million citations on the computerized scientific literature resource, Medline, and 3,000 more are added to the popular bibliographic database each month. The availability of new knowledge also vastly exceeds the capacity of the institutions that deliver and finance health care to access and use it. It is difficult for these hierarchical organizations to respond to past problems, much less adapt to new developments. The fact that thousands of deaths were reported to occur each year as a result of medical errors in hospitals and that neither the public nor the health care community seemed aware of the magnitude of the problem is a reflection of the size, complexity, and disorder that characterizes the system. Compare that fact with the response to a single airplane crash, after which every fragment of evidence is collected to determine the cause and prevent its reoccurrence.

The enormous potential for good that the U.S. health care system enjoys comes with deep concerns. How will the recipients of new technology be chosen? Who will address the ethical dilemmas that lie behind the ability to genetically alter humans? When will the need to set stricter standards of competence when people's lives are at stake be faced by the medical profession? When will the government rein in the unlimited profits of pharmaceutical firms that price their drugs beyond the means of those who need them the most? These and similar issues are central to a constructive reformation of the U.S. health care system.

Last, but certainly not least, we now have a federal government effort to reform, and hopefully improve, the structure of the U.S. health care system. The 2010 health care reform legislation, described in Chapter 2, represents a pragmatic approach to closing the gaps in insurance coverage by building on a mix of employer, private, and a public plan in a health insurance exchange. The legislation strengthens Medicare and expands Medicaid and is expected to stimulate important changes in the delivery of health care to improve efficiency and productivity.[32]

No matter how successful it turns out to be, the fact that any health care reform legislation was passed after our long history of other presidential attempts and failures makes this an historic occasion. As the old saying goes, however, "the proof of the pudding is in the eating." Let's wait and see how the bureaucrats, amid all the pushing and pulling of the vested interests, put this historic legislation into play.

These are exciting times for students of health care. Never has so large a change in so important an industry so intimately affected so many people. It is a time for introspection regarding one's values, circumspection regarding one's advocacy for any one position, and careful inspection of any experimental changes that come about. Will the health care reforms now in progress resolve or worsen the key issues of access, costs, and quality? Can we possibly achieve an ideal health policy scenario, such as that proposed by Shortell et al., in which there is fiscal and clinical accountability for defined populations, resources allocated according to a region's consumer needs, and up-front negotiations among all relevant parties about what services will be delivered to what people at what price?[33] Only time and skilled leadership will tell.

References

1. Gleick J. Chaos: making a new science. In: Sifonis JG, Goldberg B, Eds. *Corporation on a Tightrope: Balancing Leadership, Governance, and Technology in an Age of Complexity.* New York: Viking; 1987:1–19.
2. Shortell SM, Reinhardt UE. Creating and executing health policy in the 1990s. In: Shortell SH, Reinhardt UE, Eds. *Improving Health Policy and Management: Nine Critical Research Issues for the 1990s.* Ann Arbor, MI: Health Administration Press; 1992:5–6.
3. Ledue C. Number of uninsured Americans could grow by 10M in five years. *Health Finance News.* Princeton, NJ; March 16, 2010. Available from http://www.healthcarefinancenews.com/news/number-uninsured-americans-could-grow-10m-five-years. Accessed April 4, 2010.

4. Committee on Quality of Health Care in America, Institute of Medicine. Kohn LT, Corrigan JM, Donalsdon MS, Eds. *To Err Is Human, Building A Safer Health System.* Washington, DC: National Academy Press; 2000.

5. Millenson ML. The silence. *Health Affairs.* 2003;22:103–112.

6. Clancy CM, Scully T. A call to excellence. *Health Affairs.* 2003;22:113–115.

7. Institute for Healthcare Improvement. AHRQ Web M&M. Morbidity & Mortality Rounds on the WEB. Available from http://www.ihi.org/ihi/aboutus/people.aspx. Accessed December 6, 2006.

8. Hefler S, Smith S, Won G, et al. Health spending projections for 2001–2011: the latest outlook. *Health Affairs.* 2002;21:207–218.

9. Kitchener M, Ng T, Miller N, et al. Medicaid home and community-based services: national program trends. *Health Affairs.* 2005;24:206–212.

10. Kent DL, Haynor DR, Longstreth WT, et al. The clinical efficacy of magnetic resonance imaging. *Ann Intern Med.* 1994;120:856–875.

11. Starfield B. U.S. child health: what's amiss, and what should be done about it? *Health Affairs.* 2004;23:165–170.

12. Wolf DA. Population change: friend or foe of the chronic care system? *Health Affairs.* 2001;20:64–78.

13. Wagner EH, Austin BT, Davis C, et al. Improving chronic illness care: translating evidence into action. *Health Affairs.* 2001;20:28–42.

14. Reinhardt UE. The economic and moral case for letting the market determine the health workforce. In: Osterweis M, McLaughlin CJ, Manasse HR, et al., Eds. *The U.S. Health Workforce: Power, Politics, and Policy.* Washington, DC: Association of Academic Health Centers; 1996:3–13.

15. Cooper RA, Getzen TE, McKee HJ, et al. Economic and demographic trends signal an impending physician shortage. *Health Affairs.* 2002;21:140–154.

16. Bureau of Labor Statistics, U.S. Department of Labor. Occupational outlook handbook, 2010–2011 edition. Registered nurses. Available at http://www.bls.gov/oco/ocos083.htm. Accessed January 12, 2010.

17. Hooker RS, Berlin LE. Trends in the supply of physician assistants and nurse practitioners in the United States. *Health Affairs.* 2002;21:174–180.

18. Amara R, Bodenhorn K, Cain M, et al. Health and healthcare 2010: the forecast, the challenge. In: Engehart JK, Ed. *The Institute for the Future.* San Francisco: Jossey-Bass; 2000:73–84.

19. Robinson JC. The commercial health insurance industry in an era of eroding employer coverage. *Health Affairs.* 2006;25:1475–1486.

20. Carroll A, Ambrose JM. Any-willing-provider laws: their financial effect on HMOs. *J Health Politics, Pol Law.* 2002;27(6):927–946.

21. Aiken LH, Clark SP, Sloane DM. Hospital restructuring: does it adversely affect care and outcomes? *JHHSA.* 2000;30(10):457–465.

22. Bell DS, Marken RS, Meili RC, et al. Rand electronic prescribing expert advisory panel. *Health Affairs.* 2004;1:305–317.

23. Menachemi N, Brooks RG. Reviewing the benefits of electronic health records and associated patient safety technologies. *J Med Syst.* 2006;30: 159–168.

24. Department of Health and Human Services, Centers for Disease Control and Prevention. Public health guidance for community level preparedness and response to acute respiratory syndrome, version 2 (June 8, 2004). Available at www.publichealthlaw.net/MSEHPA/MSEHPA2.pdf. Accessed December 10, 2004.

25. Matthews JW. Legal preparedness for bioterrorism. *J Legal Med Ethics.* 2002;30:52–53.

26. Parvanta CF, Freimuth V. Health communication at the Centers for Disease Control and Prevention. *Am J Health Behav.* 2000;24:337–347.

27. Salinsky E, Garsky EA. The case for transforming governmental public health. *Health Affairs.* 2006;25:1017–1028.

28. Gelijns AC, Brown LD, Magnell C, et al. Evidence, politics, and technological change. *Health Affairs.* 2005;24:29–40.

29. Haislmaier E. A cure for the health care crisis. *Issues Sci Technol.* 1990; 6:59–63.

30. O'Connor P. States Push Ahead on Healthcare Reform and Policy Issues Preempting Some Provisions of Congressional Efforts. *Kaiser Health News.* Available from http://www.kaiserhealthnews.org/Daily-Reports/2010/February/09/State-Policy-Developments.aspx. Accessed March 29, 2010.

31. Carson J. Not-for-profits: more scrutiny. *Modern Healthcare.* January 4, 2010;32:28.

32. Davis K, Guterman SW, Collins SR, et al. Starting on the path to a high performance health system: analysis of health system reform provisions of reform bills in the House of Representatives and Senate. The Commonwealth Fund, December 2009. Available from http//www.commonwealthfund.org/content/Publications/Fund-Report. Accessed January 8, 2010.

33. Shortell SM, Morrison EM, Friedman B, et al. *Strategic Choices for America's Hospitals: Managing Change in Turbulent Times.* San Francisco: Jossey-Bass; 1990:301–327.

Abbreviations and Acronyms

AACN American Association of Colleges of Nursing

AAFP American Academy of Family Physicians

AAMC Association of American Medical Colleges

AAN American Academy of Nursing

AARP American Association of Retired Persons

ACEHSA Accrediting Commission on Education for Health Services Administrators

ACF Administration on Children and Families

ACGME Accreditation Council for Graduate Medical Education

ACHE American College of Healthcare Executives

ACP American College of Physicians

ACR Advanced Certified Rolfer

ACS American College of Surgeons

ACYF Administration for Children, Youth, and Families

ADAMHA Alcohol, Drug Abuse, and Mental Health Administration

ADD Administration on Developmental Disabilities

ADLs Activities of Daily Living

AFDC Aid to Families with Dependent Children

AFL-CIO American Federation of Labor and Congress of Industrial Organization

AHA American Hospital Association

AHC Academic Health Center

AHCPR Agency for Health Care Policy and Research (formerly Agency for Healthcare Research and Quality)

AHP Accountable Health Plan

AHRQ Agency for Healthcare Research and Quality (formerly Agency for Health Care Policy and Research)

AHSR Association for Health Services Research (formerly Academy for Health Services Research and Health Policy)

AID U.S. Agency for International Development

AIDS Acquired Immunodeficiency Syndrome

ALOS Average Length of Stay

AMA American Medical Association

AMC Academic Medical Center

ANA Administration for Native Americans; American Nurses Association

AoA Administration on Aging

APA American Psychiatric Association; American Psychological Association

APEX/PH Assessment Protocol for Excellence in Public Health

APHA American Public Health Association

APTA American Physical Therapy Association

ASAHP Association of Schools of Allied Health Professions

ASH Assistant Secretary for Health

ASHED AIDS School Health Education Database

ASHP Adolescent and School Health Programs

ASIM American Society of Internal Medicine

ASSIST American Stop Smoking Intervention Study

ASTHO Association of State and Territorial Health Officials

ATF Bureau of Alcohol, Tobacco, and Firearms

ATSDR Agency for Toxic Substances and Disease Registry

AUPHA Association of University Programs in Health Administration

BAC Blood Alcohol Concentration

BBA Balanced Budget Act of 1997

BC/BS Blue Cross and Blue Shield

BCHS Bureau of Community Health Services

BHP Bureau of Health Professions

BHRD Bureau of Health Resources Development

BIA Bureau of Indian Affairs

BLS Bureau of Labor Statistics

BPHC Bureau of Primary Health Care

BRFSS Behavioral Risk Factor Surveillance System

CAH Critical Access Hospital

CAM Complementary and Alternative Medicine

CAT Computerized Axial Tomography

CBER Center for Biologics Evaluation and Research

CCN Community Care Network; Critical Care Nurse

CCRC Continuing Care Retirement Community

CDC Centers for Disease Control and Prevention

CDER Center for Drug Evaluation and Research

CDF Children's Defense Fund

CDRH Center for Devices and Radiological Health

CEO Chief Executive Officer

CEU Continuing Education Unit

CFO Chief Financial Officer

CFSAN Center for Food Safety and Applied Nutrition

CHAMPUS Civilian Health and Medical Program of the Uniformed Services

CHC Community Health Center

CHID Combined Health Information Database

CHIP Child Health Insurance Program

CHP Comprehensive Health Planning

CME Continuing Medical Education

CMHC Community Mental Health Center

CMS Center for Medicare & Medicaid Services (formerly HCFA, the Health Care Financing Administration)

COBRA Consolidated Budget Reconciliation Act

COGME Council on Graduate Medical Education

CON Certificate of Need

CPI Consumer Price Index

CPR Customary, Prevailing, and Reasonable (fees)

CPSC Consumer Product Safety Commission

CPT Current Procedure Terminology

CPT-4 Current Procedural Terminology, 4th edition

CQI Continuous Quality Improvement

CRCC Commission on Rehabilitation Counselor Certification

CT Computed Tomography

CTP Certified Trager Practitioner

CVM Center for Veterinary Medicine

DC Doctor of Chiropractic

DHEW Department of Health, Education, and Welfare

DHHS Department of Health and Human Services

DME Durable Medical Equipment

DNR Do Not Resuscitate

DNS/DNSc Doctor of Nursing Science

DO Doctor of Osteopathy

DOE Department of Education

DOI Department of Interior

DOJ Department of Justice

DOL Department of Labor

DOT Department of Transportation

DRG Diagnosis-Related Group

DVA Department of Veterans Affairs

EACH Essential Access Community Hospital

EAP Employee Assistance Program

ECA Epidemiologic Catchment Area

ECF Extended Care Facility

EMS Emergency Medical Services

EPA Environmental Protection Agency

EPO Epidemiology Program Office

EPSDT Early and Periodic Screening, Diagnosis, and Treatment

ER Emergency Room

ERISA Employee Retirement Income Security Act

ESRD End-Stage Renal Disease

FAHS Federation of American Health Systems

FAS Fetal Alcohol Syndrome

FDA Food and Drug Administration

FDIR Food Distribution Program on Indian Reservations

FEHBP Federal Employee Health Benefits Program

FEMA Federal Emergency Management Association

FFS Fee for Service

FHSR Foundation for Health Services Research

FHWA Federal Highway Administration

FIC Fogarty International Center

FMG Foreign Medical Graduate

FNS Food and Nutrition Service

FQHC Federally Qualified Health Center

FSAs Flexible Spending Accounts

FTC Federal Trade Commission

FTE Full-Time Equivalent

FY Fiscal Year

GDP Gross Domestic Product

GHAA Group Health Association of America

GHC Group Health Cooperative

GHI Group Health Insurance

GME Graduate Medical Education

GMENAC Graduate Medical Education National Advisory Committee

GNP Gross National Product

HACCP Hazard Analysis Critical Control Point

HANES Health and Nutrition Examination Survey

HBCU Historically Black Colleges and Universities

HBV Hepatitis B Virus

HCA Hospital Corporation of America

HCFA Health Care Financing Administration

HCV Hepatitis C Virus

HDL High-Density Lipoprotein Cholesterol

HEDIS Health Plan Employer Data and Information Set

HETC Health Education and Training Center

HEW Health, Education, and Welfare (Department of)

HHS Health and Human Services (Department of)

HIAA Health Insurance Association of America

HIP Health Insurance Plan

HIPAA Health Insurance Portability and Accountability Act

HIS Health Interview Survey

HIV Human Immunodeficiency Virus

HMO Health Maintenance Organization

HNIS Human Nutrition and Information Service

HPDP Health Promotion and Disease Prevention

HPEAA Health Professions Educational Assistance Act

HRA Health Resources Administration

HRAs Health Reimbursement Accounts

HRQL Health-Related Quality of Life

HRSA Health Resources and Services Administration

HSA Health Systems Agency

HSAs Health Savings Accounts

HTPCP Healthy Tomorrows Partnership for Children Program

HUD Department of Housing and Urban Development

IADLs Instrumental Activities of Daily Life

ICD International Classification of Diseases

ICD-9-CM *International Classification of Diseases,* 9th Revision, Clinical Modification

ICU Intensive Care Unit

IDDM Insulin-Dependent Diabetes Mellitus

IHPO International Health Program Office

IHS Indian Health Service

IMGs International Medical Graduates

IMR Infant Mortality Rate

INPHO Information Network for Public Health Officials

IOM Institute of Medicine

IPA Individual Practice Association

IPN Integrated Provider Network

IPO Independent Practitioner Organization

LCME Liaison Committee on Medical Education

LDL Low-Density Lipoprotein Cholesterol

LIHEAP Low-Income Home Energy Assistance Program

LOS Length of Stay

LPN Licensed Practical Nurse

LTC Long-Term Care

MBHCC Managed Behavioral Health Care Company

MCHB Maternal and Child Health Bureau

MCN Migrant Clinicians Network

MCO Managed Care Organization

MD Medical Doctor

MDC Major Diagnostic Category

MDS Minimum Data Set

MEDLARS Medical Literature Analysis and Retrieval System

MEDTEP Medical Treatment Effectiveness Program

MEHP Minority Environmental Health Program

MHTS Minority Health Tracking System

MLP Midlevel Practitioner

MRI Magnetic Resonance Imaging

MSA Metropolitan Statistical Area; Medical Savings Account

MSEHP Model State Emergency Health Powers Act

MSHA Mine Safety and Health Administration

MSO Management Services Organization

MVP Medicare Volume Performance

NACAA National Association of Consumer Agency Administrators

NACHM National Advisory Commission on Health Manpower

NACHO National Association of County Health Officials

NAHC National Association for Home Care

NAIEP National AIDS Information and Education Program

NAM National Association of Manufacturers

NAMCS National Ambulatory Care Survey

NAMHC National Advisory Mental Health Council

NAMI National Alliance for the Mentally Ill

NAPO National AIDS Program Office

NCADI National Clearinghouse for Alcohol and Drug Information

NCAI National Congress of American Indians

NCCAN National Center on Child Abuse and Neglect

NCCDPHP National Center for Chronic Disease Prevention and Health Promotion

NCEH National Center for Environmental Health

NCHGR National Center for Human Genome Research

NCHS National Center for Health Statistics

NCHSR National Center for Health Services Research

NCI National Cancer Institute

NCID National Center for Infectious Diseases

NCIPC National Center for Injury Prevention and Control

NCPIE National Council on Patient Information and Education

NCPS National Center for Prevention Services

NCQA National Committee on Quality Assurance

NCRR National Center for Research Resources

NCTR National Center for Toxological Research

ND Doctor of Naturopathy; Doctor of Nursing

NEI National Eye Institute

NF Nursing Facility

NHDS National Hospital Discharge Survey

NHE National Health Expenditures

NHIC National Health Information Center

NHIS National Health Interview Survey

NHLBI National Heart, Lung, and Blood Institute

NHSC National Health Service Corps

NIA National Institute on Aging

NIAAA National Institute on Alcohol Abuse and Alcoholism

NIAID National Institute of Allergy and Infectious Diseases

NIAMS National Institute of Arthritis and Musculoskeletal and Skin Diseases

NICHD National Institute of Child Health and Human Development

NIDA National Institute on Drug Abuse

NIDCD National Institute on Deafness and Other Communication Disorders

NIDDK National Institute of Diabetes and Digestive and Kidney Diseases

NIDR National Institute of Dental Research

NIDRR National Institute on Disability and Rehabilitation Research

NIEHS National Institute of Environmental Health Sciences

NIGMS National Institute of General Medical Sciences

NIH National Institutes of Health

NIMH National Institute of Mental Health

NINDS National Institute of Neurological Disorders and Stroke

NINR National Institute of Nursing Research

NIOSH National Institute of Occupational Safety and Health

NLM National Library of Medicine

NLN National League for Nursing

NLTN National Laboratory Training Network

NMIHS National Maternal and Infant Health Survey

NMR Nuclear Magnetic Resonance

NQF National Quality Forum

NVSS National Vital Statistics System

OAM Office of Alternative Medicine

OASIS Outcomes and Assessment Information Set

OBRA Omnibus Budget Reconciliation Act

OCS Office of Community Services

OCSE Office of Child Support Enforcement

ODPHP Office of Disease Prevention and Health Promotion

OECD Organization of Economic Development

OEO Office of Economic Opportunity

OFA Office of Family Assistance

OHTA Office of Health Technology Assessment

OIH Office of International Health

OMB Office of Management and Budget

OMH Office of Minority Health

ORHP Office of Rural Health Policy

ORT Operation Restore Trust

OSH Office of Smoking and Health

OSHA Occupational Safety and Health Administration

OT Occupational Therapy

OTA Office of Technology Assessment

OWH Office on Women's Health

PA Physician Assistant

PAC Political Action Committee

PACE Program of All-Inclusive Care for the Elderly

PAR Preadmission Review

PCP Primary Care Provider; Primary Care Physician

PET Positron Emission Tomography

PGP Prepaid Group Practice

PharmD Doctor of Pharmacy

PHO Physician–Hospital Organization

PHP Prepaid Health Plan

PHS Public Health Service

PIRC Preventative Intervention Research Center

PMPM Per Member Per Month

PMPY Per Member Per Year

POE Point of Enrollment

PORT Patient Outcomes Research Team

POS Point of Service

PPA Preferred Provider Arrangement

PPCM Primary Care Case Management

PPHA Pennsylvania Public Health Association

PPO Preferred Provider Organization

PPRC Physician Payment Review Commission

PPS Prospective Payment System

PRO Peer Review Organization

ProPAC Prospective Payment Assessment Commission

PSO Provider Service Organization; Provider-Sponsored Organization

PSQ Patient Satisfaction Questionnaire

PSRO Professional Standards Review Organization

PT Physical Therapy

PTMPY Per Thousand Members Per Year

QA Quality Assurance

RAPs Radiologists, Anesthesiologists, and Pathologists

RBRVS Resource-Based Relative Value Scale

RMP Regional Medical Program

RN Registered Nurse

RPCH Rural Primary Care Hospital

RPP Registered Polarity Practitioner

RRA Registered Records Administrator

RRC Residency Review Committee

RSPA Research and Special Programs Administration

RUG Resource Utilization Group

RVS Relative Value Scale

RVUs Relative Value Units

SAMHSA Substance Abuse and Mental Health Services Administration

SCHIP State Children's Health Insurance Program

SEIU Service Employees International Union

SHMO Social Health Maintenance Organization

SMI Supplemental Medical Insurance

SNF Skilled Nursing Facility

SSA Social Security Administration

SSI Supplemental Security Income

STD Sexually Transmitted Disease

TEFRA Tax Equity and Fiscal Responsibility Act

Title XVIII Medicare

Title XIX Medicaid

TPA Third-Party Administrator

TPN Total Parenteral Nutrition

TQM Total Quality Management

UCR Usual, Customary, and Reasonable Reimbursement

UR Utilization Review

USDHEW U.S. Department of Health, Education, and Welfare

USDHHS U.S. Department of Health and Human Services

USFMG U.S. Foreign Medical Graduate

USPHS U.S. Public Health Service

VA Veterans Administration; Department of Veterans Affairs

VNA Visiting Nurses Association

WHO World Health Organization

WIC Women's Infant's and Children's Special Supplemental Food Program

Web Sites

U.S. Government

Agency for Healthcare Research and Quality:
http://www.ahrq.gov

Centers for Disease Control and Prevention:
http://www.cdc.gov

Centers for Medicare & Medicaid Services:
http://www.medicare.gov

Department of Health and Human Services:
http://www.HHS.gov

Department of Veterans Affairs, Veterans Health Administration:
http://www.va/gov/health_benefits

National Center for Complementary and Alternative Medicine:
http://www.nccam.nih.gov

National Center for Health Statistics:
http://www.cdc.gov/nchs

National Guideline Clearinghouse:
http://www.guideline.gov

National Institutes of Health:
http://www.nih.gov

National Library of Medicine:
   http://clinicaltrials.gov and http://www.nlm.nih.gov/medlineplus

Office of Disease Prevention and Health Promotion:
   http://www.healthfinder.gov

State Children's Health Insurance Program:
   http://cms.hhs.gov/schip

U.S. Administration on Aging:
   http://www.aoa.dhhs.gov

U.S. Congressional Budget Office:
   http://www.cbo.gov

U.S. Department of Health and Human Services:
   http://www.hhs.gov and http://healthfinder.gov

U.S. Department of Labor, Bureau of Labor Statistics:
   http://stats.bls.gov

U.S. Food and Drug Administration:
   http://www.fda.gov

Other Organizations

Alliance for Quality Health Care:
   http://www.nyhealthfinder.com

American Academy of Family Physicians:
   http://www.familydoctor.org

American Accreditation Healthcare Commission:
   http://www.urac.org

American Association of Health Plans:
   http://www.aahp.org

American Association of Retired Persons:
   http://www.aarp.org/health

American Board of Medical Specialties:
   http://www.certifieddoctor.org

American Cancer Society:
   http://www.cancer.org

American Health Care Association:
http://www.ahca.org

American Heart Association:
http://www.americanheart.org

American Lung Association:
http://www.lungusa.org

American Medical Association:
http://www.ama-assn.org/aps/amahg.htm

Annals of Long Term Care:
http://www.mmhc.com

The Commonwealth Fund:
http://www.cmwf.org

Families USA:
http://www.familiesusa.org

Health Care Careers and Jobs Center:
http://www.healthcarejobs.org

Internet Collection of Reviewed Articles:
http://www.medscape.com

The Joint Commission:
http://www.jointcommission.org

Kaiser Family Foundation and Health Research and Educational Trust:
http://www.kff.org

Long-Term Care Provider.com News and Analysis:
http://www.longtermcareprovider.com

Mayo Clinic:
http://www.mayoclinic.com

Medscape:
http://www.medscape.com

Modern Healthcare:
http://www.modernhealthcare.com

National Alliance for Caregiving:
http://www.caregiving.org

National Alliance for the Mentally Ill:
http://www.nami.org

National Association for Home Care:
   http://www.nahc.org

National Center for Assisted Living:
   http://www.ncal.org

National Committee for Quality Assurance:
   http://www.ncqa.org

National Council on Aging:
   http://www.HealthCareCoach.com

Index

Italicized page locators indicate a figure; tables are noted with a *t*.